Socialism, Capitalism and Alternatives

FRINGE

Series Editors
Alena Ledeneva and Peter Zusi, School of Slavonic and
East European Studies, UCL

The FRINGE series explores the roles that complexity, ambivalence and immeasurability play in social and cultural phenomena. A cross-disciplinary initiative bringing together researchers from the humanities, social sciences and area studies, the series examines how seemingly opposed notions such as centrality and marginality, clarity and ambiguity, can shift and converge when embedded in everyday practices.

Alena Ledeneva is Professor of Politics and Society at the School of Slavonic and East European Studies of UCL.

Peter Zusi is Associate Professor of Czech and Comparative Literature at the School of Slavonic and East European Studies of UCL.

Socialism, Capitalism and Alternatives

Area Studies and Global Theories

Edited by Peter J. S. Duncan
and Elisabeth Schimpfössl

First published in 2019 by
UCL Press
University College London
Gower Street
London WC1E 6BT

Available to download free: www.uclpress.co.uk

Text © Contributors, 2019
Images © Contributors, 2019

The authors have asserted their rights under the Copyright, Designs and Patents Act 1988 to be identified as the authors of this work.

A CIP catalogue record for this book is available from The British Library.

This book is published under a Creative Commons 4.0 International license (CC BY 4.0). This license allows you to share, copy, distribute and transmit the work; to adapt the work and to make commercial use of the work providing attribution is made to the authors (but not in any way that suggests that they endorse you or your use of the work). Attribution should include the following information:

Duncan, P.J.S. and Schimpfössl, E. (eds.). 2019. *Socialism, Capitalism and Alternatives: Area Studies and Global Theories*. London: UCL Press. DOI: https://doi.org/10.14324/111.9781787353824

Further details about Creative Commons licenses are available at http://creativecommons.org/licenses/

Any third-party material in this book is published under the book's Creative Commons license unless indicated otherwise in the credit line to the material. If you would like to reuse any third-party material not covered by the book's Creative Commons license, you will need to obtain permission directly from the copyright holder.

ISBN: 978-1-78735-384-8 (Hbk.)
ISBN: 978-1-78735-383-1 (Pbk.)
ISBN: 978-1-78735-382-4 (PDF)
ISBN: 978-1-78735-385-5 (epub)
ISBN: 978-1-78735-386-2 (mobi)
DOI: https://doi.org/10.14324/111.9781787353824

Contents

List of figures ... vii
List of tables ... ix
List of contributors ... xi
Preface ... xv
Acknowledgements ... xvii

Introduction ... 1
Peter J. S. Duncan and Elisabeth Schimpfössl

PART I Capitalism in action

1 Semi-dependent capitalism: Russia ... 15
   Ruslan Dzarasov

2 Diversifying the super-rich: *Forbes*-listed Russians from a Muslim background ... 33
   Catherine Suart

3 The culture of elite philanthropy: Russia and the United Kingdom compared ... 49
   Timothy Monteath and Elisabeth Schimpfössl

4 Between the public and the private: Socialism, capitalism and street socialisation in Georgia ... 66
   Costanza Curro

PART II China today and as a future alternative

5 Making it in China: The determinants of economic success in a socialist market system ... 89
   Ion Marandici

6 The revival of Marxism in China: Could it herald a Communist Reformation? 108
Heiko Khoo

7 China's emerging liberal partnership order and Russian and US responses: Evidence from the Belt and Road Initiative in Eurasia 131
Peter Braga and Stephen G. F. Hall

PART III   Alternatives in the West

8 Neo-liberalism, Keynesianism and the current crisis 161
Geoffrey Hosking

9 Political alternatives on the Western Left: Podemos, Syriza, Sanders and Corbyn 181
Peter J. S. Duncan

Conclusion 213
Peter J. S. Duncan and Elisabeth Schimpfössl

Index 221

List of figures

1.1 Relationship between international rankings according to the HDI and per capita GNI of the USSR (1987) and the former Soviet republics (2015). Rankings are placed in descending order (i.e., the best ranking is in the lowest left position). Source: *Human Development Report 1990*, 119; *Human Development Report 2016: Human Development for Everyone*, 198–201.   20

5.1 The number of billionaires in China, 1999–2018. Source: Graphs by author based on data from Rupert Hoogewerf, *Hurun Report*, Hong Kong/Shanghai, 2018. www.hurun.net/en/ArticleShow.aspx?nid=14678 (accessed 13 May 2018); *Forbes* Magazine, China's Rich List, 2003–2017, www.forbes.com/china-billionaires/ (accessed 13 May 2018).   93

5.2 The average marginal effects for age and education and the predictive margins for party affiliation across age groups. Source: Author's interviews.   98

5.3 Beliefs in intergenerational mobility and change in economic situation. Source: Author's interviews.   99

List of tables

2.1	List of Russia's business elite with Muslim identities (2016). Source: Author's own research files.	34
2.2	Political posts held by members of the Muslim business elite. Source: Author's own research files.	38
5.1	Frequencies of the independent and dependent variables. Source: Author's interviews.	102
5.2	Determinants of income levels: Ordered probit regression results. Source: Author's interviews.	104

List of tables

2.1 List of Russia's business elite with Muslim identities (2016). Source: Author's own research files.   34
2.2 Political posts held by members of the Muslim business elite. Source: Author's own research files.   38
5.1 Frequencies of the independent and dependent variables. Source: Author's interviews.   102
5.2 Determinants of income levels: Ordered probit regression results. Source: Author's interviews.   104

List of contributors

Peter Braga is a PhD candidate at the UCL School of Slavonic and East European Studies. Peter's publications have been featured in the *Journal of Belarusian Studies*. His book, *China's New Silk Road, Central Asia, and the Gateway to Europe*, co-authored with Dr Kaneshko Sangar, will be published in 2020 by Routledge (Taylor & Francis Group). Peter researches authoritarian persistence, China–East Europe relations, and emerging powers.

Costanza Curro's research interests include moral economies, masculinity, mobility and the transformation of space in post-socialist cities. She has a PhD in social anthropology from the UCL School of Slavonic and East European Studies. Her thesis, titled 'From Tradition to Civility: Georgian Hospitality after the Rose Revolution', explores hospitality practices as potential sources of civil values amid social, political and economic disintegration brought into place by the post–Rose Revolution political project of radical modernisation. She has published articles in the *Journal of Consumer Culture*, the *International Journal of Sociology and Social Policy* and *Caucasus Survey*, and contributions to edited volumes on informal practices, gender and post-socialism, and post-socialist urban mobilities.

Peter J. S. Duncan is Associate Professor of Russian Politics and Society at the UCL School of Slavonic and East European Studies. In 2009–10 he was a Leverhulme Research Fellow. Among his publications are *The Soviet Union and India* (1989); *Soviet-British Relations since the 1970s* (co-edited, 1990); *The Road to Post-Communism: Independent Political Movements in the Soviet Union 1985–1991* (co-author, 1992); *Towards a New Community: Culture and Politics in Post-Totalitarian Europe* (co-edited, 1993);

Convergence and Divergence: Russia and Eastern Europe into the Twenty-First Century (edited, 2007); and *Russian Messianism: Third Rome, Revolution, Communism and After* (paperback, 2014).

Ruslan Dzarasov is professor and head of the Department of Political Economy at the Plekhanov Russian University of Economics, Moscow, and is a senior research fellow at the Central Institute of Economics and Mathematics of the Russian Academy of Sciences, Moscow. He is an economist and expert on Russian capitalism, post-Keynesianism and Marxism. Dzarasov is the author of *The Conundrum of Russian Capitalism: The Post-Soviet Economy in the World System* (2013). He has published articles in the *Cambridge Journal of Economics* and *Debate: Journal of Contemporary Central and Eastern Europe*, and about 30 other scholarly works in English and Russian.

Stephen G. F. Hall is a doctoral student in political science at the UCL School of Slavonic and East European Studies. His research interests focus on authoritarianism, learning and the post-Soviet space. His doctoral research concentrates on the authoritarian learning of regimes in Belarus, Moldova, Russia and Ukraine. His publications include (all 2017) 'Learning from Past Experience: Yanukovych's Implementation of Authoritarianism after 2004', in the *Journal of Eurasian Studies;* 'Preventing a Colour Revolution: The Belarusian Example as an Illustration for the Kremlin?' and (co-authored) 'Authoritarian Learning: A Conceptual Overview', both in *East European Politics.*

Geoffrey Hosking is Emeritus Professor of Russian History at the UCL School of Slavonic and East European Studies. Among his publications are *A History of the Soviet Union* (3rd ed., 1992); *Rulers and Victims: The Russians in the Soviet Union* (2006); *Russia and the Russians* (2nd ed., 2012); *Trust: A History* (2014). He is currently studying the ways in which generalised social trust is generated and/or undermined in different countries.

Heiko Khoo runs the weekly Karl Marx walking tour in London but he is best known for 32 years of soapbox oratory at Speakers' Corner, Hyde Park. His academic focus is on the Marxist critique of Stalinism. His recently completed PhD thesis provides a Marxist critique of Janos Kornai's theory of China. He makes the weekly Speakers' Corner radio show for Resonance 104.4 FM in London and has written an op-ed column for China.org.cn since 2009.

Ion Marandici is a lecturer with the Department of Political Science at Rutgers University. At Rutgers, he teaches courses in comparative politics, international relations, and quantitative research methods. Since earning a doctorate in political science, his areas of research and writing have included the political economy of reforms and state capture in Eastern Europe, Russia, and China; economic and ethnic voting; unrecognised states; and perceptions of China in the United States. His doctoral dissertation examined the wealthy elites and state autonomy in post-communist states. His website is www.ionmarandici.com.

Timothy Monteath is pursuing his PhD in Sociology at the London School of Economics and Political Science. His doctoral research focuses on the high end of London's residential property market and the wealthy elite who own these properties. More broadly, he is interested in questions of wealth accumulation and inequality and is currently working on a number of research projects in this area. In pursuing this research, he has also developed a keen interest in the use of novel digital datasets and computational methods as a means of understanding contemporary inequalities.

Elisabeth Schimpfössl is author of *Rich Russians: From Oligarchs to Bourgeoisie* (2018). Her current research focuses on elite philanthropy, both in Russia and the United Kingdom, and has been published, for example, in *Cultural Politics*. Schimpfössl has also conducted collaborative research into media and journalism in Eastern Europe, with a focus on self-censorship as well as the role of Russia's media elite, published in *The Russian Review, Russian Politics* and *Demokratizatsiya*. She has a doctorate from the University of Manchester and is currently lecturer in sociology and policy at Aston University, Birmingham, United Kingdom.

Catherine Suart is a training and investigations consultant specialising in intelligence gathering. Catherine's work spans a variety of jurisdictions and sectors, but her principal interest remains in Russia and its neighbouring countries, where she has spent eight years supporting complex cross-border disputes and asset recovery assignments for the corporate intelligence industry. Catherine began her Russian studies at Trinity College, Cambridge, before completing an MA in Russian and Post-Soviet Politics at the UCL School of Slavonic and East European Studies.

Preface

The UCL Press FRINGE series presents work related to the themes of the UCL FRINGE Centre for the Study of Social and Cultural Complexity.

The FRINGE series is a platform for cross-disciplinary analysis and the development of 'area studies without borders'. 'FRINGE' is an acronym standing for **F**luidity, **R**esistance, **I**nvisibility, **N**eutrality, **G**rey zones, and **E**lusiveness – categories fundamental to the themes that the Centres support. The oxymoron in the notion of a 'FRINGE CENTRE' expresses our interest in (1) the tensions between 'area studies' and more traditional academic disciplines; and (2) social, political, and cultural trajectories from 'centres to fringes' and inversely from 'fringes to centres'.

The series pursues an innovative understanding of the significance of fringes: rather than taking 'fringe areas' to designate the world's peripheries or non-mainstream subject matters (as in 'fringe politics' or 'fringe theatre'), we are committed to exploring the patterns of social and cultural complexity characteristic of fringes and emerging from the areas we research. We aim to develop forms of analysis of those elements of complexity that are resistant to articulation, visualisation, or measurement.

The present volume addresses the challenge of how one might think through coherent alternatives to the entrenched conceptual categories of 'capitalism' and 'socialism', around which discussion of politics and society has centred for at least a century. This task remains stubbornly difficult, even while those categories become ever less suited to describe novel and unsettling political developments across the globe. Starting from analysis of the recent history and current dynamics of 'post-socialist' Russia and

Central and Eastern Europe, the volume confronts the global challenge we face in articulating alternatives to capitalism, socialism and threatening populist regimes.

Alena Ledeneva and Peter Zusi,
School of Slavonic and East European Studies, UCL

Preface

The UCL Press FRINGE series presents work related to the themes of the UCL FRINGE Centre for the Study of Social and Cultural Complexity.

The FRINGE series is a platform for cross-disciplinary analysis and the development of 'area studies without borders'. 'FRINGE' is an acronym standing for Fluidity, Resistance, Invisibility, Neutrality, Grey zones, and Elusiveness – categories fundamental to the themes that the Centres support. The oxymoron in the notion of a 'FRINGE CENTRE' expresses our interest in (1) the tensions between 'area studies' and more traditional academic disciplines; and (2) social, political, and cultural trajectories from 'centres to fringes' and inversely from 'fringes to centres'.

The series pursues an innovative understanding of the significance of fringes: rather than taking 'fringe areas' to designate the world's peripheries or non-mainstream subject matters (as in 'fringe politics' or 'fringe theatre'), we are committed to exploring the patterns of social and cultural complexity characteristic of fringes and emerging from the areas we research. We aim to develop forms of analysis of those elements of complexity that are resistant to articulation, visualisation, or measurement.

The present volume addresses the challenge of how one might think through coherent alternatives to the entrenched conceptual categories of 'capitalism' and 'socialism', around which discussion of politics and society has centred for at least a century. This task remains stubbornly difficult, even while those categories become ever less suited to describe novel and unsettling political developments across the globe. Starting from analysis of the recent history and current dynamics of 'post-socialist' Russia and

Central and Eastern Europe, the volume confronts the global challenge we face in articulating alternatives to capitalism, socialism and threatening populist regimes.

Alena Ledeneva and Peter Zusi,
School of Slavonic and East European Studies, UCL

Acknowledgements

This volume grew out of a conference held in 2015 to mark the centenary of the foundation of the School of Slavonic and East European Studies (SSEES), which since 1999 has been part of UCL. The conference was called 'Socialism, Capitalism and the Alternatives: Lessons from Russia and Eastern Europe'.

Christopher J. Gerry (now Dean of St Antony's College, Oxford) conceived the idea for the conference, but after his departure to work in St Petersburg we became the main academic organisers. We are grateful for the support we received from the successive SSEES directors, Slavo Radoševič and Jan Kubik, who allocated generous finance. The conference could not have taken place without the unstinting efforts of Christine Fernandes, Sarah-Jane Gregori, Claudia Roland, Chloe Thomas, Lisa Walters, Maria Widdowson, Lesley Pitman and other SSEES staff members. Zena Howard organised unprecedented (for SSEES) press publicity for the event.

Alena Ledeneva and Peter Zusi, founders of the FRINGE Centre established by SSEES at the UCL Institute of Advanced Studies, saw the potential of the conference as the basis for a volume in the FRINGE Series and commissioned us to edit it. Since then Peter Zusi, in particular, has been a vital source of intellectual support. Anonymous reviewers provided valuable advice. Chris Penfold and Lara Speicher of UCL Press encouraged us in the project. We thank them all, but emphasise that any mistakes and deficiencies in this book are solely our own responsibility.

Elisabeth Schimpfössl is grateful to the Leverhulme Trust for enabling this research through the award of a Leverhulme Early Career Fellowship.

Finally, we wish to thank Sasha Zernova (who married Duncan while this volume was being prepared) for her support.

Introduction

Peter J. S. Duncan and Elisabeth Schimpfössl

In 1989 the Berlin Wall came down. Two years later, the Soviet Union disintegrated. This collapse of communism in Eastern Europe and the Soviet Union discredited the idea of socialism for generations to come. It was seen as representing the final and irreversible victory of capitalism over socialism. This triumphant dominance was barely challenged for nearly the next two decades. But then the 2008 crisis hit and threw the Western world into a state of turmoil. More than a decade on, things are far from being back to 'normal'; on the contrary, everything has come even more apart at the seams. Wars are raging, populists are taking over the reins and our ecology is going downhill.

This volume begins with a number of separate studies of some of the consequences of the introduction of capitalism into the former Soviet Union and China. It continues by examining possible alternatives to the existing organisation of the world economy, particularly as posed by the Chinese Belt and Road Initiative. It further considers alternatives to the policies currently pursued domestically and discusses ways of achieving these changes.

Socialism and capitalism competing

As gloomy and disturbing as the twenty-first century has been so far, it would be pretentious to claim that our times are exceptional in their level of grimness. In retrospect, we know that the good times were the exception to the norm, not the other way around. This is particularly true for the boom years following the Second World War. Prematurely, many came to be convinced that lasting prosperity was from then on the order of the day. At the very latest, the 2008 crisis (if not already three-and-a-half decades prior to it) brought home that capitalism means misery for millions of people.

The grievances of today have triggered doubts among the young generations all over the globe that the world has to be like this. Such sentiments have expressed themselves in a variety of social movements, from the Arab Spring to the Occupy movement. Alongside these movements, ideas have reappeared – many of which are almost as old as the problem created by capitalism – among them calls for considering socialism as an alternative as outlined most famously by Karl Marx and Friedrich Engels.

In 1848, in their Communist Manifesto, Marx and Engels called on the working class to unite in order to create a socialist society. This call was international. Socialism would only be possible in countries that had laid the material basis for abundance under capitalism, they reiterated. Seventy years later, Lenin still held the same conviction. Even after he had been on the forefront of the first socialist seizure of power in 1917, he was adamant that for the revolution in Russia to survive it needed a far more advanced Germany or Britain to follow suit.

That a country like Germany might have its own revolution was not a far-fetched idea at this moment in time. Millions of people in the belligerent countries had been radicalised by their wartime experience. Whether the men in the trenches or the women in the factories, they understood that the fate of their nations depended on them. The ruling classes understood this too. The danger of revolution and unrest made the latter concede to a number of demands they had so long managed to circumvent. In the wake of revolutionary movements, former empires became republics and countries all over Europe introduced social reforms, such as unemployment insurance, social housing and war disabled relief.

While prior to the war, governments brought themselves to implement social welfare reforms in order to constrain the influence of social-democratic parties (most famously, Bismarck with his social welfare policies), now many social democratic parties became the closest allies, if not pivotal, in undermining and containing the revolutionary craving of their often much more militant followers by soothing them with reform policies. After these revolting masses were let down by their party once too often, they lost their spirit. The 1929 Wall Street Crash and the depression of the 1930s further disintegrated society. These factors combined allowed fascist movements to rise. Decisively for the catastrophes to come was that in Germany the conservative right opted for Hitler to save their skin.

The Second World War led to yet another radicalisation of working people all over Western and Eastern Europe and beyond. The threat of a social revolution was back on the agenda, alarmingly so to the rulers of the time. Stalin – who was about to swallow many countries in Eastern Europe – would have seen a genuine socialist revolution as a mortal threat to his totalitarian regime, while the Western rulers feared an end to their economic domination. These fears resulted in an expansion of the welfare state that was unseen in history and never seen again. Governments began caring for their citizens 'from the cradle to the grave'. Strengthened by full employment and favourable labour legislation, in most West European countries trade unions grew in numbers of members and in their political and economic influence.

For some time, it looked as if the 'mixed economy' of welfare-state capitalism had banished unemployment and delivered universal and long-lasting prosperity. Against this backdrop, it seemed reasonable to many working people to demand a fairer share of the cake. By that time, in the late 1960s, students also passionately vocalised their impatience with rigid hierarchies and dusty social mores. But then in 1973, the price of oil quadrupled. This unexpected earthquake shook one Western economy after the other.

In response to the oil crisis and the subsequent instability of markets, neo-liberal policies gained dominance. Thatcherism and Reaganomics in the 1980s came to determine not only their countries of origin but also influenced developments globally. Parallel to this, trade unions lost much of their industrial power. Social welfare was cut back, traditional industries closed down, state-owned services privatised and the financial markets deregulated. The fall of the Berlin Wall in 1989 and the collapse of the Soviet Union in 1991 further escalated the ideological offensive against public ownership and state provision of welfare and services in many capitalist countries. Austerity programmes, which had initially been launched by conservative governments, were continued by social-democratic governments, most notoriously by New Labour in Britain and the SPD in Germany, which goes a long way to explain their gradual decrease in popularity in the coming decades.

From 1989 into the 1990s, the neo-liberal economic template was implemented in most of the post-communist states of Eastern Europe and the former Soviet Union. The International Monetary Fund (IMF) devised programmes for the transition to a market economy, following the same mantras of liberalisation and deregulation, macroeconomic stabilisation and privatisation. Sometimes even the same advisors travelled from country to country, bringing what was termed the Washington Consensus first to Poland and later to Russia. In Central and Eastern Europe, where a legal consciousness was relatively strong, economic and institutional reforms produced economic growth fairly quickly, albeit alongside widening inequality.[1] In the post-Soviet states, the lack of rule of law, the prevalence of corruption and strong bureaucratic networks – all factors impeding the full implementation of 'shock therapy' – led to economic decline, here with even more sharply rising inequality.

In Russia and Ukraine, businessmen with close connections to the state created private banks and bought much of the state-owned oil, gas and metals assets cheaply, creating a class of 'oligarchs'. In Russia, from 2000 onwards, Putin moved against some of these oligarchs to deprive them of their influence on the media and to increase the role of the state in the ownership and control of the economy, to the benefit of his former KGB colleagues, other personal cronies and himself. In most other respects, however, Putin has followed the calls of the neo-liberals for low flat taxes on incomes; low taxes on corporations; slashing of social spending to be replaced by private insurance; freer labour markets achieved by cutting back workers' and trade union rights; allowing the sale of land to individuals and corporations; raising the pension age; and joining the World Trade Organization.[2]

The increasing role of private enterprise in China and the opening up of the country to the world economy led to China replacing Japan as the main challenger to US economic dominance in the 1990s. This was not affected by the 1997 Asian financial crisis, which had ramifications around the world, including in Russia, but hardly affected the neo-liberal hegemony. Combining a neo-liberal economic policy with a neoconservative belief in the omnipotence of America, the administration of George W. Bush led the country into wars in Afghanistan in 2001 and Iraq in 2003. Regime change proved easy, but it was much harder to keep the newly installed governments in control of their countries. America's world hegemony was severely challenged following these conflicts. The subsequent sharp increases in oil and gas prices strengthened not only the feudal Arab monarchies but also the Putin regime, giving the Kremlin a popular basis of support.

Populism as an alternative?

Despite long decades of capitalism seeming invincible, neo-liberalism suffered its own crisis of credibility. In the aftermath of the 2008 Western financial crisis, millions of people lost their jobs or their homes, real wages fell and health and social spending was curtailed, as governments resorted to austerity policies to reduce their deficits. In the United Kingdom, major banks and financial institutions became insolvent or survived only because they were propped up with government funding. Meanwhile, the rich got richer year by year – in some parts of the world, astronomically so.[3]

The political impact of the 2008 crisis varied between different countries. In the United States, it was a major factor in the defeat of the Republicans and the election of the Democrat Barack Obama as the first black president in 2008. In Britain, on the other hand, Gordon Brown's pursuit of austerity policies led to Labour's defeat in 2010 and the election of a much more austere Conservative-Liberal Democrat coalition, led by David Cameron. In the eurozone, Angela Merkel's Germany led the trend towards austerity and pressured other states into subscribing to it too, which resulted in years of economic stagnation.

Austerity policies from above eventually incited a range of radical social and political movements of resistance from below. The year 2011 began with the flowering of the Arab Spring. In May the 'indignant citizens' movements emerged on the squares of Spain and Greece. In the autumn, the Occupy movement appeared across the United States and the City of London. In December, hundreds of thousands of Russians protested against fraudulent parliamentary elections. Putin's response on his return to the presidency in May 2012 was to clamp down brutally on the opposition and launch a campaign to uphold 'traditional' conservative, religious values, promoting a statist form of Russian nationalism and continuing neo-liberal economic policies.[4] In most Western countries, the protest movements had important political results. The indignant citizens created Podemos in Spain and boosted Syriza in Greece. In 2015, Bernie Sanders announced his candidacy for the Democratic nomination for America's president as a democratic socialist, and Jeremy Corbyn, the far-left candidate, was elected leader of the Labour Party.

One of the most dramatic consequences these developments have had is the rise of populism as expressed in Brexit, Trump and the far right throughout Europe. In France, where the left is split several ways, the right-wing populist Marine le Pen went through to the final round in the 2017 presidential election, being beaten there by Emmanuel Macron who advocated a neo-liberal economic policy. As Jan-Werner Müller argues, typically, the populists of our time rage against the elites and the establishment, even though many stem directly from them. They launch campaigns against elite corruption and 'treasonous' trade deals and claim the exclusive right to represent the people, among other things by promising to return their national sovereignty to them. Further, they declare immigrants to be the main source of their people's ills; for example by equalising Islam with terrorism, thereby appealing to the chauvinist and racist prejudices of the more backward part of the population. Such hatred often goes hand-in-hand with anti-Semitism. Once in power (which is often gained with the active support of the traditional conservative right), populist governments undermine checks and balances, clamp down on trade unions and civil society organisations, and use referenda that allow for popular participation in politics as supposed instruments of real democracy. This is often accompanied by some kind of showdown with the alleged enemies of the people, whom they accuse of conspiring against the nation with the backing of the mainstream media which spread 'fake news'.[5]

Such a scenario is hardly what Marx and Engels would have wanted to see as the consequence of having neo-liberal ideas discredited.

Area studies and global theories

This edited volume is not intended to provide summary overviews of the history and essence of global theories revolving around socialism and capitalism. Instead, it brings together research studies from the 2010s, which deal with capitalism in action against the backdrop of a new international situation. On the one hand, for more than a quarter of a century the Soviet Union and the Eastern Bloc are no more; and on the other hand, China is more powerful than ever.

The global repercussions of both regions' trajectories demonstrate the still persisting significance of research that is located in the multidisciplinary field of area studies. In the English-speaking world, area studies has just celebrated its centenary. The University of London created the School of Slavonic and East European Studies (SSEES) in 1915 and the School of Oriental and African Studies (SOAS) in 1916. The area studied by SSEES – the former Soviet Union and Eastern Europe – has functioned as a laboratory for the experiment of making the transition from centrally planned economies to various forms of capitalism. This also implied that boundaries became much more malleable than in the decades prior to this. For area studies, this has wide-reaching implications. Such sudden geopolitical and ideological remapping (for example, former Eastern Bloc countries becoming members of the European Union) has thrown into question the traditional separation of the East European area from Europe as a whole.

Moreover, global trends often manifest themselves in concrete area or country situations. The area studies tradition is to analyse the interaction of the cultural, historical, social, economic, political and ideological influences on a specific dynamic. One early example of someone taking an area studies approach, albeit not using the term, was Karl Marx. He developed his theory of the state on the basis of the study of the state in France in works such as *The Class Struggles in France* and *The Eighteenth Brumaire of Louis Bonaparte*. Many present-day area studies practitioners might not see themselves in the Marxist tradition, but not unlike him, they have again turned their attention to the global significance of their research beyond the confines of their traditional region or country of study.[6]

Our prime geographical focus is nevertheless on those two great powers, one in decline, the other rising. We also consider the implications of these developments for Western societies. The volume covers three major areas. Part One revolves around the impact of capitalism on countries that had centrally planned economies. Part Two focuses on the alternative posed by China's outstanding economic growth – its domestic consequences, and how it is projecting its economic power to challenge the current international economic order. Part Three identifies features in contemporary society that point towards alternatives that have the potential to challenge the existing socio-economic relationships in Western states.

There is a substantial literature on the 'varieties of capitalism'. Hall and Soskice deal exclusively in two models of capitalism. One is the 'liberal market economy'; that is, the Anglo-American version. The second is the 'coordinated market economy', more normally known as the mixed economy or social-market economy; that is, the version found in Scandinavia and Germany.[7] Others have added Eastern Europe to this mix.[8] In another twist, János Kornai views varieties of capitalism by their political regimes.[9]

Similarly, we can talk of 'varieties of socialism'. The Soviet model of central planning and one-party rule was only one of many possibilities. Within Eastern Europe, there were experiments with market socialism in Hungary and self-management in Yugoslavia. The model of 'socialism with Chinese characteristics' has taken the role of the market much further.[10] Within the Marxist tradition, many tendencies reject Leninist concepts of the need for a single ruling party.[11] Beyond the Marxists, the nineteenth-century concept of cooperative socialism shows resilience in the forms of the contemporary cooperative movement and worker-owned enterprises such as John Lewis. Many Western socialists favour a pluralist system, with a combination of nationalised, municipal, cooperative and private business providing support for well-funded public health, social, educational and environmental services.

Despite the geographical foci that this volume deals with, it nevertheless has global reach. The opening chapter by Ruslan Dzarasov shows how contemporary Russian society is a semi-dependent capitalism, depending on the core capitalist countries for its markets while simultaneously exercising hegemonic power regionally. This reinforces the relevance of world systems theory, classifying Russia as part of the semi-periphery. Here our application of area studies confirms a particular approach to global economic relationships.

The last years saw a continuous increase in social inequality. This trend was accelerated by the 2008 financial crisis, which hit almost everyone but the wealthiest. In 2014, a global debate on inequality was initiated following the publication of Thomas Piketty's *Capital in the Twenty-First Century*. Piketty argues that capitalism automatically produces extreme inequality. He warns that the increasing imbalance in global wealth has the potential to cause major instability and to threaten democracy. He recommends that the state should intervene to counteract this.[12]

Two chapters in this volume examine how the rich in Russia have accumulated their wealth and how they legitimise it. Catherine Suart dissects the origins of the wealth held by the Muslim business elite in Russia. She also explores how these oligarchs strive to legitimise their power and exercise political influence. Power legitimisation is also the topic of the next chapter. Elisabeth Schimpfössl and Timothy Monteath investigate the philanthropic practices exercised by Russia's hyper-rich and compare them to those of the British elite.[13]

There is growing interest in the impact on society around the world of informal practices. A major contribution towards the study of this is *The Global Encyclopaedia of Informality*, published in the UCL Press Fringe Series.[14] A final chapter in the first part of the present volume analyses the impact of neo-liberal reforms on the traditional informal structures prevalent in Eastern Europe and the former Soviet Union. Costanza Curro discusses the survival of the *birzha*, the informal youth networks in Georgia.

The principal challenge to Western capitalist dominance of the world economy in general and American dominance in particular comes not, as yet, from systemic alternatives arising from within the West, but from China, the focus of Part Two. This part is opened by a chapter that deals with the rise of China's billionaires and their close relationship with the Communist Party officials. Its author, Ion Marandici, finds that higher income levels correlate with party membership and education.

Heiko Khoo poses the key question whether China today is capitalist or socialist and whether it offers a viable alternative to both Soviet-style socialism and to free-market capitalism. He applies the theories and definitions of capitalism and socialism developed by the Hungarian reform economist János Kornai. Khoo argues that the rise of China challenges the hegemony of liberal democracy and the free market which is held to underpin it. China's leader Xi Jinping is the most influential Marxist in today's world, but outside China few people read his writings or speeches, and many Western Marxists consider China to be capitalist. Nevertheless, the impact of his ideas and actions is decisive in shaping the fate of China. Khoo locates Xi's line today in the tradition of the New Economic Policy (NEP), introduced by Lenin in Russia in 1921. According to Khoo, Xi's emphasis on Marxism as China's guiding ideology is connected to a radical campaign against corruption that is designed to strengthen the communist party's popular support and appease social discontent. His defence of the central role of public ownership and his outright opposition to parliamentary democracy indicate that China will remain a communist state for the foreseeable future.

The next chapter on China deals with the country's role on a global scale. Xi Jinping's Belt and Road Initiative seems to pose a challenge to Western neo-liberal trading patterns.[15] Peter Braga and Stephen Hall ask whether the Belt and Road Initiative poses an alternative system, as opposed to an alternative communications network. They conclude that it does not, but that China will use the project to stimulate changes in the global system to its own advantage.

The two chapters in Part Three bring us back to Western Europe and North America, where the discrediting of neo-liberalism has led to a renewed interest in ideas of a mixed economy. More effective state intervention should both revive growth and reduce inequality.[16] Among other concepts, Keynesianism is beginning to make a comeback. Writing in 2018, Robert Skidelsky, the biographer of John Maynard Keynes, is among several who have warned that the world economy is heading for another crash. He has called for a partial return to Keynesianism with governments borrowing in order to invest.[17] Keynes had argued that, in order to avoid recessions, which he saw as endemic in the capitalist system, the government should be ready to borrow money and raise the level of aggregate effective demand. In Western Europe between 1945 and 1973, Keynesian theory was generally seen as the answer to Marx's theory of inevitable capitalist crisis.

Geoffrey Hosking's chapter, which focuses on Britain as an example but is of global significance, concretely shows the impact of neo-liberal policy. He shows that the resulting inequalities have led to a loss of faith in the political system and rising right-wing populism. In arguing for a return to Keynesian policies, he points out some of the mistakes made by governments in the past, which prevented these policies from working properly.

Others have questioned whether a return to Keynesianism is viable in the twenty-first century and suggested that it is capitalism itself which needs to be replaced, not simply the neo-liberal model. Some have argued that capitalism can only continue to exist by taking away democratic rights.[18] As traditional social democracy adapted itself to neo-liberal ideas and policies, its support amongst the working class tended to decline.[19] This was sometimes challenged by new, radical movements on the left which occasionally inspired large numbers of young people into political activity and in a short time achieved substantial support: for example, Podemos in Spain, Syriza in Greece, Jeremy Corbyn in Britain and Bernie Sanders in America.[20] Pete Duncan's chapter discusses the successes and limitations of these four movements.

Notes

1. Sebastian Leitner and Mario Holzner, 'Economic Inequality in Central, East and Southeast Europe', *Intervention: European Journal of Economics and Economic Policies* 5, no. 1 (2008), 155–88.
2. For a neo-liberal programme articulated early in the Putin era, much of which has been implemented, see Vladimir Mau, *From Crisis to Growth* (London: Centre for Research into Post-Communist Economies, 2005), especially ch. 10. Mau is now Rector of the presidential Russian Academy for the National Economy and State Service in Moscow. For a celebration of neo-liberal achievements in the former Soviet bloc, and a call for their greater application in the former Soviet Union, see Ånders Aslund, *How Capitalism was Built: The Transformation of Central and Eastern Europe, the Caucasus and Central Asia*, 2nd ed. (Cambridge: Cambridge University Press, 2013), 358–65.
3. Few still subscribe to the declaration of the final global triumph of capitalism as expressed in Francis Fukuyama's *The End of History and the Last Man* (New York: Free Press, 1992), an idea which its author has abandoned in the meantime (see Fukuyama, *Political Order and Political Decay: From the Industrial Revolution to the Globalisation of Democracy* (London: Profile Books, 2015)).
4. Ilya Budraitskis, 'Contradictions in Russian Cultural Politics: Conservatism as an Instrument of Neoliberalism', in *The Art of Civil Action*, ed. Philipp Dietachmair and Pascal Gielen, accessed 15 January 2019, http://www.criticatac.ro/lefteast/russian-contradiction/.
5. Jan-Werner Müller, *What is Populism?* (London: Penguin, 2017).
6. For example, Geoffrey Hosking, having studied the phenomenon of trust within Russia, then moved on to write a book on the global importance of trust. Geoffrey Hosking, *Trust: A History* (Oxford: Oxford University Press, 2014).
7. Peter A. Hall and David Soskice, eds., *Varieties of Capitalism: The Institutional Foundations of Comparative Advantage* (Oxford: Oxford University Press, 2001).
8. Dorothee Bohle and Béla Greskovits, *Capitalist Diversity on Europe's Periphery* (Ithaca, NY: Cornell University Press, 2012).
9. János Kornai, *The Socialist System: The Political Economy of Communism* (Oxford: Clarendon Press, 2007).
10. For an analysis of the workings of the different models of 'real existing socialism', see Alec Nove, *The Economics of Feasible Socialism* (London: Allen & Unwin, 1983) and Heiko Khoo's chapter in this volume.

11 Leszek Kolakowski, *Main Currents of Marxism: Its Origins, Growth and Dissolution,* 3 vols. (Oxford: Oxford University Press, 1978).
12 Thomas Piketty, *Capital in the Twenty-First Century* (Cambridge, MA: The Belknap Press of Harvard University Press, 2014). The crisis had already evoked an academic debate on the costs of inequality; in particular, see Richard Wilkinson and Kate Pickett, *The Spirit Level: Why Equality is Better for Everyone* (London: Allen Lane, 2009); Joseph E. Stiglitz, *The Price of Inequality: The Avoidable Causes and Hidden Costs of Inequality* (New York: Norton, 2012); James K. Galbraith, *Inequality and Instability: A Study of the World Economy just before the Great Crisis* (New York: Oxford University Press, 2012); Branko Milanovic: *Global Inequality: A New Approach for the Age of Globalization* (Cambridge, MA: The Belknap Press of Harvard University Press, 2016); and Chrystia Freeland, *Plutocrats: The Rise of the New Global Super-Rich and the Fall of Everyone Else* (London: Penguin, 2012).
13 On the process of privatisation in Russia and its consequences, see Chrystia Freeland, *Sale of the Century: The Inside Story of the Second Russian Revolution* (London: Little, Brown, 2000); David E. Hoffman, *The Oligarchs: Wealth and Power in the New Russia* (New York: Public-Affairs, 2011); Thane Gustafson, *Wheel of Fortune: The Battle for Oil and Power in Russia* (Cambridge, MA: The Belknap Press of Harvard University Press, 2012); Stephen Fortescue, *Russia's Oil Barons and Metal Magnates: Oligarchs and the State in Transition* (Basingstoke, UK: Palgrave Macmillan, 2006); and Elisabeth Schimpfössl, *Rich Russians: From Oligarchs to Bourgeoisie* (New York: Oxford University Press, 2018).
14 *The Global Encyclopaedia of Informality*, ed. Alena Ledeneva (London: UCL Press, 2018).
15 Peter Frankopan, *The New Silk Roads: The Present and Future of the World* (London: Bloomsbury, 2018).
16 *The Alternative: Towards a New Progressive Politics*, ed. Lisa Nandy MP, Caroline Lucas MP, and Chris Bowers (London: Biteback, 2016); and Colin Crouch, *Making Capitalism Fit for Society* (Cambridge: Polity Press, 2013).
17 Robert Skidelsky, *Money and Government: A Challenge to Mainstream Economics* (London: Allen Lane, 2018). See also David Sainsbury, *Progressive Capitalism: How to Achieve Economic Growth, Liberty and Social Justice* (London: Biteback, 2013); *Beyond Neoliberalism, Nationalism and Socialism: Rethinking the Boundary between State and Market,* ed. Thomas Aubrey (London: Rowman & Littlefield, 2017).
18 Wolfgang Streeck, *How Will Capitalism End? Essays on a Failing System* (London: Verso, 2016).
19 Ernesto Laclau and Chantal Mouffe, *Hegemony and Socialist Strategy: Towards a Radical Democratic Politics*, 2nd ed., paperback (London: Verso, 2014); and Stephanie L. Mudge, *Leftism Reinvented: Western Parties from Socialism to Neoliberalism* (Cambridge, MA: Harvard University Press, 2018).
20 Paul Mason, *Why it's STILL Kicking Off Everywhere: The New Global Revolutions* (London: Verso, 2013).

Bibliography

Aslund, Ånders. *How Capitalism was Built: The Transformation of Central and Eastern Europe, the Caucasus and Central Asia.* 2nd ed. Cambridge: Cambridge University Press, 2013.
Aubrey, Thomas, ed. *Beyond Neoliberalism, Nationalism and Socialism: Rethinking the Boundary between State and Market.* London: Rowman & Littlefield, 2017.
Bohle, Dorothee, and Béla Greskovits. *Capitalist Diversity on Europe's Periphery.* Ithaca, NY: Cornell University Press, 2012.
Budraitskis, Ilya. 'Contradictions in Russian Cultural Politics: Conservatism as an Instrument of Neoliberalism'. In *The Art of Civil Action*, edited by Philipp Dietachmair and Pascal Gielen. Accessed 15 January 2019, http://www.criticatac.ro/lefteast/russian-contradiction/.
Crouch, Colin. *Making Capitalism Fit for Society.* Cambridge: Polity Press, 2013.
Fortescue, Stephen. *Russia's Oil Barons and Metal Magnates: Oligarchs and the State in Transition.* Basingstoke, UK: Palgrave Macmillan, 2006.
Frankopan, Peter. *The New Silk Roads: The Present and Future of the World.* London: Bloomsbury, 2018.

Freeland, Chrystia. *Plutocrats: The Rise of the New Global Super-Rich and the Fall of Everyone Else*. London: Penguin, 2012.
Freeland, Chrystia. *Sale of the Century: The Inside Story of the Second Russian Revolution*. London: Little, Brown, 2000.
Fukuyama, Francis. *The End of History and the Last Man*. New York: Free Press, 1992.
Fukuyama, Francis. *Political Order and Political Decay: From the Industrial Revolution to the Globalisation of Democracy*. London: Profile Books, 2015.
Galbraith, James K. *Inequality and Instability: A Study of the World Economy just before the Great Crisis*. New York: Oxford University Press, 2012.
Gustafson, Thane. *Wheel of Fortune: The Battle for Oil and Power in Russia*. Cambridge, MA: The Belknap Press of Harvard University Press, 2012.
Hall, Peter A., and David Soskice, eds. *Varieties of Capitalism: The Institutional Foundations of Comparative Advantage*. Oxford: Oxford University Press, 2001.
Hoffman, David E. *The Oligarchs: Wealth and Power in the New Russia*. New York: PublicAffairs, 2011.
Hosking, Geoffrey. *Trust: A History*. Oxford: Oxford University Press, 2014.
Kolakowski, Leszek. *Main Currents of Marxism: Its Origins, Growth and Dissolution*. 3 vols. Oxford: Oxford University Press, 1978.
Kornai, János. *The Socialist System: The Political Economy of Communism*. Oxford: Clarendon Press, 2007.
Labour Party. *Alternative Models of Ownership*. 2018. Accessed 25 November 2018, labour.org.uk/wp-content/uploads/2017/10/Alternative-Models-of-Ownership.pdf.
Laclau, Ernesto, and Chantal Mouffe. *Hegemony and Socialist Strategy: Towards a Radical Democratic Politics*. 2nd ed., paperback. London: Verso, 2014.
Ledeneva, Alena, ed. *The Global Encyclopaedia of Informality*. London: UCL Press, 2018.
Leitner, Sebastian, and Mario Holzner. 'Economic Inequality in Central, East and Southeast Europe'. *Intervention: European Journal of Economics and Economic Policies* 5, no. 1 (2008), 155–88.
Mason, Paul. *Why it's STILL Kicking Off Everywhere: The New Global Revolutions*. London: Verso, 2013.
Mau, Vladimir. *From Crisis to Growth*. London: Centre for Research into Post-Communist Economies, 2005.
Milanovic, Branko. *Global Inequality: A New Approach for the Age of Globalization*. Cambridge, MA: The Belknap Press of Harvard University Press, 2016.
Mudge, Stephanie L. *Leftism Reinvented: Western Parties from Socialism to Neoliberalism*. Cambridge, MA: Harvard University Press, 2018.
Müller, Jan-Werner. *What is Populism?* London: Penguin, 2017.
Nandy, Lisa, Caroline Lucas, and Chris Bowers, eds. *The Alternative: Towards a New Progressive Politics*. London: Biteback, 2016.
Nove, Alec. *The Economics of Feasible Socialism*. London: Allen & Unwin, 1983.
Piketty, Thomas. *Capital in the Twenty-First Century*. Cambridge, MA: The Belknap Press of Harvard University Press, 2014.
Sainsbury, David. *Progressive Capitalism: How to Achieve Economic Growth, Liberty and Social Justice*. London: Biteback, 2013.
Schimpfössl, Elisabeth. *Rich Russians: From Oligarchs to Bourgeoisie*. New York: Oxford University Press, 2018.
Skidelsky, Robert. *Money and Government: A Challenge to Mainstream Economics*. London: Allen Lane, 2018.
Stiglitz, Joseph E., *The Price of Inequality: The Avoidable Causes and Hidden Costs of Inequality*. New York: Norton, 2012.
Streeck, Wolfgang. *How Will Capitalism End? Essays on a Failing System*. London, New York: Verso, 2016.
Wilkinson, Richard, and Kate Pickett. *The Spirit Level: Why Equality is Better for Everyone*. London: Allen Lane, 2009.

Part I
Capitalism in action

1
Semi-dependent capitalism
Russia

Ruslan Dzarasov

Modern Russian society can be defined as a semi-dependent form of capitalism. This means that on the one hand, it depends heavily on the core capitalist countries, while on the other, it aspires to play a regional hegemonic role. All contradictions in Russia's economy, domestic and foreign policy stem from this intermediate position in the capitalist world-system.

Creeping Stalinism: The economic foundation of post-Soviet society

The roots of the present-day model of capitalism in Russia lie in two major factors: (1) degeneration of the Soviet bureaucracy, and (2) the influence of global financialised capitalism.

Leon Trotsky in his insightful work *The Revolution Betrayed* demonstrated that contrary to Stalin's proposition, Soviet society was by no means socialist. Actually, it was no more than a transitional formation which amounted merely to an attempt at constructing socialism. In the absence of a victorious world revolution, this society could well revert to capitalism. Trotsky also singled out the source of this degeneration, in the special position of the ruling bureaucracy: 'Privileges are worth little if they cannot be handed on to one's children by way of inheritance. Therefore, the privileged bureaucracy will sooner or later seek to take ownership of the enterprises it now manages, to turn them into private property.'[1]

Cambridge University Professor David Lane speaks of two main social groupings which aided in the transition of the Soviet system to capitalism: the 'administrative class', consisting of the Soviet bureaucracy, and the 'appropriating class', made up of the intelligentsia who had an interest in using markets to benefit from their professional knowledge.[2] To these two social categories can be added the black-market entrepreneurs who had gradually developed behind the ostensibly monolithic façade of the Soviet system.[3] In the course of Gorbachev's Perestroika, these groupings tacitly formed a powerful pro-capitalist social bloc, which facilitated the demise of the Soviet system and its transition to capitalism.

A no less important factor shaping the new social system was the unprecedented Western influence on the process of transformation in the former Soviet republics. The defeat of the Soviet Union in the Cold War had compromised the socialist system of values, helping to create a situation in which Russian society uncritically adopted a bourgeois system of values which presupposed the broad introduction of private property. It was against the backdrop of its victory in the Cold War that ruling groups in the West, above all in the United States, were able to exert a decisive behind-the-scenes influence on the formation of the post-Soviet societies.

This formation was based on the principles of the notorious Washington Consensus, which underlay the policies pursued by Western (primarily American) financial organisations in their dealings with developing countries.[4] As the American researcher Janine Wedel argued, the Russian reforms were mapped out by a few Harvard University experts with close links to the US government. They were implemented in Russia by the politically dominant group of pro-Western politicians belonging to the close coterie of the first Russian president, Boris Yeltsin.[5]

It follows from the above that implementation of the Russian reforms saw the desire of Soviet state functionaries to become private-property owners merging with the ambition of the Western ruling elite to impose their system of values on their historical adversary.

The foundations of the new social system were laid by privatisation. Its nature can be seen in the materials of an official report by the Accounting Chamber of the Russian Federation.[6] The report states that privatisation was based neither on the selection of particular state assets whose effectiveness might have been increased by their transfer to private hands, nor on the creation of equal opportunities for all layers of the population. As a result, the preconditions were created for countless breaches of the law during the privatisation process. In the course of this process, an enormous transfer of wealth from the state to the private sector was carried out. Its scale can be gauged from the fact that the privatisations yielded the government less than 5 per cent of the market price of the former state enterprises.[7] An important dimension of this process was that privatisation further strengthened informal control over the assets of the new owners (see more on this below). This was only the continuation of informal control over state enterprises enjoyed by the Soviet bureaucracy from Stalin's time.

Other reform policies had the same thrust. The liberalising of prices – that is, their freeing from control by the state – in fact facilitated transfer of labour income into private hands through price increases on the part of the new owners. To fight inflation, the authorities started the so-called financial stabilisation approach, reduced to restrictive monetary policy. The money stock was squeezed at the expense of real wages, pensions and social transfer payments. All this resulted in the enormous decline in aggregate demand, leading in turn to an equally great decrease in gross domestic product (GDP).

To better understand the nature of the post-Soviet social system, one should focus on the aims of the new capitalist elite in terms of the type of income that they extract from the assets under their control, which reflects a particular model of corporate governance established in modern Russia. It is highly authoritarian in nature, because it is based on a high rate of concentration of property rights.[8] However, the real concentration of power at Russian enterprises is even greater than is assumed by the formal concentration of property rights. The most important feature of the Russian model of corporate governance is that it is largely based on informal control.

Dominant groups controlling Russian productive assets developed a sophisticated network of power relations, allowing them to influence both the internal and external environment of their enterprises. One should call the network of these predominantly informal institutions an 'infrastructure of control'. Its external elements typically include a sophisticated chain of offshore firms disguising the real owners of enterprises; ties to corrupt state functionaries lobbying for their business interests; and protection provided by so-called roofs – state law enforcement agencies, private security firms and criminal structures. The main aim of the external elements of the infrastructure of control is to protect the 'property rights' of the established dominant groups against encroachments by hostile groups. The internal elements of the infrastructure include top-down management with a highly centralised decision-making process; overgrown departments of monitoring and control; and internal security services. These institutions were designed to suppress worker protests and opportunist actions by hired employees. The whole infrastructure of control ensures reliable control on the part of owners over the financial flows of their enterprises.[9] It follows from the above that the highly authoritarian character of Russian big business assumes extra-economic compulsion.

The largely informal character of the Russian model of corporate governance has numerous and vital consequences for business strategies, social relations and national economic development. It is impossible to fix legally informal control over enterprises, and hence it is equally impossible to bequeath it to inheritors. However, informal control can always be challenged. Waves of property redistribution between rival groups of dominant owners roll regularly across the landscape of Russian big business. The majority of these takeovers are hostile in nature and carried out with the help of coercion from state organs and/or criminal groups. Alternatively, the state can use so-called state corporations to transfer property from alien to friendly business groups. This means that ownership and control in Russian business are fundamentally unstable.

One of the most important results of this instability of property rights in modern Russia is the shift of the typical corporate strategy to a short-term time horizon. This determined short-term rent as the predominant type of income maximised by the majority of Russian corporations. This rent can be quantitatively defined as 'free cash flow' net of interest payments on loans and also dividends of non-controlling shareholders. Rent extraction assumes offshore figurehead trading intermediaries. The latter are usually registered in some offshore jurisdictions with a favourable tax regime. Typically, Russian owners do not supply the products of the controlled enterprises directly to the domestic market. First, they sell goods to their own offshore trading companies at prices lower than the market level. Intermediaries later resell the products at market prices. As a result, profit is accumulated in the accounts of the trade intermediaries and later is transferred to private accounts of the final beneficiaries. Alternatively, the latter can establish firms supplying raw materials, parts and/or equipment to the controlled enterprises at prices higher than the market level. The result is the same. Funds are withdrawn from enterprises and transferred to private offshore accounts. This system was especially evident on the eve of the global financial meltdown of 2008, when oil revenues of Russian capitalism were at their highest. According to some data, 90 per cent of Russian big business is registered in offshore sites and 80 per cent of the deals in Russian securities are carried out through the same jurisdictions.[10] According to the Russian Central Bank, in the period from 1994 to the first quarter of 2018, the net export of private capital from Russia amounted to $714 billion.[11]

The rent type of incomes appropriated by Russian capitalists should be distinguished from the entrepreneurial profit dominating economies of the centre. The latter depends on the difference between costs and revenues. The rent in question only partially depends on this factor because it is extracted due to control over the firm's financial flows. The above means that sources of this income may be formed at the expense of wages, salaries of rank-and-file managers, investment funds, depreciation funds, violation of contractual commitments, and tax evasion – sometimes even embezzlement of loans and any other kinds of financial flows. Some of these sources represent costs rather than revenues. Dependence of this short-term rent extraction on the largely informal infrastructure of control makes this type of income close to Marxian feudal rent, which is appropriated by extra-economic coercion. Hence, the rent of Russian capitalists should be placed somewhere in between the entrepreneurial profit of the centre and the feudal rent of the periphery. The aims of Russian firms reflect the semi-peripheral nature of Russian capitalism.

Figure 1.1 shows in generalised form the impact of the transition to peripheral (or semi-peripheral) capitalism on the social and economic development of the former Soviet republics. All of the former Soviet republics lag behind the USSR in terms of both Human Development Index (HDI) and per capita GDP rankings, with Estonia being the only exception. (And even Estonia is behind the USSR in terms of per capita gross national income (GNI) rank.)

Split elite and authoritarian state

Beginning in the mid-2000s, Western analysts started actively discussing the return of Russia to the authoritarian path of development and resumption of the Cold War.[12] Such a change is usually regarded as a result of the personal influence of Vladimir Putin, especially in connection with his past KGB experience. In fact, the political system of modern Russia, like its foreign policy, is only the natural result of the new social-economic system of semi-peripheral capitalism, which replaced the Soviet system.

According to the famous theory of hegemony developed by Antonio Gramsci, the mechanism of democracy under capitalism assumes a certain compromise of the ruling class with subjugated classes and social groups. It includes the observation of certain social-economic rights of the labouring classes, petty bourgeoisie and intellectual circles.[13] This service is provided by the social welfare state. It allows the ruling class to present its own interests in society as national interests shared by everyone. An important precondition of this social compromise is formation of the general class consciousness of capitalists in a given society,

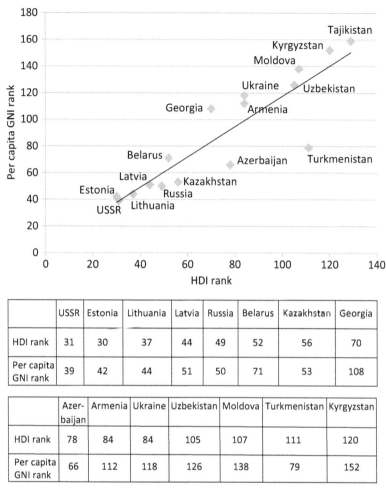

Fig. 1.1 Relationship between international rankings according to the HDI and per capita GNI of the USSR (1987) and the former Soviet republics (2015). Rankings are placed in descending order (i.e., the best ranking is in the lowest left position). Source: *Human Development Report 1990*, 119; *Human Development Report 2016: Human Development for Everyone*, 198–201.

which assumes limiting the interests of individual capitalists when they contradict the general, whole-class interests. Only with this backdrop can a relatively independent (from particular representatives of the ruling class) democratic state appear.[14]

The modern semi-peripheral capitalism established in Russia is a far cry from the preconditions for bourgeois democracy. As mentioned above, its private ownership is based on an infrastructure of control – that is, on supra-economic coercion and violence. This type of private property, reflecting the joint effect of degeneration of the Soviet system and Western influence (see above), became the major institution strengthening the violation of human rights in modern Russia. First, these are rights of hired labour. Distribution of the national income is determined by the power of big capital in its coarse form. It implies transfer of part of the income created by the labour of the Russian population (and in the case of oil revenues, by labour in other countries) to the world financial markets. Such a regime is incompatible with a genuine democracy. Indeed, under a democratic regime people would not tolerate not only some particular politicians, but the social system of peripheral capitalism as such. Thus, the foundations of the authoritarian political regime are rooted not in past experiences of Mr Putin, but in the nature of the new social system which was partially inherited from the degeneration of the Soviet system and formed under the crucial influence of the West.

As is well known, the radical market reforms of the early 1990s, and privatisation in particular, were challenged by the Russian Supreme Soviet – the first truly democratically elected parliament in modern Russian history. This led to an eventual showdown between the parliament and President Yeltsin, supported by the West, in October 1993. It was a decisive moment for the fate of democracy in modern Russia. For the sake of going forward with radical market reforms, the liberal pro-Western power elite resorted to shooting up the first legally elected parliament in modern Russian history.[15] It is worth mentioning that Yeltsin's edict, which disbanded the Supreme Soviet, justified this move by the Supreme Soviet's 'direct resistance to implementation of social and economic reforms'.[16] The parliamentary opposition, while pursuing its own aims, at the same time protested against the radical market reforms on behalf of the wider Russian public. Shooting up the parliament removed the last obstacles on the way to formation of the new capitalist class – notorious Russian oligarchs – and secured the authoritarian political regime favourable to their economic power and corresponding to it. It is exactly the type of pseudo-democratic power free from the societal control necessary to establish the external elements of the infrastructure of control. The shooting up of the democratically elected parliament, whatever conservative trends it demonstrated, was an undisguised act of civil war. It was carried out with the tacit support of the American administration. The memoirs of Strobe Talbott, the deputy US Secretary of State responsible for policy towards Russia in the Clinton administration, testify that in the moment of this acute crisis the US administration was concerned only with preserving in power

Mr Yeltsin, who was making important unilateral concessions in vital strategic issues.[17] Results of this 'victory' were fixed in the new authoritarian Constitution which cut the rights of the State Duma and the new Russian Parliament, and disproportionately extended presidential power.

Mr Putin only applied the mechanism of authoritarianism created by his powerful predecessor with the full support of the West. It is important to emphasise that this mechanism itself reflects the objective character of the social-class relations established in the country in post-Soviet times. More than that, present Russian capitalism has inner features which prevent its democratic evolution.

As was shown above, due to the fundamental instability of its control over assets, Russian big business is oriented towards short-term rent rather than long-term growth. This creates obstacles for the process of recognition of general interests by the Russian property-owning class. That is why such aims as modernisation, social stability, a worthy place at the world market and the like are not shared by all business groups. The recurring process of redistribution of property rights demonstrates the constant 'war of all against all' in the milieu of big business. Essentially, Russian oligarchs represent a mechanical aggregation of rival, hostile groups. Such a situation prevents the development of the joint class consciousness of the current Russian bourgeois class in a meaningful form. In the absence of the joint interests of the ruling class, there is no real place for genuine social compromise with other social classes and groups. It appears that there are no socio-economic foundations for the hegemony of the current Russian bourgeoisie.

There are no preconditions for the formation of a relatively independent bourgeois state either. The principle of 'equidistance of power from oligarchs' proclaimed by Putin is no more than a slogan. A number of his cronies joined the Forbes 'Golden hundred' of Russians, when Mr Putin came to power.[18] The external elements of the infrastructure of control, 'roofs' provided by the state functionaries and lobbyist structures, mean that in fact they have a double system of responsibilities. Ostensibly they are responsible to the state hierarchy, while actually they stick to the interests of business groups to which they are linked by informal networks of power and money relations. External elements of control are very costly, but they are vital to preserve control over enterprises. From this it follows that bribes (which facilitate informal links between power and money) are intrinsic to the system and represent part of the investment of capital by Russian big business. That is why it is impossible to overcome corruption in the society of semi-peripheral capitalism without challenging this social system as such.

Thus, modern Russia demonstrates an atomised proprietary class and fragmented state. Having come into being in the 1990s, it was followed by economic decline and plummeting living standards that threatened the disintegration of the very fabric of society. This was saliently demonstrated by the 'parade of sovereignties' (which means that many Russian regions proclaimed their independence from the central power) which rolled over Russia in the early 1990s. All this was only a window of opportunity for the local elites' takeover of the former state assets in 'their' territories. It was this growing vacuum of power which was stopped by Mr Putin's strengthening of his personal power regime.

Putin carried out an administrative reform strengthening control of the central government bodies in the hierarchy of power; cancelled election of the regional heads, replacing it by direct appointment; increased expenditures on the military, secret services and law enforcement agencies; ousted from the country a few powerful oligarchs who challenged his personal power, and so on. In the absence of real preconditions for bourgeois democracy and any influential social protest movements, Putin's authoritarianism helped to fill the vacuum of power and stopped the anarchic disintegration of the country. This explains his popularity among the Russian population. However important in their time, these achievements are only relative and temporary.

One must say that Putin's reforms left intact the foundations of the social system established in Russia after the fall of the Soviet system. The US expert on Russia, Marshall Goldman, wittily called modern Russia 'Petrostate'.[19] Indeed, the relative political and social stability of our society achieved in the 2000s rested on partial redistribution of oil revenues. It was this which allowed a significant increase of expenditures on defence, the state apparatus, education and healthcare. Subsidies to some regions, which were largely embezzled, bought loyalty of the local elites. However, these measures do not solve the long-term problems of the inefficient social system.

Indeed, the domestic policy of the Russian state is ambiguous and contradictory. One of the most salient contradictions in modern Russia is the fact that the sharp anti-American rhetoric of the mass media coexists with staunchly neo-liberal economic policy based on American recipes. Even more than that, government bodies responsible for economic policy are headed by pro-American functionaries. Their main instruments of economic policy are (a) restrictive monetary policy and (b) a balanced budget approach. These are seen as the main preconditions for financial stabilisation which is expected to facilitate economic growth. Restrictive monetary policy is designed to suppress inflation, but it also serves to establish a foreign currency rate favourable for exporters. To prevent appreciation of the rouble, the Russian Central Bank buys 'excess' foreign currency and invests it in the world financial markets (largely in US assets). The budget deficit is decreased at the expense of cutting expenditures on the national economy, national defence, education, science and healthcare. Obviously, it is a conventional neo-liberal agenda. It was not changed even under the conditions of anti-Russian economic sanctions imposed on the country in retaliation for its firm position in the Ukraine crisis (see the next section).

In obvious contradiction to this approach stands the so-called manual management of the national economy on the part of the Kremlin group, which entails 'point management' of the presidential administration. The Kremlin group is an influential state body in modern Russia that sometimes challenges the government, infringing on its sphere of influence. A number of Russian oligarchs dependent on the Kremlin act as vehicles of the latter's economic policy. Dependent structures of big business are unofficially, but earnestly 'advised' to invest in one or another project considered important for national economic development by the Kremlin administration. This policy corresponds to Putin's international strategy (see below). For instance, under current conditions pro-Kremlin oligarchs are guided to create enterprises in the Russian Far East to supply raw materials and semi-processed products to China. Another important vehicle of the Kremlin's economic policy is represented by 'state corporations'. These bulky and rigid structures represent state holdings whose assets were appropriated under strong pressure from the state. They are notoriously inefficient but increase the economic influence of the Kremlin.

Obviously, 'manual management' goes against the conventional principles of the neo-liberal approach of the Russian government. Economic policy eventually reflects some compromise between two approaches intermediated by Putin. Naturally, this compromise fails to provide any clearly articulated long-term strategy of economic or social development of the country. The very fact of the deep split in the Russian elite reflects the essential properties of semi-peripheral capitalism. They also condition a contradictory approach to foreign policy.

Neo-revisionist foreign policy: The clash of capitalisms?

One may single out two groups of the Russian ruling class, who cooperate and compete in shaping Russian domestic and foreign policy. They can be defined according to the direction of their integrationist strategy.

'Atlantic integrationists' are oriented towards strengthening their ties with the West. Their opponents can be called 'Eurasian integrationists', because they try to entrench Russia's independent stance in the world arena. The first group is largely represented by notorious Russian oligarchs, who extract their rent in Russia and then invest large parts of it in the West. Even when they buy enterprises abroad, these are savings rather than investments because their profitability is usually much lower than that of their Russian assets. (This does not mean that Russian business is more efficient. Big business simply redistributes income in its favour using non-economic means.) Trying by all means to integrate into the Western ruling elite, these oligarchs are dependent on the West. The second group largely consists of oligarchs associated with the so-called Kremlin group. Functionaries from law enforcement agencies occupy a prominent position in this group. The two orientations of Russian foreign policy are only another dimension of the split peculiar to the ruling class of a semi-peripheral capitalism. Russian foreign policy is determined by behind-the-scenes collusion and compromise of these two powerful groups. This explains its inconsistency and wavering.

Mainstream Western political analysts depict Russian foreign policy as a revisionist one, attempting to undermine the current world economic order. It is substantiated by the fact that it allegedly tries to restore the Soviet Union in a new form. In December 2012, then US Secretary of State Hillary Clinton condemned Russia for the alleged attempt 'to re-Sovietize the region' of the former USSR: 'It's not going to be called that. It's going to be called customs union, it will be called Eurasian Union and all of that,' she explained. 'But let's make no mistake about it. We know what the goal is and we are trying to figure out effective ways to slow down or prevent it.'[20] However, Russian policy is by no means a revisionist one. In fact, Putin challenges neither Western domination in the world in general, nor US hegemony in particular. He is rather trying to defend Russian national interests in the existing framework of the current world order. According to Richard Sakwa from Kent University (UK), such a strategy, based on an attempt to change the *practice* of Western domination rather than *undermine* it, should be called 'neo-revisionist'.[21]

This can be seen from the recent history of Russian foreign policy. In his first tenure in power (2000–4) Putin's policy more or less continued the 'Yes' diplomacy of his predecessor in relations with the West. He made a few important unilateral concessions, signing the Strategic Arms Reduction Treaty (START, 2002), which contained conditions unilaterally favourable for the United States; closing Russian military bases in Vietnam; closing the electronic surveillance centre in Cuba; helping to establish US military bases in Central Asia; and cooperating on Afghanistan and in some other issues. In response, the then-new Russian president expected that the West would recognise the leading role of Russia in the former Soviet space. However, this never happened. What followed was seen in Moscow as creeping but persistent strategic encirclement of Russia; the most treacherous was considered the expansion of NATO to the East despite oral guarantees that this military bloc would never move 'an inch' to the East. Quite important was the US decision to deploy an anti-missile defence system in Europe allegedly directed against the menace of North Korean forces, but obviously against Russia. One of the most threatening developments to Russian interests was a number of 'coloured revolutions' organised by the United States in the former Soviet space. Against this backdrop, the invitation to join NATO granted to Ukraine 'represented a fundamental threat to Russia's national security. It would have rendered Russia indefensible and threatened to destabilise the Russian Federation itself. When the United States went so far as to suggest that Georgia be included as well, bringing NATO deeper into the Caucasus, the Russian conclusion – publicly stated – was that the United States in particular intended to encircle and break Russia'.[22]

A clear signal that Moscow was reconsidering its policy of unilateral concessions was sent to the West by Putin in his famous 'Munich speech', made at the 43rd Munich Security Conference in 2007. The Russian president condemned the US policy of establishing a 'unipolar world' and reminded the West of its obligations on the non-expansion of NATO.[23] Despite the fact that the speech did not contain any aggressive statements, the very claim of Russian leadership to an independent international policy annoyed the Western political establishment.[24] The next year, dramatic events in the Caucasus put this new strategy to a severe test.

In August 2008, the pro-American Georgian regime of Mikheil Saak'ashvili invaded the breakaway republic of South Ossetia in the Southern Caucasus. This had been an autonomous region, while Abkhazia had been an autonomous republic in Soviet Georgia. Both proclaimed independence and had been attempting to join Russia ever since the breakdown of the Soviet Union, on the same moral and judicial grounds by which Georgia received its own independence. The military attempt to suppress the maverick region followed after tacit support and encouragement on the part of the United States, despite unofficial warnings on the part of Russia that this would not be tolerated.[25] The Russian army quickly interfered, putting an abrupt end to the Georgian adventure and securing independence for the two republics. As was observed by the well-informed

British *Times* newspaper, the reasons for this clash were deeper than just local ethnic conflict: 'Oil may not be the cause of the war between Georgia and Russia, but it is a central element in the wider geo-strategic picture, and a source of incendiary tension that has helped to inflame the area.'[26]

The Eurasian Economic Union (EAEU) is an international organisation of regional economic integration formed in 2015 by Belarus, Kazakhstan and the Russian Federation, and joined the same year by Armenia and Kyrgyzstan. The EAEU proclaims the free movement of goods, services, capital and workforce, and conducts a coordinated, agreed policy in particular sectors of the economy. Post-Soviet republics view the concept of Eurasian integration as a way of mobilising their joint resources for modernisation of their countries confronted with strong external challenges, defined in terms of both geopolitics and geo-economics.[27] The EAEU population amounts to 183.8 million, its joint GDP to $1.8 trillion; industrial production in 2017 was 2.2 per cent of world output; and foreign trade with the outside world in 2014 was $877.6 billion (3.7 per cent of world exports and 2.3 per cent of world imports).[28] The world share of EAEU economies is quite modest. Nevertheless, integration has facilitated mutually beneficial economic (especially trade) relations. Russia is the main driving force behind the EAEU. However, while its share in foreign trade of the fellow-members of the union is great, their share in Russia's imports is low.[29] This means that for Russia, geopolitical aspects of the union are more important than economic aspects. Indeed, it is the most important Russian initiative of recent years in the former Soviet space.

Even more challenging was the Ukraine crisis, which erupted in late 2013. This country plays the key role in Mr Putin's design of the EAEU project and in any attempt to restore Russia's role in the former Soviet space. According to a US military expert, Ukraine plays an enormously significant role in energy resources transportation to the West and helps to prevent the revival of anything like a superpower in the former USSR.[30] This made Ukraine a battleground for the strategic clash of Russia and the West long before the Maidan uprising of 2013–14. The United States had long exercised their 'soft power' in this country, which cost them $5 billion, according to the famous confession of the then US Deputy Secretary of State Victoria Nuland.[31] The Maidan uprising itself was quite justified as an expression of people's outrage against the corruption and gross inefficiency of the country's leadership. However, it was exploited and directed from behind the scenes by the West, mainly by America. Russian interference was both predictable and justified as defence of Russian interests against Western interference behind the façade of a new coloured revolution. Reunification of Crimea was a pre-emptive strike, which thwarted the ousting of the Russian navy from its major naval base on the Black Sea in Sevastopol.[32] However, Russian support of the Donbas uprising of the pro-Russian population against the dictatorship of the Ukrainian nationalists was limited, since Putin abstained from open recognition of the two breakaway republics and from granting them full-scale military support.[33]

The Russian role in the Syrian conflict should be seen in connection with the Ukraine crisis. For a long time, Russia was working behind the scenes to form the alliance of Iran, Hezbollah and Syria in support of the friendly Assad regime.[34] However, Russian direct involvement was facilitated by the stalemate of the Ukraine crisis. Putin needed some tool to divert the US military, economic and political resources from Central Europe to some other region more important for American interests. He found Syria, saving Assad from destruction and turning back the course of the Syrian civil war. Doing this, the Russian president attempted to compel the West to recognise Russia as an indispensable player in the international arena.

Putin's foreign policy is quite pragmatic, pursuing economic interests rather than cherishing imperial dreams. In particular, the abovementioned 'manual management' is used by the Kremlin group in the Russian Far East to join the supply chain of Chinese industry. A number of enterprises are established in the region to supply raw materials and semi-processed goods to the industrial heart of China. The problem is that these goods are already being supplied to China by Australia, and extraction of Australian mineral resources is controlled by powerful Western financial groups. The Kremlin suggests a certain share in Russian business in this region to these financial groups to placate them and obtain their support for the project. An additional dimension of this policy is the Kremlin's hope to enlist the support of powerful segments of the Western elite in broader areas of international policy.[35] It is the type of scheming pertinent to Mr Putin. He would never make such a blunder as poisoning former KGB defectors by chemical warfare agents or direct interference in the US elections. Mr Putin prefers much subtler ways of behind-the-scenes influence, which leaves no traces.

However clever and skilful such types of scheming may seem, it can promote Russian interests only in the short or at most medium term because it fails to address the roots of Russian problems – the deficiencies of a semi-peripheral capitalism.

Conclusion

Summing up the above, one must note that Russian capitalism is a far cry from what was dreamed about by the Soviet population on the eve of transition to the new social system. The image of the new society was appealing because of its pledge of democracy, economic prosperity and human rights. However, radical market reforms produced semi-dependent capitalism. Its economy is based on transfer of part of the wealth created by the labour of its population to the dominant capitalist countries. It is the real condition of access to the capitalist world-system. As a result of this, the Russian economy, and economies of all other former Soviet republics as well, inevitably suffer backwardness, economic inefficiency and the mass impoverishment of the population. Big business is based on rent-seeking behaviour, undermining the accumulation of capital and economic growth. The high rate of exploitation of labour is incompatible with human rights and real democracy. The authoritarian state is the only alternative to social chaos. Under conditions of the Great Stagnation,[36] the struggle for redistribution of global wealth exacerbates. This increases the number of international conflicts in which Russia is involved. Under such conditions, inefficient, semi-dependent Russian capitalism is unable to defend national interests in the framework of the existing world order.

Notes

1. Lev Trotskii, *Predannaia revoliutsiia. Chto takoe SSSR i kuda on idet?* (Moscow: Moskovskii rabochii, 1991 [1936]), 210.
2. David Lane, *Elites and Classes in the Transformation of State Socialism* (New Brunswick, NJ: Transaction Publishers, 2011), 43.
3. Stanislav Menshikov, *The Anatomy of Russian Capitalism* (Washington, DC: Executive Intelligence Review News Service, 2007), 9.
4. By the 1990s, world experience already had demonstrated that the formula of 'liberalisation plus stabilisation' (that is, privatisation and a restrictive monetary policy) served to aggravate poverty and misery in the developing countries. Michael Chossudovsky, *The Globalisation of Poverty: Impact of IMF and World Bank Reforms* (London: Zed Books, 1997).
5. Janine Wedel, *Collision and Collusion: The Strange Case of Western Aid to Eastern Europe* (New York: Palgrave, 2001), ch. 4.
6. Sergei Stepashin, ed., *Analiz protsessov privatizatsii gosudarstvennoy sobstvennosti v Rossiiskoi Federatsii za period 1993–2003 gody* (Moscow: Olita, 2004).
7. Stanislav Menshikov, *Anatomiia rossiiskogo kapitalizma* (Moscow, Mezhdunarodnye Otnosheniia, 2004), 61–62.
8. Tatyana Dolgopyatova, 'Evolution of the Corporate Control Models in the Russian Companies: New Trends and Factors', *SUHSE Working Paper WP1/2005/04* (Moscow: State University–Higher School of Economics, 2005).
9. Ruslan Dzarasov, 'Insider Control and Investment Behaviour of Russian Corporations' (PhD thesis, Staffordshire University, UK, 2007), 78.

10. Robert Nigmatulin, ed., *Modernizatsiia Rossii: problemy i puti ikh resheniia* (Moscow: ZATS Modernizatsiia, 2012), 53.
11. 'The net inflow/outflow of private capital (according to the data of the Balance of Payments of Russian Federation)', Central Bank of the Russian Federation, accessed 17 August 2018, www.cbr.ru/statistics/?PrtId=svs.
12. Edward Lucas, *The New Cold War: How the Kremlin Menaces both Russia and the West* (New York: Palgrave Macmillan, 2008).
13. Joseph V. Femia, *Gramsci's Political Thought: Hegemony, Consciousness, and the Revolutionary Process* (Oxford: Clarendon Press, 1981).
14. Ralph Miliband, *Marxism and Politics*. Marxist Introductions. (Oxford: Oxford University Press, 1977).
15. Antonio Rubbi, *Yeltseniada: Pervoye desiatiletye postsovetskoi Rossii* (Moscow: Mezhdunarodnye otnoshenia, 2004), 188–205.
16. *Moskva. Osen'-93: Khronika Protivostoianiia* (Moscow: Respublika, 1995), vii.
17. Strobe Talbott, *The Russia Hand: A Memoir of Presidential Diplomacy* (New York: Random House, 2002).
18. Boris Nemtsov and Vladimir Milov, *Putin 10 Let. Itogy* (Moscow: Solidarnost', 2010), 6.
19. Marshall Goldman, *Petrostate: Putin, Power and the New Russia* (New York: Oxford University Press, 2008).
20. Bradley Klapper, 'Clinton fears efforts to "re-Sovietize" in Europe', *The Seattle Times*, 6 December 2012, accessed 29 August 2018, www.seattletimes.com/nation-world/clinton-fears-efforts-to-re-sovietize-in-europe/.
21. Richard Sakwa, *Frontline Ukraine: Crisis in the Borderlands* (London: I.B. Tauris, 2015).
22. George Friedman, 'The Russo-Georgian War and the Balance of Power', *Geopolitical Intelligence Report*, 12 August 2008, accessed 26 November 2018, worldview.stratfor.com/article/russo-georgian-war-and-balance-power.
23. Vladimir Putin, 'Vystuplenie i diskussiia na Miunkhenskoi konferentsii po voprosam politiki bezopasnosti 10 fevralia 2007 g', *Prezident Rossii*, 10 February 2007, accessed 4 September 2018, www.kremlin.ru/events/president/transcripts/24034.
24. Thom Shanker and Mark Landler, 'Putin Says U.S. is Undermining Global Stability', *New York Times*, 11 February 2007.
25. Thomas Omestad, 'Putin's Russia Acts as a Great Power Again', *US News & World Report*, 22 August 2008.
26. Ben Macintyre, 'Georgian Oil Pipeline: The Frontline', *The Times*, 13 August 2008.
27. See papers written by leaders of Russia, Belarus and Kazakhstan who initiated the EAEU: Vladimir Putin, 'Novyi integratsionnyi proekt dlia Evrazii – budushchee, kotoroe rozhdaetsia segodnia', *Izvestiia*, 3 October 2011; A. Lukashenko, 'O sud'bakh nashei integratsii', *Izvestiia*, 17 October 2011; N. Nazarbaev, 'Evraziiskii Soyuz – ot idei k istorii budushchego', *Izvestiia*, 25 October 2011.
28. Eurasian Economic Union, 'EAEU, 2016', accessed 4 September 2018, www.eaeunion.org/#about.
29. Elena Ustyuzhanina, 'The Eurasian Union and Global Value Chains', *European Politics and Society* 17, supp. 1 [The Eurasian Project in Global Perspective] (2016): 35–45.
30. R. Craig Nation, *NATO's Relations with Russia and Ukraine* (Carlisle, PA: U.S. Army War College, 2000).
31. Victoria Nuland, 'Victoria Nuland Admits Washington Has Spent $5 Billion to "Subvert Ukraine"', 9 February 2014, accessed 7 May 2018, www.youtube.com/watch?v=U2fYcHLouXY.
32. Rodolfo Ragonesi, 'The Crimean Question', *Times of Malta.com*, 14 April 2014, accessed 7 May 2016, www.timesofmalta.com/articles/view/20140414/opinion/The-Crimean-question.514876.
33. Richard Sakwa, *Frontline Ukraine: Crisis in the Borderlands* (London: I.B. Tauris, 2015).
34. Talal Nizameddin, 'Squaring the Middle East Triangle in Lebanon: Russia and the Iran-Syria-Hezbollah Nexus', *The Slavonic and East European Review* 86, no. 3 (July 2008): 475–500.
35. Personal communication of the author with an expert in Russian big business in the Far East, who requested that his identity not be disclosed.
36. This refers to the view that recent sources of economic growth are becoming exhausted. See Tyler Cowen, *The Great Stagnation* (New York: Dutton, 2011).

Bibliography

Chossudovsky, Michael. *The Globalisation of Poverty: Impact of IMF and World Bank Reforms*. London: Zed Books, TWN Third World Network, 1997.

Cowen, Tyler. *The Great Stagnation*. New York: Dutton, 2011.

Dolgopyatova, Tatyana. 'Evolution of the Corporate Control Models in the Russian Companies: New Trends and Factors'. *SUHSE Working Paper WP1/2005/04*. Moscow: State University–Higher School of Economics, 2005.

Dzarasov, Ruslan. 'Insider Control and Investment Behaviour of Russian Corporations'. PhD thesis, Staffordshire University, UK, 2007.

Eurasian Economic Union. 'EAEU, 2016'. Accessed 4 September 2018, www.eaeunion.org/#about.

Femia, Joseph V. *Gramsci's Political Thought: Hegemony, Consciousness, and the Revolutionary Process*. Oxford: Clarendon Press, 1981.

Friedman, George. 'The Russo-Georgian War and the Balance of Power'. *Geopolitical Intelligence Report*, 12 August 2008. Accessed 26 November 2018, worldview.stratfor.com/article/russo-georgian-war-and-balance-power.

Goldman, Marshall. *Petrostate: Putin, Power and the New Russia*. New York: Oxford University Press, 2008.

Human Development Report 1990 (New York: Oxford University Press, 1990).

Human Development Report 2016: Human Development for Everyone (Washington, DC: Communications Development Incorporated, 2016).

Klapper, Bradley. 'Clinton Fears Efforts to "re-Sovietize" in Europe'. *The Seattle Times*, 6 December 2012. Accessed 29 August 2018, www.seattletimes.com/nation-world/clinton-fears-efforts-to-re-sovietize-in-europe/.

Kotz, David, and Fred Weir. *Russia's Path from Gorbachev to Putin: The Demise of the Soviet System and the New Russia*. Abingdon, UK: Routledge, 2007.

Lane, David. *Elites and Classes in the Transformation of State Socialism*. New Brunswick, NJ: Transaction Publishers, 2011.

Lucas, Edward. *The New Cold War: How the Kremlin Menaces both Russia and the West*. New York: Palgrave Macmillan, 2008.

Lukashenko, A. 'O sud'bakh nashei integratsii'. *Izvestiia*, 17 October 2011.

Macintyre, Ben. 'Georgian Oil Pipeline: The Frontline'. *The Times*, 13 August 2008.

Menshikov, Stanislav. *Anatomiia rossiiskogo kapitalizma*. Moscow: Mezhdunarodnye otnosheniia, 2004.

Menshikov, Stanislav. *The Anatomy of Russian Capitalism*. Washington, DC: Executive Intelligence Review News Service, 2007.

Miliband, Ralph. *Marxism and Politics*. Marxist Introductions. Oxford: Oxford University Press, 1977.

Morozov, Sergei. *Diplomatiia Putina*. Moscow: Izdatel'stvo 'Krylov', 2008.

Moskva. Osen'-93: Khronika Protivostoianiia. Moscow: Respublika, 1995.

Nation, R. Craig. *NATO's Relations with Russia and Ukraine*. Carlisle, PA: U.S. Army War College, 2000.

Nazarbaev, N. 'Evraziiskii Soyuz – ot idei k istorii budushchego'. *Izvestiia*, 25 October 2011.

Nemtsov, Boris, and Vladimir Milov. *Putin 10 Let. Itogy*. Moscow: Solidarnost', 2010.

Nigmatulin, Robert, ed. *Modernizatsiia Rossii: problemy i puti ikh resheniia*. Moscow: ZATS Modernizatsiia, 2012.

Nizameddin, Talal. 'Squaring the Middle East Triangle in Lebanon: Russia and the Iran-Syria-Hezbollah Nexus'. *The Slavonic and East European Review* 86, no. 3 (July 2008): 475–500.

Nuland, Victoria. 'Victoria Nuland Admits Washington Has Spent $5 Billion to "Subvert Ukraine"'. 9 February 2014, accessed 7 May 2018, www.youtube.com/watch?v=U2fYcHLouXY.

Omestad, Thomas. 'Putin's Russia Acts as a Great Power Again'. *US News & World Report*, 22 August 2008.

Putin, Vladimir. 'Novyi integratsionnyi proekt dlia Evrazii – budushchee, kotoroe rozhdaetsia segodnia'. *Izvestiia*, 3 October 2011.

Putin, Vladimir. 'Vystuplenie i diskussiia na Miunkhenskoi konferentsii po voprosam politiki bezopasnosti 10 fevralia 2007 g'. *Prezident Rossii*, 10 February 2007. Accessed 4 September 2018, www.kremlin.ru/events/president/transcripts/24034.

Ragonesi, Rodolfo. 'The Crimean Question'. *Times of Malta.com*, 14 April 2014. Accessed 7 May 2016, www.timesofmalta.com/articles/view/20140414/opinion/The-Crimean-question.514876.

Reddaway, Peter, and Dmitri Glinski. *The Tragedy of Russia's Reforms: Market Bolshevism against Democracy*. Washington, DC: United States Institute of Peace Press, 2001.

Rubbi, Antonio. *Yeltseniada: Pervoe desiatiletie postsovetskoi Rossii*. Moscow: Mezhdunarodnye otnoshenia, 2004.

Sakwa, Richard. *Frontline Ukraine: Crisis in the Borderlands*. London: I.B. Tauris, 2015.

Shanker, Thom, and Mark Landler. 'Putin Says U.S. is Undermining Global Stability'. *New York Times*, 11 February 2007.

Stepashin, Sergei, ed. *Analiz protsessov privatizatsii gosudarstvennoy sobstvennosti v Rossiiskoi Federatsii za period 1993–2003 gody*. Moscow: Olita, 2004.

Talbott, Strobe. *The Russia Hand: A Memoir of Presidential Diplomacy*. New York: Random House, 2002.

Trotskii, Lev. *Predannaia revoliutsiia. Chto takoe SSSR i kuda on idet?* Moscow: Moskovskii Rabochii, 1991 [1936].

Ustyuzhanina, Elena. 'The Eurasian Union and Global Value Chains'. *European Politics and Society* 17, supp. 1 [The Eurasian Project in Global Perspective] (2016): 35–45.

Wedel, Janine R. 'Clique-Run Organizations and U.S. Economic Aid: An Institutional Analysis'. *Demokratizatsiya: The Journal of Post-Soviet Democratization* 4, no. 4 (Fall 1996).

Wedel, Janine R. *Collision and Collusion. The Strange Case of Western Aid to Eastern Europe*. New York: Palgrave, 2001.

2
Diversifying the super-rich
Forbes-*listed Russians from a Muslim background*

Catherine Suart

Introduction

In September 2015, ahead of the Muslim holiday of Eid al-Adha (Feast of Sacrifice), President Putin attended the official inauguration of the reconstructed Moscow Cathedral Mosque. Alongside the presidents of Turkey and the Palestinian Authority stood Dagestan-born businessman Suleiman Kerimov (45th on the Russian *Forbes* rich list),[1] who had donated over half the mosque's construction funds "as charity towards Allah".[2] Such philanthropy was not new to Russia's business elite,[3] but the overt association with the mosque and Islamic practices was a rare acknowledgment of Muslim identity among Russia's hyper-rich. This chapter examines how such Muslim identities have shaped and diversified Russia's business elite, as ranked by the most credible of the remaining Russian rich lists, published by *Forbes Russia* in 2016.[4] It provides a new religious framework for exploring the popular topic of wealth generation and political influence in the early years of capitalism in Russia, and uses the same approach to examine more recent topics of scholarly interest such as power legitimisation and philanthropy, as investigated by Elisabeth Schimpfössl and Timothy Monteath in chapter 3.[5]

Of the 200 businessmen and women listed by *Forbes Russia* in 2016, 21 had Muslim identities (see Table 2.1). Throughout this chapter, they are referred to collectively as the Muslim Business Elite (MBE). The methodology for this identification was based on an inclusivist, sociological approach to Muslim identity,[6] including both Mosque-goers and those raised in 'Muslim-heritage' cultures or regions.[7] This approach accommodates the broad array of ethnic groups that make up Russia's Muslim population, which have largely developed in isolation from one another,[8]

Table 2.1 List of Russia's business elite with Muslim identities (2016)

Name	2016 rating	Ethnicity	Age*	Place of birth	Initial source of wealth
Alisher Usmanov	3	Uzbek	63	Chust, Uzbek SSR	Trade
Vagit Alekperov	9	Azerbaijani	66	Baku, Azerbaijan SSR	Oil & Gas
Mikhail Gutseriev	16	Ingush	58	Akimolinsk, Kazakh SSR	Finance
Iskander Makhmudov	21	Uzbek	52	Bukhara, Uzbek SSR	Trade
Suleiman Kerimov	45	Lezgin (Dagestan)	50	Derbent, Dagestan ASSR	Trade
Mikhail Shishkhanov	46	Ingush	44	Chechen-Ingush ASSR	Finance
Sait-Salam Gutseriev	48	Ingush	57	Akimolinsk, Kazakh SSR	Finance
Farkhad Akhmedov	51	Azerbaijani	61	Baku, Azerbaijan SSR	Oil & Gas
Aras Agalarov	55	Azerbaijani	60	Baku, Azerbaijan SSR	Trade
Ruslan Baisarov	89	Chechen	48	Veduchi, Chechen-Ingush ASSR	Trade
Ziyavudin Magomedov	93	Avar (Dagestan)	47	Makhachkala, Dagestan ASSR	Trade
Airat Shaimiev	126	Tatar	54	Muslyumovo, Tatar ASSR	Oil & Gas
Radik Shaimiev	127	Tatar	51	Kazan, Tatar ASSR	Oil & Gas
Rustem Sulteev	131	Tatar	62	Tatar ASSR	Trade
Albert Shigabutdinov	132	Tatar	63	Pervouralsk, RSFSR	Trade
Ziyad Manasir	140	Jordanian	50	Amman, Jordan	Trade
Aleksei Semin	152	Tatar	48	Kazan, Tatar ASSR	Finance
Deni Bazhaev	155	Chechen	20	Moscow, Russian Federation	Inheritance
Musa Bazhaev	156	Chechen	50	Grozny, Chechen-Ingush ASSR	Oil & Gas
Arsen Kanokov	160	Kabardian	59	Shithala, Kabardino-Balkar ASSR	Trade
Rustam Tariko	168	Tatar	54	Menzelinsk, Tatar ASSR	Trade

* Accurate as of 1 September 2016. The average age of the MBE is 53. Of the 193 businessmen for whom *Forbes* provides ages, the average is 53.5.
Source: Author's own research files.

and the secularisation of many Muslim practices during the anti-religious campaigns of the Soviet Union. As Dominic Rubin observes in his recent travelogue of Russia's Muslim heartlands, 'the closer one gets to individuals, the more individual and idiosyncratic "Russian Islam" begins to seem'.[9] Casting the net in such a way groups together wealthy businessmen such as Vagit Alekperov (9) and Alisher Usmanov (3), who run some of Russia's most strategically important companies, and more regionally powerful players such as Airat (126) and Radik Shaimiev (127). While other studies of the business elite may categorise these individuals differently, their unification here allows this study to focus on the dynamics between religion and capitalism within as broad a group as possible.

Information pertaining to the religious identities of the *Forbes*-listed individuals was compiled from personal interviews in newspaper, radio and television archives,[10] according to four research categories: 1) self-identification; 2) family identification;[11] 3) religious observances;[12] and 4) traditional religion of ethnic group. In all, the 21 individuals represent nine different ethnic groups traditionally affiliated with Muslim identities: Tatar (6), Chechen (3), Ingush (3), Azerbaijani (3), Uzbek (2), Kabardian (1), Avar (1), Lezgin (1), Jordanian (1). The strongest of these research categories, self-identification, included Chechen businessman Ruslan Baisarov (89), Uzbek businessman Alisher Usmanov (3),[13] and former president of Kabardino-Balkaria Arsen Kanokov (160), who considers himself to be a law-abiding (*pravovernyi*) Muslim and undertakes the Muslim pilgrimage to Mecca (Hajj).[14]

Business as usual

How Russia's business elite generated their initial wealth has fascinated scholars since the fall of the Soviet Union. Those who made their money in the murky years of the early 1990s have received particular attention in an attempt to unravel the close and complex relationship between business, organised crime, and the state. Muslim businessmen and their religious identities, however, have rarely dominated the debate,[15] despite the fact that the majority began their commercial activities at the very same time and many of them have been open about their initial source of wealth in public interviews.[16]

Foreign trade was one of the principal methods through which many of Russia's business elite entered the commercial world at the end of the Soviet period. It was one of the three areas to benefit from the 1988 Law on Cooperatives introduced by Mikhail Gorbachev, which permitted private ownership in the services, manufacturing and foreign trade sectors through the establishment of cooperatives. No special permission was required to establish a cooperative and it legalised the trading of goods which had previously been bought and sold on the black or grey markets.[17] As a result, from 1988 through the early 1990s, the law enabled those with and without privileged access to start making money.[18]

Over half the MBE made their initial wealth in foreign trade. Low-value consumer goods such as cigarettes and food were quickly replaced in 1991 and 1992 by electrical appliances, computers and other office equipment and, in the case of Uzbek businessman Iskander Makhmudov (21), larger commodities such as coal and metal. Some of the most successful traders were Tatar businessmen Albert Shigabutdinov (132) and Rustem Sulteev (131), who established one of the biggest foreign trading cooperatives in Tatarstan. Others saw trade as a stepping-stone to other industries, and for one member of the MBE, the change in commercial activity was explicitly driven by religious beliefs. In an interview with *Vedomosti* in 2003 in which he discussed his early business activities, Alisher Usmanov (3) stated that he chose to stop trading cigarettes because 'as a Muslim [he] could not sell poison'.[19]

In the early 1990s, banking and finance also became a growing area for private commercial activity following the introduction of the Central Bank Law and the new Commercial Banking Law in December 1990, marking the beginning of Russia's market-based financial system.[20] These laws created a two-tier banking system by separating the Central Bank's operations from commercial banking functions, and allowed for the relatively straightforward establishment of new commercial banks by resident or foreign entities.[21] A number of the MBE took advantage of this new banking legislation and shifted their focus from trade to finance in the early 1990s. Ingush businessman Mikhail Gutseriev (16) established one of the first cooperative banks in Moscow and used it to hold the accounts of companies registering in the newly created free economic zone of Ingushetia.[22] As he boasted in an interview with a *Financial Times* correspondent in 1994, 'twenty-three billion roubles [more than US $10 million at the time] flowed into our accounts today alone. And it's like this every single day'.[23] Dagestani businessman Ziyavudin Magomedov (93)[24] also reported that he made his first 'serious money' in finance, having traded computers and other electrical appliances while still at university from 1988 to 1990. In 1993 he created Interfinance Company alongside his brother Magomed Magomedov and cousin Akhmed Bilalov and began managing internal currency bonds from foreign trade associations, accumulating US $15 million of their own money and US $50–$60 million under management by 1994.[25]

The large privatisation auctions were an area in which the MBE made fewer financial gains than their non-Muslim counterparts of the mid-1990s in Russia. The main exceptions were the four TAIF shareholders, who benefitted from the second wave of privatisations in 1994 when the Tatar government created Tatar American Investments and Finance (TAIF) to hold the government's stakes in newly privatised assets such as Tatneft and Nizhnekamensknefteķhim. Albert Shigabutdinov (132) and Rustem Sulteev (131) were given a 14 per cent stake and they now control the company alongside Airat (126) and Radik Shaimiev (127).

Commercial lobbying

While the TAIF shareholders inevitably benefitted from the lobbying of the former President of Tatarstan and father of the Shaimiev brothers, Mintimir Shaimiev,[26] the remaining MBE do not appear to have turned to their home regions for political support and lobbying. Instead, those who entered politics to lobby for their commercial interests did so through the same route as their non-Muslim counterparts.

The close relationship between business and the state in Russia has been cited as one of the defining methods by which the business elite made their wealth.[27] At the fall of the Soviet Union, lobbying and political influence were still highly personalised, and personal political connections were crucial to obtaining favourable decisions.[28] This personalised interaction between state and enterprise was inherited by the business elite in post-Soviet Russia, and remains part of the perceived *sistema* of governance in Russia.[29] The business elite started to enter the political stage on a personal level after 1994, when their newly-formed business and financial groups had grown strong enough to carry sufficient economic and political influence.

Of the 21 members of the MBE, six have held high-level political positions in post-Soviet Russia (Table 2.2).

Of these positions, the State Duma offered the greatest opportunity for businessmen to lobby for their commercial interests, and access to Russia's lower house was rumoured to be frequently facilitated by the Liberal Democratic Party of Russia (LDPR).[30] Many of Russia's business elite entered politics this way to lobby for commercial interests, and the MBE were no exception. Ingush businessman Mikhail Gutseriev (16),

Table 2.2 Political posts held by members of the Muslim business elite

MBE member	Political position	Dates position held
Suleiman Kerimov	State Duma deputy	1999–2007
	Federation Council senator (representing the Republic of Dagestan)	2008–present
Mikhail Gutseriev	State Duma deputy	1995–9
Sait-Salam Gutseriev	State Duma deputy	1999–2008
Farkhad Akhmedov	Federation Council senator (representing the Krasnodar Region 2004–7 and the Yamalo-Nenets Autonomous Region 2007–9)	2004–9
Arsen Kanokov	State Duma deputy	2003–5
	President of the Republic of Kabardino-Balkaria	2005–13
	Federation Council senator (representing the Republic of Kabardino-Balkaria)	2013–present
Albert Shigabutdinov	State Council member (for the Republic of Tatarstan)	2009–14

Source: Author's own research files.

for example, explicitly stated that he entered politics to further his business interests: 'I understood that we [. . .] were getting too big to keep on fighting the *chinovniks* [bureaucrats]. We had to join them.'[31] All four members of the MBE who were State Duma deputies were elected on the LDPR party list, despite the fact that ideologically the LDPR was highly racist and suspicious of what it referred to as the 'Southern problem'.[32]

In addition to those who chose politics as a lobbying instrument, many businessmen never directly engaged in personal politics. As Russian scholar Andrei Yakovlev argues, there were in fact many businesses which deliberately kept their distance from the state.[33] From the 2000s onwards, this strategy was adopted by more and more businesses as Putin discouraged the business elite from engaging in politics.[34] They began to promote themselves as 'self-made' businessmen to counter the negative connotations of the term 'oligarch', and many spoke publicly about their lack of political activity. In a televised interview, Uzbek trader Iskander Makhmudov (21), for example, rejected the term 'oligarch', claiming he had no connection with the government.[35]

Outside the political arena, the business elite also promoted and supported their businesses through the Russian Union of Industrialists and Entrepreneurs (RUIE). This business association was arguably at its most influential in the aftermath of the August 1998 financial crisis, when many of the business elite joined the RUIE in an attempt to coordinate the general recovery of the Russian economy. Although significantly weakened under Putin, the RUIE has remained one of the primary lobbies for the business elite in Russia, and many of the MBE number among its management board and continue to engage with its various committees and councils. Vagit Alekperov (9) was one of the first high-profile members of the association's management board in September 2000 and has remained an active member since, alongside four other members of the MBE: Alisher Usmanov (3), Mikhail Gutseriev (16), Aras Agalarov (55) and Ziyavudin Magomedov (93).

The MBE have engaged far less actively with the recently established Association of Muslim Businessmen of the Russian Federation (AMBRF), founded in 2014 to represent and promote the commercial interests of Muslim businessmen in Russia and abroad. Unlike the Russian Jewish Congress (RJC), which was founded by a number of the Jewish business elite in 1996 to promote Jewish interests in Russia and which continues to be actively supported by these elite, the AMBRF currently has very limited interaction with members of the MBE.

Lobbying from within

Conversely, the MBE appear to have embraced one of the key *modus operandi* of Russia's business and political elite in the post-Soviet space by lobbying for their commercial interests using those who know them best: family.

A third of the MBE have more than one family member on the *Forbes Russia* list: the Gutserievs (Mikhail (16), Sait-Salam (48) and their nephew Mikhail Shishkhanov (46)), the Shaimievs (Radik (127) and Airat (126)) and the Bazhaevs (Musa (156) and Deni (155)). In *Forbes Russia's* 2017 calculation of the 10 wealthiest families in Russia, all three families were included, alongside Ziyavudin Magomedov (93) and his brother Magomed.[36] The combined wealth of these four families was estimated by *Forbes* to be US $15.3 billion, greater than the combined wealth of the remaining six families (US $12.7 billion).

The majority of the MBE also involve their immediate family members in key (board-level) management positions, and the proportion of children brought in to run part of their businesses is high.[37] Notably,

Suleiman Kerimov's (45) son Said runs much of his business activities to enable him to continue his role on the Federation Council, and Aras Agalarov's (55) son Emin is Executive Vice President of Crocus Group. Female relatives have also been well-represented: Vagit Alekperov's (9) sister Nelli Alekperova is President of the Lukoil charity fund; Radik Shaimiev's (127) daughter Kamila was on the management board of TAIF, a decision that Kamila reports had been made by the family;[38] and Rustem Sulteev's (131) daughter Diana is on the management board of another of his commercial interests, the Bank Avers. This contrasts with many other companies represented on the *Forbes Russia* list, where family members less frequently hold such senior positions.[39]

The importance of family for Muslims in business has been widely covered by scholars in the field. Rodney Wilson observed that there is a reluctance among Muslim businessmen to see family businesses moving to external shareholders.[40] Indeed, Mikhail Gutseriev (16) has asserted that his business empire is a 'brotherhood' in which all assets, regardless of who acquired them, are divided between himself, his nephew Mikhail Shishkhanov (46) and brother Sait-Salam Gutseriev (48), with 51 per cent, 24.5 per cent and 24.5 per cent respectively.[41] More recently, this has also included his son Said. Although Mikhail Gutseriev (16) does not acknowledge any Muslim influence in this structure, there is a similarity with the Islamic principle of *musharakah*. Literally meaning sharing, in the context of business *musharakah* refers to a joint enterprise in which partners (or parties) to the enterprise share profits and losses, regardless of the amount invested.

Giving back

In addition to understanding how Russia's business elite generated their initial wealth, scholars are increasingly examining how these businessmen spend it, a subject which has fascinated Western and Russian tabloid journalists since their glitzy displays of wealth in the early 1990s. Elisabeth Schimpfössl, in her research on Russia's social upper class, demonstrates that the rise of philanthropy is an important component in their current quest for 'culturedness',[42] and like their non-Muslim counterparts, the MBE are active in their philanthropic activities, both through corporate social responsibility programmes and personal foundations.[43]

Philanthropy among the Russian business elite is typically focussed on a wide range of social initiatives – most prominently children, sport, culture, education and healthcare[44] – and a number of the MBE follow this model of charitable giving, such as Mikhail Gutseriev's (16) charitable foundation SAFMAR. Patriotism also plays an important role in the engagement in (and promotion of) these initiatives, and many of the more public acts of philanthropy directly or indirectly benefit the Russian state. In 2007, for example, one of the most philanthropic members of the MBE, Alisher Usmanov (3), bought all 450 lots at a Sotheby's Russian auction and donated them to Konstantinovsky Palace outside Saint Petersburg.[45]

A number of the MBE have expanded this national patriotism to a form of regional patriotism, which has not been evident in their business investments. This regional commitment to social development is most clearly illustrated in Dagestan and Chechnya, where the Dagestani businessman Suleiman Kerimov (45) and, until shortly after his arrest, his fellow Dagestani Ziyavudin Magomedov (93), and the Chechens Ruslan Baisarov (89) and Musa Bazhaev (156), invest considerable funds for social projects in the regions.[46] As well as supporting a number of charities in Dagestan, Suleiman Kerimov (45) also supports charities promoting his ethnic clan, the Lezgins, and the Lezgin language.[47]

Whereas the business elite on the whole has remained somewhat conservative in its vocal support of religious organisations, many channel their support through charitable donations, in particular to the renovation of churches and other religious buildings.[48] This is particularly visible among the MBE. Over half of the MBE have supported religious causes as part of their philanthropic activities and 11 have supported the construction of mosques. Philanthropy is considered a central tenet of many religions, and Islam is no exception. Many Muslims regard charity as a form of worship and, according to traditional conceptions of Islam, it is one of the five pillars of the faith.

The most active member of the MBE in his charitable support of religious and specifically Muslim organisations and institutions is Suleiman Kerimov (45), through his charitable foundation, The Suleiman Kerimov Foundation.[49] In addition to buildings, the Suleiman Kerimov Foundation supports a number of different Muslim celebrations and religious festivals, sponsoring thousands of Dagestani pilgrims to travel to Mecca for Hajj each year. In 2011 a similar trip for inhabitants of the republic of Kabardino-Balkaria was organised and sponsored by the republic's former president, Arsen Kanokov (160). These events are similar to the activities of the RJC, which since 2012 has been organising pilgrimages to Israel to celebrate Passover.[50] Unlike the Hajj pilgrimages, however, members of the Jewish business elite, including Mikhail Fridman (2) and Andrei Rappaport (67), regularly take part in the pilgrimage, spending three days in the desert in the run-up to Passover.[51]

Very few of the MBE, however, direct their religious philanthropic activities just at Muslim causes, and the majority, including Suleiman Kerimov (45), Ziyavudin Magomedov (93) and Arsen Kanokov (160), have also supported institutions of other religious denominations. Mikhail Gutseriev (16) has supported Russian Orthodoxy, Judaism and Buddhism, as well as Islam. This coincides with the central goals of Mikhail Gutseriev's (16) principal charitable foundation, SAFMAR, promoting the revival of spiritual values to achieve 'a constructive dialogue between [. . .] traditional confessions in Russia'.[52] This is in contrast to many of the Jewish business elite, such as the heads of the financial investment conglomerate, the Alfa Group, whose charitable activities in the area of religion solely focus on the support of Jewish causes and activities.

Other MBE highlight religious tolerance and diversity in Russia as the purpose of their religious charitable activities. Former president of the Republic of Kabardino-Balkaria, Arsen Kanokov (160), revealed in an interview with Anna Politkovskaya in 2005 that he wanted to promote religious tolerance in the republic by constructing Russian Orthodox churches and Muslim mosques in close proximity.[53] Vagit Alekperov (9) has also used the construction of religious buildings to promote peaceful interaction between religious groups in areas where his company LUKoil operates,[54] and Iskander Makhmudov's (21) metals and mining company UGMK details 'spiritual revival' as one of the principal goals of its corporate social responsibility.

Conclusion

It is within this last area of investigation – philanthropy – that we begin to see both marked similarities in the engagement of the MBE and clear distinctions with their non-Muslim counterparts. Over half the MBE support Muslim organisations, most frequently by financing mosques but also by supporting Hajj pilgrimages and Muslim festivals, and in recent years such donations have received growing support from local and federal authorities. Unlike their Jewish counterparts, the MBE's engagement with other religions shows an acute awareness of the historical and current challenges associated with a minority religion such as Islam in Russia, and a desire to improve its reputation and standing in the country.

Public acknowledgements of the influence of Islam on the MBE's business activities remain rare; only the Uzbek businessman Alisher Usmanov

(3) has reported that he had stopped trading cigarettes, a haram substance, in the 1990s because he was a Muslim. More indirect manifestations, however, appear in a range of areas, including the propensity for close family members to occupy senior management positions within the MBE's businesses and the similarity between the profit-sharing structures of Mikhail Gutseriev (16) and the Muslim business practices of *musharakah*.

Suleiman Kerimov's (45) sponsorship of the Moscow Cathedral Mosque not only improved his relationship with the Kremlin,[55] it strengthened his association with Russia's Muslim authorities, and following his arrest in France in November 2017 on charges of tax evasion, these authorities spoke out in his support. Political influence has often been sought by the business elite to promote their business interests and secure patronage from the state, but the support of both the federal and Muslim authorities in response to this act of religious philanthropy shows a level of engagement with the Muslim business community previously absent in Russia's early years of capitalism.

The intermittent influence of Muslim identities identified within this chapter highlights the importance of the study of religion in the context of Russia's business elite and their interaction with the capitalist dynamics of the country. One-third of the MBE identified during this research have been on the *Forbes Russia* rich list since it was launched in 2005, having survived numerous financial crises and regime changes since they first entered business in the early 1990s. They form part of what Alena Ledeneva describes as Russia's *sistema*, and the prominence and influence of these MBE on the business and political landscape of Russia will likely continue, if not grow, as Putin elevates Islam alongside Russian Orthodoxy as one of the country's central religions and seeks to maintain close control over Russia's ethnically Muslim regions.

Notes

1. This and all further numbers in brackets refer to the 2016 *Forbes Russia* ranking assigned to the individuals.
2. 'Mosques should not become a museum', Russia Mufties Council, accessed 18 May 2018, muslim.ru/en/articles/142/3232/.
3. As demonstrated by the renovation of the Russian Orthodox Christ the Saviour Cathedral in Moscow in the 1990s: Marc Bennetts, *I'm Going to Ruin Their Lives: Inside Putin's War on Russia's Opposition* (London: Oneworld Publications, 2014), 134.
4. Rich lists receive considerable criticism from individuals in academic and commercial circles alike. The addition of Sayfeddin Roustamov to the rich list in 2018, whose wealth had previously been hidden behind offshore companies, illustrates some of the limitations imposed by financial transparency and valuation. For discussion of the setbacks of rich lists and other sources of data on the rich, see: Anthony B. Atkinson, 'Concentration among the Rich', *United Nations University* 151 (2006): 5–10.

5   To reflect the broad sociological approach to the terms 'Muslim' and 'Islam' used during this research, and to highlight the multiple dynamic factors that contribute to a definition, or self-definition of an individual as 'Muslim', I use the term 'Muslim identities', rather than the singular 'identity'.
6   This is closest in form to Nasar Meer's reading of it as a 'quasi-ethnic sociological formation': Nasar Meer, *Citizenship, Identity and the Politics of Multiculturalism: The Rise of Muslim Consciousness* (Basingstoke, UK: Palgrave Macmillan, 2010), 62.
7   William Rowe, 'Cultural Muslims: The Evolution of Muslim Identity in Soviet and Post-Soviet Central Asia', in *Geographies of Muslim Identities: Diaspora, Gender and Belonging*, ed. Cara Aitchinson, Mei-Po Kwan, and Peter Hopkins (Aldershot, UK: Ashgate Publishing, 2007), 141–64.
8   As illustrated in a study of contrasting Muslim identities in Tatarstan and Dagestan; see Elena Omelchenko and Gusel Sabirova, 'Islam and the Search for Identity', in *Islam in Post-Soviet Russia,* edited by Hilary Pilkington and Galina Yemelianova (London: Routledge Curzon, 2003), 167–82.
9   Dominic Rubin, *Russia's Muslim Heartlands – Islam in the Putin Era* (Glasgow: C. Hurst & Co., 2018), 11.
10 This was complemented with information from personally approved websites such as official company, charity or personal websites, and where necessary, secondary reporting from a wide range of journalistic and academic sources.
11 For example, Aras Agalarov's son, Emin, has stated that he is a 'proud Muslim': Brian Boyd, 'Not Eminem: Just Emin', *The Irish Times*, 22 March 2015, accessed 21 May 2018, www.irishtimes.com/culture/music/not-eminem-just-emin-1.2147234.
12 Mikhail Gutseriev, an ethnic Ingush, does not speak publicly about any religious affiliation, but the wedding of his son Said Gutseriev in 2016 and funeral of his other son Chingiskhan Gutseriev in 2007 both involved Muslim ceremonies. Ruslan Baisarov married his second wife, Kristina Orbakaite, according to Sharia law: Yuriy Nosovskiy, 'Multireligioznyi kokteil semi Orbakaite', *Pravda,* 12 November 2012, accessed 11 May 2018, www.pravda.ru/faith/religions/orthodoxy/12-11-2012/1134344-orbakaite-0/.
13 Irina Reznik, 'Interv'yu: Alisher Usmanov, general'nyi direktor OOO "Gazprominvestkholdinga", *Vedomosti*, 14 January 2003, accessed 20 May 2018, www.vedomosti.ru/newspaper/articles/2003/01/14/intervyu-alisher-usmanov-generalnyj-direktor-ooo-gazprominvestholdinga.
14 'Arsen Kanokov sleduet predpisaniyam islama', *Islam News*, 26 August 2011, accessed 23 May 2018, www.islamnews.ru/news-80481.html.
15 See, for example, Chrystia Freeland, *Sale of the Century: The Inside Story of the Second Russian Revolution* (London: Little, Brown, 2000).
16 See Reznik, 'Interv'yu: Alisher Usmanov'; Chrystia Freeland, 'Meet Mikhail', *The Globe and Mail*, 28 April 2000, accessed 12 May 2018, www.theglobeandmail.com/report-on-business/rob-magazine/meet-mikhail/article4163094/?page=all.
17 For the full text see: A. Gromyko, 'Zakon SSSR ot 26 Maya 1988, No. 8998-XI "O kooperatsii v SSSR"', *Base Garant*, 26 May 1988, accessed 16 May 2018, base.garant.ru/10103075/.
18 Here I use the term 'privileged' to include Communist Party members, Komsomol members and those born into families of the Soviet *nomenklatura*.
19 Reznik, 'Interv'yu: Alisher Usmanov'.
20 Inna Vysman, 'New Banking Legislation in Russia: Theoretical Adequacy, Practical Difficulties, and Potential Solutions', *Fordham Law Review* 62, no. 1 (1993): 265.
21 Hans-Henning Schröder, 'El'tsin and the Oligarchs: The Role of Financial Groups in Russian Politics between 1993 and July 1998', *Europe-Asia Studies* 51, no. 6 (1999): 964.
22 'Chem izvesten Mikhail Gutseriev', *Kommersant*, 24 April 2010, accessed 19 May 2018, www.kommersant.ru/doc/1360325.
23 Freeland, 'Meet Mikhail'.
24 In March 2018, Ziyavudin Magomedov was arrested in Russia and charged with racketeering and embezzlement of state funds. Since then, further charges have been brought against him and his brother. Ziyavudin Magomedov denies the charges but remained in pre-trial custody in August 2019.
25 Yekaterina Derbilova, 'K finansovym poteryam ya vsegda otnosilsya filosofski', *Vedomosti*, 6 February 2012, accessed 21 May 2018, www.vedomosti.ru/newspaper/articles/2012/02/06/v_biznese_ya_sam_sebe_pomogayu_ziyavudin_magomedov_osnovnoj.

26 Mintimir Shaimiev was President of the Republic of Tatarstan from 1990 to 2010.
27 See, for example, Peter Rutland, *Business and the State in Contemporary Russia* (Boulder, CO: Westview Press, 2001).
28 Peter Rutland, 'Business Elites and Russian Economic Policy', *Royal Institute of International Affairs* (1992): 13.
29 For a detailed analysis of *sistema*, see Alena V. Ledeneva, *Can Russia Modernise? Sistema, Power Networks and Informal Governance* (Cambridge: Cambridge University Press, 2013).
30 Elena Ivanova, 'Interv'yu: Vladimir Zhirinovsky, predsedatel LDPR', *Vedomosti*, 12 June 2007, accessed 21 May 2018, www.vedomosti.ru/newspaper/articles/2007/07/12/intervyu-vladimir-zhirinovskij-predsedatel-ldpr.
31 Freeland, *Sale of the Century,* 100–3.
32 Zhirinovsky's 1993 political pamphlet 'The Last Dash to the South' proposed, among other things, the reoccupation of post-Soviet Central Asia and the Southern Caucasus and the annexation of Turkey, Iran and Afghanistan to Russia.
33 Andrei Yakovlev, 'The Evolution of Business – State Interaction in Russia: From State Capture to Business Capture?' *Europe-Asia Studies* 58, no. 7 (2006): 1034.
34 See, for example, Ben Aris, 'Oligarchs' Power over Kremlin Has Come to an End, Says Putin', *The Telegraph*, 29 July 2000, accessed on 11 May 2018, www.telegraph.co.uk/news/worldnews/europe/russia/1350892/Oligarchs-power-over-Kremlin-has-come-to-an-end-says-Putin.html.
35 Aleksandr Gentelev, 'Makhmudov: Ya ne oligarkh', *YouTube*, 21 November 2012, accessed 13 May 2018, www.youtube.com/watch?v=JMnDh6hPU8A.
36 Elena Berezandskaya, 'Bogateyshiye semeinye klany Rossii – 2017', *Forbes Russia,* 30 August 2017, accessed 19 May 2018, www.forbes.ru/milliardery-photogallery/349563-bogateyshie-semeynye-klany-rossii-2017-reyting-forbes?photo=9.
37 High-profile examples among the non-Muslim elite include Igor Rotenberg, who took over a number of his father's businesses to limit the impact of US sanctions.
38 Albert Galeev, 'Vnuchka pervovo prezidenta Tatarstana', *Tatler*, 19 February 2018, accessed 14 May 2018, www.tatler.ru/geroi/vnuchka-pervogo-prezidenta-tatarstana-kamilya-shajmieva-i-ee-modnye-startapy.
39 A sample of the main companies of the top 10 businessmen on the list, for example, lists no immediate family members on the companies' board of directors. Companies searched: Novatek, Alfa Group, Metalloinvest, Norilsk Nickel, Severstal, Rusal, NLMK and Lukoil.
40 Rodney Wilson, 'Islam and Business', *Thunderbird International Business Review* 48 (2006): 109–23.
41 Maria Abakumova, 'Biznes pod podushkoi', *Forbes Russia*, 3 January 2016, accessed 7 April 2018, www.forbes.ru/forbes/issue/2016-01/308091-biznes-pod-podushkoi.
42 Elisabeth Schimpfössl, 'Russia's Social Upper Class: From Ostentation to Culturedness', *The British Journal of Sociology* 65, no. 1 (2014): 63–81.
43 Six of the MBE have been decorated by the Russian state specifically for their charitable activities: Alisher Usmanov, Mikhail Gutseriev, Suleiman Kerimov, Aras Agalarov, Musa Bazhaev and Arsen Kanokov.
44 Julia Khodorova, 'Philanthropy in Russian Society Today', *International Journal of Not-for-Profit Law* 8, no. 3 (2006): 13–15.
45 Luke Harding, 'Russian Oligarch Halts Auction to Buy Complete Rostropovich Art Collection', *The Guardian*, 18 September 2007, accessed 11 May 2018, www.theguardian.com/world/2007/sep/18/russia.artnews.
46 Musa Bazhaev funds the Ziya ensemble, which is a children's dance ensemble in Chechnya. Ruslan Baisarov sponsored the construction of a ski resort in Chechnya. Ziyavudin Magomedov dedicated a section of his charitable foundation to My Dagestan. Suleiman Kerimov's charitable foundation is largely focused on education, children and religious causes in Dagestan.
47 'Grants', Suleiman Kerimov Foundation, accessed 17 May 2018, www.kerimovfoundation.org/index.php?id=21.
48 In this, Muslim traditions bear a close relationship to medieval Christian ones, whereby rulers and other wealthy patrons contribute to the construction of religious buildings.
49 According to their 2014 annual return, 65 per cent of the foundation's donations were spent on religious charities.

50   The first president of the RJC was Vladimir Gusinsky (1996–2001) who was one of the 'seven bankers'. The current presidium includes many businessmen represented on the *Forbes Russia* 2016 List, including Mikhail Fridman, Len Blavatnik, God Nisanov (mountain Jew from Azerbaijan), German Khan and Boris Mints.
51   Niva Goldberg, 'Eighteen Russian Oligarchs Descending On Israeli Desert For Pesach', *Jewish Business News*, 10 April 2014, accessed on 23 May 2018, jewishbusinessnews.com/2014/04/10/eighteen-russian-oligarchs-descending-on-israeli-desert-for-pesach/.
52   'Annual Review 2016', SAFMAR, accessed 12 May 2018, safmarinvest.ru/userfiles/file/SAFMAR-AR-2016_ENG_interactive.pdf.
53   Anna Politkovskaya, 'Arsen Kanokov: V respublike my imeem ne storoniki a sochustvuyush-chikh', *Novaya Gazeta*, 31 October 2005, accessed 7 May 2018, politkovskaya.novayagazeta.ru/pub/2005/2005-094.shtml.
54   Rustam Rakhmatullin, 'Sobornuyu mechet Kogalyma posetil president OAO LUKoil Vagit Yusufovich Alekperov', *Musulmane Rossii*, 5 March 2012, accessed 16 May 2018, www.dumrf.ru/common/regnews/2735.
55   Magomed Shamkhalov, 'Mechet vyvela Suleimana Kerimova iz kremlevskoy opaly', *On Kavkaz*, 24 September 2015, accessed 7 May 2018, onkavkaz.com/news/287-mechet-vyvela-suleimana-kerimova-iz-kremlevskoi-opaly.html.

Bibliography

Abakumova, Maria. 'Biznes pod podushkoi'. *Forbes Russia*, 3 January 2016. Accessed 1 June 2016, www.forbes.ru/forbes/issue/2016-01/308091-biznes-pod-podushkoi.

Aitamurto, K. 'Protected and Controlled: Islam and "Desecularisation from Above"'. *Europe-Asia Studies* 68, no. 1 (2016): 182–202.

Aitchinson, C., M.-P. Kwan, and P. Hopkins, eds. *Geographies of Muslim Identities: Diaspora, Gender and Belonging*. Aldershot, UK: Ashgate Publishing, 2007.

Aris, Ben. 'Oligarchs' power over Kremlin has come to an end, says Putin'. *The Telegraph*, 29 July 2000. Accessed 11 May 2018, www.telegraph.co.uk/news/worldnews/europe/russia/1350892/Oligarchs-power-over-Kremlin-has-come-to-an-end-says-Putin.html.

'Arsen Kanokov sleduet predpisaniyam islama'. *Islam News*, 26 August 2011. Accessed 23 May 2018, www.islamnews.ru/news-80481.html.

Atkinson, Anthony B. 'Concentration among the Rich'. *United Nations University* 151 (2006): 5–10.

Bennetts, Marc. *I'm Going to Ruin Their Lives: Inside Putin's War on Russia's Opposition*. London: Oneworld Publications, 2014.

Berezandskaya, Elena. 'Bogateyshiye semeinye klany Rossii – 2017'. *Forbes Russia*, 30 August 2017. Accessed 19 May 2018, www.forbes.ru/milliardery-photogallery/349563-bogateyshie-semeynye-klany-rossii-2017-reyting-forbes?photo=9.

Boyd, Brian. 'Not Eminem. Just Emin'. *The Irish Times*, 22 March 2015. Accessed 21 May 2018, www.irishtimes.com/culture/music/not-eminem-just-emin-1.2147234.

'Chem izvesten Mikhail Gutseriev'. *Kommersant*, 24 April 2010. Accessed 19 May 2018, www.kommersant.ru/doc/1360325.

Chua, Amy. *World on Fire: How Exporting Free Market Democracy Breeds Ethnic Hatred and Global Instability*. London: Arrow, 2003.

Dawisha, Karen. *Putin's Kleptocracy: Who Owns Russia?* New York: Simon & Schuster, 2014.

Derbilova, Yekaterina. 'K finansovym poteryam ya vsegda otnosilsya filosofski'. *Vedomosti*, 6 February 2012. Accessed 21 May 2018, www.vedomosti.ru/newspaper/articles/2012/02/06/v_biznese_ya_sam_sebe_pomogayu_ziyavudin_magomedov_osnovnoj. Basingstoke, UK: Palgrave, 2014.

Duncan, P.J.S. 'Contemporary Russian Identity between East and West'. *The Historical Journal* 48, no. 1 (2005): 277–94.

Duncan, P.J.S. 'Oligarchs, Business and Russian Foreign Policy: From El'tsin to Putin'. *Centre for the Study of Economic and Social Change in Europe* 83 (2007).

Fortescue, Stephen. *Russia's Oil Barons and Metals Magnates*. Basingstoke, UK: Palgrave Macmillan, 2010.

Freeland, Chrystia. 'Meet Mikhail'. *The Globe and Mail*, 28 April 2000. Accessed 12 May 2018, www.theglobeandmail.com/report-on-business/rob-magazine/meet-mikhail/article4163094/?page=all.

Freeland, Chrystia. *Sale of the Century: The Inside Story of the Second Russian Revolution*. London: Little, Brown, 2000.

Frye, Timothy. 'Capture or Exchange? Business Lobbying in Russia'. *Europe-Asia Studies* 54, no. 7 (2010): 1017–36.

Galeev, Albert. 'Vnuchka pervovo prezidenta Tatarstana'. *Tatler*, 19 February 2018. Accessed 14 May 2018, www.tatler.ru/geroi/vnuchka-pervogo-prezidenta-tatarstana-kamilya-shajmieva-i-ee-modnye-startapy.

Gentelev, Aleksandr. 'Makhmudov: Ya ne oligarkh'. *YouTube*, 21 November 2012. Accessed 13 May 2018, www.youtube.com/watch?v=JMnDh6hPU8A.

Goldberg, Niva. 'Eighteen Russian Oligarchs Descending on Israeli Desert for Pesach'. *Jewish Business News*, 10 April 2014. Accessed 23 May 2018, jewishbusinessnews.com/2014/04/10/eighteen-russian-oligarchs-descending-on-israeli-desert-for-pesach/.

Gromyko, A. 'Zakon SSSR ot 26 Maya 1988, No. 8998-XI "O kooperatsii v SSSR"'. *Base Garant*, 26 May 1988. Accessed 16 May 2018, base.garant.ru/10103075/.

Hanson, Philip, and Elizabeth Teague. 'Big Business and the State in Russia'. *Europe-Asia Studies* 57, no. 5 (2005): 657–80.

Harding, Luke. 'Russian Oligarch Halts Auction to Buy Complete Rostropovich Art Collection'. *The Guardian*, 18 September 2007. Accessed 11 May 2018, www.theguardian.com/world/2007/sep/18/russia.artnews.

Hunter, Shireen T. *Islam in Russia: The Politics of Identity and Security*. London: M.E. Sharpe, 2004.

Ivanova, Elena. 'Interv'yu: Vladimir Zhirinovsky, predsedatel' LDPR'. *Vedomosti*, 12 June 2007. Accessed 21 May 2018, www.vedomosti.ru/newspaper/articles/2007/07/12/intervyu-vladimir-zhirinovskij-predsedatel-ldpr.

Khodorova, Julia. 'Philanthropy in Russian Society Today'. *International Journal of Not-for-Profit Law* 8, no. 3 (2006): 13–15.

Kryshtanovskaya, Olga, and Stephen White. 'The Rise of the Russian Business Elite'. *Communist and Post-Communist Studies* 38, no. 3 (2005): 293–307.

Ledeneva, Alena V. *Can Russia Modernise? Sistema, Power Networks and Informal Governance*. Cambridge: Cambridge University Press, 2013.

Livshin, Alexander, and Richard Weitz. 'Civil Society and Philanthropy Under Putin'. *International Journal of Not-for-Profit Law* 8, no. 3 (2006): 7–12.

Malashenko, Alexey, and Aziza Nuritova. 'Islam in Russia'. *Social Research* 76, no. 1 (2009): 321–58.

Meer, Nasar. *Citizenship, Identity and the Politics of Multiculturalism: The Rise of Muslim Consciousness*. Basingstoke, UK: Palgrave Macmillan, 2010.

Nosovskiy, Yuriy. 'Multireligioznyi kokteil semi Orbakaite'. *Pravda*, 12 November 2012. Accessed 11 May 2018, www.pravda.ru/faith/religions/orthodoxy/12-11-2012/1134344-orbakaite-0/.

Omelchenko, Elena, and Gusel Sabirova. 'Islam and the Search for Identity'. In *Islam in Post-Soviet Russia*, edited by Hilary Pilkington and Galina Yemelianova, 167–82, London: Routledge Curzon, 2003.

Politkovskaya, Anna. 'Arsen Kanokov: V respublike my imeem ne storoniki a sochustvuyushchikh'. *Novaya Gazeta*, 31 October 2005. Accessed 7 May 2018, politkovskaya.novayagazeta.ru/pub/2005/2005-094.shtml.

Rakhmatullin, Rustam. 'Sobornuyu mechet Kogalyma posetil president OAO LUKoil Vagit Yusufovich Alekperov'. *Musulmane Rossii*, 5 March 2012. Accessed 16 May 2018, www.dumrf.ru/common/regnews/2735.

Reznik, Irina. 'Interv'yu: Alisher Usmanov, general'nyi direktor OOO 'Gazprominvestkholdinga''. *Vedomosti*, 14 January 2003. Accessed 20 May 2018, www.vedomosti.ru/newspaper/articles/2003/01/14/intervyu-alisher-usmanov-generalnyj-direktor-ooo-gazprominvestholdinga.

Rowe, William, 'Cultural Muslims: The Evolution of Muslim Identity in Soviet and Post-Soviet Central Asia'. In *Geographies of Muslim Identities: Diaspora, Gender and Belonging,* edited by Cara Aitchinson, Mei-Po Kwan, and Peter Hopkins, 141–64. Aldershot, UK: Ashgate Publishing, 2007.

Rubin, Dominic. *Russia's Muslim Heartlands – Islam in the Putin Era*. Glasgow: C. Hurst & Co., 2018.

Russia Mufties Council. 'Mosques Should Not Become a Museum'. Accessed 18 May 2018, muslim.ru/en/articles/142/3232/.
Rutland, Peter. *Business and the State in Contemporary Russia*. Boulder, CO: Westview Press, 2001.
Rutland, Peter. 'Business Elites and Russian Economic Policy'. *Royal Institute of International Affairs* (1992).
SAFMAR. 'Annual Review 2016'. SAFMAR. Accessed 12 May 2018, safmarinvest.ru/userfiles/file/SAFMAR-AR-2016_ENG_interactive.pdf.
Schimpfössl, Elisabeth. 'Russia's Social Upper Class: From Ostentation to Culturedness'. *The British Journal of Sociology* 65, no. 1 (2014): 63–81.
Schroder, Hans-Henning. 'El'tsin and the Oligarchs: The Role of Financial Groups in Russian Politics between 1993 and July 1998'. *Europe-Asia Studies* 51, no. 6 (1999): 957–88.
Shamkhalov, Magomed. 'Mechet vyvela Suleimana Kerimova iz kremlevskoy opaly'. *On Kavkaz*, 24 September 2015. Accessed 7 May 2018, onkavkaz.com/news/287-mechet-vyvela-suleimana-kerimova-iz-kremlevskoi-opaly.html.
Suleiman Kerimov Foundation. 'Grants'. Accessed 17 May 2018, www.kerimovfoundation.org/index.php?id=21.
Vysman, Inna. 'New Banking Legislation in Russia: Theoretical Adequacy, Practical Difficulties, and Potential Solutions'. *Fordham Law Review* 62, no. 1 (1993).
White, Stephen, Richard Sakwa, and Henry E. Hale, eds. *Developments in Russian Politics 8*.
Wilson, Rodney. 'Islam and Business'. *Thunderbird International Business Review* 48 (2006): 109–23.
Yakovlev, Andrei. 'The Evolution of Business – State Interaction in Russia: From State Capture to Business Capture?' *Europe-Asia Studies* 58, no. 7 (2006): 1033–56.

3
The culture of elite philanthropy
Russia and the United Kingdom compared

Timothy Monteath and Elisabeth Schimpfössl

This chapter explores the philanthropic practices of Russian and British wealthy elites. The two differ significantly, from the context of their formation to their contemporary characteristics, yet, they also show important parallels: both countries have experienced ever-increasing and by now extreme inequality of wealth. A large proportion of this wealth is being concentrated in the hands of a small group of hyper-rich individuals. Both countries' economies have been stagnating in recent years. This has resulted in a politics of austerity, hastening the states' retreat from the provision of social infrastructure.

These parallels form the background against which we examine the two elites' philanthropic giving. Following a brief introduction to the history of first, the Russian, then the British hyper-rich and their formation, we set out to identify the major distinctions in their philanthropy and explore possible reasons and explanations for similarities and differences. We conclude with a discussion on what these practices might mean for society at large.

Concept and literature

As the importance of philanthropy has grown in recent decades, so too has the research into who is giving and why. An increasingly dominant stream of research within philanthropy studies has focused on the practical question of how to improve the methods and impact of charity endeavours. Philanthrocapitalists have been the most vocal advocates of effectivity in charity.[1] The basic ideology behind any such approaches conceives wealth as a blessing: without wealthy people, so the argument goes, there cannot be any large-scale charitable initiatives.

A number of experts have challenged such logics, in particularly those of philanthrocapitalism, which they see as directly reinforcing social inequality.[2] Their criticisms split broadly into two lines of argument. First, in many countries, charities and foundations receive tax relief and other forms of fiscal incentives. While on a small scale, initiatives of this kind might appear harmless, and even desirable, on a large scale and over the long term, such policies mean large losses of tax revenues to the treasury. This, together with money being distributed by the hyper-wealthy according to their whims, has detrimental effects on democracy. Wealthy individuals end up not only having a disproportionately larger say in the distribution of societal goods, but in fact they are subsidised by the taxpayer in doing so.[3] Second, critics argue that the dynamics of philanthropy reinforce social inequality, rather than supporting those in need. This argument was forcefully presented in a 1990 study by Teresa Odendahl, who claimed that the rich primarily fund their own by directing their giving to organisations of particular interest to themselves, such as the educational institutions they graduated from.[4] Odendahl's findings were subsequently substantiated by many other academics in a variety of contexts, among them Rob Reich, who found that private schools and public schools in wealthy areas receive far greater philanthropic support than similar schools in poor areas.[5]

Not unlike Odendahl and her successors, we seek to engage with philanthropy through the wider social context through which elite giving occurs; that is, we approach the topic through the study of elites. As a subfield of research into philanthropy, elite philanthropy studies have mostly focused on the United States, which reflects both the global distribution of wealth and the importance of philanthropy among wealthy Americans. Examples for scholars following this tradition are Francie Ostrower and Diana E. Kendall, who investigated philanthropy in the context of power relations, the legitimisation of privileges, the cementation of social dominance and wealth transfer across generations.[6] Paul Schervish has devoted his work to contemplating the more philosophical aspects of giving among the wealthy and how conceptions of mortality inform the motives and aims of philanthropists.[7]

Following these approaches, we scrutinise the giving of the top business elites within two national and cultural settings. Scholars researching philanthropy in Britain are scattered all over the country, often in business schools or in third-sector organisations.[8] As for Russia, research into philanthropy is nascent. With its rise in the 2000s and early 2010s, when Russia saw an extraordinary growth in elite philanthropy – partly thanks to the oil boom, partly forced by the Kremlin and Putin's call for 'social responsibility' – a small cohort of researchers, mostly based in think tanks and charity organisations, started documenting and researching rich people's giving.[9]

Methodology and empirical data

Our sample of philanthropists is drawn from the top 257 entries listed in the 2017 *The Sunday Times* rich list and the 200 richest individuals featured by *Forbes Russia* in 2017.[10] Collectively, these individuals own an estimated £500 billion and $459 billion respectively, with a minimum personal wealth of £500 million.

Studying the hyper-wealthy presents a number of methodological challenges. First, many of them are both highly visible and shrouded in mystery. An overall picture of their wealth can be easy to estimate, but the details are usually stubbornly elusive, with much of their fortunes dissolving into offshore tax havens and highly complex financial arrangements.[11] Researchers are thus reliant on the annual rich lists produced by media organisations, among them *The Sunday Times* and *Forbes*.[12] Rich list estimates are based on openly available information of publicly traded companies and include company holdings, land and property, significant artworks and other similar assets.[13] Alongside money held offshore, much inherited wealth remains hidden. It is near impossible to identify wealth accumulated in the past and over generations, as shown by research into the estates of deceased hyper-rich individuals.[14] Nevertheless, although the estimates produced by *Forbes* and *The Sunday Times* are by no means definitive, 'at least they exist', argues Thomas Piketty, and 'it would be absurd and counterproductive' to ignore these estimates and the overall trends they depict.[15]

In our data collection, we draw upon the template that Breeze and Lloyd employed in their 2013 study.[16] We replaced a small number of their categories with some considered in *The Sunday Times* giving list. 'Instances' of giving, defined as either a major one-off public act of giving or continued financial support of a specific cause or charity, form the smallest research entity. Most of these instances are recorded in the public realm. We also include personal, but publicly accessible involvement with registered charities. Ignoring the exact amount given in each specific case obviously distorts the results towards frequency of donations to the detriment of the amount given. It nevertheless allows us to generate an overall snapshot of the areas the wealthy prioritise.

Specialisation versus oligarchization?

The most glaring difference between the two elites is the number of causes they give to. Our data showed that British philanthropists tend to specialise their activities on a small number of causes, whereas their Russian peers give strikingly widely. That is, the majority of the UK-based philanthropists confine their energy to a small number of concerns. They average three causes, with one of them standing out as their major effort and the others being additional pet projects. In contrast to that, rich Russians' donations are spread over nearly six different causes, without necessarily having one cause they focus on most.

This striking difference might have an explanation which goes well beyond the immanent tastes and preferences of wealthy philanthropists in both countries. We suggest that these diverse patterns could potentially indicate that wealthy Russians perpetuate a tendency to oligarchization in their giving, while the (much older and more established) British elite has long undergone a process of differentiation and specialisation.

Oligarchization: Russia's richest 200

Many of Russia's billionaires today rose to riches during the privatisation that followed the collapse of the Soviet Union in 1991. Those who did so and managed to seize large-scale industrial assets, which were formerly in state ownership, soon became known as the oligarchs. Their biggest political coup was to organise then-President Boris Yeltsin's re-election in 1996.[17]

Their grip on political power declined with the rise of Putin in the new century. Meanwhile, their overarching might being shattered, many of these oligarchs, as well as up-and-coming entrepreneurs, saw their personal wealth grow to astronomical levels, primarily thanks to rapidly rising oil prices. Soon into his rule, Putin ensured that these individuals committed to sustain Russia's infrastructure, which had shrunk dramatically after a decade of severe neglect. Under the slogan of 'social responsibility', Russia's super-wealthy were enlisted to contribute to state-approved projects, mostly in welfare and education. Philanthropic activities that ran counter to the Kremlin's interests were hamstrung. The most drastic reprimand was received by Mikhail Khodorkovsky, whose independent choices are said to have been one of the triggers leading to his imprisonment in

2003. This so-called Khodorkovsky Affair taught the rest a long-lasting lesson as to what it takes to remain in Putin's good books.

Philanthropic giving grew steadily throughout the 2000s. The 2008 global financial crisis did not slow this trend down significantly, and the wealthy's philanthropic spending shot up even more in the 2010s.[18] By far not all of this generosity was down to political pressure; it was also due to a growing desire among the hyper-rich to improve their image and shake off a reputation for being ruthless and selfish.[19]

The first oligarch to set up his own foundation was Vladimir Potanin in 1999. Since then many others have followed, and today there are about 40 private foundations in Russia. This urge to set up foundations was initially down to the underdevelopment of Russian non-governmental organisations (NGOs), which were little trusted and deemed corrupt and hence unsuitable to be tasked with acting as intermediaries. Even though this has changed since, many philanthropists still reject the idea of outsourcing the operational side of their charity to intermediary charity organisations.[20]

In particular, since the economic crisis in December 2014, large privately run foundations have gained new meaning. A drop in oil prices and a stark devaluation of the rouble left regional budgets empty and people without jobs. In many regions, whole towns depend on one single business empire. In some regions, foundations attached to businesses have tried to absorb the harm done to the local population following their own recent downsizing and layoffs, without, however, increasing their budget.[21] Concerns about the local population are only motivated by those business leaders' desire to preserve social peace; they are also triggered by a paternalism that is deeply anchored in Russian history. Serfdom was only abolished in Russian in 1861, comparatively late. A mentality of obedience and subordination among the peasantry, which made up over 80 per cent of the population, survived into the early twentieth century and returned during Soviet rule. Even the most ruthless business leader tends to have a certain understanding of history and suspects that the Russian people's obedience might in the long run rely on some minimum of care from above.

The role big foundations play in many Russian regions emerges in our data through a large percentage of causes classified as 'community giving'. Almost 20 per cent among Russia's richest 200 give to local causes, compared to just under 9 per cent among their UK counterparts. The overarching role of these foundations goes a long way to explain the wide range of causes over which the hyper-wealthy spread their philanthropic giving. To make sense, however, of why many of these foundations do not limit their activities to social care but often cover a whole range of cultural projects (15 per cent support the community arts) requires looking back into Soviet times.[22]

Philanthropy informed by the Soviet and post-Soviet past

Some individuals who run foundations have come to fancy themselves as moral leaders. One of their typical role models is the late nineteenth-century intelligentsia and their quest to enlighten the Russian people. Part and parcel of such re-enactments is to organise cultural projects and engage ordinary people in the foundation's fundraising to raise their civic understanding. Other endeavours simply aim at keeping the youth off the street.[23]

Odd, maybe even cynical, as such motives might seem, they are easily explained by the social backgrounds many wealthy Russians were born into – the Soviet intelligentsia – that is, professionals engaged in the cultural and educational sectors as well as academically trained medics, technicians and engineers. Reviving the Soviet intelligentsia values their parents held dear allows today's rich to construct a self-identity that has anchoring in the past.[24] Highlighting Soviet intelligentsia background is less (self-) betrayal than it might seem at first. Rather, it illustrates a shift from an emphasis on supposedly being self-made to one foregrounding a cultured upbringing, bookishness, the arts, high morals and a strong work ethos.

Family backgrounds in the Soviet intelligentsia also partly explain why science research greatly enjoys support among the richest 200 Russians. Fourteen per cent of them fund science projects or fellowships, compared to only 3.5 per cent of their British peers. Another explanation for such a priority is that many of Russia's hyper-rich started their professional careers in Soviet science or engineering; many hold doctorates in these fields. This stands in sharp contrast to the UK hyper-rich. Among them, previous science careers are extremely rare; even educational trajectories beyond master's level are atypical. This might partly explain why UK philanthropists prioritise medical research (nearly 9 per cent). Such giving is often motivated by personal experience or incidents in one's family. In Russia, medical research is supported by only 1.5 per cent of the 200 richest Russians. These low numbers might stem from the reality that rich Russians do not use the health system in Russia, especially if seriously ill, but get treated abroad, which disperses their gratitude and health concerns over the globe.

Intelligentsia roots might also form one explanation as to why 24 per cent of the 200 richest give to religious causes, compared to only 6.6 per cent in the United Kingdom. Some intelligentsia circles in the Soviet Union were close to the religious underground, who tended to harbour anti-Soviet sentiments. The general religious revival since the 1990s, which is strongly connected to Russian national identity, may be another factor. Some cynically trace rich people's strong support for religion back to the 'unholy' methods by which many had accumulated their wealth; helping the church should wash away their sins. Especially the construction of churches has attracted a lot of rich people's money. Curious here is that, when people make donations to the renovation or construction of churches, their own faith might well be secondary. The Russian Orthodox Church receives donations from across the denominations, including Jews, Muslims and atheists.[25]

The most distinctive difference between Russian and British rich is the former's overwhelming support for children. Thirty-nine per cent of the 200 richest Russians give money to projects targeting children in one form or the other, compared to only 10 per cent among the richest 257 people in Britain. That makes 'children' the category leading by a large distance from art philanthropy, the second most popular cause at 31 per cent. In comparison, 'children' did not even make it into the first five of the causes supported by the UK-based rich.

This overwhelming concern about children, and only them, takes us back to the 1990s, when some of today's billionaires found themselves among the winners of the economic transformation. When asking rich Russians why they support children and not adults, one can often hear that this is because they consider children as the only trustworthy group in society. The distrust towards all the rest is a result of 70 years of Soviet rule, followed by the 1990s, which brought social cohesion to a breakdown, sharply raised the crime and mortality rates among new businessmen and pushed millions into poverty. Apart from that, support for children is seen as an investment in the future – unless the children are disabled. Despite the Russian Orthodox teaching to perform good deeds for the sake of passive alms takers,[26] there is a clear priority among wealthy Russians to promote the strong, healthy and gifted over the weak and feeble.

Specialisation: The British elite

As Breeze points out, the United Kingdom sees herself as the birthplace of contemporary philanthropy, emerging from a strong tradition of charitable giving that developed over the course of the nineteenth century.[27] Long predating the appearance of modern cultural attitudes were the legal structures that form the foundation of charities as we know them today. They were taking shape already in the sixth century AD with the common law tradition that allowed for early educational and religious institutions to be formed.[28] By the late seventeenth century, the structure of the trust calcified into its modern legal form. This structure ensures that gifts may be left in perpetuity by distinguishing between a gift giver, the beneficiary of a gift and a trust who manages a gift on their behalf.[29] This legal framework underpins the structure of charities today, and continues to be of crucial importance to their functioning; for example, by placing the ultimate responsibility for all of a charity's actions into the hands of its board of trustees.[30]

In the late seventeenth and eighteenth centuries, during the Industrial Revolution, practices of charity (as described by Breeze) began to take hold and became deeply rooted in culture and society. Charity was transformed from individual acts of kindness into recognisable and organised movements. This development was not limited to giving by the wealthy but took place across all levels of the social hierarchy.[31] The means through which this occurred showed significant variation, from religious missions sponsored by churches to worker-organised 'friendly societies'. While many of these organisations' activities have been far broader than a strict charitable remit, it was through their common benevolent purpose that a new societal norm of charitable giving began to take shape.[32]

Those who owed their fortunes and elevated social positions to the toil of others were often particularly attuned to the damage that was being done in the heat of the Industrial Revolution. Indeed, many of today's leading charitable organisations in the United Kingdom, such as the Rowntree Foundation and the Peabody Trust, owe their origins to the fortunes of late nineteenth-century philanthropists.[33] Strong religious fervour was a motivating factor for many such philanthropists, with industrialists like George Cadbury or Titus Salt seeking to alter the lives of their workers not only through charity, but through the creation of new 'utopian' towns in which their workers could live – a form of philanthropic giving antecedent to the corporate social responsibility of today.[34] Tellingly, however, while these towns remain, their purpose has long been dismantled by the asset-stripping capitalism which Britain pioneered.[35]

The great levelling of the world wars ended the 'golden age' of philanthropy, when monumental personal fortunes foundered, and the political landscape shifted towards the nationalisation of societal goods. In this climate, charity and charitable organisations did not become obsolete, but their relevance and influence declined. In the words of historian David Owen, they turned into 'junior partners in the welfare firm'.[36] Following the post-war consensus, the surviving charitable sector sought to transform itself to fit with the times and needs of a new era. As a result, by the early 1970s, when Britain emerged from the exceptional political and economic circumstances that followed the Second World War, the charitable sector had been transformed from Victorian values to a new system that favoured self-help, specialist conditions, lobbying and secularisation.[37]

The eruption of financial capital in the 1980s truly revived the function of philanthropy as a significant source of prestige for the elite. The financial deregulation of the Big Bang of 1986, and the neo-liberal economic policies that enabled it, allowed unrestrained fortunes to again be made on a tremendous scale and at a prodigious rate. With this dynamic, a new breed of philanthropists was created who eschewed the paternalism of previous Victorian benefactors to focus on the utility of their giving (either to themselves, or the recipients). Their ethos was in tune with the new values and standards of a rapidly professionalising and secularising charitable sector.

The landscape of who occupied the richest echelons of British society had also begun to change. A more international and commercially mobile elite emerged. Yet, far from fulfilling the meritocratic promises of the new neo-liberal ideology, the fortunes made following the Big Bang tended to be made by those who already possessed the necessary capital, both economic and cultural, to capture the value unlocked by this new economic environment.[38] In other words, those at the pinnacle of this new hyper-wealthy elite were mostly drawn from the upper strata of society, which, while having shed the strict hierarchical posturing of their Victorian counterparts, place their family wealth and educational background far above the majority of British society.[39]

British philanthropists today

The explosion of wealth unlocked in this process is evident in the sources of wealth in our sample of the UK's hyper-wealthy. Among these 200 individuals, 18 per cent have primarily made their fortunes through finance, a percentage far higher than in any other industry.[40] When property trading and holdings are taken into account as a source of wealth, this number increases to 41 per cent of our sample – a figure that demonstrates the importance of real estate as a driver of wealth inequality and the role of financialisation in swelling its value.[41] Despite the new fortunes that have arisen in the United Kingdom in the last 30 years, little difference has been observed in the patterns of giving between 'emerging' and 'established' philanthropists.[42]

Britain's long tradition of giving, its economic clout and large number of multimillionaires, is reflected in the amount that elite philanthropists give. In 2014, donations made in the United Kingdom of over £1 million totalled £1.56 billion, compared to $405 million in Russia.[43] As mentioned earlier, British philanthropists are highly specialised in their giving, on average supporting only three causes, while their Russian counterparts give to nearly twice as many. This specialisation can be explained by at least four features that distinguish the UK elites from Russia's: First, many donors have distinctive corporate business backgrounds and prioritise 'effective' giving over a broader range of paternalistic support. Second, especially for the large proportion of philanthropists who have made their money in the financial sector, their motivations for giving remain detached from their primary moneymaking. Third, these factors are highly compatible with the long-established tradition of donating to intermediary organisations. The charity sector in the United Kingdom is highly developed, and charity organisations, NGOs and think tanks enjoy a great level of trust and support among the wealthy.[44] Last but not least, the UK welfare system is still highly functional, which relieves wealthy donors of many social 'obligations' and allows them to pursue their pet projects.

The giving of UK philanthropists is noticeably more internationalised than that of Russia. In our UK sample, 10 per cent were actively involved in international aid and development efforts in the global south, compared to only 1 per cent of the Russian rich (all three of whom are exiles in London) who gave to projects outside of Russia. Among UK philanthropists, development aid concerns are on a par with giving towards children, which stands in stark contrast to the overwhelming support given to the young by Russian philanthropists. The internationalism of British donors is reflective of Britain's long history of international business and philanthropy beyond its own borders, much of which remains entangled with its colonial history.[45] A similar pattern is evident in support for civil society organisations that are focused on human rights and social justice issues, to which 7 per cent of our British sample gave. (Of the 3.5 per cent of Russians who gave to causes that fell under the same category, their focus was strongly linked to their own backgrounds and biographies.[46])

In a number of areas in which UK philanthropists are particularly active, their giving is skewed away from the needs and concerns of the most unfortunate. One area in which this is particularly evident is in giving to educational causes. In both our Russian and British sample, education is one of the most popular causes, standing at 27.5 per cent and 25 per cent respectively. What is remarkable in the United Kingdom, however, is that the vast majority of such donations flows into higher education. Indeed, in 2015 Coutts reported that higher education institutions had received 65 significant donations in the preceding year, totalling £485 million. By comparison, all other forms of non-university education received only nine such donations, amounting to a total of £27 million.[47] The size of these donations and their discrepancy with philanthropy towards other forms of education demonstrate the power and prestige of elite universities and their alumni networks. Furthermore, many of these donations do not directly impact the educational remit of universities but are instead channelled towards capital works projects or research institutes, which can bear the name of the donor.[48]

A similar pattern of philanthropy targeting elite institutions can be seen in the arts. Compared to the 34 per cent of our Russian sample, only 14 per cent of our UK philanthropists were involved in providing significant support to the arts sector. The greatest difference between the two countries is in the type of art being supported. In the United Kingdom, the vast majority of arts philanthropy is focused on a small number of elite art institutions, many of them centred in London. Their involvement in the arts is primarily private collecting rather than charitable giving.[49] Although Russia's rich display similar preferences, many foundations run by the wealthy have community art projects included in their set of social care projects, which account for almost half of their philanthropy in this sector. In contrast, in the UK, 'community art' was a category of philanthropy which we found not to be relevant.

Conclusion

Elite philanthropy was questioned most forcefully and explicitly by Odendahl in her 1990s study on American elites, who exposed their donations for education and art institutions as benefitting primarily their own and thus reproducing social inequality rather than fighting it. Scathing as this verdict might sound, none of it is down to 'character' or 'personality'. Piketty warns of our almost automated quest to identify the 'good' rich and attack the bad ones.[50] Such attempts to separate the wheat from the chaff simply obscure a system that generates the glaring inequalities we see today and, in our case, the need for charity in the first place as well as the fact that the ability to provide help is in the hands of a small minority.

The most glaring difference between the giving of the richest 200 people on the *Forbes Russia* list and the richest 257 UK-based individuals and families as listed by *The Sunday Times* is clearly not grounded in personality, but in each country's respective economic and social history. British philanthropists' giving is specialised, which mirrors an economic structure that is highly developed, diversified and differentiated. In contrast, the natural-resources-dependent Russian economy is dominated by conglomerates, the portfolios of which cover a wide range of business activities. Many owners reign over their empires like mini-tsars. Having appeared during the course of Britain's industrialisation, charity organisations have acted as intermediaries between benefactors and beneficiaries since Victorian times. Russia's nascent civil society sector is still underdeveloped, little trusted and widely ignored by wealthy benefactors, who prefer running their own foundations and keeping them under tight control. Britain's hyper-rich are globalised in several senses of the word: in their composition, corporate activities, and history – both their colonial history and their involvement in world markets. In contrast, although highly dependent on exports and global finances, Russia's philanthropists are ideologically inward-looking. Their paternalistic attitudes to the people are based on reciprocity and compliance, something which is deeply ingrained in Orthodox traditions and stems from Byzantine ideas of almsgiving.

Acknowledgements

Elisabeth Schimpfössl is grateful to the Leverhulme Trust for enabling this research through the award of a Leverhulme Early Career Fellowship.

Notes

1   Matthew Bishop and Michael Green, *Philanthrocapitalism: How the Rich Can Save the World and Why We Should Let Them* (London: A. & C. Black, 2008). Other works in this tradition are: Joel Fleishman, *Putting Wealth to Work: Philanthropy for Today or Investing for Tomorrow?* (New York: PublicAffairs, 2017); Ács J Zoltán, *Why Philanthropy Matters: How the Wealthy Give, and What it Means for Our Economic Well-Being* (Princeton, NJ: Princeton University Press, 2013); Lester M. Salamon, ed., *New Frontiers of Philanthropy: A Guide to the New Tools and Actors Reshaping Global Philanthropy and Social Investing* (Oxford: Oxford University Press, 2014); and Norime MacDonald and Luc Tayart de Borms, eds., *Global Philanthropy* (London: MF Publishing, 2010). Many major banks have been quick to respond

to this trend by establishing philanthropy departments (see, for example: Bank of America, Coutts, Barclays, HSBC, JPMorgan, BNP Paribas).
2. David Callahan, *The Givers: Wealth, Power, and Philanthropy in a New Gilded Age* (New York: Alfred A. Knopf, 2017); Linsey McGoey, *No Such Thing as a Free Gift: The Gates Foundation and the Price of Philanthropy* (London: Verso, 2015); Linsey McGoey, 'Philanthrocapitalism and its critics', *Poetics* 40 (2012): 185–99; and Michael Edwards, *Small Change: Why Business Won't Save the World* (San Francisco: Berrett-Koehler Publishers, 2010).
3. The US tax system follows this logic particularly actively, and with the most obvious cost for society. Elements of such fiscal arrangements can be found in most of the world's tax systems, however, including the United Kingdom. Critical voices have been raised in academic literature on that issue. See, for example, Iain Hay and Samantha Muller, 'Questioning Generosity in the Golden Age of Philanthropy: Towards Critical Geographies of Super-Philanthropy', *Progress In Human Geography* 38, no. 5 (2013): 635–53.
4. Teresa Odendahl, *Charity Begins at Home: Generosity and Self-Interest among the Philanthropic Elite* (New York: Basic Books, 1990).
5. Rob Reich, 'Philanthropy and its Uneasy Relation to Equality', in *Taking Philanthropy Seriously: Beyond Noble Intentions to Responsible Giving*, 27–59, ed. William Damon and Susan Verducci (Bloomington: Indiana University Press, 2006).
6. Francie Ostrower, *Why the Wealthy Give: The Culture of Elite Philanthropy* (Princeton, NJ: Princeton University Press, 1995); and Diana E. Kendall, *The Power of Good Deeds: Privileged Women and the Social Reproduction of the Upper Class* (Lanham, MD: Rowman & Littlefield, 2002).
7. Paul Schervish and Keith Whitaker, *Wealth and the Will of God: Discerning the Use of Riches in the Service of Ultimate Purpose* (Bloomington: Indiana University Press, 2010); Paul Schervish, 'Major Donors, Major Motives: The People and Purposes Behind Major Gifts', *New Directions for Philanthropic Fundraising* 16 (1997): 85–112; and Paul Schervish, 'The Moral Biographies of the Wealthy and the Cultural Scripture of Wealth', in *Wealth in Western Thought: The Case for and Against Riches*, ed. Paul Schervish (Westport, CT: Praeger 1994), 167–208.
8. An example for a centre based in a business school is the Centre for Charitable Giving and Philanthropy (CGAP) at Cass, City University of London. Other important places are the Marshall Institute at the London School of Economics and the Centre for Philanthropy at Kent University. The latter is home to Beth Breeze who, together with Theresa Lloyd, produced the most comprehensive overview of elite philanthropy in Britain: *Richer Lives: Why Rich People Give* (London: Directory of Social Change, 2013). This was preceded by Theresa Lloyd's *Why Rich People Give* (London: Association of Charitable Foundations, 2004). Charity organisations themselves also produce important research. See, for example, Rhodri Davies, *Public Good by Private Means: How Philanthropy Shapes Britain* (London: CAF, 2015).
9. Leading in questions of elite philanthropy in Russia is Julia Khodorova, for example, with *Russia Giving: Research on Individual Giving in Russia* (Moscow: Charity Aid Foundation Russia, 2014). See also the results in the study carried out by the Skolkovo Center for Management, *Issledovanie Vladel'tsev Kapitalov Rossii* (Moscow: Center for Management, Wealth and Philanthropy, 2015). In the late 1990s, an early historical-philosophical discussion was launched by a seminal article by Natalia Dinello, 'Philanthropy in Russia and the United States: Elites and Philanthropy in Russia', *International Journal of Politics, Culture and Society* 12, no. 1 (1998): 109–33. The rise of wealthy men's giving in the early 2000s, as well as their preferences for giving, were analysed by Jamey Gambrell in 'Philanthropy in Russia: New Money under Pressure', *Carnegie Reporter* 3, no. 1 (2004), www.carnegie.org/ reporter/ 09/ philanthropy/ index.html, and Alexander Livshin and Richard Weitz, 'Civil Society and Philanthropy Under Putin', *International Journal of Not-for-Profit Law* 8, no. 3 (2006): 7–12.
10. 'The Sunday Times Rich List 2018', features.thesundaytimes.co.uk/richlist/live/richlist; and '200 Bogateishikh Biznesmenov Rossii 2017', www.forbes.ru/rating/342579-200 -bogateyshih-biznesmenov-rossii-2017.
11. Oliver Bullough, *Moneyland: Why Thieves and Crooks Now Rule the World and How to Take It Back* (London: Profile Books, 2018).
12. Facundo Alvaredo, Anthony B. Atkinson, and Salvatore Morelli, 'The Challenge of Measuring UK Wealth Inequality in the 2000s', *Fiscal Studies* 37, no. 1 (2016): 13–33.

13 Journalists themselves might regard their figures 'more of an art than a science', according to *The Sunday Times* rich list compiler Robert Watts, Skype interview, 13 May 2016. *The Sunday Times* rich list's rules of engagement: www.thetimes.co.uk/article/sunday-times-rich-list-2018-rules-of-engagement-nvw0lwzck.
14 Thomas Piketty, *Capital in the Twenty-First Century* (Cambridge, MA: The Belknap Press 2014), 441–2.
15 Piketty, *Capital,* 432; and Facundo Alvaredo, Anthony B. Atkinson, and Salvatore Morelli, 'Top Wealth Shares in the UK over More than a Century', *Journal of Public Economics*, In Honor of Sir Tony Atkinson (1944–2017), 162 (2018): 26–47.
16 Breeze and Lloyd, *Richer Lives*, 108.
17 Our definition of 'oligarchs' follows Jeffrey A. Winters, *Oligarchy* (Cambridge: Cambridge University Press, 2011).
18 'Million Dollar Donors Report 2014', *Coutts* 2015, accessed 15 January, philanthropy.coutts .com/ en/ reports/ 2014/ russia/ findings.html.
19 Elisabeth Schimpfössl, *Rich Russians: From Oligarchs to Bourgeoisie* (New York: Oxford University Press, 2018). This was not unlike the robber barons of the late nineteenth century in the United States or the new entrepreneurs in the Victorian period. For the latter, see Dianne Sachko Macleod, *Art and the Victorian Middle Class: Money and the Making of Cultural Identity* (Cambridge: Cambridge University Press, 1996).
20 Khodorova, *Russia Giving*, 19.
21 Irina Sedykh, the wife of metallurgy tycoon Anatolii Sedykh, the main shareholder of United Metallurgical Company (OMK), Russia's second-largest pipe producer and biggest maker of train wheels, in an interview with Elisabeth Schimpfössl on 11 June 2015, raised her awareness about the consequences layoffs have for those affected: Every single worker losing his job cannot look after the three (on average) people dependent on him, she said. She and her husband's charity foundation (OMK-Participation) try to mitigate the consequences.
22 Theatre productions and cultural festivals feature prominently in the annual programme of the Mikhail Prokhorov Foundation in the Siberian city of Krasnoyarsk. Mikhail Prokhorov led Russia's rich list in 2009 with assets of $22.6 billion (down to $8.9 billion in 2017). The foundation is led by his sister Irina Prokhorova, who is also the founder of *New Literary Observer*, the main intellectual journal and publishing house in Russia.
23 Elisabeth Schimpfössl, 'Russian Philanthrocapitalism', *Cultural Politics* 12, no. 1 (2019).
24 Schimpfössl, 'Russian Philanthrocapitalism'.
25 Schimpfössl, *Rich Russians*, 107–10.
26 Dinello, 'Philanthropy in Russia and the United States'.
27 Beth Breeze, Peter Halfpenny, and Karl Wilding, 'Giving in the United Kingdom: Philanthropy Embedded in a Welfare State Society', in *The Palgrave Handbook of Global Philanthropy*, ed. Pamala Wiepking and Femida Handy (New York: Palgrave Macmillan, 2005).
28 Frederic W. Maitland, 'The Origin of Uses', *Harvard Law Review* 8, no. 3 (1894): 127–37.
29 John Langbein, 'The Contractarian Basis of the Law of Trusts', *Yale Law Journal* 105 (1995).
30 Jeremy Kendall and Martin Knapp, 'Defining The Nonprofit Sector: The United Kingdom', in *Working Papers of the Johns Hopkins Comparative Nonprofit Sector Project*, ed. Lester M. Salamon and Helmut K. Anheier (Baltimore, MD: The Johns Hopkins Institute for Policy Studies, 1993).
31 Jeremy Kendall and Martin Knapp, *The Voluntary Sector in the United Kingdom* (Manchester, UK: Manchester University Press, 1995).
32 David Owen, *English Philanthropy, 1660–1960* (London: Oxford University Press, 1965).
33 Owen, *English Philanthropy*.
34 Craig N. Smith, 'Corporate Social Responsibility: Whether or How?' *California Review of Management* 45, no. 4 (2003): 52–76.
35 See, for example, James Meek, *Private Island*: *Why Britain Now Belongs to Someone Else* (London: Verso, 2014).
36 Owen, *English Philanthropy*.
37 Kendall and Knapp, *The Voluntary Sector*.
38 Stewart Lansley, 'Britain's Wealth Explosion', *Accountancy Business and the Public Interest* 5, no. 2 (2006): 2–15.
39 Tom Nicholas, 'The Myth of Meritocracy: An Inquiry into the Social Origins of Britain's Business Leaders since 1850', *Economic History Working Papers LSE* 53/99 (1999).

40   The next closest sources of wealth are retail and fashion at 7 per cent and pharmaceuticals at 3 per cent.
41   Manuel B. Aalbers, *The Financialization of Housing* (London: Routledge, 2016).
42   Breeze, *Richer Lives*, 107.
43   To put these figures into a comparative perspective, there are 61,199 ultra-high net worth individuals (those with $10 million+ in liquid assets) living in the UK, compared to 12,986 such individuals living in Russia. Anthony Shorrocks, James Davies, and Rodrigo Lluberas, *World Wealth Report 2018* (London: Credit Suisse Research Institute, 2018).
44   Breeze, *Richer Lives*, 211.
45   David Lambert and Alan Lester, 'Geographies of Colonial Philanthropy', *Progress in Human Geography* 28, no. 3 (2004): 320–24.
46   Among these donors, all bar two were involved in supporting the Jewish diaspora in the former Soviet space. Vladimir Melnikov is deeply devoted to his Russian-Orthodox faith and gives in this area. The only person who supports human rights causes in a more traditional sense of the term is the former long-term prisoner and London exile Mikhail Khodorkovsky.
47   'Million Dollar Donors Report 2015', *Coutts* 2016, accessed 27 November 2018, http://philanthropy.coutts.com/en/reports/2015/executive-summary.html.
48   On problematic donations within higher education, see Rob Reich, *Just Giving: Why Philanthropy is Failing Democracy and How It Can Do Better* (Princeton, NJ: Princeton University Press, 2018).
49   For a further discussion of this divide, see Alessia Zorloni, *Art Wealth Management: Managing Private Art Collections* (Berlin: Springer, 2016).
50   Piketty, *Capital*, 443–47.

Bibliography

Aalbers, Manuel B. *The Financialization of Housing*. London: Routledge, 2016.
Alvaredo, Facundo, Anthony B. Atkinson, and Salvatore Morelli. 'The Challenge of Measuring UK Wealth Inequality in the 2000s'. *Fiscal Studies* 37, no. 1 (2016): 13–33.
Alvaredo, Facundo, Anthony B. Atkinson, and Salvatore Morelli. 'Top Wealth Shares in the UK over More Than a Century'. *Journal of Public Economics*, In Honor of Sir Tony Atkinson (1944–2017), 162 (2018): 26–47.
Bishop, Matthew, and Michael Green. *Philanthrocapitalism: How the Rich Can Save the World and Why We Should Let Them*. London: A. & C. Black, 2008.
Breeze, Beth, Peter Halfpenny, and Karl Wilding. 'Giving in the United Kingdom: Philanthropy Embedded in a Welfare Society.' In *The Palgrave Handbook of Global Philanthropy*, edited by Pamala Wiepking and Femida Handy, 285–306. New York: Palgrave Macmillan, 2005.
Breeze, Beth, and Theresa Lloyd. *Richer Lives: Why Rich People Give*. London: Directory of Social Change, 2013.
Bullough, Oliver. *Moneyland: Why Thieves and Crooks Now Rule the World and How to Take It Back*. London: Profile Books, 2018.
Callahan, David. *The Givers: Wealth, Power, and Philanthropy in a New Gilded Age*. New York: Alfred A. Knopf, 2017.
Davies, Rhodri. *Public Good by Private Means: How Philanthropy Shapes Britain*. London: CAF, 2015.
Dinello, Natalia. 'Philanthropy in Russia and the United States: Elites and Philanthropy in Russia'. *International Journal of Politics, Culture and Society* 12, no. 1 (1998): 109–33.
Edwards, Michael. *Small Change: Why Business Won't Save the World*. San Francisco: Berrett-Koehler Publishers, 2010.
Fleishman, Joel. *Putting Wealth to Work: Philanthropy for Today or Investing for Tomorrow?* New York: PublicAffairs, 2017.
Gambrell, Jamey. 'Philanthropy in Russia: New Money under Pressure'. *Carnegie Reporter* 3, no. 1 (2004).
Hay, Iain, and Samantha Muller. 'Questioning Generosity in the Golden Age of Philanthropy: Towards Critical Geographies of Super-Philanthropy'. *Progress In Human Geography* 38, no. 5 (2013): 635–53.

Kendall, Diana E. *The Power of Good Deeds: Privileged Women and the Social Reproduction of the Upper Class*. Lanham, MD: Rowman & Littlefield, 2002.

Kendall, Jeremy, and Martin Knapp. 'Defining the Nonprofit Sector: The United Kingdom'. In *Working Papers of the Johns Hopkins Comparative Nonprofit Sector Project 5*, edited by Lester M. Salamon and Helmut K. Anheier. Baltimore, MD: The Johns Hopkins Institute for Policy Studies, 1993.

Kendall, Jeremy, and Martin Knapp. *The Voluntary Sector in the United Kingdom*. Manchester, UK: Manchester University Press, 1995.

Khodorova, Julia. *Russia Giving: Research on Individual Giving in Russia*. Moscow: Charity Aid Foundation Russia, 2014.

Lambert, David, and Alan Lester. 'Geographies of Colonial Philanthropy'. *Progress in Human Geography* 28, no. 3 (2004): 320–24.

Langbein, John. 'The Contractarian Basis of the Law of Trusts'. *Yale Law Journal* 105 (1995): 625–75.

Lansley, Stewart. 'Britain's Wealth Explosion'. *Accountancy Business and the Public Interest* 5, no. 2 (2006): 2–15.

Livshin, Alexander, and Richard Weitz. 'Civil Society and Philanthropy Under Putin'. *International Journal of Not-for-Profit Law* 8/3 (2006): 7–12.

Lloyd, Theresa. *Why Rich People Give*. London: Association of Charitable Foundations, 2004.

MacDonald, Norime, and Luc Tayart de Borms, eds. *Global Philanthropy*. London: MF Publishing, 2010.

Macleod, Dianne Sachko. *Art and the Victorian Middle Class: Money and the Making of Cultural Identity*. Cambridge: Cambridge University Press, 1996.

Maitland, Frederic W. 'The Origin of Uses'. *Harvard Law Review* 8, no. 3 (1894): 127–37.

McGoey, Linsey. *No Such Thing as a Free Gift: The Gates Foundation and the Price of Philanthropy*. London: Verso, 2015.

McGoey, Linsey. 'Philanthrocapitalism and its critics'. *Poetics* 40 (2012): 185–99.

Meek, James, *Private Island: Why Britain Now Belongs to Someone Else*. London: Verso, 2014.

'Million Dollar Donors Report 2014'. *Coutts* 2015. Accessed 15 January 2015, philanthropy.coutts.com/en/reports/2014/russia/findings.html.

'Million Dollar Donors Report 2015'. *Coutts* 2016. Accessed 27 November 2018, philanthropy.coutts.com/en/reports/2015/executive-summary.html.

Nicholas, Tom. 'The Myth of Meritocracy: An Inquiry into the Social Origins of Britain's Business Leaders since 1850'. *Economic History Working Papers LSE* 53/99 (1999).

Odendahl, Teresa. *Charity Begins at Home: Generosity and Self-Interest among the Philanthropic Elite*. New York: Basic Books, 1990.

Ostrower, Francie. *Why the Wealthy Give: The Culture of Elite Philanthropy*. Princeton, NJ: Princeton University Press, 1995.

Owen, David. *English Philanthropy, 1660–1960*. London: Oxford University Press, 1965.

Piketty, Thomas. *Capital in the Twenty-First Century*. Cambridge, MA: The Belknap Press 2014.

Reich, Rob. *Just Giving: Why Philanthropy is Failing Democracy and How It Can Do Better*. Princeton, NJ: Princeton University Press, 2018.

Reich, Rob. 'Philanthropy and its Uneasy Relation to Equality'. In *Taking Philanthropy Seriously: Beyond Noble Intentions to Responsible Giving*, edited by William Damon and Susan Verducci, 27–49. Bloomington, IN: Indiana University Press, 2006.

Salamon, Lester, ed. *New Frontiers of Philanthropy: A Guide to the New Tools and Actors Reshaping Global Philanthropy and Social Investing*. Oxford: Oxford University Press, 2014.

Schervish, Paul. 'Major Donors, Major Motives: The People and Purposes Behind Major Gifts'. *New Directions for Philanthropic Fundraising* 16 (1997): 85–112.

Schervish, Paul. 'The Moral Biographies of the Wealthy and the Cultural Scripture of Wealth'. In *Wealth in Western Thought: The Case for and against Riches,* edited by Paul Schervish, 167–208. Westport, CT: Praeger, 1994.

Schervish, Paul, and Keith Whitaker. *Wealth and the Will of God: Discerning the Use of Riches in the Service of Ultimate Purpose*. Bloomington, IN: Indiana University Press, 2010.

Schimpfössl, Elisabeth. *Rich Russians: From Oligarchs to Bourgeoisie*. New York: Oxford University Press, 2018.

Schimpfössl, Elisabeth. 'Russian Philanthrocapitalism'. *Cultural Politics* 15, no. 1 (2019): 105–20.

Shorrocks, Anthony, James Davies, and Rodrigo Lluberas. *World Wealth Report 2018*. London: Credit Suisse Research Institute, 2018.
Skolkovo Center for Management. *Issledovanie Vladel'tsev Kapitalov Rossii*. Moscow: Center for Management, Wealth and Philanthropy, 2015.
Smith, Craig N. 'Corporate Social Responsibility: Whether or How?' *California Review of Management* 45, no. 4 (2003): 52–76.
'The Sunday Times Rich List 2018'. *The Sunday Times.* April 2018. Accessed 27 November 2018, features.thesundaytimes.co.uk/richlist/live/richlist.
'200 Bogateishikh Biznesmenov Rossii 2017'. *Forbes Russia*. May 2017. Accessed 27 November 2018, www.forbes.ru/rating/342579-200-bogateyshih-biznesmenov-rossii-2017.
Winters, Jeffrey A. *Oligarchy*. Cambridge: Cambridge University Press, 2011.
Zoltán, Ács J. *Why Philanthropy Matters: How the Wealthy Give, and What it Means for Our Economic Well-Being*. Princeton: Princeton University Press, 2013.
Zorloni, Alessia. *Art Wealth Management: Managing Private Art Collections*. Berlin: Springer, 2016.

4
Between the public and the private
Socialism, capitalism and street socialisation in Georgia

Costanza Curro

Introduction: Everyday practices and the public/private divide

This chapter investigates street hangouts known as *birzha* ('stock exchange' in Russian). *Birzha* is a form of male street socialisation which has been prominent in Georgia since Soviet times. *Birzha* is made up of young men sitting, chatting, drinking, exchanging items and securing various deals at street corners or other open spaces in urban neighbourhoods (although, as we shall see, the phenomenon has rural origins). *Birzha* is a 'school of the street'[1] at which young men learn the foundational principles of Georgian manhood, but it is also deemed to be the initial step into a potential criminal career.[2]

This practice outlived the fall of socialism and navigated the troubled 1990s and the years following the 2003 Rose Revolution. At each of these recent historical stages, *birzha* has adapted to and counteracted different moral, social, political and economic orders. In different ways, these orders saw street hangouts as an eyesore in the framework of attempted modernisation projects from the top down – whether from a socialist or neo-liberal capitalist perspective.

Drawing upon research conducted in Georgia in 2008–2009, 2014 and 2017, as well as on the analyses by Georgian and international media and of relevant literature from social and political science, this chapter investigates transformations of *birzha* against such dramatically changing backgrounds. This analysis casts a light on the resilience and response of everyday practices embedded in specific moral, cultural and social grounds to different political and economic regimes, focusing in particular on the rise of neo-liberalism in the region as a purportedly successful doctrine to fix the flaws of post-communist societies.

My research identifies *birzha* as an ambivalent practice between the public and the private spheres. Following Lofland's reference to the *Webster's Third New International Dictionary of the English Language*'s definition of 'public space', I understand the 'public' as what is 'accessible or visible to all members of the community'.[3] This definition does not apply only to physical, but also to social spaces, as well as to practices, institutions and resources. By contrast, the 'private' is accessible to and useable by only certain individuals and groups (for example, the family and the house as private space *par excellence*), and under certain conditions (such as payments for private education or private healthcare).

The ambivalent position of *birzha* between the public and the private realms is empirically illustrated by three instances. First, *birzha* hangouts flourish between the public streets of the neighbourhoods and the private space of the house. Second, mainstream political narratives throughout Georgia's recent history (in particular, since the 2003 Rose Revolution) have associated the informal networks of 'private' friendship and comradeship created at *birzha* with crime and corruption, which, especially during the 1990s 'transition' to market capitalism, had a strong grip on the public sphere of politics and economics.[4] Finally, private relationships of trust, reciprocity and mutual responsibility underpinning *birzha* have worked as a fundamental form of psychological, social and material support amidst political and economic hardship, making up for public institutions' inability to cater for citizens' needs.[5]

The political narratives that underpinned the Rose Revolution and its aftermath considered the years between the fall of socialism and the political and social upheaval which brought Mikheil Saak'ashvili to power to be a flawed transition to capitalism and democracy. A system which was corrupt under communist rule outlived the demise of the Soviet Union, reproducing the same dynamics and often endorsing the same people who had served the previous regime. Greedy private interests encroached on public institutions and prevented the efficient delivery of public goods and services to the population. For 'real' change to take place and boost the country's 'modernisation', a thorough process of reforms needed to wipe out all the poisonous legacies of socialism and its immediate aftermath. Inspired by Western neo-liberalism, these reforms attempted to establish clear boundaries between the public and the private and targeted not only politics and economics, but also people's cultural and moral values, as well as everyday practices in which Georgian citizens engaged. While favouring private initiative and minimising the role of the state in economic affairs, the post-revolutionary government aimed to make public institutions transparent and accountable, and strengthened the rule of law and the image of the state as the main source of authority and order.[6]

In this context, *birzha* was out of place for two main reasons. First, street hangouts of young men lying about, drinking and engaging in dubious deals were at odds with the image of a clean and safe place and a rapidly modernising society, which the government wanted to transmit to its own citizens as well as to foreign observers, donors and policymakers. Second, practices providing informal support for people's everyday life would no longer be needed with efficient public institutions and a secured private sphere in which a market economy could flourish. A strong rule of law and a lively and flexible economy would create order and wealth for the ultimate benefit of all citizens.[7]

However, the bold neo-liberal reforms which the government implemented to modernise the country, and the authoritarian stance which social practices at odds with this project were dealt with, dismantled social security across society and undermined citizens' trust in the post-revolutionary political institutions' actual democratic and transparent nature. Deep inconsistencies at the heart of the government's modernisation project became increasingly apparent, eventually leading to the defeat of Saak'ashvili and his United National Movement (*Ertiani Natsionaluri Modzraoba*, or ENM) in the 2012 and 2013 elections.

After an overview of my research methods, this chapter presents *birzha* in its historical, cultural, spatial and social dimensions. I highlight the ambivalence of this practice as a fundamental institution for young male Georgians coming of age, but also as a semi-criminal phenomenon. I also analyse the blurred boundaries between public and private physical, social and political spaces along which *birzha* develops. Second, *birzha* is investigated in its ambivalent relationship with the cultural, social, political and economic order of the socialist era and the 1990s. The Soviet regime officially condemned *birzha* as a practice at odds with its principles. Yet, particularly in its late years, the system tolerated private practices and networks which catered for citizens' needs vis-à-vis a public sphere characterised by endemic shortage and political authoritarianism. In the 1990s, organised crime and corruption took over public institutions, while sheer poverty and civil and ethnic conflict ravaged the country. In this context, *birzha* played a vital role in the neighbourhood's life to facilitate informal access to goods and services, which the official system failed to provide. However, *birzha* was also 'part of the problem' inasmuch as links between street hangouts and the criminal world, which paralysed political and economic institutions and plagued society with violence, were apparent.

Third, the chapter discusses the post–Rose Revolution modernisation project and its attempts to establish clear-cut boundaries between the public and the private as an essential source of transparency, order and prosperity. This project identified *birzha* as opposed to the idea of law-abiding and hard-working citizens (and youth in particular) which the post-revolutionary political elites had in mind. Confident in its own popularity, the government dealt with *birzha* in an arbitrary way, targeting street hangouts with extreme harshness. However, failure to improve the life conditions of a large part of the population, and the oppressive nature that citizens increasingly ascribed to the government's attitudes and actions, alienated people's support from Saak'ashvili's leadership, uncovering contradictions in the post-revolutionary modernisation project.

In the conclusion, I highlight the resilience of *birzha* in today's Georgia, which indicates that the implementation of bold neo-liberal reforms, coupled with the arbitrary use of power against unwanted individuals and practices as a way to modernise the country, did not deliver the expected results. In a morally, culturally, socially, politically and economically fragmented context, many Georgian citizens still rely on ties developed through everyday practices to access material and non-material goods. These ties are often endowed with higher trust and respect than official institutions, which have largely failed to empower many people in their economic well-being and democratic participation, providing just a partial alternative with respect to the previous systems.

Researching *birzha*

My interest in *birzha* began in a fortuitous way. I was doing research in Tbilisi in 2008 and 2009 on a different topic and was being hosted by a family which lived in a residential neighbourhood on the outskirts of the capital, mostly made up of middle- and low-income households. I noticed that teenagers and young men hanging out in the streets were a permanent feature of that and other areas of Tbilisi. Residents referred to such gatherings, which seemed inseparable from the neighbourhood's physical and social landscape, as *birzha*. Regardless of people's various degrees of involvement in street life, knowledge of street norms was widespread among the neighbourhood's inhabitants. Stories and gossip about events concerning the local *birzha* circulated widely among locals.

Ordinary residents' acquaintance with *birzha* was essential for the outcomes of my research. 'Second-hand' information was provided by people detached from *birzha* in time and space, such as older men recalling their youthful experiences or mothers and wives worried about men wasting time in the street. Thanks to these respondents, I could partly counterbalance the limits imposed by the almost exclusively male access to *birzha*. Moreover, due to the status of *birzha* as a phenomenon more or less close to the criminal world, many of my friends and acquaintances warned me to stay away from 'those issues'. *Birzha* was considered, if not a dangerous business, at least a despicable reality with which respectable people (especially if female and a foreigner) should not get mixed up in. The association of *birzha* with semi-legal and illegal activities also meant that *birzha* members tended to be suspicious of a stranger's interest in their street community and therefore not keen to disclose information.

The analysis presented here is based on three main methods: (partial) observation of *birzha* as a feature of several of Tbilisi's neighbourhoods; perceptions and definitions collected in conversations with young male friends and acquaintances (aged 16 to 27), who were more or less closely related to *birzha*, but did not necessarily think of themselves as being part of it; narratives of *birzha* provided by outsiders (and, in some cases, former insiders), such as older men and women of all ages.

Birzha: Moral values and social norms of Georgian street communities

Birzha refers to groups of male teenagers or young men who meet regularly in urban open spaces such as squares, courtyards and playgrounds. The Russian word literally means 'stock exchange'. In Georgian, *birzha* is used colloquially; in the *Dictionary of Georgian Slang*, the term is defined as an 'open-pit gathering of idle youth'.[8] The reference to the financial world may sound ironic as generally participants are economically inactive (students or unemployed). However, *birzha* is where valuable exchange of social capital takes place.

Another meaning of *birzha* from nineteenth-century Russian slang denotes a place where people line up in hope for a temporary job.[9] Similarly, ethnographies of the post-Soviet space (in this case Lithuania) indicate that a group of men waiting in the street for informal short-term employment is called a '*darbo birzha*', the formal Lithuanian term for 'unemployment agency'.[10] The little literature available on the topic describes *birzha* as a pervasive phenomenon among urban male youth, a pivotal stage in the process of identification within local communities, as well as a potential initial step into a criminal career.[11]

In the context of Georgia, the understanding of *birzha* is disputed. According to several participants, *birzha* is neither exclusively male and juvenile nor peculiarly urban but is widely considered to be a phenomenon of rural origins, which was successfully urbanised. Literary sources point to the pre-Soviet institution of adoptive brotherhood (*modzmeoba*), in which spiritual kinship serves as the basis for social and political allegiances between Caucasian highlanders.[12]

Today, *birzha* is visible in the streets and squares in urban neighbourhoods, *ubani* in Georgian (sometimes also referred to as *kvartali*, from the Russian *kvartal*). *Birzha* spreads across the urban space, penetrating liminal areas. In the urban landscape, liminal spaces or 'interstices'[13] are zones that 'are essentially away from a "public gaze" [sic] whilst simultaneously situated within a public space'.[14] Liminal spaces occupy a 'minoritarian' position with respect to other spaces that are 'either more institutionalized, and therefore economically and legally powerful, or endowed with a stronger identity, and therefore more recognizable or typical'.[15] Yet, liminality produces identities, practices, norms and power relations in its own right.

In the neighbourhoods of Tbilisi, variously sized groups of men populate the thresholds between house and street, between family and state: street corners, playgrounds, stairways, courtyards, block gates, cellars and basements. As a phenomenon pervasive in spaces which are neither public nor private, *birzha* lives in the tension between the private realm of domesticity and close relationships and the public sphere of the state and other official institutions. As will be discussed below, the moral, cultural, social, political and economic structure of *birzha* has generated practices that have represented an alternative, and often an opposition, to Georgia's official system at various stages of the country's recent history.[16]

Birzha is defined as the principal school for masculinity, which marks an essential stage in the transition from teenager to manhood.[17] For males, membership in *birzha* comes as a birth right, regardless of ethnicity, religion or socio-economic status.[18] Inclusion is conditional on compliance with street norms, whose pivotal points are honour, honesty, manly attitudes and respect for the elderly, and which are predicated on a rigid hierarchy of identities and roles. The fundamental authority in the *birzha* hierarchy is the *dzveli bich'i* ('old boy'), a young man aiming for a career in the criminal world.[19] His key features are an utter disregard for official rules and authorities, mastery of street norms, proneness to using violence to solve conflicts, and prison experience. *Dzveli bich'i* status is regarded as the first level of a criminal hierarchy which culminates in the figure of the 'thief-in-law', *k'anonieri kurdi*, a semi-mythical kind of bandit that has its origins in Stalin's labour camps and developed in various forms across the Soviet Union.[20]

In my research, I came across flexible meanings of *birzha*, which transcend the narrow reference to semi-criminal street gangs. In the perspective of several of my participants, *birzha* partially overlapped with *dzmak'atsoba*.[21] *Dzmak'atsoba* is a stronger and manlier relationship than the neutral 'friendship', *megobroba*, and refers to the link with a *dzmak'atsi* – from *dzma* ('brother') and *k'atsi* ('man'). In the words of Giorgi (42, profession unknown), a *dzmak'atsi* is 'more than a friend, more than a brother'. The strongest kind of *dzmak'atsoba* is with your 'friend from childhood' (*bashvobis dzmak'atsi*), and according to Giorgi, 'it's a friendship that should last forever, and it's really sad if you lose this mate'. A *dzmak'atsi* is someone to whom 'you can entrust your mother, your sister and your wife'. But if the mutual loyalty is betrayed, even such an important friend can become the most despised foe. In Giorgi's view, 'when a *dzmak'atsi* lets you down and betrays your trust, he ought to be killed. In my life I have learned that almost nobody is worthy of being called *dzmak'atsi*'.

As Giorgi's words indicate, trust is pivotal to personal ties within *birzha*, and to relationships between *dzmak'atsi* in general. These relationships oblige one to be totally honest with other *birzha* members, take responsibility for oneself and face the consequences of breaking street laws. Severe violations include deceiving or betraying *birzha* members, especially collaborating with the police or other state institutions; verbally offending or physically attacking another *birzha* member or somebody close to him (particularly a female member of his family); and letting down a *dzmak'atsi* and failing to respect older residents of the neighbourhood (whether or not affiliated to *birzha*). Yet, solidarity between *dzmak'atsi* is also intertwined with (sometimes physical) competitiveness between *birzhas* from different neighbourhoods and even members of the same *birzha*. Success in enhancing one's position among peers is linked to cunning behaviour, proneness to risks, mastery of street laws and strong ties with influential *dzveli bich'i* or the neighbourhood's elderly.

Relationships in the street are regulated by reciprocity. *Birzha* is informed by ongoing exchanges of material and non-material items. The term indicates multi-directional giving and taking, and business deals, both small and large, take place in the street. Sharing is a common feature: members of the street community are expected to circulate cigarettes, clothes and other belongings among peers. Since *birzha* mostly consist of young people, who usually do not own much, sharing is of high importance. Those who are better off than others (even if only temporarily, because they have found a short-term job or have taken a loan or received a gift from friends or family) make their resources available to the group.

Money can be used to purchase drinks and food, to pay for a taxi for a trip out of town, to feast in a restaurant or to go out to clubs or bars. In Tbilisi, a widespread custom is to buy fresh beer directly from the local brewery on the banks of the river Mt'k'vari and treat fellow *birzha* members to it, together with dry smoked fish and rye bread. One can often spot groups of men drinking beer on the brewery's premises, sitting on the pavement or on the parapet by the riverside. Others take large plastic bottles full of beer back to their neighbourhoods and share it with friends while sitting outdoors.

Birzha is a fundamental institution for young Georgian men to create close relationships with their peers across their neighbourhoods. These relationships are based on mutual trust, total dedication and honesty towards street communities, and a willingness to share goods, feelings and experiences with other *birzha* members. Streets and squares of Georgian cities and towns are the stage for equitable exchanges, through which young people come of age sharing moral, cultural and social values. However, while the exclusive and often hierarchical structure of *birzha* establishes strong ties within street communities, it cuts out other members of society. Furthermore, the more or less tight links between *birzha* and organised crime throughout recent Georgian history have contributed to create an image of street communities – variously emphasised by political authorities and partially resonating across the population – as idle and lost youths who encroach on public space for their murky and selfish business. The following section discusses the key features of the ambivalent relation between *birzha* and the official system in the Soviet era and throughout the 1990s.

Birzha under socialism and in the 1990s

In Soviet and post-Soviet times up to the Rose Revolution, *birzha* occupied the 'grey zones' between public and private social and physical spaces.[22] The Soviet-type social and political structure envisages 'the realm of *officialdom*' on the one hand, including the ruling elite, *apparat* and *nomenklatura*, and 'the *domestic* realm of family and friendship' on the other hand, resting upon kinship ties, intimacy networks and shared value commitments. Yet, in between there is a '"*social* realm" encompassing the enormous and complex domain developing between the top level of the Party-state and family and friends networks – that is, the domain of work, routine administration, and "official" associational life'.[23] Only on the surface is this intermediate space organised through ideological, meritocratic or authoritarian principles; its core structure develops 'along lines of bargaining, reciprocal favours, mutual dependencies, networks of connections, dissimulation, circumvention of regulations and procedures'.[24] Although emerging from the private space of family and friend relationships, this 'private-public realm' or 'second public'[25] is at the same time clearly separated from the official public.

In socialist systems, the public sphere largely overlapped with the state, and only activities controlled by the authorities were allowed publicly.[26] In this context, the grey zones between public and private inhabited by *birzha* formed a niche relatively free of the system's regimentation. *Birzha* was an alternative form of youth association to those promoted by Soviet authorities, such as the Young Pioneers and the Komsomol.[27] In contrast to public images of socialist youth as the most active part of the population in realising the collective goals of Soviet society, *birzha* valued loyalty to personal ties more highly than loyalty to the state and the Party. Images of hard-working and healthy Soviet youth clashed with the perceived inactivity and debauchery of *birzha* members.

In Soviet cityscapes, 'open "public" spaces [were] perceived as something alien and belonging to the state, not to the inhabitants', turning an ideal 'everyone's space' into 'no one's space'.[28] *Birzha* catered for a different kind of collective interaction in urban spaces, as a way in which 'ordinary residents appropriated public places beyond the mainstream paradigms and master narratives of the city image'.[29] By carving out social and physical grey zones partially spared from state control, *birzha* created spaces for those young men to whom socialist symbolic and material power was alien.[30] However, while ideologically stigmatised by official authorities, *birzha* was hardly subject to actual repression from the Soviet state. The latter (especially in its later years) in fact tolerated informal networks and practices grounded in grey zones between the public and the private, inasmuch as citizens' access to informal means 'enabled the system to function and made it tolerable'.[31]

When the Soviet Union came to an end, in Georgia the public sphere of politics and the economy was taken over by the private interests of organised criminal groups or paramilitary squads. They infiltrated and paralysed the state, which prevented public institutions from fulfilling their basic functions.[32] Corruption became pervasive in all aspects of public life, from politics and business to education, from the police to the health system. The blurred lines between public and private encouraged the abuse of public resources for the benefit of private interests.[33] While pointing out the greed of corrupt politicians and businessmen as a major cause of the country's miserable conditions, citizens themselves often resorted to petty bribery as the easiest, and sometimes the only possible way to secure essential goods and services.[34]

The physical and social public space was ravaged by violence and decay.[35] In a neighbourhood life of struggle and sharing, *birzha* had a prominent role. It facilitated access to goods and services which the shortcomings of official institutions otherwise made unattainable, moving easily within and across boundaries and merging the public with the private. In addition, *birzha* was a way for young men to cultivate ideas and practices of masculinity in a context in which unemployment, heavy drinking, criminality and drug addiction severely challenged men's ability to live up to the traditional male role of breadwinner and wise and honourable member of the community.[36] On the one hand, many young men referred to being part of *birzha* in the 1990s and circumventing official rules as a form of protest against the system.[37] On the other hand, *birzha* was linked to the criminal world, which had considerable political and economic power. As a result, in several citizens' perspectives *birzha* stood out more as an expression of, rather than a form of, resistance to corruption and violence.[38]

Clearing grey zones: *Birzha* after the Rose Revolution

Following the political narratives that surrounded the Rose Revolution, the system which developed out of the Soviet regime in the 1990s was democratic and capitalist in theory, but in fact offered no real alternative to what went before. Corruption and the prominent influence of organised crime in the political and economic sphere prevented the creation of accountable public institutions and a lively public realm in which citizens could participate. The development of secure private property and business, which would boost a market economy, was also hampered.

The post-revolutionary political leadership, which ruled the country from 2003 to 2012, envisaged the 'transition' from socialism to capitalism and democracy as a movement from backwardness to modernity. Transparency, as the opposite of the corrupt 'private use of public good',[39] was the banner under which the government implemented reforms which aimed to get rid of ambivalent grey zones in politics, economics and the law. Following core neo-liberal principles, a vast process of privatisation and deregulation went hand in hand with a radical restructuring of public institutions and services, such as the police and local authorities.[40]

The modern and transparent society framed by post-revolutionary political narratives stood in opposition to the blurred boundaries informing citizens' relationship with the state and the rule of law. These narratives depicted the Georgian population as pervaded by a 'culture of informality', which supposedly affected all social mechanisms. People's habit of circumventing formal rules to 'get things done' was not a by-product of institutional inefficiencies, but a way of thinking that had corrupted citizens' moral principles. In an interview with the German filmmaker Stefan Tolz in 2013, Saak'ashvili attacked his people's way of relating to official rules, stressing that dramatic changes at the institutional level must go hand in hand with a radical transformation of the population's moral and cultural ground:

> But everybody has to pay [taxes], it's [not] something that has ever been heard of here. Or when everybody had to put seatbelts on, unheard of in our part of the world. Or nobody could take bribes, you know, very unusual. And you know when you ask people say, even today when we did opinion polls and you ask people: What is a crime? People say: 'Oh killing somebody is a crime, raping is a crime, not paying taxes not really a crime, I mean just taking bribes, oh well, he has to feed his family, right? This official, he took like 500 euros, so what a big deal.' People were saying that in opinion polls. Overcoming that I guess, that takes a couple of generations.[41]

Many studies of both Soviet and 1990s Georgia discuss citizens' alienation from political institutions as a crucial factor in determining the spread of practices that circumvent official norms.[42] It is argued that 'state laws have been avoided not only because they were bad but because the population could manage better without them'.[43] The Rose Revolution, as depicted in collective narratives, political analyses and media coverage, was expected to reverse this trend, and 'perhaps for the first time in Georgia's modern history, establish the congruity of private and public well-being'.[44]

In the communist era, the mistrust which informed the relationship between state and citizens stemmed from the perception of public institutions as the expression of a hostile power. In the 1990s, the public sphere of the state, rather than representing the 'common good', was seen by citizens as the arena in which greedy officials fought for their private interests, neglecting the miserable conditions of a large part of the population. The Rose Revolution pledged to make the public realm, embodied by state institutions, finally accountable.

The modern public and private, which represented a radical alternative to the socialist system and its poisonous legacies, were to be inhabited by modern individuals. The ideal citizens of post-revolutionary Georgia were patriotic but also cosmopolitan, independent, ambitious and law-abiding. People's everyday practices mattered for defining social profiles that fitted, or did not fit, the country's radical renovation. Social practices had to conform to modernisation narratives, embodying trust in institutions, respect for the law, an ambitious way of thinking and an efficient lifestyle.[45] Most importantly, people's practices were expected to stick to the clear-cut division between the public and the private.

For a number of reasons, the post-revolutionary government identified *birzha* as one of the main targets of its modernisation project. First, *birzha* was a blatant expression of the despised features of the past: petty crime, over-drinking, drug use and inactivity. Second, *birzha* and the criminal world competed with the state for moral, social, political, legal and economic authority – especially among the youth, whom the government had placed at the forefront of the modernisation project.[46] An indication of the popularity of street life and the criminal world among young people is the fact that 25 per cent of Georgian schoolchildren interviewed in 1993 declared that they wanted to be thieves-in-law when they grew up.[47]

Third, young men who hung out in public spaces, getting drunk, talking loudly and negotiating dubious deals, spoiled the image of cleanness and safety which the government wanted external observers and visitors to see. *Birzha* embodied liminal use of public spaces, transcending the divide between the public and the private which the political leadership aimed to establish as a fundamental sign of the country's modernity.

The zero-tolerance approach taken by the government aimed to remove undesirable practices, of which *birzha* was a paradigmatic expression, and those who engaged in them from the city's physical and cultural landscape. In his 2006 address to parliament, Saak'ashvili referred to the tough policies being implemented against petty crime as aiming to 'clean our streets of this rubbish'.[48] The Georgian Criminal Code was reformed to include harsher sanctions against petty theft and minor drug-related offences.[49] During Saak'ashvili's rule, many of my young male research participants were worried about the increasing presence of police patrols (*p'at'ruli*) in the streets.[50] Some people avoided going out at night, even to the local shop. This behaviour was motivated by the belief that young males hanging out after a certain hour in certain areas were suspicious. Data confirm the government's repressive stance against people and practices considered unsuitable to the modernisation project. The harsh sanctions imposed for petty crime during Saak'ashvili's presidency led to the prison population becoming one of the highest per capita in the world.[51]

Conclusion: Everyday practices as the alternative?

The political order brought about by the Rose Revolution presented itself as the only real alternative to the flaws of the communist system, which had endured the fall of the Soviet Union and had precipitated the country into poverty, crime and conflict throughout the 1990s. Post-revolutionary political narratives identified the blurred boundaries between the public and the private as an essential feature of these flaws and the main hindrance to the country's modernisation. Transparency and order were the foundational pillars not only of a projected modern society, politics and economics, but also of modern citizens' moral and cultural ground.

A large part of the population, however, questioned the means by which the government tried to modernise society. Many of my participants were disappointed by the developments of the Rose Revolution not only because of the lack of improvement in people's socio-economic conditions but also because they perceived state authority as an arbitrary power which made it dangerous to walk in the streets of the neighbourhood after dusk, discuss politics in public, or go to a protest rally.[52] The growing inequality brought into place by swift privatisation and deregulation[53] went hand in hand with the severe violation of democratic and civil liberties, regardless of the post-revolutionary government's official rhetoric. This increasingly alienated citizens' trust in post-revolutionary political elites and in the implementation of political and economic models which these elites believed to be the only viable alternative to the backwardness and lawlessness inherited from socialism and its aftermath.

Theoretical analyses and empirical contributions on everyday practices in post-socialism systems have called into question the fading away of these practices as a form of support resulting from the development of free market and democratic rights, which would provide a political and economic environment able to cater for the needs of all citizens. Instead, these studies have pointed out that, in spite of optimistic expectations, 'shock therapies' and subsequent economic policies implemented after the fall of socialism did not bring about immediate development and well-being for everyone, but in most cases had a devastating effect on the already precarious lives of millions of people. In such contexts, although changing to adapt to different circumstances, everyday practices have maintained their role as a means of psychological, social, political and economic support amidst growing inequality and uncertainty.[54]

Reforms implemented by the post-revolutionary government aimed to efface the ambivalence between the public and the private and introduce respect for the law, meritocracy, ambition and transparency as foundational values of modern Georgian society. Sanctions and repression targeted those individuals and social phenomena which did not fit this project. Yet, the post-revolutionary government's vision of the end of 'transition' as the demise of grey zones in favour of clear-cut distinctions proved to be inconsistent. Indeed, at the end of Saak'ashvili's rule in 2012, groups of young men hanging out at *birzha* had become a less conspicuous feature across the cityscape. Yet, the harsh policies implemented by the government against *birzha* did not have a long-term effect, and transformations in the prominence and visibility of street communities are more closely connected to increased social and geographical mobility among young people.[55] In the years following the United National Movement's electoral defeat in 2012, *birzha* has proved to be a resilient practice among many young men coming of age. This happens in spite of enduring hostility from the political authorities and the ambivalent status of *birzhas* within their own neighbourhoods, in which they are met by residents' tolerance mixed with suspicion.[56]

Birzha's ability to adapt to and outlive different social, political and economic orders indicates that projects of top-down reform of a society have overlooked the importance and strength of everyday practices embedded in relationships of trust, reciprocity and solidarity. These practices develop from ties cultivated in the private sphere of the house, the neighbourhood, and the circle of friends and colleagues, but are also parallel and complementary to public institutions, catering for needs which the official system is unable, or unwilling, to fulfil. The case of post–Rose Revolution Georgia, while grounded in its own specifics, provides grounds for comparison with other countries in the post-socialist space which have experienced the rise of neo-liberalism and the importation of Western political and economic models as the best available options for moving forward from socialist legacies. As the analysis of *birzha* vis-à-vis the official system indicates, this approach has significant flaws, which call into question the suitability of such political and economic models for the realities to which they have been applied. The top-down implementation of several post-socialist reforms has often disregarded the role of embedded practices and relationships as fundamental cultural, social, political and economic alternatives to the official system. This obliviousness has contributed to create the fragmentation and marginalisation that different social and political contexts across the region experience today.

Notes

1. J. Koehler, 'The School of the Street: Organising Diversity and Training Polytaxis in a (Post-) Soviet Periphery', *Anthropology of East Europe Review* 17, no. 2 (1999b): 41–55. See also J. Koehler, *Die Schule der Strasse: Georgische Cliquen zwischen Kämpfen um Ehre und organisierter Kriminalität* (Berlin: Das Arabische Buch, 1999a).
2. C. Curro, 'Davabirzhaot! Conflicting Claims on Public Space in Tbilisi between Transparency and Opaqueness', *International Journal of Sociology and Social Policy* 35, no. 7/8 (2015): 497–512. See also M. D. Frederiksen, 'Good Hearts or Big Bellies: *Dzmak'atsoba* and Images of Masculinity in the Republic of Georgia', in *Young Men in Uncertain Times,* edited by V. Amit and N. Dyck (New York: Berghahn Books, 2012), 165–87. See also E. Zakharova, 'Street Life in Tbilisi as a Factor of Male Socialization', *Laboratorium: Russian Review of Social Research* 2, no. 1 (2010).
3. L. Lofland, *The Public Realm: Exploring the City's Quintessential Social Territory* (London: Routledge, 1998), 8.
4. G. Slade, *Reorganising Crime: Mafia and Anti-Mafia in Post-Soviet Georgia* (Oxford: Oxford University Press, 2014). See also G. Slade, 'The Threat of the Thief: Who Has Normative Influence in Georgian Society? Dispatches', *Global Crime* 8, no. 2 (2007): 172–79. See also A. K'up'at'adze, 'Georgia's Fight against Organized Crime: Success or Failure?', *Caucasus Analytical Digest*, 9 (2009): 9–12. See also A. K'ukhianidze, 'Corruption and Organized Crime in Georgia before and after the Rose Revolution', *Central Asian Survey* 28, no. 2 (2009): 215–34.
5. J. Round and C. Williams, 'Coping with the Social Costs of "Transition": Everyday Life in Post-Soviet Russia and Ukraine', *European Urban and Regional Studies* 17, no. 2 (2010): 183–96. See also A. Smith and A. Rochovská, 'Domesticating Neo-Liberalism: Everyday Lives and the Geographies of Post-Socialist Transformations', *Geoforum* 38, no. 6 (2007): 1163–78; A. Ledeneva, *Russia's Economy of Favours: Blat, Networking and Informal Exchange* (Cambridge: Cambridge University Press, 1998); M. E. Chatwin, *Socio-Cultural Transformation and Foodways in the Republic of Georgia* (Commack, NY: Nova Science Publishers, 1997).
6. P. Evans and W. Sewell, 'The Neoliberal Era: Ideology, Policy, and Social Effects', in *Social Resilience in the Neoliberal Era,* edited by P. Hall and M. Lamont (Cambridge: Cambridge University Press, 2013): 35–68.
7. D. Gugushvili, *Do the Benefits of Growth Trickle down to Georgia's Poor? A Case for a Strong Welfare System* (PhD thesis, University of Kent, 2014).
8. L. Bregadze, *Kartuli jargonis leksik'oni* (*Dictionary of Georgian Slang*) (Tbilisi: Gapur Sulakauris Gamomtsemloba, 2005).
9. Dal' 1955, as quoted in Zakharova, 'Street Life in Tbilisi'.
10. I. Harboe Knudsen, 'The Lithuanian "Unemployment Agency": On *Bomzhai* and Informal Working Practices', in *Ethnographies of Grey Zones in Eastern Europe: Relations, Borders and Invisibilities,* edited by I. Harboe Knudsen and M. D. Frederiksen (London: Anthem Press, 2015), 141–56.
11. C. Curro, 'A Critical Assessment of Informal Practices as Resistance: The Case of *Birzha* in Georgia', *Caucasus Survey* 5, no. 1 (2017): 65–84. See also C. Curro, 'From Goods to Emotions: The Transformation of Informal Practices in the Republic of Georgia', in *The Informal Economy: Exploring Drivers and Practices,* edited by I. Horodnic, P. Rodgers, C. Williams, and L. Momtazian (London: Routledge, 2017). See also Curro, 'Davabirzhaot!'; E. Zakharova, 'The Tbilisi Street as a Legal and Political Phenomenon in Georgia', in *State and Legal Practice in the Caucasus,* edited by S. Voell and I. Kaliszewska (London: Ashgate, 2015), 69–82;

Zakharova, 'Street Life in Tbilisi'; M. D. Frederiksen, *Young Men, Time, and Boredom in the Republic of Georgia* (Philadelphia: Temple University Press, 2013); Frederiksen, 'Good Hearts or Big Bellies'; Koehler, 'The School of the Street'; Koehler, *'Die Schule der Strasse'*.

12 V. Bardavelidze, 'The Institution of *Modzmeoba* (Adoptive Brotherhood): An Aspect of the History of the Relations between Mountain and Valley Populations in Georgia', in *Kinship and Marriage in the Soviet Union: Field Studies,* edited by T. Dragadze (London: Routledge, 1984), 173–88.

13 A. M. Brighenti, *Urban Interstices: The Aesthetics and the Politics of the In-Between* (Farnham, UK: Ashgate, 2013), xv.

14 S. Parkin and R. Coomber, 'Public Injecting Drug Use and the Social Production of Harmful Practice in High-Rise Tower Blocks (London, UK): A Lefebvrian Analysis', *Health and Place* 17, no. 3 (2011): 717.

15 Brighenti, 'Urban Interstices', xvi.

16 Curro, 'A Critical Assessment of Informal Practices'.

17 Zakharova, 'The Tbilisi Street'. See also Zakharova, 'Street Life in Tbilisi'; Koehler, 'The School of the Street'; Koehler, *'Die Schule der Strasse'*.

18 Zakharova, 'Street Life in Tbilisi'.

19 J. Finckenauer and L. Kelly, 'Juvenile Delinquency and Youth Subcultures in the Former Soviet Union', *International Journal of Comparative and Applied Criminal Justice* 16, no. 1–2 (1992): 247–61.

20 Slade, 'The Threat of the Thief'. See also Slade, 'Reorganizing Crime'; Frederiksen, 'Young Men, Time and Boredom'; Zakharova, 'Street Life in Tbilisi'; K'up'at'adze, 'Georgia's Fight against Organized Crime';T. Frisby, 'The Rise of Organized Crime in Russia: Its Roots and Social Significance', *Europe-Asia Studies* 50, no. 1 (1998): 27–49.

21 Frederiksen, 'Young Men, Time and Boredom'. See also Frederiksen, 'Good Hearts or Big Bellies'.

22 Harboe Knudsen and Frederiksen, eds., 'Ethnographies of Grey Zones in Eastern Europe'. See also S. Roy 'The Grey Zone: The "Ordinary" Violence of Extraordinary Times', *Journal of the Royal Anthropological Institute* 14, no. 2 (2008): 316–33; A. Robertson, 'The Anthropology of Grey Zones', *Ethnos* 71, no. 4 (2006): 569–73.

23 M. Garcelon, 'The Shadow of the Leviathan: Public and Private in Communist and Post-Communist Society', in *Public and Private in Thought and Practice: Perspectives on a Grand Dichotomy,* edited by J. Weintraub and K. Kumar (Chicago: University of Chicago Press, 1997): 317 (emphasis in original).

24 Garcelon, 'The Shadow of the Leviathan', 317.

25 I. Oswald and V. Voronkov, 'The "Public–Private" Sphere in Soviet and Post-Soviet Society: Perception and Dynamics of "Public" and "Private" in Contemporary Russia', *European Societies* 6, no. 1 (2004): 97–117. See also E. Zdravomyslova and V. Voronkov, 'The Informal Public in Soviet Society: Double Morality at Work', *Social Research* 69, no. 1 (2002): 49–69.

26 A. Zhelnina, 'Public Spaces as Spaces of Fear and Alienation? Youth in Public Spaces in St. Petersburg, Russia', *Isaconf*, 2nd ISA Forum of Sociology, *Social Justice and Democratisation*, 1–4 August 2012, University of Buenos Aires, Argentina.

27 C. Walker and S. Stephenson, 'Youth and Social Change in Eastern Europe and the Former Soviet Union', in *Youth and Social Change in Eastern Europe and the Former Soviet Union*, edited by C. Walker and S. Stephenson (London: Routledge, 2012), 1–13. See also Zakharova, 'Street Life in Tbilisi'.

28 A. Zhelnina, 'Learning to Use "Public Space": Urban Space in Post-Soviet St. Petersburg', *The Open Urban Studies Journal* 6 (2013): 58.

29 T. Darieva and W. Kaschuba, 'Sights and Signs of Postsocialist Urbanism in Eurasia: An Introduction', in *Urban Spaces after Socialism: Ethnographies of Public Spaces in Eurasian Cities,* edited by T. Darieva, W. Kaschuba, and M. Krebs (Frankfurt: Campus Verlag, 2011): 11.

30 J. Kubik, *Power of Symbols against the Symbols of Power: The Rise of Solidarity and the Fall of State Socialism in Poland* (University Park, PA: Penn State Press, 1994).

31 Ledeneva, 'Russia's economy of favours', 3. See also G. Mars and Y. Altman, 'The Cultural Bases of Soviet Georgia's Second Economy', *Soviet Studies* 35, no. 4 (1983): 546–60.

32 Slade, 'Reorganizing Crime'. See also K'up'at'adze, 'Georgia's Fight against Organized Crime'; K'ukhianidze, 'Corruption and Organized Crime in Georgia'.

33 L. Shelley, E. Scott, and A. Latta, eds., *Organized Crime and Corruption in Georgia* (New York: Routledge, 2007).
34 A. Polese, '"If I Receive It, It Is a Gift; if I Demand It, Then It Is a Bribe": On the Local Meaning of Economic Transactions in Post-Soviet Ukraine', *Anthropology in Action* 15, no. 3 (2008): 47–60.
35 N. Dudwick, 'No Guests at Our Table: Social Fragmentation in Georgia', in *When Things Fall Apart: Qualitative Studies of Poverty in the Former Soviet Union*, edited by N. Dudwick, E. Gomart, and A. Marc (Washington, DC: World Bank Publications, 2002): 213–57.
36 Curro, 'From Goods to Emotions'. See also Frederiksen, 'Good Hearts or Big Bellies'.
37 Zakharova, 'Street Life in Tbilisi'.
38 Curro, 'A Critical Assessment of Informal Practices'.
39 See also Transparency International, working definition of corruption as 'the abuse of entrusted power for private gain', applying both to the public and the private sector, https://www.transparency.org/cpi2011/in_detail.
40 L. Di Puppo, 'Police Reform in Georgia: Cracks in an Anti-Corruption Success Story', *U4 Practice Insight* 2 (2010): 1–5. See also K'up'at'adze, 'Georgia's Fight against Organized Crime'.
41 *Full Speed Westward* [Film Documentary/Video], directed by S. Tolz (Germany: Cologne Filmproduktion, 2013).
42 F. Muehlfried, 'A Taste of Mistrust', *Ab Imperio* 4 (2014): 63–68. See also S. Jones, 'The Rose Revolution: A Revolution without Revolutionaries?', *Cambridge Review of International Affairs* 19, no. 1 (2006): 33–48. See also K. Tuite, 'The Autocrat of the Banquet Table: The Political and Social Significance of the Georgian *supra*', *Language, History and Cultural Identities in the Caucasus*, 17–19 June 2005, IMER, Malmoe University, Sweden: 9–35; Chatwin, 'Socio-Cultural Transformation and Foodways'.
43 Jones, 'The Rose Revolution', 44.
44 Jones, 'The Rose Revolution', 44.
45 C. Swader, *The Capitalist Personality: Face-to-Face Sociality and Economic Change in the Post-Communist World* (London: Routledge, 2013).
46 D. Ó Beacháin, D. Polese, and A. Polese, '"Rocking the Vote": New Forms of Youth Organizations in Eastern Europe and the Former Soviet Union', in *Youth and Social Change in Eastern Europe and the Former Soviet Union*, edited by C. Walker and S. Stephenson (London: Routledge, 2012), 108–24. See also Jones, 'The Rose Revolution'.
47 Slade, 'The Threat of the Thief', 179.
48 G. Slade, 'Georgian Prisons: Roots of Scandal', *Open Democracy*, available at https://www.opendemocracy.net/gavin-slade/georgias-prisons-roots-of-scandal, 2012; Civil.ge for 2006, https://civil.ge/archives/111714.
49 A. Glonti, 'Reducing Imprisonment Rates and Prevention of Criminality in Contemporary Georgia', *European Scientific Journal* 8, no. 2 (2012): 91–98.
50 Curro, 'Davabirzhaot!'.
51 A. K'up'at'adze and G. Slade, 'The Failed Mental Revolution: Georgia, Crime, and Criminal Justice', *Open Democracy*, available at https://www.opendemocracy.net/gavin-slade-alexander-kupatadze/failed-mental-revolution-georgia-crime-and-criminal-justice, 2014. See also Slade, 'Georgian Prisons'.
52 M. D. Frederiksen and K. Gotfredsen, *Georgian Portraits: Essays on the Afterlives of a Revolution* (London: Zero Books, 2017). See also P. Manning, 'Rose-Coloured Glasses? Colour Revolutions and Cartoon Chaos in Postsocialist Georgia', *Cultural Anthropology* 22, no. 2 (2007): 171–213.
53 L. Rekhviashvili, 'Marketization and the Public-Private Divide', *International Journal of Sociology and Social Policy* 35, no. 7/8 (2015): 478–96. See also N. Gujaraidze, 'Hidden Costs of Privatization' (Tbilisi: Green Alternative, 2014); Gugushvili, 'Do the Benefits of Growth Trickle down to Georgia's Poor?'.
54 L. Rekhviashvili and A. Polese, 'Introduction: Informality and Power in the South Caucasus', *Caucasus Survey* 5, no. 1 (2017): 1–10. See also H. Aliyev, 'The Effects of the Saakashvili Era Reforms on Informal Practices in the Republic of Georgia', *Studies of Transition States and Societies* 6, no. 1 (2014): 19–33; J. Morris and A. Polese, *The Informal Post-Socialist Economy: Embedded Practices and Livelihoods* (London: Routledge, 2013); Round and Williams, 'Coping with the social costs of "transition"'; Smith and Rochovská, 'Domesticating Neo-Liberalism'; Ledeneva, 'Russia's Economy of Favours'.
55 Curro, 'From Goods to Emotions'. See also Zakharova, 'Street Life in Tbilisi'; K. Roberts and G. Pollock, 'New Class Divisions in the New Market Economies: Evidence from the Careers of

Young Adults in Post-Soviet Armenia, Azerbaijan and Georgia', *Journal of Youth Studies* 12, no. 5 (2009): 579–96.
56 Curro, 'A Critical Assessment of Informal Practices'. See also Curro, 'From Goods to Emotions'; Curro, '*Davabirzhaot!*'; Zakharova, 'Street Life in Tbilisi'; Zakharova, 'The Tbilisi Street'.

Bibliography

Aliyev, H. 'The Effects of the Saakashvili Era Reforms on Informal Practices in the Republic of Georgia'. *Studies of Transition States and Societies* 6, no. 1 (2014): 19–33.

Bardavelidze, V. 'The Institution of *Modzmeoba* (Adoptive Brotherhood): An Aspect of the History of the Relations between Mountain and Valley Populations in Georgia'. In *Kinship and Marriage in the Soviet Union: Field Studies*, edited by T. Dragadze, 173–88. London: Routledge, 1984.

Bregadze, L. *Kartuli jargonis leksik'oni* (*Dictionary of Georgian Slang*). Tbilisi: Gapur Sulakauris Gamomtsemloba, 2005.

Brighenti, A. M. *Urban Interstices: The Aesthetics and the Politics of the In-Between*. Farnham, UK: Ashgate, 2013.

Chatwin, M. E. *Socio-Cultural Transformation and Foodways in the Republic of Georgia*. Commack, NY: Nova Science Publishers, 1997.

Curro, C. 'A Critical Assessment of Informal Practices as Resistance: The Case of *Birzha* in Georgia'. *Caucasus Survey* 5, no. 1 (2017): 65–84.

Curro, C. '*Davabirzhaot!* Conflicting Claims on Public Space in Tbilisi between Transparency and Opaqueness'. *International Journal of Sociology and Social Policy* 35, no. 7/8 (2015): 497–512.

Curro, C. 'From Goods to Emotions: The Transformation of Informal Practices in the Republic of Georgia', in *The Informal Economy: Exploring Drivers and Practices*, edited by I. Horodnic, P. Rodgers, C. Williams, and L. Momtazian. London: Routledge, 2017.

Darieva, T., and W. Kaschuba. 'Sights and Signs of Postsocialist Urbanism in Eurasia: An Introduction'. In *Urban Spaces after Socialism: Ethnographies of Public Spaces in Eurasian Cities*, edited by T. Darieva, W. Kaschuba, and M. Krebs, 9–30. Frankfurt: Campus Verlag, 2011.

Di Puppo, L. 'Police Reform in Georgia: Cracks in an Anti-Corruption Success Story'. *U4 Practice Insight* 2 (2010): 1–5.

Dudwick, N. 'No Guests at Our Table: Social Fragmentation in Georgia'. In *When Things Fall Apart: Qualitative Studies of Poverty in the Former Soviet Union*, edited by N. Dudwick, E. Gomart, and A. Marc, 213–57. Washington, DC: World Bank Publications, 2002.

Dunn, E. C., and M. D. Frederiksen. 'Introduction'. *Slavic Review* 73, no. 2 (2014): 241–45.

Engvall, J. 'Against the Grain: How Georgia Fought Corruption and What It Means'. Washington, DC: Central Asia-Caucasus Institute and Silk Road Studies Program, 2012.

Evans, P., and W. Sewell. 'The Neoliberal Era: Ideology, Policy, and Social Effects'. In *Social Resilience in the Neoliberal Era*, edited by P. Hall and M. Lamont, 35–68. Cambridge: Cambridge University Press, 2013.

Finckenauer, J., and L. Kelly. 'Juvenile Delinquency and Youth Subcultures in the Former Soviet Union'. *International Journal of Comparative and Applied Criminal Justice* 16, no. 1–2 (1992): 247–61.

Frederiksen, M. D. 'Good Hearts or Big Bellies: *Dzmak'atsoba* and Images of Masculinity in the Republic of Georgia', in *Young Men in Uncertain Times*, edited by V. Amit and N. Dyck, 165–87. New York: Berghahn Books, 2012.

Frederiksen, M. D. *Young Men, Time, and Boredom in the Republic of Georgia*. Philadelphia: Temple University Press, 2013.

Frederiksen, M. D., and K. Gotfredsen. *Georgian Portraits: Essays on the Afterlives of a Revolution*. London: Zero Books, 2017.

Frisby, T. 'The Rise of Organized Crime in Russia: Its Roots and Social Significance', *Europe-Asia Studies* 50, no. 1 (1998): 27–49.

Garcelon, M. 'The Shadow of the Leviathan: Public and Private in Communist and Post-Communist Society'. In *Public and Private in Thought and Practice: Perspectives on a Grand Dichotomy*, edited by J. Weintraub and K. Kumar, 303–32. Chicago: University of Chicago Press, 1997.

Glonti, A. 'Reducing Imprisonment Rates and Prevention of Criminality in Contemporary Georgia'. *European Scientific Journal* 8, no. 2 (2012): 91–98.

Gugushvili, D. *Do the Benefits of Growth Trickle down to Georgia's Poor? A Case for a Strong Welfare System.* PhD thesis, University of Kent, 2014.

Gujaraidze, N. 'Hidden Costs of Privatization'. Tbilisi: Green Alternative, 2014.

Harboe Knudsen, I. 'The Lithuanian "Unemployment Agency": On *Bomzhai* and Informal Working Practices'. In *Ethnographies of Grey Zones in Eastern Europe: Relations, Borders and Invisibilities*, edited by I. Harboe Knudsen and M. D. Frederiksen, 141–56. London: Anthem Press, 2015.

Harboe Knudsen, I., and Frederiksen, M. D., eds. *Ethnographies of Grey Zones in Eastern Europe*. London: Anthem Press, 2015.

Jones, S. 'The Rose Revolution: A Revolution without Revolutionaries?', *Cambridge Review of International Affairs* 19, no. 1 (2006): 33–48.

Koehler, J. *Die Schule der Strasse: Georgische Cliquen zwischen Kämpfen um Ehre und organisierter Kriminalität*. Berlin: Das Arabische Buch, 1999a.

Koehler, J. 'The School of the Street: Organising Diversity and Training Polytaxis in a (Post-) Soviet Periphery'. *Anthropology of East Europe Review* 17, no. 2 (1999b): 41–55.

Kubik, J. *Power of Symbols against the Symbols of Power: The Rise of Solidarity and the Fall of State Socialism in Poland*. University Park, PA: Penn State Press, 1994.

K'ukhianidze, A. 'Corruption and Organized Crime in Georgia before and after the Rose Revolution'. *Central Asian Survey* 28, no. 2 (2009): 215–34.

K'up'at'adze, A. 'Georgia's Fight against Organized Crime: Success or Failure?'. *Caucasus Analytical Digest*, 9 (2009): 9–12.

K'up'at'adze, A., and G. Slade. 'The Failed Mental Revolution: Georgia, Crime, and Criminal Justice'. *Open Democracy,* available at https://www.opendemocracy.net/gavin-slade-alexander-kupatadze/failed-mental-revolution-georgia-crime-and-criminal-justice, 2014.

Ledeneva, A. *Russia's Economy of Favours: Blat, Networking and Informal Exchange*. Cambridge: Cambridge University Press, 1998.

Lofland, L. *The Public Realm: Exploring the City's Quintessential Social Territory*. London: Routledge, 1998.

Manning, P. 'Rose-Coloured Glasses? Colour Revolutions and Cartoon Chaos in Postsocialist Georgia'. *Cultural Anthropology* 22, no. 2 (2007): 171–213.

Mars, G., and Y. Altman, 'The Cultural Bases of Soviet Georgia's Second Economy'. *Soviet Studies* 35, no. 4 (1983): 546–60.

Morris, J., and A. Polese. *The Informal Post-Socialist Economy: Embedded Practices and Livelihoods*. London: Routledge, 2013.

Muehlfried, F. 'A Taste of Mistrust'. *Ab Imperio* 4 (2014): 63–68.

Ó Beacháin, D., D. Polese, and A. Polese. '"Rocking the Vote": New Forms of Youth Organizations in Eastern Europe and the Former Soviet Union'. In *Youth and Social Change in Eastern Europe and the Former Soviet Union*, edited by C. Walker and S. Stephenson, 108–24. London: Routledge, 2012.

Oswald, I., and V. Voronkov. 'The "Public–Private" Sphere in Soviet and Post-Soviet Society: Perception and Dynamics of "Public" and "Private" in Contemporary Russia'. *European Societies* 6, no. 1 (2004): 97–117.

Parkin, S., and R. Coomber. 'Public Injecting Drug Use and the Social Production of Harmful Practice in High-Rise Tower Blocks (London, UK): A Lefebvrian Analysis'. *Health and Place* 17, no. 3 (2011): 717–26.

Polese, A. '"If I Receive It, It Is a Gift; if I Demand It, Then It Is a Bribe": On the Local Meaning of Economic Transactions in Post-Soviet Ukraine'. *Anthropology in Action* 15, no. 3 (2008): 47–60.

Rekhviashvili, L. 'Marketization and the Public-Private Divide'. *International Journal of Sociology and Social Policy* 35, no. 7/8 (2015): 478–96.

Rekhviashvili, L., and A. Polese. 'Introduction: Informality and Power in the South Caucasus'. *Caucasus Survey* 5, no. 1 (2017): 1–10.

Roberts, K., and G. Pollock. 'New Class Divisions in the New Market Economies: Evidence from the Careers of Young Adults in Post-Soviet Armenia, Azerbaijan and Georgia'. *Journal of Youth Studies* 12, no. 5 (2009): 579–96.

Robertson, A. 'The Anthropology of Grey Zones'. *Ethnos* 71, no. 4 (2006): 569–73.

Round, J., and C. Williams. 'Coping with the Social Costs of "Transition": Everyday Life in Post-Soviet Russia and Ukraine'. *European Urban and Regional Studies* 17, no. 2 (2010): 183–96.

Roy, S. 'The Grey Zone: The "Ordinary" Violence of Extraordinary Times'. *Journal of the Royal Anthropological Institute* 14, no. 2 (2008): 316–33.

Shelley, L., E. Scott, and A. Latta, eds.. *Organized Crime and Corruption in Georgia*. New York: Routledge, 2007.

Slade, G. 'Georgian Prisons: Roots of Scandal', *Open Democracy*, available at https://www.opendemocracy.net/gavin-slade/georgias-prisons-roots-of-scandal, 2012.

Slade, G. *Reorganising Crime: Mafia and Anti-Mafia in Post-Soviet Georgia*. Oxford: Oxford University Press, 2014.

Slade, G. 'The Threat of the Thief: Who Has Normative Influence in Georgian Society? Dispatches', *Global Crime* 8, no. 2 (2007): 172–79.

Smith, A., and A. Rochovská. 'Domesticating Neo-Liberalism: Everyday Lives and the Geographies of Post-Socialist Transformations', *Geoforum* 38, no. 6 (2007): 1163–78.

Swader, C. *The Capitalist Personality: Face-to-Face Sociality and Economic Change in the Post-Communist World*. London: Routledge, 2013.

Tolz, S., director. *Full Speed Westward* [Film Documentary/Video]. Germany: Cologne Filmproduktion, 2013.

Transparency International, https://www.transparency.org/cpi2011/in_detail.

Tuite, K. 'The Autocrat of the Banquet Table: The Political and Social Significance of the Georgian supra'. Language, History and Cultural Identities in the Caucasus, 17–19 June 2005, IMER, Malmoe University, Sweden: 9–35.

Walker, C., and S. Stephenson. 'Youth and Social Change in Eastern Europe and the Former Soviet Union'. In *Youth and Social Change in Eastern Europe and the Former Soviet Union*, edited by C. Walker and S. Stephenson, 1–13. London: Routledge, 2012.

Zakharova, E. 'Street Life in Tbilisi as a Factor of Male Socialization'. *Laboratorium: Russian Review of Social Research* 2, no. 1 (2010).

Zakharova, E. 'The Tbilisi Street as a Legal and Political Phenomenon in Georgia'. In *State and Legal Practice in the Caucasus*, edited by S. Voell and I. Kaliszewska, 69–82. London: Ashgate, 2015.

Zdravomyslova, E., and V. Voronkov. 'The Informal Public in Soviet Society: Double Morality at Work'. *Social Research* 69, no. 1 (2002): 49–69.

Zhelnina, A. 'Learning to Use "Public Space": Urban Space in Post-Soviet St. Petersburg'. *The Open Urban Studies Journal* 6 (2013): 57–64.

Zhelnina, A. 'Public Spaces as Spaces of Fear and Alienation? Youth in Public Spaces in St. Petersburg, Russia'. *Isaconf*, 2nd ISA Forum of Sociology. *Social Justice and Democratisation*. 1–4 August 2012. University of Buenos Aires, Argentina.

Part II
China today and as a future alternative

5
Making it in China
The determinants of economic success in a socialist market system

Ion Marandici

China's politicians like to emphasise that they are building a socialist market economy based on the ideology of socialism with Chinese characteristics. Unlike other post-communist transitions to capitalism, China's radical economic transformations during the neo-liberal era did not generate a large pool of economic losers. On the contrary, over the last three decades, seven hundred million Chinese escaped poverty. Yet at the same time, China's impressive economic growth has been associated with the rise of a wealthy elite, which gradually is being co-opted by the party-state. Relying on elite-level and survey data, this study goes beyond socio-demographic characteristics and investigates whether party membership, education, beliefs in upward mobility and support for an interventionist state correlate with income levels. The final section discusses the implications of the observed trends for the future of the Chinese economic model.

From planned economy to socialist market economy

Xi Jinping is the General Secretary of the Communist Party of China (CPC) and President and 'core leader' of the People's Republic of China (PRC). In October 2017, in front of the delegates of the XIX Party Congress, Xi gave an important speech entitled 'Thought on Socialism with Chinese Characteristics for a New Era'. Soon thereafter, the phrase 'Xi Jinping Thought' was incorporated into the party and state constitutions, an honour reserved so far only to Mao Zedong and Deng Xiaoping. In his long speech, Xi promised to uphold socialism with Chinese characteristics in order to finish the country's 'socialist modernization and national rejuvenation' by 2050.[1] The phrase 'socialism with Chinese characteristics' was coined by Deng Xiaoping three decades ago. Even though current officials mention it as the essential goal of the party-state, it is difficult to pinpoint its precise meaning. So far, the expression seems to refer to the transition of the Chinese planned economy to a socialist market economy, a hybrid system blending market and command economy elements.

During the last seven decades, China underwent two systemic transformations. From 1949 to 1976, under Mao's leadership, it largely followed the Soviet model of development. It collectivised agriculture, created its own heavy industry, eliminated private enterprises, controlled prices and monopolised foreign trade and state banking. These are classic command economy policies borrowed from the Soviet Union. After the Sino-Soviet split, China embarked on a course of gradual rapprochement with the United States. The stagnation of the early 1970s prompted some party officials to voice pro-market views, running against the prevailing statist ideology. Rejected by Mao, those market-friendly communists were quickly side-lined for their attempts to push the country onto the capitalist path.

After Mao's death, the reformers, including Deng Xiaoping, advanced to top positions in the party. Deng initiated the policy of reform and opening up (*gaige kaifang*), which remains the foundation of China's transition to market. The experiment of the special economic zones, though successful, generated fears among the ideological hardliners, who thought that the Middle Kingdom was moving toward capitalism. To defend his policy proposals against Maoist critiques, in 1982 Deng highlighted the need to adapt Western development models to local conditions:

> In carrying out our modernization program, we must proceed from Chinese realities. Both in revolution and in construction, we should also learn from foreign countries and draw on their experience, but mechanical application of foreign experience and copying of foreign models will get us nowhere. We have had many lessons in this respect. We must integrate the universal truth of Marxism with the concrete realities of China, blaze a path of our own and build a socialism with Chinese characteristics.[2]

In 1983, Deng went even further suggesting that 'some people in rural areas and cities should be allowed to get rich before others'.[3] Later on, at the XIV Party Congress, the party leaders officially endorsed the project of a socialist market economy. More recently, former CPC General Secretary Hu Jintao outlined in a key party congress speech that *public ownership* and the *guiding role of the party* in building a moderately prosperous society (*xiaokang shehui*) by 2020 remain two of the central elements of the existing economic system.[4]

Yet the evolution of China's socialist market economy remains a big unknown. It would be hazardous to speculate on its sustainability solely by deciphering the official party line. Within the development paradigm adopted by the party, the state will continue to play the major role in steering domestic economic transformation through five-year plans. Productivity gains and large-scale capital investment, combined with the propensity of Chinese households to save, have produced high rates of economic growth. In 2012, the private sector was responsible for 70 per cent of the country's manufacturing output and 80 per cent of the jobs in urban areas.[5] So far, China's state-led development resembles the late-modernisation success stories of the 'four Asian tigers' – Hong Kong, Singapore, South Korea and Taiwan. During the next decade, the Chinese economy might slow down as the country abandons export-led growth and embraces a model of growth based on domestic consumption. Currently, China seems far from the chronic economic stagnation plaguing the command economies before their demise. As such, the idea that a communist-led China achieved economic growth without relying significantly on foreign direct investment and without dismantling the state, challenges the Washington consensus – the neo-liberal orthodoxy popular until recently among policymakers in some of the former Communist countries.[6]

When compared to other post-communist transitions, China's road to market differs in two respects. First, in some of the former communist countries, transitions to market have generated an anti-market backlash exploited by adept political entrepreneurs. By contrast, marketisation enjoys popular support in China. Some scholars characterised this phenomenon as "reforms without losers."[7] According to World Bank data, in 1990, 756 million Chinese (66 per cent of the population) lived on less than US $1.90/day (i.e., below the international poverty line).[8] A quarter of a century later, using the same benchmark, the same data show that only 10 million Chinese (0.7 per cent of the population) were poor. Indeed, the state has enacted economic reforms allowing more than 700 million individuals to escape poverty. In doing so, it has profoundly altered the fabric of society and created a pro-market constituency.

Second, China's leaders adopted a dual-track approach, developing labour-intensive sectors and supporting exports, while protecting inefficient sectors from international competition. Such an approach enabled the political elites to harvest the fruits of trade liberalisation and avoid massive layoffs. In 1998, preparing its WTO accession, China was constrained to launch deeper market reforms. But even then, the state exited competitive sectors and privatised the smaller state-owned enterprises (SOEs), while keeping the large ones under its control (*zhua da fang xiao*). As a result of this increase in efficiency, higher revenues allowed the state to compensate the groups negatively impacted by economic reforms. That is why the Chinese political elites could pursue further marketisation without having to fear an anti-market backlash.

The future of the market in China depends to a large extent on the level of acceptance it enjoys in society. Among elites, there is a solid consensus on the necessity to continue reforms. But the cosy relationship between the indigenous capitalists and state officials amidst rising income disparities led some scholars to expect an outburst of social unrest. Whyte rejects such expectations as unrealistic and demonstrates that 'China's social volcano of potential anger at growing distributive injustice was clearly still dormant in 2009.'[9] Survey data from 2012 confirm that 75 per cent of Chinese support market reforms despite the growing inequality.[10]

Nevertheless, the transition to market did breed dissatisfaction. Some intellectuals criticised the continuing privatisation of state property and the conspicuous consumption prevalent among the wealthy elites. Cui Zhiyuan, Gan Yang, Wang Shaoguang and Wang Hui formed the New Left (*xin zuopai*), a loose group calling for alternative models of development that would mitigate the negative side effects of the pro-market policies.[11] Likewise, discontent with reforms is simmering among those who religiously revere Mao Zedong. When Mao Yushi, a liberal economist, published an article criticising Mao's economic policies, diehard Maoists requested that state authorities put him on trial.[12] Despite such scattered pockets of discontent, popular support in favour of further marketisation remains strong.

The rise of the billionaires

Economic growth has been accompanied by the rise in wealth and income inequality. So that by now, the concentration of wealth in China has reached levels comparable to those in advanced capitalist countries.

In 2016, the country's official Gini coefficient of 0.47 stood above the coefficients of the former Communist states.[13] Moreover, for several years, income inequality in China remained higher than in the United States. Since 2008, as a result of governmental efforts, income inequality has slightly declined, but it still surpasses the levels observed in most of the developed countries.

The newly emerged billionaires situated at the top of the wealth distribution benefitted most from the economic transformations. Two organisations – *Hurun* and *Forbes* – identify and rank the Chinese magnates. As shown in figure 5.1, their estimates diverge. Compared to *Forbes*, *Hurun* counts annually more Chinese billionaires. Despite some discrepancies, both graphs illustrate an unmistakable trend – the rapid rise of a national wealthy elite. In 2015, according to *Hurun*, more billionaires lived in China than in the United States.[14]

In the new context, private wealth may turn into a power resource. As certain individuals become extremely wealthy, they acquire more autonomy from the state and may use their resources to gain influence over regional officials. So far, the wealthy elites seem content to play the role of "allies of the state" rather than act as agents of change.[15] But as

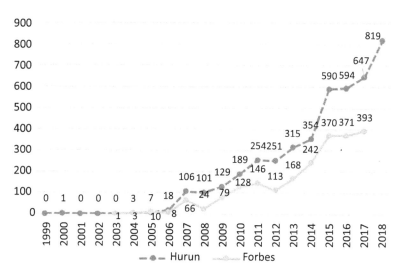

Fig. 5.1 The number of billionaires in China, 1999–2018. Source: Graphs by author based on data from Rupert Hoogewerf, *Hurun Report*, Hong Kong/Shanghai, 2018. www.hurun.net/en/ArticleShow.aspx?nid =14678 (accessed 13 May 2018); *Forbes* Magazine, China's Rich List, 2003–2017, www.forbes.com/china-billionaires/ (accessed 13 May 2018).

Beijing continues to promote governors based in part on their economic performance, regional officials realise that the billionaires in their provinces are indispensable for the achievement of economic growth and the preservation of their power positions within the party-state.

Over the last three decades, the relationship between the party-state and entrepreneurs evolved from suspicion to co-optation. The 1989 Tiananmen protests constituted a watershed moment in this regard. Some entrepreneurs provided food and transportation for demonstrators, thus irritating the party hardliners. Consequently, from 1989 to 2002, entrepreneurs were banned from joining the party. Moreover, pro-privatisation advocates such as Zhao Ziyang, the General Secretary of the Communist Party of China (CPC), were accused of overempathising with the student protesters and lost their influence within the party. Interestingly enough, in 1991 the conservative faction was discussing the idea of establishing direct party ownership of state assets in order to prevent the formation of rival power centres.[16] After a three-year hiatus, Deng's Southern Tour weakened the conservatives led by Chen Yun and market reforms accelerated again.[17] In retrospect, it is noteworthy that the anti-market reaction after Tiananmen temporarily slowed down the transition to market, but did not lead to a wholesale reversal of reforms.

As the importance of the private sector grew, the mood in the party changed. To achieve a broader representation of societal interests, the party began courting and co-opting successful entrepreneurs. In 2002, the then CPC General Secretary Jiang Zemin formulated the doctrine of *Three Represents*, which encouraged the new social actors, among them businesspeople, to join the party.[18] Five years later, 5 per cent of all party members were private entrepreneurs.[19] In 2013, out of 85 million members, 25 million were farmers, herders and fishers; 20 million were management staff and technicians working in enterprises; 7 million were workers; and 7 million were state and party officials.[20] The adoption of the *Three Represents* opened the doors of the CPC to the newly emerged billionaires, allowing the wealthy elites to gain representation in the party.

CPC's party-building strategy trailed the growth of the private sector as well. Non-public enterprises are required by law to set up party committees and cells. While the law has been in place for more than two decades, its strict implementation began a decade ago.[21] In 2012, a party official triumphantly announced that 'party units have been established in about 983,000 private enterprises, including 47,000 foreign-funded companies'.[22] Official data from 2017 show that the party has embedded itself in

1.88 million non-public enterprises and in 93 per cent of all SOEs.[23] It follows then that the party has penetrated more than 10 per cent of all private enterprises. This pragmatic party-building strategy allowed CPC to establish its permanent presence in the private sector.

State institutions co-opt billionaires, too. Some of them become members of the National People's Congress (NPC) and the Chinese People's Political Consultative Conference (CPPCC), others join state-sponsored business associations. In 2008, 17 billionaires joined the NPC, while in 2013, the figure nearly doubled.[24] I reviewed the biographies of the top 100 wealthiest individuals identified by *Hurun* in 2015 and found out that 58 per cent held politically important offices in the past. So far, most of them are recruited by provincial people's congresses and regional party officials via invitation.[25] Overall, the selection process lacks transparency as it is not entirely clear what criteria are used to pick the future NPC and CPPCC delegates.

The two parallel processes – the co-optation of the wealthy elites by the party and the de facto colonisation of the private sector with party cells – point to the growing interdependence of the political and wealthy elites. However, despite the CPC efforts, China's wealthy do not feel secure. In 2013, 60 per cent of high-net-worth individuals were seriously thinking about investment migration.[26] For now, in the absence of an inheritance tax in China, billionaires can easily transfer wealth to their children. The *fuerdai*, the second generation of wealthy Chinese, compete with their parents' generation in attracting media attention to their consumerist excesses at home and abroad.

To survive, socialism with Chinese characteristics needs more frugality. Besides the offspring of the wealthy elites, party cadres at higher levels engage in conspicuous status-confirming behaviour. CPC is not interested in the transformation of the party and state officials into a new class of mandarins. In 2012, Xi promoted the 'eight-point regulation', a nervous effort to subject the behaviour of the party cadres to a set of thrift and integrity rules. The guidelines ban spending on luxury goods, impose stricter standards on the use of public funds, specify limits on travel expenses, prompt officials to organise modest banquets, prohibit the construction of extravagant government buildings and control the frequency of public appearances of the nomenklatura.[27] By October 2017, the party recorded a total of 193,168 thrift violations and reprimanded 145,059 officials for disregarding the policy.[28] While the crackdown on conspicuous consumption will not stem the tide of consumerism sweeping nowadays across China, it might moderately improve the public's perception of party officials.

Does it pay to be a party member?

It is unclear whether the rising income inequality will perpetuate itself and block social mobility in the future. Hence, an intriguing aspect of China's economic transition concerns the determinants of income at the household level. Are demographic characteristics, political affiliation, and certain beliefs linked to higher income groups?

Previous studies have identified a variety of income predictors. Xin proved that party membership has a minor, but positive impact on household wealth.[29] Xie and Jin demonstrate that employment with the party-state exerts a positive effect on household wealth.[30] Besides political ties, education might figure as a determinant of income.[31] Traditionally, parents in China put a high premium on education, regarding it as a contributing factor to social mobility. Western university degrees are preferred over domestic ones. High-ranking officials send their offspring to American and European universities. For example, President Xi Jinping's daughter studied at Harvard. The son of Wen Jiabao, China's former head of government, and other princelings graduated from universities in the West. Upon the careful analysis of party careers, a recent study found out that the CPC promotes educated individuals to higher party positions.[32]

To further explore whether party affiliation and education influence economic success in the general population, I used statistical techniques to analyse survey data recently published by the Pew Research Center.[33] Table 5.1 displays the frequencies for each variable used in the analysis (see Appendix).

Since household income may be regarded as an important indicator of economic success, it figured as the dependent variable in this brief study. Respondents placed their household income within one of the following five brackets: 'less than 10,000 yuan' (14.4 per cent), '10,001–15,000 yuan' (4.9 per cent), '15,001–30,000 yuan' (25.9 per cent), '30,001–50,000 yuan' (14.7 per cent) and '50,001 and up' (36.2 per cent).[34]

Party membership and education figure as the main independent variables. Both party membership and education should be positively correlated with household income. Roughly 6 per cent of the respondents self-identified as party members, which corresponds to the percentage of party members in the overall population. Likewise, the level of education among respondents falls within one of the following seven categories: 'below primary school', 'primary school', 'junior school', 'high school', 'college', 'Bachelor's' and 'Master's'. Overall, 17 per cent of those interviewed received an undergraduate or graduate degree. To test whether other variables have an impact on household income, four demographic control variables were included in the analysis – gender, residence, region ('eastern', 'central' and 'western'), and ethnicity (Han and non-Han).[35]

Besides demographic characteristics, I was interested to test whether expectations about the role of the state in society are linked to income levels. To capture the preferences of the population regarding state intervention, survey respondents were asked the following question: What is more important in Chinese society: that everyone be free to pursue their life's goals without interference from the state or that the state plays an active role in society so as to guarantee that nobody is in need? Thirty-five per cent of the respondents prefer a less intrusive state (that is, freedom from state intervention), while 49 per cent opt for a stronger state providing for people in need (that is, equality). Even though most Chinese prefer state-sponsored redistribution and protection, one-third of the respondents opted for freedom from state intervention.

Beliefs in upward mobility may be associated with household income levels. To measure the belief in upward mobility, interviewees were asked the following question: How easy or difficult is it in China for a young person to get a better job and to become wealthier than his or her parents were – very easy, somewhat easy, somewhat difficult or very difficult? Fifty-seven per cent of respondents stated optimistically that it is easy/somewhat easy to get a job and become wealthier than their parents.[36]

To test whether party membership, education, and mobility and statist beliefs predict household income levels, an ordered probit regression was implemented using STATA. I started the analysis with a baseline model and then entered additional variables of interest, as well as an interaction term. Table 5.2 (see Appendix) displays detailed estimates of the effects of each of the variables on income levels. Age, education, residence, region, party membership, belief in upward mobility, and the interaction term between party affiliation and orientation towards the state predict household income.[37]

To ease the interpretation of results, I plot in figure 5.2 the average marginal effects and predictive margins of the relevant predictors across the five income levels. Age has a negative effect on income, which is particularly notable at incomes above 30,000 yuan (figure 5.2A). By contrast, education has a positive effect on income (figure 5.2B). Specifically, education best predicts incomes above 50,000 yuan. Similarly, the chances to reach the upper income brackets are higher in cities and towns compared to villages. Given the existing literature on the urban-rural income gap, this finding is hardly surprising. Furthermore, in line with previous studies,

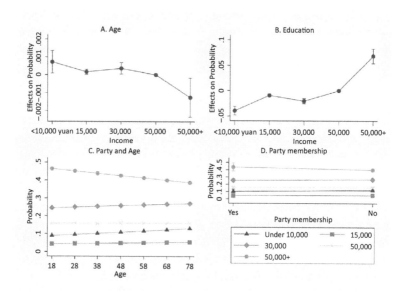

Fig. 5.2 The average marginal effects for age and education and the predictive margins for party affiliation across age groups. Source: Author's interviews.

regions matter as well. Compared to respondents situated in the Eastern region, those in the less developed Western and Central parts of the country are less likely to move up to higher income brackets.

Party membership has a significant and differentiated impact on income level. The odds ratio of 0.8 in Model 1 and Model 2 reveals that non-members compared to party members are 20 per cent less likely to have higher incomes. However, the predictive margins in figure 5.2D point to the non-linear effect of party membership across different income levels. While party membership seems clearly to be a bonus for households with incomes over 50,000 yuan, it has a slight negative impact on those in the first (below 10,000) and third income brackets (15,000–30,000). No effect can be observed in the case of the second (large X) and fourth income group (squares).

To track how the effect of party membership changes with age, I have plotted the predictive margins of party membership on income across age groups in Figure 5.2C. For those in the highest income bracket, the bonus effect of party membership diminishes with age. By contrast, we observe a small increase in the impact of party membership on individuals in the first (under 10,000 yuan) and third income groups (15,000–30,000 yuan) over time.

The beliefs in upward mobility correlate incompletely with income levels. Such beliefs have no impact on the second and fourth income groups. On the other hand, the upper-income individuals think that it is relatively easy to climb up the economic ladder. Still, we cannot assert with certainty the direction of causality. It is not clear whether strong beliefs in upward mobility help these individuals reach the highest income bracket, or whether such beliefs are acquired after their income increases. When it comes to attitudes toward state intervention, the interaction term in Model 4 (see table 5.2) between party membership and state intervention is significant beyond the 5 per cent level. Those in the lower income brackets who are unaffiliated with the party expect the state to protect those in need. Interestingly enough, this group exhibits stronger support for an interventionist welfare state compared to party members in the same income bracket.

Next, I was interested in exploring the relationship between social mobility beliefs and perceptions of economic change at the individual level. Intuitively, one would expect that the losers in the economic transition should hold weak beliefs in upward mobility. I ran a cross-tabulation to explore this conjecture (see figure 5.3). To capture individual perceptions

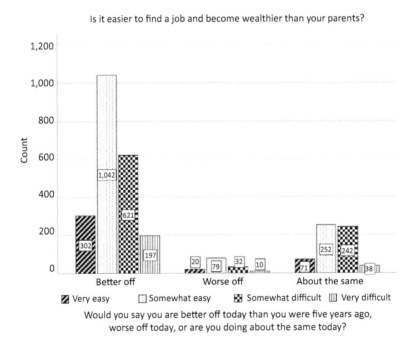

Fig. 5.3 Beliefs in intergenerational mobility and change in economic situation. Source: Author's interviews.

MAKING IT IN CHINA   99

of economic change, survey participants were asked whether their financial situation has improved or deteriorated over the last five years. The majority of respondents mentioned that, compared to 2007, their financial situation was better in 2012. Sixty-two per cent of those who were better off stated that it was easier to find a job and get wealthy than during their parents' time. Surprisingly, 70 per cent of those who were worse off in 2012 believed that it was easy or somewhat easy to get wealthier than their parents. Thirty-seven per cent of those whose situation improved and 29 per cent of those worse off found it very difficult or somewhat difficult to get wealthy in China. If anything, compared to losers (that is, individuals whose economic situation deteriorated), the winners were slightly less confident that finding a job was easier than during their parents' time. Unexpectedly, we found that optimistic beliefs in intergenerational mobility remain resilient even when individuals face economic hardship.

Implications for the future of the China model

State-sponsored capitalism in China today is stuck midway between a command economy and a market system. The five-year plans, the guiding role of the CPC, the state-controlled banking sector, the dominance of the large state-owned corporations, all remind us of the traditional command economy. On the other hand, the rise of billionaires, the privatisation reforms, the growing private sector, the conspicuous consumption of Western luxury goods, the hard-budget constraints for small and medium enterprises, the support of free trade in an era of increasing American protectionism, and the heavy investments in US treasury bonds, all feature as novel elements of the socialist market system. So far, this mixed economy has produced high levels of economic growth as well as sharp wealth disparities.

Four implications can be drawn from this exploration of China's unequal economic growth. First, it is important to call attention to the flexibility of the CPC in the absence of real political liberalisation. It has slowly but surely adapted to the new economic environment. Knowing that private entrepreneurs complain about unfair competition from state-owned enterprises, key businesspeople from the private sector were invited to connect with the party-state. The party even began setting up cells within the leading domestic and foreign private companies. However, it is not the emergence of the private sector per se, but the conspicuous consumption patterns pervasive among the wealthy elites and party cadres that raise the greatest problem for the CPC. In the long run, despite the party-state's incontestable success in reducing poverty, consumerist excesses among political and economic elites might give rise to the perception that the existing socio-economic inequalities are unfair. To counteract this by-product of economic growth, CPC's frugality campaign aims at aligning the behaviour of party officials with the egalitarian ethos of the official ideology.

Second, the relationship between politicians and capitalists is one of asymmetrical interdependence. The new wealthy elites and the party-state are already bound together by a dense web of institutional and structural ties. More than half of the 100 wealthiest Chinese occupy or have occupied a public office, among them Jack Ma, the wealthiest Chinese and founder of Alibaba. Crucially, they are co-opted to public positions after, rather than before, they become wealthy. There are only several cases in which party-state officials became billionaires after 'plunging into the sea' of commerce (*xiahai*). In their relationship with the party-state, the wealthy elites enjoy a privileged position. While the party-state may use coercion and engage in selective nationalisation, it largely depends on the wealthy elites to achieve economic growth, maintain high employment levels, ensure political stability and expand the country's global reach. With the nomenklatura firmly in power, China's insecure capitalists are nudged to expand and invest globally. Some of them hedge their bets and acquire a second citizenship, but in the long run, this interdependent relationship between the party-state and the extremely rich will inevitably consolidate into one of the cornerstones of the Chinese economic model.

Third, despite the existence of corrupt practices, the Chinese system incorporates meritocratic elements. The preceding statistical analysis has revealed that education, among other factors, functions as the strongest predictor of income. Undoubtedly, *guanxi* (that is, informal networks), as numerous scholars have pointed out, play an important role in Chinese society. Still, education stands out as more important than party affiliation as a determinant of income. The crucial ramification of this finding is that in the midst of radical economic transformations, the party-state successfully shaped an environment in which income is at least partially a function of education. In other words, the existing system tends to reward highly educated individuals.

Finally, these findings have to be interpreted in light of Xi's Chinese Dream initiative (*Zhongguo meng*) and the larger theme of national rejuvenation (*Zhonghua minzu weida fuxing*). Leaving aside their ideological content, both initiatives aim at instilling pride in China's economic accomplishments, always contrasted with the 'hundred years of national humiliation'. It is not clear whether the population has bought into the promise of the Chinese Dream, an expression conjuring up the middle-class American Dream. In this sense, it is remarkable that most Chinese hold robust, optimistic beliefs in upward mobility. The strong beliefs in upward mobility remain resilient even when an individual experiences a deterioration of her economic situation. Most Chinese perceive sufficient opportunities for upward mobility within the current hybrid system. Despite unequal growth, most of the population supports the mixed economy, while continuing to hold durable statist beliefs. At the same time, the resilient optimistic beliefs regarding upward mobility in the context of rising wealth and income inequality may simply be a matter of perception. Americans, for instance, hold extremely strong beliefs in the meritocracy of their economic system in spite of its low social mobility when compared to other Western economies. Further research would need to elucidate how the strong beliefs in upward mobility among China's population contribute to the stability of the current economic and political system. Until then, such perceptions should be cautiously interpreted as indicators of an optimistic popular mood prevailing inside the Middle Kingdom during its rapid economic rise.

Appendix

Table 5.1 Frequencies of the independent and dependent variables

			Weighted N	Percent
Dependent Variable	Household annual income	Less than 10,000 yuan	319	12.0
		10,001 to 15,000 yuan	134	5.0
		15,001 to 30,000 yuan	721	27.1
		30,001 to 50,000 yuan	413	15.5
		50,001 and up	1071	40.3
		Total	2658	100.0
Factor	Gender	Female	1349	50.8
		Male	1309	49.2
		Total	2658	100.0
	CPC member	No	2504	94.2
		Yes	154	5.8
		Total	2658	100.0

Table 5.1 (continued)

			Weighted N	Percent
	Ethnicity	Han	2543	95.7
		Non-Han	115	4.3
		Total	2658	100.0
	Region	East	1473	55.4
		Centre	608	22.9
		West	577	21.7
		Total	2658	100.0
	Belief in Upward Mobility	Somewhat easy	1272	47.9
		Somewhat difficult	823	31.0
		Very easy	368	13.8
		Very difficult	195	7.3
		Total	2658	100.0
	Residence	City	1080	40.6
		Town	469	17.6
		Rural location	1109	41.7
		Total	2658	100.0
	State Intervention	Nobody in need	1550	58.3
		Freedom to pursue life's goals without interference	1108	41.7
		Total	2658	100.0
Covariates	Age (Range)	18–86	2658	100.0
Education		Below primary school	112	4.2
		Primary school	388	14.6
		Junior school	835	31.4
		High school	872	32.8
		College	305	11.5
		Bachelor's degree	140	5.3
		Master's degree	6	.2
		Total	2658	100

Source: Author's interviews.

Table 5.2 Determinants of income levels: Ordered probit regression results

		Model 1		Model 2		Model 3		Model 4	
		B	Exp (B)	B	Exp (B)	B	Exp (B)	B	Exp (B)
DV Intercepts	Lower income	.34	1.4	.31	1.36	.214	1.239	.48**	1.6
	Middle	.65**	1.91	.619*	1.86	.525**	1.69	.79***	2.20
	Upper middle	1.87***	6.48	1.84***	6.31	1.75***	5.768	2.02***	7.527
	Upper income	2.49***	12.12	2.46***	11.79	2.38***	10.79	2.64***	14.12
Gender[a]		−.001	.999	.001	1.001	−.006*	.994	.011	1.011
CPC member[b]		−.220*	.803	−.219*	.803	−.208	.812	.480***	1.617
Ethnicity[c]		.117	1.126	.114	1.121	.111	1.117	.123	1.131
Region[d]	East	.681***	1.976	.676***	1.967	.667***	1.947	.657***	1.930
	Central	.398***	1.488	.389***	1.476	.385***	1.470	.372***	1.252
Residence[e]	City	1.81***	6.15	1.81***	6.14	1.84***	6.29	1.83***	6.24
	Town	1.08***	2.95	1.08***	2.96	1.09***	2.98	1.08***	2.97
Age		−.004*	.996	−.004*	.996	−.004*	.996	−.004*	.996
Education		.277***	1.319	.277***	1.320	.277***	1.319	.281***	1.325
State support				−.041	.960	−.033	.967	.067	1.070
Upward Mobility[f]	Very Easy					−.218*	.804	−.238*	.788
	Somewhat Easy					−.027	.974	−.036	.964
	Somewhat Difficult					−.166*	.847	−.175*	.840
Non-CPC Member*State support[g]								−.67***	.508
Initial Log Likelihood		−3567.7		−3567.7		−3567.7		−3567.7	
Log Likelihood		−2789.5		−2789.2		−2782.9		−2777.8	
Likelihood Ratio		1736.2***		1736.9***		1749.3***		1759.6***	

Notes: Effect estimates presented as odds ratios. Reference categories: [a] Female, [b] CPC member, [c] Han Chinese, [d] West, [e] Village, [f] Very difficult, [g] CPC*State support.
Significance levels: *p ≤ .05, **p ≤ .01, ***p ≤ .001
Source: Author's interviews.

Notes

1 'Backgrounder: Xi Jinping Thought on Socialism with Chinese Characteristics for a New Era', *Xinhua News Agency*, 17 March 2018, accessed 4 March 2019, www.xinhuanet.com/english/2018-03/17/c_137046261.html.
2 Deng Xiaoping, 'Opening Speech at the Twelfth National Congress of the Communist Party of China', 1 September 1982, in *Selected Works of Deng Xiaoping (1982–1992)*, vol. 3., ed. People's Daily, accessed 23 March 2018, www.people.com.cn/english/dengxp/contents3.html.
3 Deng Xiaoping, *Selected Works of Deng Xiaoping (1982–1992)*, accessed 23 March 2018, www.people.com.cn/english/dengxp/home.html.
4 Hu Jintao, 'Report at the 18th Party Congress', *Xinhua News Agency*, 8 November 2012, accessed 21 December 2015, news.xinhuanet.com/english/special/18cpcnc/2012-11/17/c_131981259_3.htm.
5 Nicholas Lardy, 'The Changing Role of the Private Sector in China', Proceedings of RBA Annual Conference, in *Structural Change in China: Implications for Australia and the World Reserve Bank of Australia*, ed. Iris Day and John Simon (2016), 37–41.
6 Thomas Piketty, *Capital in the Twenty-First Century* (Cambridge, MA: Belknap Press of Harvard University Press, 2014), 70.
7 Lawrence J. Lau, Yingyi Qian, and Gérard Roland, 'Reform without Losers: An Interpretation of China's Dual-Track Approach to Transition'. *Journal of Political Economy* 108 (2000): 123; Justin Yifu Lin, *Demystifying the Chinese Economy* (Cambridge: Cambridge University Press, 2012), 9.
8 World Bank Poverty Data (Washington, DC: World Bank, October 2018), accessed 24 February 2019, http://povertydata.worldbank.org/poverty/country/CHN.
9 Martin King Whyte and Dong-Kyun Im, 'Is the Social Volcano Still Dormant? Trends in Chinese Attitudes toward Inequality', *Social Science Research* 48, no. 1 (2014): 74.
10 Pew Global Attitudes Survey (Washington, DC: Pew Research Center, 2012), accessed 30 May 2015, www.pewglobal.org/category/datasets/2012/.
11 Chaohua Wang, ed., *One China, Many Paths* (New York: Verso, 2003), 9–46.
12 'Boundlessly Loyal to the Great Monster', *The Economist,* 26 May 2011. http://www.economist.com/node/18744533?story_id=18744533.
13 OECD, *Going for Growth: Economic Policy Reforms* (Paris: OECD, 2017), 162, accessed 10 May 2018, www.oecd.org/eco/growth/Going-for-Growth-China-2017.pdf.
14 Olivia Lowenberg, 'Beijing Has Now More Billionaires Than New York City', *Christian Science Monitor*, 24 February 2016, accessed 13 May 2018, www.csmonitor.com/Business/2016/0224/Beijing-now-has-more-billionaires-than-New-York-City-study-says; Rupert Hoogewerf, 'Number of Billionaires in China 1999–2018', *Hurun Organization*, accessed 2 May 2018, www.hurun.net/en/ArticleShow.aspx?nid=14678.
15 Jie Chen and Bruce J. Dickson, *Allies of the State: China's Private Entrepreneurs and Democratic Change* (Cambridge, MA: Harvard University Press, 2010), 25–35.
16 Richard McGreggor, *The Party: The Secret World of China's Communist Rulers* (London: Penguin Books, 2010), 34–41.
17 Ezra Vogel, *Deng Xiaoping and the Transformation of China* (Cambridge, MA: Harvard University Press, 2011), 664–90.
18 Chen and Dickson, 28.
19 Cheng Li, 'China's Communist Party State: The Structure and Dynamics of Power in Politics in China', in *Politics in China*, ed. William Joseph (Oxford: Oxford University Press, 2014), 178.
20 'China's Communist Party Membership Exceeds 85 Million', *Xinhua News Agency,* 1 July 2013, accessed 1 May 2018, english.cpc.people.com.cn/206972/206974/8305636.html.
21 TL (Scholar), interviewed by author, Taipei: National Chengchi University, 2 May 2016.
22 'Entrepreneurs' Presence Grows at CPC Congress', *China's Daily*, 12 November 2012, accessed 15 May 2018, www.chinadaily.com.cn/china/2012cpc/2012-11/12/content_15919473.htm.
23 'CPC has 89.6 million members', Xinhua News Agency, 30 June 2018, accessed 5 March 2019, www.xinhuanet.com/english/2018-06/30/c_137292146.htm.
24 'Entrepreneurs' Presence', *China's Daily*.
25 HT (Expert), interviewed by author, Taipei: National Taiwan University, 15 April 2016.

26   Jennifer Zeng et al., 'China Private Wealth Report 2013' (China Merchants Bank and Bain & Company, 13 August 2013), 35, accessed 22 May 2018, www.bain.com/publications/articles/china-private-wealth-report-2013.aspx.
27   'Central Government Convenes a Meeting Presided by Xi Jinping', *People's Daily*, 4 December 2012, accessed 18 April 2018, cpc.people.com.cn/n/2012/1205/c64094-19793530.html; 'China to Punish Extravagance in Official Galas', *Xinhua News Agency*, 15 August 2013, accessed 1 May 2018, english.cpc.people.com.cn/206972/206974/8365826.html.
28   'Ba xiang guiding biaoqing bao shuaping pengyouquan shou ri dianji shubaiwan', *Xinhua News Agency*, 4 December 2017, accessed 5 April 2018, www.xinhuanet.com/politics/2017-12/04/c_1122051109.htm.
29   Meng Xin, 'Political Capital and Wealth Accumulation', in *China: New Engine of World Growth*, ed. Ross Garnaut and Ligang Song (Canberra: ANU Press, 2012), 327.
30   Yu Xie and Yongai Jin, 'Household Wealth in China', *Chinese Sociological Review* 47 (2015): 203–29.
31   Biwei Su and Almas Heshmati, *Analysis of the Determinants of Income and Income Gap between Urban and Rural China*, Discussion Paper 7162 (Bonn: Institute for the Study of Labor, January 2013): 10.
32   Victor Shih, Christopher Adolph, and Mingxing Liu, 'Getting Ahead in the Communist Party: Explaining the Advancement of Central Committee Members in China', *American Political Science Review* 106 (2012): 166–87.
33   From 18 March to 15 April 2012, 3,177 face-to-face interviews were conducted in Mandarin with individuals aged 18 years and older. The data were collected via a multi-stage cluster sample stratified by China's three economic zones – east, west and centre (except Tibet, Xinjiang, Hong Kong and Macao). The urban population, slightly overrepresented in the sample, comes from 12 cities and 12 towns located in the three regions. The survey's margin of error lies at +/− 4.3 per cent. Cases with missing information on certain variables were eliminated through list-wise deletion. The "Don't Know" and "No Response" categories of the outcome variable were coded as system-missing and excluded from the analysis. In all, 2,658 cases were suitable for the weighted regression analysis. See 'Pew Global Attitudes Survey', 18 March–20 April 2012.
34   The incomes in the sample are slightly higher than those in the overall population. One potential reason for this minor discrepancy may be the overrepresentation of urban households. Since the distribution of income in the sample approximates the population incomes, the data were used without modifications. Out of the 3,177 respondents, 127 individuals either refused to answer the question on income or could not identify their income bracket. Hence, those cases were excluded from the analysis.
35   In terms of ethnicity, 96 per cent of respondents declared themselves Han. Besides Han, 15 different ethnicities were mentioned by respondents. By collapsing all the minorities into a non-Han category, I created a binary variable called *ethnicity*. Han ethnics were coded as 1, while non-Han respondents were assigned a score of 2.
36   In 2016, a Pew survey asked the following question: 'When children today in China grow up, do you think they will be better off or worse off financially than their parents?' Seventy-eight per cent of the respondents expected to be better off and only 11.5 per cent thought that their children will be 'worse off'. See *Global Trends and Attitudes*, Pew Research Center, Spring 2016.
37   The explanatory power increased across the four models. The predictive power in Model 4 jumped from −3567.7 to the maximised log-likelihood value of −2777.9 at iteration 6. The likelihood ratio (LR) for the ordered probit model is significant at p < .001. The successive addition of predictors improves the likelihood ratio from 1736.2 (Model 1) to 1759.6 (Model 4).

Bibliography

Chen, Jie, and Bruce J. Dickson. *Allies of the State: China's Private Entrepreneurs and Democratic Change*. Cambridge, MA: Harvard University Press, 2010.
Deng Xiaoping, *Selected Works of Deng Xiaoping (1982–1992)*. Edited by People's Daily Online. Vol. 3. Accessed 23 March 2018, www.people.com.cn/english/dengxp/home.html.

Lardy, Nicholas. 'The Changing Role of the Private Sector in China', Proceedings of RBA Annual Conference. In *Structural Change in China: Implications for Australia and the World Reserve Bank of Australia*. Edited by Iris Day and John Simon (2016).
Lau, Lawrence J., Yingyi Qian, and Gérard Roland. 'Reform without Losers: An Interpretation of China's Dual-Track Approach to Transition'. *Journal of Political Economy* 108 (2000): 121–43.
Li, Cheng. 'China's Communist Party State: The Structure and Dynamics of Power in Politics in China'. In *Politics in China*. Edited by William Joseph. Oxford: Oxford University Press, 2014.
Lin, Justin Yifu. *Demystifying the Chinese Economy*. Cambridge: Cambridge University Press, 2012.
McGreggor, Richard. *The Party: The Secret World of China's Communist Rulers*. London: Penguin Books, 2010.
National Bureau of Statistics. *China Statistical Yearbook*. Beijing: China Statistical Press. 2016.
OECD, *Going for Growth: Economic Policy Reforms*. Paris: OECD, 2017. Accessed 10 May 2018, www.oecd.org/eco/growth/Going-for-Growth-China-2017.pdf.
Piketty, Thomas. *Capital in the Twenty-First Century*. Cambridge, MA: Belknap Press of Harvard University Press, 2014.
Shih, Victor, Christopher Adolph, and Mingxing Liu. 'Getting Ahead in the Communist Party: Explaining the Advancement of Central Committee Members in China'. *American Political Science Review* 106 (2012): 166–87.
Sicular, Terry. *The Challenge of High Inequality in China*. Policy Brief. Washington, DC: The World Bank, August 2013.
Stratford, Kate, and Arianna Cowling. *Chinese Household Income, Consumption and Savings*. Bulletin, Sydney: Reserve Bank of Australia, September 2016.
Su, Biwei, and Almas Heshmati. *Analysis of the Determinants of Income and Income Gap between Urban and Rural China*. Discussion Paper 7162. Bonn: Institute for the Study of Labor, 2013.
Vogel, Ezra. *Deng Xiaoping and the Transformation of China*. Cambridge, MA: Harvard University Press, 2011.
Wang, Chaohua, ed. *One China, Many Paths*. New York: Verso, 2003.
Whyte, Martin King, and Dong-Kyun Im. 'Is the Social Volcano Still Dormant? Trends in Chinese Attitudes toward Inequality'. *Social Science Research* 48, no. 1 (2014): 62–76.
Xie, Yu, and Yongai Jin. 'Household Wealth in China'. *Chinese Sociological Review* 47, no. 3 (2015): 203–29.
Xin, Meng. 'Political Capital and Wealth accumulation'. In *China: New Engine of World Growth*. Edited by Ross Garnaut and Ligang Song, 316–29. Canberra: ANU Press, 2012.

6
The revival of Marxism in China
Could it herald a Communist Reformation?

Heiko Khoo

Introduction

Since 1979, the Communist Party of China (CPC) has presided over a system that generated the most dramatic economic development and improvement in living standards in history. The CPC uses state planning through its command over publicly owned enterprises and banks to attain its objectives.[1] However, capitalist exploitation and grotesque levels of inequality coexist with the Party's exclusive rule. Recently, the CPC general secretary and China's president, Xi Jinping, reemphasised the critical role of socialist, Marxist and communist ideas to the party's policies, projects and perspectives.

In this chapter, I will use two influential theories of socialism to examine China's system – first, that of the Soviet economist Evgeny Preobrazhensky; and second, that of the Hungarian economist János Kornai.

My own definition of socialism conforms to Preobrazhensky's, which is based on classical Marxist theory. This holds that a socialist economy will be more advanced, and its political system will be more democratic, than any capitalist system. Public ownership will dominate the economy and the management, administration and planning system will operate under the democratic control of the workforce and wider society. I also accept Leon Trotsky's Marxist critique of the Soviet Union, which offers a coherent and logical explanation as to why the Soviet system became bureaucratic and dictatorial.

According to this theoretical tradition, those states which self-identified as socialist never were. Rather they were systems undergoing transition from backward capitalism to socialism. This approach to the transition to a socialist economy underpinned Preobrazhensky's analysis of the Soviet Union under the New Economic Policy (NEP) in the 1920s. He envisaged a prolonged period in which a socialist government, through its monopolistic command over the largest and most important state enterprises and banks, gradually accumulates resources from the private sector economy and lays the material basis for a socialist economy. Preobrazhensky called this process *original socialist accumulation*. His theoretical framework also considered how class conflicts help to shape the direction in which society moves. This long view of socialist transformation allows for the possibility that either capitalism or socialism will eventually triumph. I believe that this perspective can be used to capture the fundamental features of China's state-led development and explains how it incorporates and exploits capitalist features.

However, both Trotsky and Preobrazhensky were killed, yet the bureaucratic and dictatorial system in the Soviet Union remained firmly in command and acquired new features, which they never observed. Furthermore, after 1945, similar regimes took power in China, Eastern Europe and some other countries. These governments self-defined as socialist and were also identified as socialist in mainstream Western thought.

The second definition of socialism that I use is that developed by János Kornai. His comprehensive analysis of 'real-existing socialist' states studies the basic characteristics of those systems and their variants, and it includes all those states which appeared in the twentieth century. This provides a range of invaluable tools with which to interpret and forecast events in contemporary China. Indeed, in the 1980s, Kornai's influence towered above that of any other contemporary foreign economist in Chinese debates about economic reform. Chinese economists and senior leaders keenly studied his analysis of the relationship between shortage, investment hunger, and soft budget constraints. He proposed that the eradication of shortage would follow from expanding market competition. His policy suggestions sought to facilitate moves towards a more efficient economic system.[2]

However, when Kornai's magnum opus *The Socialist System*[3] was first published in 1992, the drama of the fall of the Berlin Wall and the collapse of the socialist bloc overshadowed this sophisticated and comprehensive investigation into the causes of its failure. Hence, it was largely ignored despite being highly praised by experts in the field.[4]

I employ Kornai's definitions of socialism in most of this chapter. This is despite my own inclination to define 'real-existing socialist' systems as 'bureaucratic socialism', as distinct from a possible democratic form of socialism. This is because by using Kornai's definition of socialism to study

China, it is possible to identify common features and trends that appeared in other socialist states.

I reject Kornai's recent contention that China no longer fits within his definition of socialism and that it is now a capitalist system. I argue instead that his neglected concepts of the 'revolutionary transitional era' and of 'self-management' under socialism should be used to understand the way that social unrest affects and influences the CPC and its ideological orientation.

During the New Economic Policy in the 1920s, Preobrazhensky developed his theory of *original socialist accumulation*.[5] This provides a Marxist method with which to assess how systemic contradictions appear in conflicts between economic forms and social classes. I will use these insights to reflect on China today.

China's rapid economic development is synonymous with the growth of the working class. I examine the research of Yu Jianrong, who studies outbursts of workers and peasants' unrest, in order to consider how this might influence the balance of forces inside the CPC. I suggest that Xi Jinping's anti-corruption campaign and his revival of the centrality of Marxist ideology is a manifestation of this process. Thus, in contrast to the assumption that Marxism is a zombie philosophy in China, I believe that the ossification of Marxist ideas and the corruption of power may eventually provoke something akin to a communist Reformation; and that the CPC leadership is dusting off its claim to Marxist credentials in order to avoid such an outcome.

Systems analysis and development economics

Joseph Stiglitz and Justin Yifu Lin[6] both worked at the leadership level of the World Bank and engaged in detailed discussions with China's top policymakers. They elevated growth, equitable development and government policies above neo-liberal economic prescriptions. They rejected the big-bang Soviet and East European transition, in which the rapid anchoring of property rights was regarded as the decisive benchmark for progress, in favour of the gradualist evolution of markets and incentives as the precondition for successful market transition.

For Yifu Lin, exploiting comparative advantage (in capital, labour and other resources) necessitates the promotion of corresponding policies. The typical pattern of investment in heavy industry by socialist states (where capital is scarce) is regarded as a wasteful and costly policy that, by defying comparative advantage, negatively distorts the entire economy. Stiglitz and Yifu Lin tend to avoid explicitly employing socialist or capitalist labels to categorise China's system. Instead, their emphasis is on policy measures designed to produce development. Stiglitz believes that China's system reveals the significance of government policy, and indeed of fuzzy property relations in developmental economics, and in economic policy formulation more generally. Stiglitz says:

> For me, the central questions posed by development are systemic: How can we change the organization of society (including the organization of the economy) in ways that increase its openness to new ideas and that facilitate the change leading to increases in the well-being of most citizens? And what can we, as developmental practitioners, do to promote the change in societal organization in that direction? These are questions of the kind that used to be asked by those engaged in the analysis of comparative economic systems. But that sub-discipline focused on comparing socialist, communist, and market economies, and with the fall of the Iron Curtain, interest in the sub-discipline waned. I am suggesting that key to understanding development is in fact an analysis of comparative economic systems, with particular focus on the development context of what kind of economic system(s), institutions, and policies most promote the societal change that leads to sustained and inclusive development.[7]

Kornai and Preobrazhensky's theories of socialism

I approach the study of China by utilising a comparative analysis focusing on socialism as a means to investigate its contemporary social system and developmental dynamics. I employ two theories of socialism, which I regard as relevant and complementary. The first is that of Janos Kornai – whose theory of socialism is highly respected in academia and has been deeply influential inside China. The second is Preobrazhensky's Marxist development theory elaborated in the 1920s, which is concerned with economic development during the transition between capitalism and socialism.

Preobrazhensky's ideas were closely aligned with Leon Trotsky's. Both believed that the backwardness of the Soviet Union precluded the establishment of a socialist economy and society, unless there was an international socialist transformation. Thus, the Soviet Union was a treated as a society in transition between backward capitalism and socialism. Leon

Trotsky's Marxist critique of the Soviet system under Stalin stands out as the earliest and most penetrating explanation of the contradictory relationship between Marxism and the ideology and practice of the ruling communist party and its bureaucratic state. Trotsky saw this ideology as a falsification of Marxism used to justify the dictatorial power of a bureaucratic caste ruling over the working class in the name of socialism.[8]

Kornai is probably the most pre-eminent theorist and critic of real-existing socialist systems alive today. His definition of socialism begins where Trotsky's theory ends. Thus, he views the bureaucratic system established in the Soviet Union under Stalin as the basic archetype of socialism which, after 1953, was supplemented by reform socialism. However, unlike Trotsky and Preobrazhensky, Kornai's research examines the full life cycle of those socialist states that appeared in the twentieth century. So, whilst I concur with Trotsky's challenge to the socialist definition of the Soviet system, nevertheless I employ Kornai's concepts of socialism in this chapter, which differentiates between the dynamics of capitalism and socialism in the real systems that have held power in many countries over the last one hundred years.

Nowadays, Kornai regards socialism as a failed experiment and attributes the success of China's system to its having become capitalist. I believe that his assessment of China as a capitalist system is inconsistent and incorrect, and that his general theory of socialism provides a far superior method for anyone trying to understand China today. Furthermore, I maintain that if Preobrazhensky's theory of socialist development is combined with Kornai's theory, this reinforces and expands on Kornai's original analysis of the dynamics of socialist political economy. I also suggest that two of Kornai's neglected socialist concepts – the 'revolutionary transitional era' and 'self-management' – hold contemporary vitality and relevance for understanding social unrest, class conflicts, and ideological contradictions in contemporary China.

Kornai's pioneering method of analysis isolates the fundamental features of such socialist states and identifies how and why the existence of these core features automatically produces and reproduces the system.

Kornai isolates three primary features that distinguish capitalism from socialism.

Under socialism:

1. Rule of a communist state and ideology
2. The dominance of public ownership
3. The dominance of bureaucratic economic coordination

Under capitalism:

1. State and political power is not hostile to private property
2. Private ownership dominates
3. Market-mediated coordination of economic activity dominates

I argue that Kornai's socialist theory still provides a powerful lens with which to examine China's system, and that the image of China that emerges bears an uncanny resemblance to his core textbook examples of reform socialism. In addition, his neglected concepts of the *revolutionary-transitional era* and *self-management* merit close attention in this study.

Kornai's method of contrasting the basic characteristics of socialism and capitalism is rooted in Karl Marx's thought, and I argue that there are important similarities with the method employed by the Soviet economist Preobrazhensky. Both Kornai and Preobrazhensky analysed how contradictory pressures from both capitalist and socialist economic laws operate in a backward socialist economy.

Karl Marx as Xi Jinping's guide

Xi Jinping's speech to commemorate the 200th anniversary of Karl Marx's birth was broadcast to the world on live television. In the speech, Xi claimed that Marxism is the guiding force of the CPC, which is the true inheritor of socialist, Marxist and communist thought, as adapted and implemented in a Chinese context. He provided multiple examples of how the study of Marxism should help Communists to propagate ideas and policies in line with China's Two-Century Goals.[9]

In China's system, what those at the top say is by no means an arbitrary cacophony of noise. Speeches by China's leaders are prepared long in advance and are the product of an intense process of discussion, debate, argument and compromise. This is how the Politburo hammers out its common line, which tens of millions of party members are expected to study and propagate to the wider public. Ideas emanating from the top determine the ideology and shape the policy framework for government planning and implementation. Documents and speeches by the leadership affect the exercise of power in a way unknown in Western political systems. The party controls nearly every organisation that wields power and influence in society and guides the country's bureaucratic system of administration and governance.

Before Xi Jinping became general secretary of the party in 2012 and president of the republic in 2013, the consensus view in Western sinology and economics was that China was moving towards the elimination of Marxism and socialism from party ideology.[10] However, in his speech on Marx, President Xi boldly restated that Communists must be inspired and guided by the vision of communism[11] – which is supposed to be a society where material abundance satisfies everyone's needs; exploitation ends, the state begins to wither away, and money ceases to be the medium of economic coordination. Of course, you cannot judge someone by what they say about themselves, but it is nevertheless important to understand why they say it. Is this renewed focus on Marx merely a ritual, or does it tell us something about how the CPC's ideology relates to class relations today?

The recent repression of Marxist-inspired students at Peking University for standing up for workers' rights appears to confirm that the CPC is opposed to elementary Marxist beliefs, critical analysis and independent workers' organisations.[12] However, in all real-existing socialist states[13] critical Marxists were repressed, as were those attempting to form independent organisations.

The CPC leadership responds to Marxist critics as if they constitute a direct challenge to official doctrines and practices; advocates of liberal democratic values are not treated as a similar threat to their authority. Thus, Martin Luther's challenge to the Catholic Church comes to mind as an apposite comparison.

The dominant assumption in economics is that the dynamism of an economy comes overwhelmingly from its private sector. In relation to China, this means that socialised and publicly owned sectors are treated as if they are a drag on efficiency. Therefore, investigation into the positive contribution that comes from state intervention, public ownership, socialistic planning policies and coordination mechanisms has been sidelined or ignored.

The CPC leadership regards Marxism as an ideology whose socialist and communist objectives are broadly supported by party members, and by the poor and the working classes. Indeed, China's rulers claim that *only* Marxism can guide the party and appease its most important constituency of discontents.

In China, party and state involvement in society is ubiquitous. Policy is made through long-term plans that structure the CPC's relationship to the economy. The party dominates and controls every social organisation – from women's groups, to youth groups, trade unions, the churches, and so forth, as well as the entire state apparatus. However, private economic enterprises are permitted to function relatively independently.

When the CPC mobilises the bureaucracy to implement its policy and planning decisions, it draws on vast entities and networks in the economy and society to attain its objectives and goals. Private capitalists and party officials often collaborate through mutually beneficial nepotistic networks. But, whenever it is deemed expedient, the party curtails the freedom of private economic actors.

China's economic stimulus programme after the 2008 financial crash stands out as a model of crisis containment. A massive investment programme was launched to overcome the negative impact of the world crisis of capitalism. The expanding influence of the state versus the private economy has been well documented over the last 10 years.[14] It is manifest in two key factors. The first is the banking system, which channels the majority of corporate and individual savings into state investment to implement government policies. The second is the increased role for state enterprises and other public sector bodies. They draw on state funds to fulfil objectives defined in five-year plans and other state priorities.

China's Belt and Road Initiative constitutes the largest international investment programme by any country since the Marshall Plan after World War II, which was a geopolitical strategic investment by the United States of America designed to contain the threat of communism. With Belt and Road, Xi Jinping has shifted Chinese foreign policy from a gradual rise without rocking the boat – promoted by Deng Xiaoping after 1979 – to a new stage, where China shows off its prowess, power and strength to the world.

Change towards a more democratic system, accompanied by the rule of law, constitutionalism, and a free-market economy, remains the endgame of most capitalist visions for China's transition. However, 40 years since China's reform began, Maoist remnants are still said to haunt the present. This idea, that socialist historical legacies are hindering China's development is a rather weak argument, as the reform era (1979–2018) has lasted 10 years longer than the Maoist era (1949–78). Yet the Communist Party remains firmly in power, public ownership continues to predominate, and economic planning steers the macro-economy despite the widespread presence of capitalist economic and social relations.

In China, the term *planned economy* refers to Mao Zedong's regime after the 1950s. However, surely a planned economy must be judged by the degree to which its macro-level economic and social development plans are actually realised? Encouraging private investment and foreign direct investment in joint ventures generated China's present mix of state-private ownership in large enterprises, as well as its macro-level plan-market relations. Moves away from ubiquitous state ownership did not result in the dominance of private ownership; and China's new planning system actually became more effective under the new constellation of ownership forms and the liberalisation of most prices.

The inability to find close analogies that capture the dynamics of the Chinese economy has perplexed analysts from a wide spectrum of theoretical perspectives. Many who regard China as capitalist advocate more profound and accelerated pro-market changes.[15] For example, the prominent US sinologist David Shambaugh argues that China must experience significant instability and decline before it can reboot and flourish, based on a much more open system.[16] However, despite multiple predictions of the collapse of China, it failed to materialise either in 1989, or after the Great Recession of 2008–9.

Kornai's theories of socialism and capitalism in relation to China

Kornai identifies socialism with two primary archetypes: classical and reform socialism. Classical socialism is based on a planned and nationalised economy combined with a totalitarian political regime – such as Stalin's Russia from the 1930s until 1953. This kind of government brooks no dissent and severely restricts market-based activity and private ownership. Kornai's second type is reform socialism, which is generally presented as a disintegrating system. It is the sort of regime that existed under Mikhail Gorbachev in the period from 1986 to 1991. There is greater intellectual and economic freedom and openness in political discourse. However, exclusive rule by the party, public ownership of the commanding heights of the economy, and bureaucratic coordination continue. Under reform socialism in Hungary and Poland from the 1960s to the 1980s, a significant private sector coexisted with the three foundations of the socialist system. Kornai shows that a loss of faith in Marxist-Leninist ideology under reform socialism eventually heralds the dissolution of communist parties and states, in advance of a revolutionary change of system to capitalism.[17]

The revolutionary transitional era is a third type of socialism in Kornai's schema, which he regards as a transient state. It is a period when enthusiasm for the revolution is at its peak. Sacrifice, commitment and faith help to mobilise the energy of the masses, and this enables the revolutionary government to establish its authority and forge a new society.

This is the type of system that existed in the first years of the Russian Revolution. At times it operates as 'self-management'. However, after the revolutionary awakening and seizure of state power, emphasis shifts to the more mundane tasks of development, economic growth and technical progress. The need to resolve questions of everyday life leads to stabilisation and bureaucratisation as mass participation in revolutionary politics slackens off. The ossification and consolidation of bureaucratic power transforms the revolutionary transitional era into a system of reform socialism or classical socialism.

Nonetheless, Kornai's sequencing of socialism does not follow a purely linear path from the revolutionary transitional era to a classical system, and then from reform socialism to systemic collapse. For example, Kornai regards the Cultural Revolution in China (1966–76) as a variant of the revolutionary transitional system. Mao Zedong unleashed this movement, which challenged bureaucratic authority and power, *after* the classical system was already consolidated.[18]

It is Kornai's current view that although the primary characteristic of socialism – communist party rule and Marxist-Leninist ideology – maintains its dominant position in China, the internal corruption of the party and its association and affinity with private business make it a de facto agent of capitalism.

In adopting this stance, Kornai modifies his proposition that exclusive communist party rule and Marxist ideology is the first structural precondition of socialism.[19] He now argues that the two basic economic factors – the predominance of public ownership and bureaucratic planning – define socialism, provided the ruling power acts in a hostile way towards capitalism. Capitalism, by contrast, is based on private ownership and market coordination guided by price signals, where the ruling power is not hostile to capitalist property. Marxist ideology and the CPC's dictatorship have therefore declined in importance in Kornai's schema. The centrality of ideology is replaced by a more amorphous concept – the degree of hostility from the ruling political power towards capitalism.

Kornai attempts to extend his method of systemic analysis to study capitalism in his book *Dynamism, Rivalry, and the Surplus Economy: Two Essays on the Nature of Capitalism*.[20] This book complements his work on socialism. He describes capitalism as a surplus economy, endowed with unique creative forces.[21] However, Kornai's closest Chinese colleague, Xu Chenggang, has carried out a systematic review of this book, using Kornai's new arguments to analyse China today.[22] But Xu is forced to conclude that although China has a surplus economy, the commanding heights remain in state hands; and society is still dominated by a communist party-led system based on state ownership. Nevertheless, Xu believes that China operates a market economy with major distortions imposed by the state sector; for example, the state banking sector lends overwhelmingly to state entities rather than to the private sector.

Xu concludes that although China has a surplus economy, it is one that operates in a system of 'state capitalism', similar to that established by Lenin's NEP in the 1920s. Indeed, Xu notes that in the late 1970s and early 1980s, Deng Xiaoping based his original concept of reform and opening on the Soviet NEP. However, Lenin's concept of state capitalism during the NEP referred to the use of capitalist methods to revive the economy and strengthen the efficiency and quality of public sector enterprises. The NEP was designed to help overcome backwardness vis-à-vis world capitalism, and to establish genuine socialist enterprises on a higher technical foundation.

China, the Soviet NEP and Preobrazhensky's theory of original socialist accumulation

Kornai defines the period of state capitalism during the NEP as the first prototype of socialism and not as a type of capitalism.[23] During the NEP, state capitalism was not regarded as the restoration of capitalism but as a means to exploit capitalist methods to defend, foster, and advance the socialist economy. In the NEP, the state sector guided economic progress in order to sustain the alliance between the workers, the party, and the majority of peasants, whilst simultaneously stimulating economic activity through the market.

At the time of the NEP, the main problem identified by critical Marxists like Preobrazhensky, organised in the Left Opposition,[24] was that the tiny urban working class would be swamped by the interests of rich peasants, market traders and middlemen. They skimmed off part of the surplus and operated as economic actors driven by profit-seeking activity. These activities spontaneously shaped and influenced the direction of investment in the economy. The Left Opposition feared that a counter-revolution serving capitalist interests would be supported by the right wing of the party.

Alongside the emergence of capitalist forces during the NEP, the particular interests of bureaucratic agencies of the party and state also grew in scope and influence. As Kornai explains, as a general rule, bureaucratic power constantly seeks its self-expansion, and where there is no organic system of control over this expansion process, the phenomena of unconstrained 'investment hunger' in a planned economy appears, which eventually produces a shortage economy.[25]

Reflecting the pressure of such bureaucratic interests, Stalin brought an end to the NEP in 1928. Private capital and the peasantry were repressed and the economy and agriculture were socialised and subordinated to state planning.[26]

Preobrazhensky, the leading economist of the Left Opposition, envisaged a long-term battle between two economic systems in a socialist state. In his view, advanced socialism should function according to universal planning principles. However, where the public economy is not developed or sophisticated enough to ensure that socialist planning is effective, planning principles must try to control and channel capitalist laws. Where the capitalist 'law of value' predominates, the economy is organised around the pursuit of profit, which spontaneously reproduces capitalist social relations. The state economy exploits its monopoly over the commanding heights of the economy and banking to unify the power of its industries and promote development according to plan. This requires the accumulation and transfer of resources from capitalist and petty capitalist entities into the hands of the state.

Preobrazhensky's theory of original socialist accumulation elaborates a Marxist method to guide the economic transformation from backward capitalism to socialism.[27] He defines the process of transition to socialism as the epoch of *original socialist accumulation*, which he expected to last for decades. In this period, planning must be used to carefully steer the economy and society to catch up with, and eventually overtake, capitalist ownership forms and market coordination. The state economy reveals its superiority and strength once a sufficient level of economic competence and development is attained. In the era of original socialist accumulation, the socialist state must ameliorate, amend and contain the impact of the law of value, to achieve party and state objectives. Successful economic policy enables the state to introduce socialist measures such as higher wages, better conditions, social services, healthcare provision, and so on.

'Never forget the class struggle!'[28]

Yu Jianrong is probably the most influential scholar monitoring social unrest in China today. He works at the Social Problems Research Centre of the Rural Development Research Institute of the Chinese Academy of

Social Sciences. His analysis, published in 2007, shows how protests in China affect the party and state.

> The CPC's historical ideology and legitimacy declares that the 'workers are the ruling class' and 'peasants are allies' (of the ruling class). Yet, the capitalists' status has been raised far more in the past decades of reform. The nation is entering a stage of being a well-off society while hundreds of millions of peasants and workers cannot make ends meet. This gap between reality and professed ideology will inevitably shake the political root of the CPC's ideology and stability of its rule. Avoiding the escalation of social conflict will require, at a minimum, a better protection of the fundamental rights and interests of all citizens, particularly workers and peasants.[29]

Yu's research into social struggles in modern China has identified several features of mounting worker discontent: the sudden and spontaneous nature of disputes, disbelief in official responses, distrust of local authorities, and faith in the national government.[30] Protests generally concentrate on rights specified in the law. Modern means of communication have enabled militancy to be energetically channelled into exposing discrepancies between the arbitrary exercise of local power and the positive legal rights of the poor. The subaltern classes have discovered powerful methods of unifying their actions and strengthening their morale, whilst avoiding the repressive measures traditionally associated with dissidence and rebellion.[31]

Resistance to privatisation and the restructuring of state-owned enterprises came to a head in the late 1990s, when overt workers' unrest by state employees often drew on Maoist ideology and slogans. These protests slowed down privatisation, 'convincing the state to hold on to a significant number of large enterprises'.[32]

Radical changes in labour contracts and welfare rights increased the power of employers and shifted welfare provision outside of factory walls by means of contributory insurance plans. New labour laws were largely ignored by private and foreign enterprises, which provided most of the new employment opportunities in urban areas. Labour unrest in the mid-1990s often took the form of 'short-sit ins outside local labour offices aimed at provoking government officials into ordering capitalists to obey labour laws'.[33]

Legal measures to address grievances have become a focal point for workers' unrest. Claims and disputes taken to arbitration rose dramatically throughout the last 20 years, both for individual and collective cases.[34] This has been particularly evident in high-growth regions. Workers and state bodies treat arbitration seriously. In the event of local officials conspiring with employers, workers commonly resort to collective action to secure the active intervention of higher-level government agencies.[35]

Yu reports that workers at the Tonghua Iron and Steel Company went on strike against a takeover bid by the privately owned Jianlong Steel Holding Company in 2009.

> On July 24, 2009 Tonghua Iron and Steel had a strike [during which] the general manager was killed. Afterwards, [workers] in old state-owned enterprises in many places came up with slogans. One of them was 'When the Tonghua Big Boss is doing [bad] things, what should one do about it?' This scared a lot of bosses at state-owned factories that were being restructured so much that they didn't show up for work. Why? They were afraid of being killed.[36]

Surprisingly perhaps, popular opinion was not opposed to the killing of the boss. The incident was widely seen as indicative of proletarian anger and popular resentment. One consequence of the strike was that the Jilin State-owned Assets Supervision and Administration Commission (SASAC) cancelled the privatisation. Zhang Wangcheng, a professor of the China Labour Studies Centre at Beijing Normal University, blamed the trade union for the failure to pre-empt the unrest and reduce tensions.[37] A month later the All-China Federation of Trade Unions (ACFTU)[38] published a statement that privatisations are illegal unless agreed by the workers' congress.[39] The objective of expanding the presence of the ACFTU and the legal role of the Staff and Workers' Representative Councils (SWRCs) as official organs of democratic management is to create pressure release valves to contain unrest within the existing system of power.

Yu Jianrong's research reveals that it tends to be people with internal knowledge and experience of the system that act as the force galvanising and expressing social unrest:

> The foundations for a mass social movement in China may already be laid as there are indications that workers, peasants and the lower class of intellectuals are forging a common identity. Up to this point, workers and peasants have not yet merged into one coherent social group, even though they share a common social status and interests. The formation of their common identity and

goals may require an outside group that can act as the bond to bring workers and peasants together. This group could be the 20 million demobilized and retired soldiers living in rural China, which possesses the social capital, organizational, networking and mobilization capabilities to be the bridge between workers and peasants.

They have already been prominently contributing to peasants' movements to reduce tax burdens and protect land rights. In some southern regions, demobilized and retired soldiers have launched movements to mobilize both workers and peasants. For example, in some regions in Hunan Province, demobilized and retired soldiers built a 100,000-person 'anti-corruption brigade' that was mainly comprised of laid-off workers, poor peasants and lower class intellectuals. In fact, corruption may be the one factor that could bring workers and peasants together since both see this as the root cause of their current predicament and misery. In all past and current social conflicts that involve a combination of workers and peasants, their demands have universally held up anti-corruption [sic] as the common enemy.[40]

For his part, Kornai regards the corruption of China's officials as a repugnant but positive factor, because the enrichment of cadres has helped to avert a direct conflict between capitalist interests and state bureaucrats, who might otherwise have provoked a civil war.[41] The sweeping anti-corruption campaign initiated by Xi Jinping is a response to the type of pressure described above. In recent years, the wages of state-owned enterprise directors were slashed and they bear no relationship to the global standards of remuneration for the CEOs of comparable enterprises internationally, or to remuneration in private enterprises in China.[42] By taking the initiative at the top, Xi seeks to neutralise the potential for militant struggles that might otherwise escalate into a broader revolutionary movement.

The social stratum that Yu regards as the key agent of change is mainly composed of disgruntled system insiders, rather than random angry people. And their focus is on defending the rights of the social classes that the party's communist ideology claims to represent. I believe that this provides a coherent explanation for why Xi Jinping is dusting off the party's Marxist ideology, as this serves to pre-empt and neutralise opposition forces that may be supported by broad layers of the urban and rural masses.

Self-management as a recurrent socialist tendency

Kornai rejects the very possibility of socialism existing in combination with democracy.[43] And he claims that this conclusion is based entirely on a 'positive' analysis, which only evaluates real-existing socialist systems established in the twentieth century. However, when discussing the early history of the Soviet Union, he notes: 'The revolutionaries really did elect representatives to the bodies of the revolutionary political movements. In many places and for some time after the revolution had been won, the bodies of the new state power were chosen in real elections . . .' a process that Kornai dismisses because it 'proved to be temporary'.[44]

Despite the temporary nature of early Soviet systems of democratic control, the basic aspirations and impulses behind this assumed a more enduring form, which Kornai labels *self-management*. He defines self-management as a trend inspired by purely socialist ideologies that challenge bureaucratic and statist power.

According to Kornai, self-management held sway in Yugoslavia from 1949 until the early 1990s. He regards this as a sub-variant of reform socialism. Self-management modifies the two core economic mechanisms in Kornai's theory of socialism: public ownership and bureaucratic coordination. Property rights that transfer power over enterprises from the managers to the workers replace public ownership; and the workers can dispose of the firm's residual income. The coordination mechanisms of the economy are based on democratic self-governing principles rather than bureaucratic decisions.

This concept of self-management encompasses a diverse and broad historical trend. It can emerge where controls over the workers under classical or reform socialism weaken. The workforce is able to exercise considerable power over its managers. This tendency also appeared at the initial stage of socialist revolutions – for example, during the Paris Commune, the Russian Revolution, and movements based on workers' councils. However, self-management tendencies can emerge at any stage in the life cycle of socialist systems and reappear even after socialism has disappeared.[45]

As far as Kornai is concerned, self-management has a negative impact on socialist systems because it undermines economic efficiency. He distinguishes between market-driven decisions, which involve the *hard budget constraint* – where profit-seeking activity seeks to minimise costs; and the opposite tendency – the *soft-budget constraint* – where workers' interests are elevated above profits. Under the soft-budget constraint, managers come under pressure to improve the conditions of the workforce and increase living standards. Labour discipline becomes lax and managers often champion the interests of their specific workplace, community and city. Part of the bureaucracy responds to this pressure by lobbying on behalf of the workers to secure concessions from their superiors, in order to maintain stability and social peace.

Kornai regards the soft-budget constraint as a general tendency in socialist countries, generated by the system-specific relation of forces inside the workplaces. Self-management, the state system in Yugoslavia, also appeared in a number of phases of social and political unrest in ways that challenged the leading role of the communist party itself; for example, Hungary in 1956. This does not gain sufficient attention in Kornai's analysis of the socialist system. Nevertheless, he shows that there is no universal or linear process in relation to the emergence of socialist types. However, the tendency towards self-management, or to some form of mass participatory democracy in socialist systems, appeared and reappeared in many of the political and social movements that challenged the ruling parties or leading factions within them.

Indeed, given that social unrest within socialist systems has a tendency to appear as self-management, this concept sheds light on the character of workers' struggles in China today and on the balance of forces in Chinese society. For example, in the process of reforming state enterprises during the 1980s and 1990s, lip service was paid to the democratic management rights of the workers as defined in the constitution. Under articles 16 and 17, state-owned and collective enterprises 'practice democratic management through congresses of workers and staff and in other ways in accordance with the law'.[46] During the restructuring of state-owned enterprises, conflicts often focused on staff and workers' representative councils,[47] which are legally entitled to veto and control management.[48] These legal rights are not simply remnants from the past. For example, it was in 2010 that the Shanghai Municipal People's Congress adopted comprehensive regulations seeking to extend the workers' congress system throughout all Shanghai enterprises, regardless of ownership type.[49]

Conclusion

China's extraordinary rate of socio-economic development is almost universally attributed to the increasing influence of the private sector, whereas the state sector of the economy is seen as the main fetter on its future development. I adopt an alternative theoretical stance, which holds that China's success is based on exploiting the advantages of public ownership to harness national resources and channel private sector activity to achieve state planning objectives. The state sector of the economy operates under the political and bureaucratic command of the CPC. This permits the mobilisation of resources in ways that capitalism is unable to. I maintain that China's system displays the main characteristics and many of the nuanced features of Kornai's analysis of socialist systems, particularly reform socialism.

Kornai's analysis of 'real-existing' socialist systems in the twentieth century provides a comprehensive and penetrating analysis that focuses on the contradictions and dynamics generated by the Soviet model. His model of classical socialism is synonymous with the system established under Stalin in the 1930s. Its basic features were emulated in many countries that took an indigenous path to socialism, but the longevity of Kornai's analysis is undermined by excluding the very possibility of any other forms of socialism, or of new combinations of previous socialist types.

I maintain that the NEP-type policies pursued by the CPC over the last 40 years created a system where capitalist tendencies are contained by the bureaucracy whose main fear is mass unrest. And whilst China fits Kornai's socialist models, as Xu Chenggang explains, the present balance of socialist and capitalist economic forces more closely resembles the Soviet NEP. This system was studied by Preobrazhensky, who elaborated the theory of original socialist accumulation in which socialist and capitalist economic and social forces engage in a long-term struggle for dominance in a post-revolutionary developing socialist economy.

Preobrazhensky regarded the conflict between ownership and coordination forms during the NEP as a manifestation of class struggle, in a period where the economic and social foundations of socialism were being established. In China today, the struggles of the workers and poor peasants revolve around issues that put the CPC under pressure to meet their demands. The party regards social unrest as a mortal danger, and the trend is for workers' demands to be partially or fully met. The party adopts state plans that are designed to satisfy the growing wants of an ever-expanding urban working class, and it tries to contain unrest within official channels.

Simultaneously, Xi Jinping's aggressive anti-corruption campaign seeks to pacify public anger at undeserved enrichment. Although growing inequality in wealth and power is mirrored inside the CPC and the state bureaucracy, this also means that the interests of lower level cadres are often aligned with the interests of the workers and peasants. By drawing on the repertoire of Marxist ideology, Xi is reasserting the party's claim to represent the interests of the working class and the peasants. However, if the conflicts generated by reform socialism give rise to mass social unrest, and this finds expression in self-management tendencies, the contradictions in Chinese society may spark the communist equivalent of the European Reformation.

Notes

1. Amongst economists specialising in China, the consensus view from the 1990s was that the market dominated and the plan had lost nearly all significance. This view has been convincingly countered in recent years. Particularly important is the study by Sebastian Heilmann and Oliver Melton, 'The Reinvention of Development Planning in China, 1993–2012', *Modern China* 39 (2013): 580–628.
2. Julian Gewirtz, *Unlikely Partners: Chinese Reformers, Western Economists, and the Making of Global China* (Cambridge, MA: Harvard University Press, 2017).
3. Janos Kornai, *The Socialist System: The Political Economy of Communism* (Oxford: Clarendon Press, 1992).
4. Daniel Chirot, 'Review of *The Socialist System: The Political Economy of Communism*, Janos Kornai', *Slavic Review* 52 (1993): 855–56.
5. Evgeny Preobrazhensky, *The New Economics* (Oxford: Clarendon Press, 1965).
6. Joseph Stiglitz, 'The State, The Market, And Development', 2016/1 UNU-WIDER Working Paper (2016); Justin Yifu Lin, *Demystifying the Chinese Economy* (Cambridge: Cambridge University Press, 2012); Justin Yifu Lin, Cai Fang, and Li Zhou, *The China Miracle: Development Strategy and Economic Reform* (Hong Kong: Hong Kong Centre for Economic Research and the International Center for Economic Growth, 2003).
7. Stiglitz, 'The State'.
8. Leon Trotsky, *The Revolution Betrayed: What Is the Soviet Union and Where Is It Going?* (London: Union Books, 1999).
9. The first is to 'build a moderately prosperous society in all respects' – that is, improving living standards for all and eradicating severe poverty by 2021 – the centenary of the party's formation; and the second is to 'build a modern socialist country that is prosperous, strong, democratic, culturally advanced and harmonious' by 2049 – one hundred years after the founding of the People's Republic. 'CPC Q&A: What Are China's Two Centennial Goals and Why Do They Matter?', accessed 30 October 2018, www.xinhuanet.com/english/2017-10/17/c_136686770.htm.
10. Kerry Brown and Una Aleksandra Bērziņa-Čerenkova's study of Xi Jinping's ideology notes that:

    In the era of Hu, China increasingly seemed to be a capitalist society in all but name, with the CPC behaving like a massive business operation, one which paid only lip service to the ideology it was meant to be serving. Under Xi, we have seen a return to more focused political commitments, based on an acknowledgement that the great prize of national rejuvenation is within sight and an awareness that the party must maintain organizational unity and discipline in order to achieve this. This future is already being mapped out with the talk of centennial goals. In this new context, ideology supplies a precious elite unity, a common language of power, while also promoting a particular vision of society.

    Kerry Brown and Una Aleksandra Bērziņa-Čerenkova, 'Ideology in the Era of Xi Jinping', *Journal of Chinese Political Science* 23, no. 3 (September 2018): 338.
11. 'Full Video: Chinese President Xi Jinping Delivers Speech on Anniversary of Marx's Birth', accessed 1 November 2018, www.youtube.com/watch?v=EN58Cl35xQQ.
12. 'A Spectre is Haunting China: Officials in Beijing Worry about Marx-Loving Students', accessed 28 September 2018, www.economist.com/china/2018/09/29/officials-in-beijing-worry-about-marx-loving-students.

13 'Real-existing socialism' was the term used by the leaders in Eastern Europe and the Soviet Union to describe the mature and relatively stable system of power in the 1970s, when the goal of communism was no longer regarded as a short- or medium-term possibility.
14 Sarah Eaton, 'The Gradual Encroachment of an Idea: Large Enterprise Groups in China', *The Copenhagen Journal of Asian Studies* 31 (2014): 5–22; Barry Naughton, 'The Return of Planning in China: Comment on Heilmann–Melton and Hu Angang'. *Modern China* 39 (November 2013): 640–52; David Shambaugh, *China's Future* (Cambridge: Polity Press, John Wiley & Sons, 2016); Sebastian Heilmann, *China's Political System* (Lanham, MD: Rowman & Littlefield, 2017); Kjeld Erik Brødsgaard and Paul Hubbard, 'China's SOE Executives: Drivers of or Obstacles to Reform?', *The Copenhagen Journal of Asian Studies* 35, no. 1 (2017): 52–75.
15 Ronald Coase and Ning Wang, *How China Became Capitalist* (Basingstoke, UK: Palgrave Macmillan, 2012); Heilmann, *China's Political System*; Shambaugh, *China's Future*; Nicholas Lardy, *Markets over Mao: The Rise of Private Business in China* (New York: Columbia University Press, 2014); Sheng Hong, Nong Zhao, and Junfeng Yang, *Administrative Monopoly in China: Causes, Behaviors, and Termination* (Singapore: World Scientific, 2015); Chenggang Xu, 'The Fundamental Institutions of China's Reforms and Developments', *Journal of Economic Literature* 49, no. 4 (2011): 1076–1151.
16 Shambaugh says that China must go through a J-curve (a theory he takes from the risk analyst Ian Bremmer) of increasing instability; then, after it becomes more open, China will stabilise and grow on a more solid foundation. David Shambaugh, *China's Future*.
17 Kornai, *Socialist System*.
18 Kornai, *Socialist System*, 20, 392–95.
19 János Kornai, *From Socialism to Capitalism: Eight Essays* (Budapest: Central European University Press, 2008).
20 János Kornai, *Dynamism, Rivalry, and the Surplus Economy: Two Essays on the Nature of Capitalism* (Oxford: Oxford University Press, 2014).
21 A surplus economy is generated where competitive pressure between private companies in a market produces goods and services. The pursuit of high returns motivates competitors to produce more than the market can consume and to do so in conditions dominated by hard budget constraints.
22 Xu Chenggang, 'Capitalism and Socialism: A Review of Kornai's *Dynamism, Rivalry, and the Surplus Economy*', *Journal of Economic Literature* 55, no. 1 (2017): 191–208.
23 Kornai, *Socialist System*, 19.
24 Leon Trotsky formed the Left Opposition in 1923, to oppose bureaucratisation of the party, encourage democratic rejuvenation through workers' democracy, and promote economic planning.
25 Kornai, *Socialist System*, 160–63.
26 Edward Hallett Carr and Robert William Davies, *Foundations of a Planned Economy, 1926–1929*, vol. 1 (London: Macmillan, 1969): 237–70.
27 Preobrazhensky, *New Economics*.
28 This was a slogan first used by Mao Zedong in 1962. It was widely deployed during the Cultural Revolution by his supporters. See 'Can China Ever Move on from Mao Zedong?', accessed 23 October 2018, www.scmp.com/week-asia/politics/article/2018050/can-china-ever-move-mao-zedong.
29 Yu Jianrong, 'Social Conflict in Rural China', *China Security* 3 (2007): 13–14.
30 Yu Jianrong, 'Maintaining a Baseline of Social Stability', Speech to Beijing Lawyers Association on 26 December 2009, accessed 23 October 2018, chinastudygroup.net/2010/04/yu-jianrong-on-maintaining-a-baseline-of-social-stability/.
31 Yu Jianrong, 'Maintaining a Baseline of Social Stability', Speech to Beijing Lawyers Association on 26 December 2009, accessed 23 October 2018, chinadigitaltimes.net/2010/03/yu-jianrong-maintaining-a-baseline-of-social-stability-part-i/.
32 Eli Friedman and Ching Kwan Lee, 'Remaking the World of Chinese Labour: A 30-Year Retrospective', *British Journal of Industrial Relations* 48 (2010): 518.
33 Tim Pringle, 'Reflections on Labor in China: From a Moment to a Movement', *South Atlantic Quarterly* 112 (2013): 196.
34 The China Labour Bulletin reported that 520,000 labour arbitration cases were registered in 2008, 50 per cent more than 2007. See 'Government Proposals to Speed up Labour

Dispute Arbitration Lack Clout', accessed 30 October 2018, clb.org.hk/content/government-proposals-speed-labour-dispute-arbitration-lack-clout.
35 Friedman and Lee, 'Remaking the World of Chinese Labour', 517–18.
36 Yu Jianrong, 'Maintaining a Baseline of Social Stability', Speech to Beijing Lawyers Association on 26 December 2009, accessed 23 October 2018, chinadigitaltimes.net/2010/03/yu-jianrong-%E4%BA%8E%E5%BB%BA%E5%B5%98-maintaining-a-baseline-of-social-stability-part-3/.
37 'Finger-pointing in Steel Mill Death', *Global Times*, accessed 20 August 2018, english.sina.com/china/2009/0728/259013.html.
38 The All-China Federation of Trade Unions (ACFTU) is the only legal trade union organisation in China. However, the union normally operates as a top-down organisation with close links to management. Its membership stood at about 90 million in 1979. 'Get Workers Unionized', accessed 15 July 2018, en.acftu.org/28620/201408/02/140802141947207.shtml. Membership surpassed 320 million in 2017. 'Wang Xiaofeng: 2.829 Million Grassroots Trade Unions Have Been Built Nationwide, Covering 320 Million Employees', accessed 21 July 2018, acftu.people.com.cn/n1/2017/0410/c197470-29200210.html.
39 'Heed Workers' Voices', *China Daily*, 8 August 2009, accessed 24 July 2018, www.chinadaily.com.cn/opinion/2009-08/19/content_8586011.htm.
40 Yu Jianrong, 'Social Conflict in Rural China', *China Security* 3 (2007): 11.
41 Kornai, *From Socialism to Capitalism*, 146–7.
42 See 'CNPC Chief Takes Year to Earn US Rival's Daily Pay', accessed 30 October 2018, www.ft.com/content/1e798454-ce5b-11e6-864f-20dcb35cede2.
43 Kornai, 'The System Paradigm Revisited', 569.
44 Kornai, *Socialist System*, 104.
45 Kornai, *Socialist System*, 461–73.
46 'Constitution of the People's Republic of China', accessed 1 July 2018, english.peopledaily.com.cn/constitution/constitution.html.
47 Chapter 5, Article 52 of the Enterprise Law defines the rights of the SWRC

1. To be informed and to examine major strategic policies such as long-term plans, annual plans, basic investments, reinvestment plans, plans for leasing and subcontracting, and so on;
2. To examine, agree to, or veto policies related to wages, bonus and industrial safety issues, and regulations pertaining to penalties and merits.
3. To examine and decide on policies related to the staff and workers' welfare, distribution of housing, and other important welfare matters.
4. To monitor and assess the performance of responsible cadres at each level and to make suggestions on how to reward, penalize, and dismiss them; and
5. To elect the factory manager according to the arrangement of the supervisory government bureaucracy, and to report the election results to the said bureaucracy for approval.

Cited in Anita Chan and Xiaoyang Zhu, 'Staff and Workers' Representative Congress: An Institutionalized Channel for Expression of Employees' Interests?', *Chinese Sociology & Anthropology* 37 (2005): 12.
48 Stephen Philion, *Workers' Democracy in China's Transition from State Socialism* (New York: Routledge, 2009); Xiaoyang Zhu and Anita Chan 'Staff and Workers' Representative Congress'.
49 'Regulations of the Shanghai Municipality on the Workers Congress', accessed 13 December 2017, gh.eastday.com/renda/node5902/node5908/node6573/u1a1729811.html.

Bibliography

All-China Federation of Trade Unions. 'Get Workers Unionized'. Accessed 15 July 2018, en.acftu.org/28620/201408/02/140802141947207.shtml.
All-China Federation of Trade Unions. 'Wang Xiaofeng: 2.829 Million Grassroots Trade Unions Have Been Built Nationwide, Covering 320 Million Employees'. Accessed 21 July 2018, acftu.people.com.cn/n1/2017/0410/c197470-29200210.html.

Brødsgaard, Kjeld Erik, and Paul Hubbard. 'China's SOE Executives: Drivers of or Obstacles to Reform?'. *The Copenhagen Journal of Asian Studies* 35, no. 1 (2017): 52–75.

Brown, Kerry, and Una Aleksandra Bērziņa-Čerenkova. 'Ideology in the Era of Xi Jinping'. *Journal of Chinese Political Science* 23, no. 3 (1 September 2018): 323–39.

Carr, Edward Hallett, and Robert William Davies. *Foundations of a Planned Economy, 1926–1929*. Vol. 1. London: Macmillan, 1969.

Chan, Anita, and Xiaoyang Zhu. 'Staff and Workers' Representative Congress: An Institutionalized Channel for Expression of Employees' Interests?'. *Chinese Sociology & Anthropology* 37 (2005): 12.

China Daily. 'Heed Workers' Voices'. Accessed 24 July 2018, www.chinadaily.com.cn/opinion/2009-08/19/content_8586011.htm.

China Labour Bulletin. 2009. 'Government Proposals to Speed Up Labour Dispute Arbitration Lack Clout'. Accessed 30 October 2018, clb.org.hk/content/government-proposals-speed-labour-dispute-arbitration-lack-clout.

Chirot, Daniel. 'Review of *The Socialist System: The Political Economy of Communism*, Janos Kornai'. *Slavic Review* 52 (1993): 855–56.

Coase, Ronald, and Ning Wang. *How China Became Capitalist*. Basingstoke, UK: Palgrave Macmillan, 2012.

'Constitution of the People's Republic of China'. Accessed 1 July 2018, english.peopledaily.com.cn/constitution/constitution.html.

Eaton, Sarah. 'The Gradual Encroachment of an Idea: Large Enterprise Groups in China'. *The Copenhagen Journal of Asian Studies* 31 (2014): 5–22.

Economist. 'A Spectre is Haunting China: Officials in Beijing Worry about Marx-Loving Students'. Accessed 28 September 2018, www.economist.com/china/2018/09/29/officials-in-beijing-worry-about-marx-loving-students.

Friedman, Eli, and Ching Kwan Lee. 'Remaking the World of Chinese Labour: A 30-Year Retrospective'. *British Journal of Industrial Relations* 48 (2010): 507–33.

Gewirtz, Julian. *Unlikely Partners: Chinese Reformers, Western Economists, and the Making of Global China*. Cambridge, MA: Harvard University Press, 2017.

Global Times. 2009. 'Finger-pointing in Steel Mill Death'. Accessed 20 August 2018, english.sina.com/china/2009/0728/259013.html.

Heilmann, Sebastian. *China's Political System*. Lanham, MD: Rowman & Littlefield, 2017.

Heilmann, Sebastian, and Oliver Melton. 'The Reinvention of Development Planning in China, 1993–2012'. *Modern China* 39 (2013): 580–628.

Kornai, János. *Dynamism, Rivalry, and the Surplus Economy: Two Essays on the Nature of Capitalism*. Oxford: Oxford University Press, 2014.

Kornai, János. *From Socialism to Capitalism: Eight Essays*. Budapest: Central European University Press, 2008.

Kornai, János. *The Socialist System: The Political Economy of Communism*. Oxford: Clarendon Press, 1992.

Kornai, János. 'The System Paradigm Revisited'. *Acta Oeconomica* 66, no. 4 (2016): 547–96.

Lin, Justin Yifu. *Demystifying the Chinese Economy*. Cambridge: Cambridge University Press, 2012.

Lin, Justin Yifu, Fang Cai, and Zhou Li. *The China Miracle: Development Strategy and Economic Reform*. Hong Kong: Hong Kong Centre for Economic Research and the International Center for Economic Growth, 2003.

Mai, Jun. 'Can China Ever Move on from Mao Zedong?' *South China Morning Post*. 2016. Accessed 23 October 2018, www.scmp.com/week-asia/politics/article/2018050/can-china-ever-move-mao-zedong.

Naughton, Barry. 'The Return of Planning in China: Comment on Heilmann–Melton and Hu Angang'. *Modern China* 39 (2013): 640–52.

Philion, Stephen E. *Workers' Democracy in China's Transition from State Socialism*. New York: Routledge, 2009.

Preobrazhensky, Evgeny. *The New Economics*. Oxford: Clarendon Press, 1965.

Pringle, Tim. 'Reflections on Labor in China: From a Moment to a Movement'. *South Atlantic Quarterly* 112 (2013): 191–202.

Shambaugh, David. *China's Future*. Cambridge: Polity Press, John Wiley & Sons, 2016.

Sheng, Hong, Nong Zhao, and Junfeng Yang. *Administrative Monopoly in China: Causes, Behaviors, and Termination*. Singapore: World Scientific, 2015.

Standing Committee of the 13th Shanghai Municipal People's Congress. 'Regulations of the Shanghai Municipality on the Workers Congress'. 2010. Accessed 13 December 2017, gh.eastday.com/renda/node5902/node5908/node6573/u1a1729811.html.

Stiglitz, Joseph. 'The State, the Market, and Development', 2016/1 *UNU-WIDER Working Paper* (2016).

Trotsky, Leon. *The Revolution Betrayed: What Is the Soviet Union and Where Is It Going?* London: Union Books, 1999.

Wildau, Gabriel. *Financial Times*. 2016. 'CNPC Chief Takes Year to Earn US Rival's Daily Pay'. Accessed 30 October 2018, www.ft.com/content/1e798454-ce5b-11e6-864f-20dcb35cede2.

Xi Jinping. 'Full Video: Chinese President Xi Jinping Delivers Speech on Anniversary of Marx's birth'. Accessed 1 November 2018, www.youtube.com/watch?v=EN58Cl35xQQ.

Xinhua. 'CPC Q&A: What Are China's Two Centennial Goals and Why Do They Matter?'. Accessed 30 October 2018, www.xinhuanet.com/english/2017-10/17/c_136686770.htm.

Xu Chenggang. 'Capitalism and Socialism: A Review of Kornai's *Dynamism, Rivalry, and the Surplus Economy*'. *Journal of Economic Literature* 55, no. 1 (2017): 191–208.

Xu Chenggang. 'The Fundamental Institutions of China's Reforms and Developments'. *Journal of Economic Literature* 49, no. 4 (2011): 1076–1151.

Yu Jianrong. 'Maintaining a Baseline of Social Stability'. Accessed 23 October 2018, chinadigitaltimes.net/2010/03/yu-jianrong-maintaining-a-baseline-of-social-stability-part-i/.

Yu Jianrong. 'Social Conflict in Rural China'. *China Security* 3 (2007): 2–17.

7
China's emerging liberal partnership order and Russian and US responses
Evidence from the Belt and Road Initiative in Eurasia

Peter Braga and Stephen G. F. Hall

> *Why should we expect the Chinese to act any differently than the US did?*
>
> John J. Mearsheimer

> *My good men! How long must our great Russia bow and cringe before China?! Just as we bowed before foul America during the Time of Troubles, so now we crawl hunchbacked before the Celestial Kingdom.*
>
> Vladimir Sorokin, *Day of the Oprichnik*

> *Reforming and perfecting the existing international system does not mean starting over. It means pushing it to develop in a more just and rational direction.*
>
> Chinese President Xi Jinping

Introduction

There is unease among neighbouring and Western states about what a rising China – its gaining political and economic strength – will mean for the world. There is fear among these states, expressed by international relations theorist John J. Mearsheimer quoted above,[1] that a rising China will become the same sort of domineering world power as the United States. This concern is starkly illustrated in Vladimir Sorokin's fictional dystopia, *Day of the Oprichnik*.[2] In the novel, Russia is not so much a nation, but a transit and resource extraction space for goods flowing westward from China.

The current international system is often described as a liberal hegemonic order, sponsored and protected by the United States.[3] A liberal order is open and loosely rules based. The ideal is for international relations to reflect such liberal traits as openness, multilateralism, human rights, democracy, market economics, economic and security cooperation, respect for state sovereignty, and so on.[4] This order is also hegemonic, or unipolar rather than multipolar, because it is maintained by a single, dominant state – the United States. This state sets clear rules and a hierarchical order according to its own vision for the world.[5]

Nonetheless, pressure is growing for a reordering of this system. Ambitious international collective action projects, such as the Belt and Road Initiative (BRI) – a Chinese-led infrastructure mega-project, which aims to coordinate maritime shipping lanes (the road) with overland transit infrastructure (the belt) from Asia to Europe – appear to be shifting the axis of global agenda setting from Washington to Beijing. There is intense debate among academics and public intellectuals on the fate of the liberal hegemonic order.[6]

But what alternative to this international order does China seek to build? And what can be said about the reactions of major powers, such as the United States and Russia, to a changing international system? This chapter argues that tentative answers to these questions can be found in Russia's and the United States' reactions to China's growing presence in Eurasia. Eurasia is the combination of the two continents of Europe and Asia, including (but not limited to) Afghanistan, Armenia, Azerbaijan, Belarus, Georgia, Kazakhstan, Kyrgyzstan, Moldova, Pakistan, Russia, Tajikistan, Turkmenistan, Ukraine, and Uzbekistan.

The answer to the first question briefly summarises academic debates on China's rise. It supports the view, contrary to hawkish interpretations of China's gain in influence, that China seeks to build an international order that closely resembles the current system, but with a greater emphasis on multipolarity, sovereignty, and non-interference in domestic affairs. Scholar Wu Xinbo has called this a liberal partnership international order.[7] China's system of diplomatic partnerships with Eurasian countries participating in the BRI serves as evidence for this hypothesis.

The answer to the second question argues that Russia seeks to maintain its status as a great power within a reordered international system. Its Greater Eurasia Project is a clear indication of this opportunistic strategy. Additionally, the United States' response to Chinese pressures upon the liberal hegemonic order has become increasingly incoherent. In the late 1990s and 2000s, its strategy fluctuated between engagement and containment. In recent years, it has leaned closer towards containment.

But the Trump administration has thrown this response into disarray. This chaos is reflected in the United States' lack of a BRI policy and in its patchy support for partners in Eurasia.

Debating China's rise

There is lively scholarly debate on China's rise and its impact for the contemporary international order. To begin with, the international order itself is a concept fundamental to both (neo)realist and (neo)institutionalist theory. Both camps see states as unitary actors, believe there is no overarching authority to enforce rules between them, and conclude states are forced to structure an international order among themselves.[8] Therefore, debates on the international order occur often within or between these two camps of theory.

For realist scholars, China's rise tends to be associated with the looming threat of war. Issues of power transition and polarity are their main concerns.[9] Some analysts fear that the transition from a US-led, unipolar international system to a multipolar or bipolar one, or to a possible future where China is the sole hegemon, will not be peaceful.[10] They are concerned the United States might attempt to balance against China's increasing strength, which will result in a military conflict; they worry about a Thucydides trap[11] between China and the United States.[12] Other realists argue that the structural conditions for a Thucydides trap are not present, so conflict is unlikely.[13]

Institutionalist scholars focus on the principles, norms, rules, and decision-making procedures of the international system. They are concerned for the international order's 'liberal traits' of democracy, human rights, free markets, and economic and security cooperation.[14] In general, institutionalist views on China's rise can be divided into three groups. The first group argues that China will continue to integrate into an expanded and somewhat rearranged liberal order.[15] China's growing interconnectedness to the current system means its own interests will increasingly align with those of the other members of the existing liberal order.[16] The next group argues that China's continued rise resembles a negotiation.[17] While China will aim to preserve the aspects of the system that made it rich, it will also seek to adapt parts of the current liberal order to better suit its needs. However, the liberal order will also adapt to China. The stakeholders of the current system will seek to protect their interests, while at the same time including China, which is also an important member. The third group takes a gloomier view. While China will not seek to overthrow the existing order, it will push for major changes to rules and norms, which are at the heart of contemporary liberal order.[18] This will not end global cooperation between states but the features of multilateral governance – such as conditions for democracy and human rights – may simply be different or absent.[19]

Chinese academia tends to be concerned with how best to suit domestic development needs to the current international order.[20] One group of academics argues that China should directly engage in altering the liberal order to suit these needs. A second group advocates returning to a low profile in world affairs, much like during the Deng Xiaoping era.[21] The third 'mainstream view' is where China makes efforts to continue its peaceful 'harmonious rise', but also works towards incremental changes.[22]

The alternative: A liberal partnership order

This chapter argues that China seeks to maintain some elements of the liberal order, while changing others to better suit its needs. The third epigraph that opens this chapter, quoting Chinese president Xi Jinping, expresses this argument.

The alternative system China aims to build is a liberal partnership order. Wu Xinbo outlines its features.[23] China wishes to preserve liberal economic elements and dilute the hegemonic requirements of the current US-led order. It wants a 'relatively more equal political order and a cooperative security order'.[24] Or, in other words, it wants a multipolar system without a sole dominant power. The ideal is for issues of global collective security to be decided among the order's leading members – via an institution such as the United Nations.[25] This order also accommodates greater 'political diversity'[26] and means that all political regime types are equal – democratic or non-democratic. Issues of human rights and regime type are a nation's internal, sovereign affairs. Any interventions or conditions on such issues count as interference in a nation's sovereignty. Political diversity and non-interference are exemplified in the regional security organisation, the Shanghai Cooperation Organization (SCO),[27] which requires 'mutual respect of sovereignty, independence, territorial integrity of States and inviolability of State borders, non-aggression, non-interference in internal affairs . . . [and] equality of all member States'.[28] Adherence to human rights or democracy are not requirements for participation – unlike NATO, for example, which was founded upon principles of democracy.[29] Thus the 'partnership' element of this order emphasises international cooperation based on shared economic and security goals.

Wu argues that Chinese partnership diplomacy is evidence of China's efforts to gradually implement an alternative order in the international system.[30] Partnership diplomacy is a system of symbolic partnerships, which the Chinese Ministry of Foreign Affairs (MFA) assigns to countries to signal the level of bilateral relations they have with China. Since the early 1990s, China gradually developed this approach to diplomacy according to the same principles of the liberal partnership order – open markets, free investment flows, respect for sovereignty, and non-interference in domestic affairs.[31] Scholars argue that partnership diplomacy is an effort to shape an international order more in accordance with China's own long-term interests.[32] Partnership diplomacy began when Chinese policymakers sought a way to develop relations with foreign countries without the binding conditions of formal alliances. It is an approach to relations that seeks to maximise opportunities and reduce risks. Now, practically every country China interacts with has an official MFA partnership.[33]

It is just now that a proto-liberal partnership order has emerged. Partnership diplomacy was developed over more than two decades in tandem with China's rise. Although there have been years of booming, high-level economic growth, only recently has China dramatically increased its international profile, with projects such as the BRI. To be clear, since the early 2000s China has actively encouraged its state-owned enterprises to increase investments overseas.[34] By contrast, the BRI is a collective action project, which requires multiple foreign partners for success. Rather than individual enterprises pursuing profits abroad, the BRI requires many participants to coordinate with China towards a common goal.

The BRI and Eurasia as a proto-liberal partnership order

The beginnings of China's liberal partnership order can be monitored in Eurasia. This is mainly because the BRI has created conditions for China to become the guiding force for an initiative that shares aspects of liberal internationalism – such as openness, multilateralism and market economics. Although the analogy is supported neither by Chinese academics nor by China, the BRI has been described as 'China's Marshall Plan'.[35] The 1947 Marshall Plan is considered one of the foundations of the current liberal hegemonic order, because it brought multiple nations together to work collectively with the United States to rebuild a more prosperous

Europe.[36] The BRI holds comparable potential for the countries of Eurasia. The region is the location of the BRI's Silk Road Economic Belt (SREB). Announced in 2013,[37] the SREB is China's effort to interlink Central Asia, Russia and Europe across the landmass of Eurasia – reminiscent of the ancient Silk Road. Most of the post-Soviet countries that span the vast distances of the SREB have low- or lower-middle income economies.[38] For countries in the region, participation in the SREB represents a potential future of greater trade, connections with the wider world, modernisation and development. For China, relations in Eurasia are essential for the success of the SREB, the BRI's flagship project.

Another reason China's emerging alternative order can be observed in Eurasia is because China actively practises partnership diplomacy in the region. All post-Soviet Eurasian countries have MFA partnerships.[39] There are various levels of MFA partnerships; each level implies different expectations and significance to a bilateral relationship. Those with BRI-related projects officially supported by China have been assigned high-level partnerships. Those without BRI projects officially supported by China have lower-level partnerships. The higher-level partnerships have 'strategic' in their title. Strategic partners are '"closer friends" than other countries, and among the strategic partners, there is also an implicit hierarchical structure'.[40] Bilateral interactions with the higher-level strategic partnerships 'include rather detailed agendas for bilateral collaboration and provide for the establishment of specific communication channels to facilitate regular exchanges between the heads of state and high-level representatives of different government units'.[41] This is not to say non-strategic partnerships are not valued by China. Strategic partners are seen to impact China's security, while non-strategic partners are less likely to do so. For example, since the announcement of the BRI, Chinese military leaders have met with BRI participants on average almost twice a year.[42] BRI non-participants met with military leaders on average once in four years, if at all. This suggests the BRI is an additional security concern for China, and thus merits additional efforts on security with BRI participants.

Partnership diplomacy coupled with the BRI makes Eurasian diplomatic relations adhere to the principles of China's liberal partnership order – openness, market economics, and economic and security cooperation. To begin with, despite the hierarchical nature of the MFA's different levels of partnerships, the Chinese concept of partnership implies a relationship of collaboration, joint undertakings and shared risks.[43] This equates openness and equality within a liberal partnership order. The BRI projects – whether transit or energy infrastructure – are meant to increase connectivity, which means an increasing 'trade', 'financial', 'infrastructure', and 'people-to-people' interaction between all partners involved.[44] This adheres to the market economy and economic cooperation within the order. So far, there is no formal security architecture for the BRI. This suggests existing multilateral security forums, such as the UN and SCO, are enough – at least at this early stage. For example, China has supported multilateral efforts within the United Nations to resolve the crisis in Ukraine.[45] Multilateral organisations fit the liberal partnership order's preference for collective approaches to security. Any political interaction consists of 'exchanges between parliaments, political parties and non-governmental organisations of different countries'.[46] That is, political interaction refers to increased encounters, but does not touch on human rights or political systems, such as liberal democracy.

Crucially, issues of human rights and political systems are private matters, rather than matters of principle. Two recent examples – one between Kazakhstan and China, and the other involving political developments in Kyrgyzstan and Ukraine – demonstrate how China handles these types of issues with its partners. In late May 2018, after months of reported disappearances, the Kazakh government confronted Chinese authorities about rumours of Kazakh citizens being detained against their will in anti-Muslim, 're-education' camps in neighbouring Xinjiang province.[47] Kazakhstan's Foreign Ministry said the two sides discussed the 'protection of the rights and interests of the citizens of the two countries, and also the mutual trips of residents of Kazakhstan and China'.[48] China responded that any detentions resulted from ethnic Kazakhs that had tried to revoke their Chinese citizenship without the proper documentation. The key takeaway is that China is dealing with Kazakhstan via diplomatic channels to carefully and quietly resolve the issue.[49] Above all, the issue is China's sovereignty – that China can conduct whatever policy it sees fit within its western territory of Xinjiang. Therefore, the problem is being solved quietly via diplomatic exchange, rather than adherence to a set of agreements on human rights.

The second example shows differences of political regime are unimportant to China. Instead, stability is what matters. When a regime change took place in Ukraine against an increasingly authoritarian regime, China did not degrade its strategic partnership with Ukraine.[50] In addition, Ukraine lost its main investment project with China, because it was located in Crimea, which Russia annexed in 2014, so China chose to scrap the project.[51] All the same, China did not downgrade its strategic partnership with Ukraine. The two sides continue to search for areas of cooperation, including within the BRI.[52] Another example relates to regime change in Kyrgyzstan. Violent protests took place in Kyrgyzstan in 2005 and 2010. However, China did not alter its relations with Kyrgyzstan. Instead, China waited for stability to return, and continued to develop its relations. Kyrgyzstan received its first strategic partnership in 2013 and its higher-level comprehensive strategic partnership in June 2018.[53] The principles of openness in economic matters and trade, equality among partners, sovereignty, and non-interference are what China seeks to uphold.

The BRI and China's partnership diplomacy in Eurasia, therefore, can be viewed as a proto-liberal partnership order. The BRI is a collective action project that exemplifies aspects of liberal internationalism, such as openness, multilateralism and market economics. In the region, China practises partnership diplomacy, which seeks to enhance cooperative relations among partners, instead of making binding agreements among allies. Together, partnership diplomacy and the BRI combine as a basic form of China's liberal partnership order. Importantly, aspects of the US-led liberal hegemonic order that China dislikes – principles of human rights and democracy – are not requirements to participate in China's alternative order.

Reactions to a changing international order

How are Russia and the United States responding to China's rise and a potential alternative international order? The following two sections, 'Russia's reaction: Desire and risk' and 'The United States' reaction: Liberal hegemonic disorder', argue that the two countries' foreign policies in Eurasia can be analysed to show contemporary reactions to and potential future trajectories of the shifting international order.

Russia's reaction: Desire and risk

Russia desires to take advantage of changes to the international order as China rises. To balance against the United States and Western Europe (the West), and to maintain its identity as a great power, Russia is seeking to become an essential element of a new, multipolar order. In doing so, Russia runs the risk of becoming a less important member of an alternative order. While there is a broad range of scholarship characterising Russia-China relations, there is general agreement that Russia's marginalised position within the current world order is driving it to deepen its cooperation with China. An example of Russia's strategy to keep itself an important member of the international order is its attempt to make itself a political arbiter of trade in Eurasia as the BRI grows. Only time will tell if this risky strategy will bring the desired results.

The study of Russia-China relations can be divided into four schools.[54] The mainstream, limitationist school stresses the differences and problematic tensions between Russia and China.[55] The alarmist school warns that China and Russia are natural allies against the West, and foresees the smooth development of a Sino-Russian security alliance.[56] Adherents of the identity literature school compare national identity and domestic society to understand how this affects Sino-Russian foreign policy. They tend to argue there is a growing convergence in Russia and China's foreign policy preferences.[57] The normalcy school argues that while Russia-China relations have fault lines, relations are founded on shared interests and are largely pragmatic.[58] Despite their differing views, these schools agree that Russia and China both seek a multipolar world. After various high-profile scandals (such as the Magnitsky affair, the Olympic doping programme), outcry against the 2014 Russian annexation of Crimea, and the implementation of Western sanctions, Russia feels increasingly ostracised. Russia has grown closer to China in a relationship of 'asymmetric interdependence'.[59] This is where China sees Russia as a supplier of military technology and resources, and junior partner. Russia needs China as an alternative market and lender, because of strained relations with the West.

An alternate international order challenges Russia to remain a relevant world power. At the same time, it presents an opportunity for Russia to rise from its apparent ostracisation in the current liberal hegemonic order. With the demise of the Soviet Union, the new Russian state under Putin has looked to replicate the pre-eminence of the Soviet period. As early as his 1999 millennium message,[60] Putin advocated that during his tenure he would place Russia among the great world powers. Putin's regime fears becoming what former US presidential advisor and diplomat Zbigniew Brzezinski called a 'black hole',[61] outshone by Europe (the EU and its allies) in the west and China in the east. For Russia, the rise of China is perceived as both a threat and an opportunity. Russia risks becoming China's junior partner for the long term. But at the same time, China could become the eastern balancer to Russia's over-reliance on Europe.

Thus, Russia has been developing a Eurasia strategy to remain relevant. The Kremlin has sought an independent policy in Eurasia, which supports China, but keeps the region under Russian influence. The first step has been to harmonise Eurasian Economic Union (EAEU) trade regulations with the BRI. Inaugurated on 1 January 2015, the EAEU is Russia's union building project for the post-Soviet space. The goal of the EAEU is to lead to 'a Russia-led political–economic bloc that would become a political–economic pole in the multipolar international order', a Eurasian Union.[62] The EAEU has five members: Armenia, Belarus, Kazakhstan, Kyrgyzstan and Russia. It is Russia's tactic to remain a leader among Eurasian states.[63] But harmonising the EAEU with the BRI is an attempt to dilute Chinese influence, because Russia is more widely included in the details of trade as the initiative develops.[64] The Kremlin's China policy is a fine balance, summed up as 'never against each other, but not always with each other'.[65]

In a further step to make the best of the BRI and China's growing presence in Eurasia, in 2016 the EAEU launched the Greater Eurasia Project.[66] It is essentially a framework of treaties to develop Eurasia into a common economic and security space.[67] The Kremlin perceives that with the integration of the EAEU and the BRI, Russia gains some control over the process and can act as a bridge to help the project reach across and into the EU.[68] This gives Russia influence both with China and Europe.[69]

In this way, Russia seeks to become an indispensable player – a vital middleman as Bobo Lo argues – for China.[70] This is the essence of the Greater Eurasia Project: to create a regulatory treaty framework to lock Russia into a 'comprehensive trade and economic partnership in Eurasia with the participation of the European Union states and China'.[71] It is intended to complement the BRI – a superstructure above the SREB to help facilitate the initiative. This strategy serves two purposes. First, to reduce pressure from the West for the short term. Second, to aid the construction of a new world order in Eurasia.[72] Combining the EAEU and the Greater Eurasia Project, Russia becomes a necessary partner for China and one of the permanent arbiters of Eurasian politics and trade. In such a scenario, Eurasian regimes get to participate in BRI trade, because Russia, the EU, and China say so. Taking advantage of China's pre-eminent economic strength, Russia maintains its status as a great power in world politics.

Chinese officials are offering their cautious support for the Greater Eurasia Project. They think the project is a short-term improvisation, rather than a long-term plan. Chinese scholars are negative about the project. They argue that the Greater Eurasian Project has vague motives and unclear boundaries. Chinese officials currently refer to the Greater Eurasia Project as the 'Eurasian Economic Partnership Agreement' instead of the 'Eurasian Comprehensive Partnership' used previously.[73] The word choice emphasises China's preference for economic interaction. This suggests they are anxious to distance themselves from anything that may be binding for project members in the future. Some Chinese experts believe the Greater Eurasian project 'is a short-term strategic shift rather than a long-term grand strategy . . . [They] foresee Russia abandoning the Greater Eurasian [project] following the rapprochement with the West'.[74]

Overall, it remains to be seen how the Sino-Russian partnership will pan out. China is after all the dominant partner, so it is possible Russia will become a junior partner without all the benefits Russian policymakers hope for. It is likely the partnership is one of mutual convenience, with both offering each other support in certain areas, but remaining independent in others.

The United States' reaction: Liberal hegemonic disorder

The United States has responded to a potentially changing liberal hegemonic order with a mix of grudging acceptance, combined with attempts to keep China in established international structures, thereby restricting China's ability to manoeuvre. It is important to note that the current Trump administration views China's rise and the BRI as threats to the existing order, carrying an alternative order with them. In a speech at the Rhode Island Naval War College in June 2018, Secretary of Defense James Mattis alerted listeners to 'China harbouring long-term designs to rewrite the existing global order'.[75] He said of China's strategy:

> The Ming Dynasty appears to be their model, albeit in a more muscular manner, demanding other nations become tribute states, kowtowing to Beijing; espousing One Belt, One Road, when this diverse world has many belts and many roads; and attempting to replicate on the international stage their authoritarian domestic model, militarizing South China Sea features while using predatory economics of piling massive debt on others.

Regardless of Chinese efforts to downplay the potential changes it will bring to the current international order, the United States is on the lookout.

This section begins with a look at academic debate on how the United States should respond to pressures placed upon the liberal hegemonic order by China's rise. Next, there is a review of the actual policy path the United States has taken in response to these pressures. This section shows the United States' response to China has been ineffective and is increasingly becoming disordered. The United States' policy has fluctuated between engagement and containment, leaning closer to the latter in recent years. The Trump administration has thrown this approach into disarray. This ineffectiveness and inconsistency are reflected in the United States' policy in Eurasia. The United States has developed a response neither to China's rise nor to the alternative system that comes with it.

In general, scholars have argued for two opposing strategies in response to Chinese pressures upon the contemporary international order. The first is hard-line containment. Realist scholars argue that the United States needs to use internal balancing (a military build-up near China) and external balancing (military alliances with China's neighbours) to counter China.[76] In the summer of 2018, US Secretary of Defense Mattis voiced his support for a strategy of internal and external balancing against China.[77] The second strategy is a compromise approach. Institutionalists have suggested a policy of 'wary interdependence',[78] also called 'congagement' (a combination of 'containment' and 'engagement').[79] This is where the United States accepts China as a great-power partner for the twenty-first century. The strategy is to include and engage China as much as possible within existing international institutions (such as the World Trade Organization and the International Monetary Fund [IMF]), so it gradually accepts the prevailing rules and norms of the contemporary order. At the same time, the United States works to contain any Chinese military build-up or aggression. On balance, it is hoped that advocates for the second strategy prevail.

In practice, the United States' response has been an attempt at congagement. Over time, this seemed to produce few meaningful results. The latter Bush administration copied much of the Clinton administration's congagement policies towards China.[80] The Obama administration began by continuing this approach. The administration stressed engagement with China through mutual cooperation and increased communication, but this strategy was mired in mutual mistrust and deemed ineffective.[81] Chinese authorities had not opened China's economy to equal competition, and a Chinese military presence continued to develop in the South China Sea.[82]

The Obama administration shifted its strategy closer towards containment. The United States increased its naval presence in the South China Sea, transferring some of its most technologically advanced naval and air force systems to the Pacific theatre.[83] Obama also inserted the United States into the Senkaku Islands dispute between Japan and China, siding with Japan.[84] These actions are not indicative of the Obama administration taking steps to improve cooperation and transparency with China. In tandem, the Obama administration promoted the Trans-Pacific Partnership (TPP) with 11 states from East Asia, South and North

America, and Oceania. This was an attempt to bolster US dominance in Asia while forcing China to make economic reforms.[85] Obama's China policy began by promoting cooperation, but rapidly became a disjointed mixture 'of highly mixed emotions and anxieties', leading to increased disapproval 'against China', which resembles a policy of containment.[86] The Obama administration's shift from congagement towards containment highlights a transition (and the decay) in US-Chinese relations.

The deterioration in relations has continued under Trump. The Trump administration's policy is incoherent – in part because it failed to hire enough China specialists at the State Department. More US naval vessels are now stationed in the South China Sea to uphold rights of naval passage.[87] A growing trade war has further strained cooperation.[88] Accusations of Chinese interference in the 2018 US elections have not helped either.[89] Despite these recent developments, in 2017 Trump met with Xi Jinping to discuss cooperation.[90] Counter-intuitively, one of Trump's first actions as president was to renege on the TPP. Many viewed this action as a US own-goal and a win for China.[91]

While the United States is not deeply involved in much of Eurasia, its approach to the region still reflects its ineffective and disordered response to China. The baseline of US foreign policy in Eurasia was established after the Soviet Union's collapse in 1991.[92] At that time, the main issues for the United States were stability and supporting transitions to market democracies. The United States then shifted to a policy of militarisation in Eurasia under the Bush administration. Focus was lost on much of the region, as Afghanistan dominated foreign policy. The Obama administration was faced with a double problem – to reduce military commitments in Eurasia as the Iraq and Afghan wars wound down, but also to address concerns about China's growing presence in the region. Policy under Trump has been erratic. It has failed to address the breadth of change in the region and has not allocated appropriate policy tools to protect US interests.

The clearest example of the failure to engage with or to counter China's growing presence in Eurasia is the fruitless Modern Silk Road Strategy (MRS), which became the New Silk Road Vision.[93] The MRS began in 2009 as an Obama-era plan to develop post-war Afghanistan. The strategy was for Afghanistan to engage in political and economic cooperation with all six of its bordering neighbours. It would promote the idea that Afghanistan was a major transit hub at the centre of Eurasia. In 2011, Secretary of State Hillary Clinton announced a highly truncated version of the MRS, the New Silk Road Vision (NSR). The NSR is a collection of projects to build economic connectivity between the Central

Asian states, Afghanistan, India, and Pakistan.[94] The aspirations outlined by Secretary Clinton have not been matched by action. But it is likely the MRS and NSR ideas sped up Beijing's BRI plans and increased its roll-out to more states and continents. Without resources paralleling China, the United States' NSR policy is unworkable.[95] Thus, the NSR highlights the disjointed nature of US foreign policy in responding to the rise of China. Secretary Clinton made a statement that could not be backed up by tangible actions.

In addition, the removal of US troops from Afghanistan and the withdrawal from the Manas airbase in Kyrgyzstan have hampered the image of the United States as an important player in Central Asia.[96] The reduction of financial support for Central Asian states by the State Department only enhanced this perception.[97]

From around the time the SREB was announced in 2013, the United States' Eurasia policies have lacked lucidity, commitment and reliability. 'US policy has been more note-worthy for its contradictions and muddled strategic framework'.[98] One such example of a muddled strategic framework by the United States occurred in August 2015, in which US Special Representative for Afghanistan and Pakistan Dan Feldman stated that 'We welcome China's engagement in Afghanistan and Pakistan, which we see not as competitive, but complementary to our own efforts'.[99] Yet, earlier in 2015, the Obama administration was advising US allies and regional partners to not join China's Asian Infrastructure and Investment Bank (AIIB) – a China-led multilateral Asia-Pacific development institution with 57 member countries formed in 2016. The AIIB is, in fact, the product of Chinese frustration with a lack of votes within the US-led development institutions, the IMF and World Bank.[100]

The Trump administration's official response to the BRI ignores much of Eurasia. It was supposedly worked on for months before being unveiled by Secretary of State Mike Pompeo. The United States would only focus on the Indo-Pacific region – defined by Pompeo as stretching 'from the United States west coast to the west coast of India'.[101] Pompeo announced financing of US $113 million dollars for 'new initiatives'. This minuscule sum pales in comparison to China's US $40 billion Silk Road Fund.[102]

Another inconsistent jolt in policy is the Trump administration's recent signal for a return to Central Asia. This comes after the Obama administration's careful withdrawal. The decision occurred because of US perceptions that China and Russia were playing a new 'Great Game' and the United States had to react in some way.[103] However, the United States is late to the game (some scholars say nearly a decade behind) and is now having to play catch-up.[104]

The United States has not held a coherent policy about the rise of China since the late 2000s. The Obama and Trump administrations have been simultaneously conciliatory and oppressive. The begrudging acceptance of China's rise by the United States has often been closer to one of intransigence. As China's political and economic influence grow in Eurasia, so will its ability to implement its alternative, liberal partnership order.

The United States has ignored Eurasia for too long. The United States' stalled NSR, coupled with its withdrawal from Afghanistan, has decreased US influence in the region. By contrast, China's BRI is in full flow, treating Eurasia as a pivotal region. If the United States is to truly engage in Eurasia, it will face stiff competition, either having to convince local states to refute Chinese and/or Russian advances, or alternatively match Chinese investment. If the United States chooses to match Chinese investment, it will lead to an astronomical sum of capital being pumped into the region. Under the disjointed foreign policy of the Trump administration – across the globe, not just Eurasia – it is highly unlikely the United States will develop a stance on China's liberal partnership order apart from scattered containment and criticisms.

Conclusion

The international order faces change. It is shifting from a unipolar system to one that, at the very least, will soon be bipolar. The contemporary order is evolving from a US-dominated system to an arrangement between the United States and China. During the Cold War, the Soviet Union led the Eastern bloc against the United States in a bipolar system. The development of the next order remains in its infancy. How it develops in the future depends on how both actors collaborate.

Some have advocated that China's gaining political and economic strength is detrimental and will lead to conflict. Others have maintained that China's preferences will evolve to support prevailing norms and it will become a stakeholder in the current order. Still others have argued that China is labouring for major changes to the core values and practices of the international system. This chapter has argued that China, for the most part, is not trying to establish a new international order. Rather, it seeks to maintain certain features of the current liberal order, while adapting others to better suit its needs. It continues to promote the liberal features of openness, multilateralism, market economics, and economic and security cooperation. It places greater emphasis on multipolarity, sovereignty, and non-interference in domestic affairs. It works to demote the current liberal order's hegemonic requirements for human rights and democracy. Chinese scholars have called this alternative system a liberal partnership international order.

This chapter has also argued that China's rise has affected two other major powers – the United States and Russia. Each country reacted in different ways to this development. Russia views itself as a great power and wants the world to become multipolar, with itself as a distinct pole. Russia is motivated in part by the West's (primarily the United States') efforts to ostracise Russia within the existing international order. Russia has sought a partnership with China that both works to displace the United States and improve its own position. Yet it is unknown how far the Sino-Russian relationship will last into the future. It is unlikely that China views Russia as anything but a regional power whose alignment may change if it becomes dissatisfied with its limited status. Russia has accepted China's rise. As pressure builds for an alternative order, Russia hopes to counter the United States' dominance. Ideally, Russia would like to be treated as a major power with its privileges maintained in the post-Soviet region.

By contrast, the United States' acceptance of China's rise has at the very best been grudging. The Bush and Obama administrations instigated a policy of congagement, attempting to both engage and contain China. As congagement came to be seen as ineffective, there has been an increasing emphasis on containment. The Trump administration views China's growing international presence as a threat. It sees China's rise as a direct challenge to the existing order. Nevertheless, the United States has failed to develop a coherent response.

Eurasia is a geopolitical theatre where China's alternative liberal partnership order, Russia's manoeuvring, and the United States' disordered policy are all visible. China uses partnership diplomacy in Eurasia to promote its brand of relations and to increase its connectivity to much of the globe. Russia views itself as the regional great power. While it has accepted Chinese economic pre-eminence, it is developing a strategy to be Eurasia's political arbiter. Its Greater Eurasia Project is a clear indication of this opportunistic approach. In recent years, the United States' policies in Eurasia have lacked clarity, commitment and reliability. Its erratic approach – ranging from support to subversion – has culminated in a lacklustre response to the BRI and estranged regional partners.

As China rises, it brings pressure for an alternative international order with it. How this order evolves remains to be seen. Russia seeks to remain a great power by making itself China's vital partner. In the process, Russia hopes to dislocate the United States' hegemonic position and to establish a multipolar order. The United States has begrudged China's rise, yet it has failed to develop an effective response. The United States is failing to embrace and adjust to change, and this increases the fragility of the liberal hegemonic order it leads. Granted, the relationship between the United States and China is filled with mutual mistrust. A reduction of containment may be perceived by US allies as growing weakness. At the same time, a refusal to engage more with China appears petty – China is rising, and the United States needs to find ways to protect its interests and accept the inevitable.

Notes

1. John J. Mearsheimer, 'The Rise of China Will Not Be Peaceful at All', *The Australian*, 18 November 2005.
2. Vladimir Sorokin, *Day of the Oprichnik*, trans. Jamey Gambrell (New York: Farrar, Straus and Giroux, 2011), 156.
3. Michael J. Mazarr, 'The Real History of the Liberal Order', *Foreign Affairs*, 7 August 2018, accessed 4 November 2018, www.foreignaffairs.com/articles/2018-08-07/real-history-liberal-order; Gilford J. Ikenberry, *Liberal Leviathan: The Origins, Crisis, and Transformation of the American World Order*, Princeton Studies in International History and Politics (Princeton, NJ: Princeton University Press, 2011), 15.
4. Ikenberry, *Liberal Leviathan*, 169–93.
5. Robert O. Keohane and Joseph S. Nye, *Power and Interdependence*, 4th ed. (Boston: Longman, 2012), 37; Robert O. Keohane, *After Hegemony: Cooperation and Discord in the World Political Economy* (Princeton, NJ: Princeton University Press, 1984), 45–6.
6. Shiping Tang, 'China and the Future International Order(s)', *Ethics & International Affairs* 32, no. 1 (2018): 31–43; Zhou Bo, 'China Is Reshaping the International Order', *Financial Times*, 16 September 2018, accessed 4 November 2018, www.ft.com/content/7f454bb6-b733-11e8-a1d8-15c2dd1280ff; Christopher J. Fettweis, 'Trump, China and International Order', *Survival* 60, no. 5 (3 September 2018): 233–42; Aaron Friedberg, 'China's Understanding of Global Order Shouldn't Be Ours', *Foreign Policy* (blog), 24 January 2018, accessed 4 November 2018, foreignpolicy.com/2018/01/24/niall-ferguson-isnt-a-contrarian-hes-a-china-apologist/.
7. Xinbo Wu, 'China in Search of a Liberal Partnership International Order', *International Affairs* 94, no. 5 (1 September 2018): 996–7.
8. Peter Lamb and Fiona Robertson-Snape, *Historical Dictionary of International Relations*, Historical Dictionaries of International Organizations (Lanham, MD: Rowman & Littlefield, 2017), 214.
9. Xinyuan Dai and Duu Renn, 'China and International Order: The Limits of Integration', *Journal of Chinese Political Science* 21, no. 2 (June 2016): 179.
10. Mearsheimer, 'The Rise of China Will Not Be Peaceful at All'; John J. Mearsheimer, 'China's Unpeaceful Rise', *Current History*, 2006; John J. Mearsheimer, 'Can China Rise Peacefully?', Text, *The National Interest* (blog), 25 October 2014, accessed 14 November 2018, nationalinterest.org/commentary/can-china-rise-peacefully-10204.
11. This is when one rising power threatens to displace an established power and a violent conflict ensues. The phrase was coined by Graham T. Allison, who was referencing the journals of Thucydides, an Athenian general.
12. Graham T. Allison, *Destined for War: Can America and China Escape Thucydides's Trap?* (Boston: Houghton Mifflin Harcourt, 2017).
13. Charles Glaser, 'Will China's Rise Lead to War? Why Realism Does Not Mean Pessimism', *Foreign Affairs* 90, no. 2 (2011): 80–91; Zbigniew Brzezinski and John J. Mearsheimer, 'Clash of the Titans', *Foreign Policy*, 2005.
14. Dai and Renn, 'China and International Order', 179–80.

15 Ikenberry, *Liberal Leviathan*, 344–7.
16 Amitav Acharya and Alastair I. Johnston, eds., *Crafting Cooperation: Regional International Institutions in Comparative Perspective* (New York: Cambridge University Press, 2007), 255–6.
17 Michael O. Slobodchikoff, 'Strong as Silk: China in the Liberal Order', in *Changing Regional Alliances for China and the West*, ed. David Lane and Guichang Zhu, Russian, Eurasian, and Eastern European Politics (Lanham, MD: Lexington Books, 2018), 229–32; Robin Niblett, 'Liberalism in Retreat', *Foreign Affairs*, 2017.
18 Amitav Acharya, *The End of American World Order* (Cambridge: Polity, 2014), 50; Charles A. Kupchan, 'The Normative Foundations of Hegemony and The Coming Challenge to Pax Americana', *Security Studies* 23, no. 2 (3 April 2014): 219–57; Martin Jacques, *When China Rules the World: The Rise of the Middle Kingdom and the End of the Western World* (London: Allen Lane, 2009), 227–8.
19 Amitav Acharya, *The End of American World Order*, 2nd ed. (Cambridge: Polity, 2018).
20 Rosemary Foot, 'Chinese Strategies in a US-Hegemonic Global Order: Accommodating and Hedging', *International Affairs* 82, no. 1 (2006): 77–94.
21 Xi Xiao, 'Guoji Zhixu Biange Yu Zhongguo Lujing Yanjiu' [On the Transformation of International Order and China's Path], *Zhengzhixue Yanjiu [CASS Journal of Political Science]* 4 (2017): 38–48; Honghua Men, 'Zhongguo Jueqi Yu Guoji Zhixu Biange' [The Rise of China and Change in International Order], *Guoji Zhengzhi Kexue [Quarterly Journal of International Politics]* 1, no. 1 (2016): 60–89.
22 Xuetong Yan, 'Wuxu Tixi Zhong de Guoji Zhixu' [International Order in an Anarchical System], *Guoji Zhengzhi Kexue [Quarterly Journal of International Politics]* 1, no. 1 (2016): 1–32.
23 Wu, 'China in Search of a Liberal Partnership International Order', 997.
24 Wu, 'China in Search of a Liberal Partnership International Order', 996.
25 Wu, 'China in Search of a Liberal Partnership International Order', 1008.
26 Wu, 'China in Search of a Liberal Partnership International Order', 997.
27 Established in June 2001, the SCO is a Eurasian organisation whose official mandate is to coordinate regional efforts to fight terrorism, separatism and extremism. See Shanghai Cooperation Organization, 'Declaration on the Establishment of the Shanghai Cooperation Organization' (Shanghai Cooperation Organization Secretariat, 15 June 2001), accessed 4 November 2018, eng.sectsco.org/load/193054/. As of 2018, SCO members include China, India, Kazakhstan, Kyrgyzstan, Pakistan, Russia, Tajikistan and Uzbekistan.
28 Shanghai Cooperation Organization, 'Charter of the Shanghai Cooperation Organization' (2002), accessed 4 November 2018, en.sco-russia.ru/load/1013181846.
29 NATO, 'The North Atlantic Treaty' (1949).
30 Wu, 'China in Search of a Liberal Partnership International Order', 1008.
31 Joseph Y. S. Cheng and Zhang Wankun, 'Patterns and Dynamics of China's International Strategic Behaviour', *Journal of Contemporary China* 11, no. 31 (May 2002): 240–4; Weilai Dai, 'China's Strategic Partnership Diplomacy', trans. Weiwei Du, *Contemporary International Relations [Xiandai Guoji Guanxi]* 26, no. 1 (2016): 101–16; Suisheng Zhao, ed., *Chinese Foreign Policy: Pragmatism and Strategic Behavior* (Armonk, NY: M. E. Sharpe, 2004); Wu, 'China in Search of a Liberal Partnership International Order', 1008.
32 Zhongping Feng and Jing Huang, 'China's Strategic Partnership Diplomacy', *SSRN Electronic Journal*, 2014.
33 MFA of the PRC, 'Guojia He Zuzhi' [Countries and Regions], Ministry of Foreign Affairs of the People's Republic of China, 2018, accessed 4 November 2018, www.fmprc.gov.cn/web/gjhdq _676201/.
34 Deborah Brautigam, *The Dragon's Gift: The Real Story of China in Africa* (Oxford and New York: Oxford University Press, 2009), 123.
35 James D. Sidaway and Chih Yuan Woon, 'Chinese Narratives on "One Belt, One Road" (一带一路) in Geopolitical and Imperial Contexts', *The Professional Geographer* 69, no. 4 (2 October 2017): 591–603.
36 Ikenberry, *Liberal Leviathan*, 189.
37 Michelle Witte, 'Xi Jinping Calls for Regional Cooperation Via New Silk Road', *The Astana Times*, 11 September 2013, accessed 4 November 2018, astanatimes.com/2013/09/xi -jinping-calls-for-regional-cooperation-via-new-silk-road/.
38 World Bank, 'World Bank Country and Lending Groups', 2017, accessed 4 November 2018, datahelpdesk.worldbank.org/knowledgebase/articles/906519-world-bank-country-and -lending-groups.

39 MFA of the PRC, 'Guojia He Zuzhi' [Countries and Regions].
40 Feng and Huang, 'China's Strategic Partnership Diplomacy', 15.
41 Georg Strüver, 'China's Partnership Diplomacy: International Alignment Based on Interests or Ideology', *The Chinese Journal of International Politics*, 26 January 2017, 45.
42 Kenneth W. Allen, Phillip C. Saunders, and John Chen, 'Chinese Military Diplomacy, 2003–2016: Master Flat File' (National Defense University Press, 17 July 2017), accessed 4 November 2018, ndupress.ndu.edu/Portals/68/Documents/stratperspective/china/PLA-diplomacy-database.xlsx?ver=2017-07-18-133407-147.
43 Hao Su, 'Harmonious World: The Conceived International Order in Framework of China's Foreign Affairs', Working Paper (Japan: The National Institute for Defense Studies (NIDS), 2009), 35, accessed 4 November 2018, www.nids.mod.go.jp/english/publication/joint_research/series3/pdf/3-2.pdf; Cheng and Wankun, 'Patterns and Dynamics of China's International Strategic Behaviour', 238.
44 Xi Jinping, 'Full Text of President Xi's Speech at Opening of Belt and Road Forum', *Xinhua News Agency*, 14 May 2017, accessed 4 November 2018, www.xinhuanet.com/english/2017-05/14/c_136282982.htm.
45 UN Security Council, 'Peaceful Resolution of Ukraine Crisis Remains Possible, Under-Secretary-General Tells Security Council during Briefing' (New York: United Nations, 13 March 2014), accessed 4 November 2018, www.un.org/press/en/2014/sc11314.doc.htm; Shannon Tiezzi, 'China Reacts to the Crimea Referendum', *The Diplomat*, 18 March 2014, accessed 4 November 2018, thediplomat.com/2014/03/china-reacts-to-the-crimea-referendum/.
46 Xi, 'Full Text of President Xi's Speech at Opening of Belt and Road Forum'.
47 Bruce Pannier, 'Analysis: Kazakhstan Confronts China over Disappearances', Radio-FreeEurope/RadioLiberty, 1 June 2018, accessed 4 November 2018, www.rferl.org/a/qishloq-ovozi-kazakhstan-confronts-china-over-disappearances/29266456.html.
48 Pannier, 'Analysis'.
49 Catherine Putz, 'Kyrgyzstan Navigates Domestic Political Firestorm, Hopes to Avoid Burning China', *The Diplomat* (blog), 7 June 2018, accessed 4 November 2018, thediplomat.com/2018/06/kyrgyzstan-navigates-domestic-political-firestorm-hopes-to-avoid-burning-china/.
50 MFA of the PRC, 'Guojia He Zuzhi' [Countries and Regions].
51 Zuokui Liu, 'The Analysis of the Relationship between China and Ukraine', 16 + 1 China CEEC Think Tank Network, 11 January 2016, accessed 4 November 2018, 16plus1-thinktank.com/1/20160111/1095.html.
52 Andriy Goncharuk et al., 'Foreign Policy Audit: Ukraine-China', Discussion Paper (Kyiv, Ukraine: Institute of World Policy, 12 October 2016).
53 Feng and Huang, 'China's Strategic Partnership Diplomacy'; Xinhua News Agency, 'China, Kyrgyzstan Agree to Establish Comprehensive Strategic Partnership', *China Daily*, 6 June 2018, accessed 4 November 2018, www.chinadaily.com.cn/a/201806/06/WS5b17c31fa31001b82571e822.html.
54 Thomas Stephan Eder, *China-Russia Relations in Central Asia: Energy Policy, Beijing's New Assertiveness and 21st Century Geopolitics*, Research (Wiesbaden: Springer VS, 2014), 57–59; Bin Yu, 'In Search for a Normal Relationship: China and Russia into the 21st Century', *The China and Eurasia Forum Quarterly* 5, no. 4 (2007): 47–81.
55 Bobo Lo, *Russia and the New World Disorder* (London: Chatham House; Washington, DC: Brookings Institution Press, 2015); Bobo Lo, *A Wary Embrace: A Lowy Institute Paper: Penguin Special: What the Russia–China Relationship Means for the World* (Docklands, Vic: Penguin Random House Australia, 2017); Alexander Gabuev, *A 'Soft Alliance'? Russia-China Relations after the Ukraine Crisis*, ECFR/126 (London: European Council on Foreign Relations, 2015), accessed 4 November 2018, www.ecfr.eu/page/-/ECFR126_-_A_Soft_Alliance_Russia-China_Relations_After_the_Ukraine_Crisis.pdf; Alexander Gabuev, 'Friends with Benefits? Russian-Chinese Relations After the Ukraine Crisis' (Moscow: Carnegie Moscow Center, 29 June 2016), accessed 4 November 2018, carnegieendowment.org/files/CEIP_CP278_Gabuev_revised_FINAL.pdf; Jeanne Lorraine Wilson, *Strategic Partners: Russian-Chinese Relations in the Post-Soviet Era* (Armonk, NY: Sharpe, 2004); Jeanne L. Wilson, 'The Eurasian Economic Union and China's Silk Road: Implications for the Russian–Chinese Relationship', *European Politics and Society* 17, sup. 1 (15 June 2016): 113–32.
56 Hasan H. Karrar, *The New Silk Road Diplomacy: China's Central Asian Foreign Policy since the Cold War*, Contemporary Chinese Studies (Vancouver: UBC Press, 2009); Constantine

Christopher Menges, *China: The Gathering Threat* (Nashville, TN: Nelson Current, 2005); Douglas E. Schoen and Melik Kaylan, *Return to Winter: Russia, China, and the New Cold War against America* (New York: Encounter Books, 2015); Charles E. Ziegler, 'Russia and China in Central Asia', in *The Future of China-Russia Relations* (Lexington: The University Press of Kentucky, 2009), 233–65.
57 Gilbert Rozman, *The Sino-Russian Challenge to the World Order: National Identities, Bilateral Relations, and East versus West in the 2010s* (Washington, DC: Woodrow Wilson Center Press, 2014).
58 Marcin Kaczmarski, 'Two Ways of Influence-Building: The Eurasian Economic Union and the One Belt, One Road Initiative', *Europe-Asia Studies* 69/7 (9 August 2017): 1027–46; Alexander Lukin, 'Russia, China, and the Emerging Greater Eurasia', in *International Relations and Asia's Northern Tier*, ed. Gilbert Rozman and Sergey Radchenko (Singapore: Springer Singapore, 2018), 75–91; Kaneshko Sangar, 'Russia and China as the Yin and Yang of 21st Century Eurasia?', in *Changing Regional Alliances for China and the West*, ed. David Lane and Guichang Zhu (London: Lexington Books, 2018), 199–223; Yu, 'In Search for a Normal Relationship: China and Russia into the 21st Century'.
59 Gabuev, 'Friends with Benefits?', 4.
60 Vladimir V. Putin, 'Rossiya Na Rubezhe Tysyacheletii' [Russia at the Turn of the Millennium], *Nezavisimaya Gazeta*, 30 December 1999, accessed 4 November 2018, www.ng.ru/politics /1999-12-30/4_millenium.html.
61 Zbigniew Brzezinski, *The Grand Chessboard: American Primacy and Its Geostrategic Imperatives*, Updated with a new epilogue (New York: Basic Books, 2016).
62 Kaczmarski, 'Two Ways of Influence-Building', 1029; Vladimir V. Putin, 'Novyi integratsionnyi proekt dlia Evrazii – budushchee, kotoroe rozhdaetsia segodnia' [A New Integration Project for Eurasia – A Future that is Being Born Today], *Izvestia*, 3 October 2011, accessed 4 November 2018, iz.ru/news/502761.
63 Fyodor Lukyanov, 'Otvet v Evraziyskom Stale' [An Answer in the Eurasian Style], *Russia in Global Affairs* (blog), 14 August 2018, accessed 4 November 2018, www.globalaffairs.ru /redcol/Otvet-v-evraziiskom-stile-19705.
64 Dmitri Trenin, 'Russia's Evolving Grand Eurasia Strategy: Will It Work?', *Carnegie Moscow Center* (blog), 20 July 2017, accessed 4 November 2018, carnegie.ru/2017/07/20/russia-s -evolving-grand-eurasia-strategy-will-it-work-pub-71588.
65 Trenin, 'Russia's Evolving Grand Eurasia Strategy'.
66 Eurasian Economic Commission, 'Perspektivy "Bol'shoi Evrazii" obsudil na Astaninskom Ekonomicheskom Forume–2017' [Prospects for 'Greater Eurasia' discussed at the Astana Economic Forum–2017], Eurasian Economic Commission, 16 June 2017, accessed 4 November 2018, www.eurasiancommission.org/ru/nae/news/Pages/16-06-2017-1.aspx.
67 Sergei Karaganov, 'From East to West, or Greater Eurasia', *Russia in Global Affairs* (blog), 25 October 2016, accessed 4 November 2018, eng.globalaffairs.ru/pubcol/From-East-to-West-or-Greater-Eurasia-18440.
68 Gregory Shtraks, 'Next Steps in the Merger of the Eurasian Economic Union and the Belt and Road Initiative', *China Brief* 18, no. 11 (19 June 2018): 14–17.
69 Trenin, 'Russia's Evolving Grand Eurasia Strategy'.
70 Lo, *Russia and the New World Disorder*, 149.
71 Vladimir V. Putin, 'Plenary Session of St Petersburg International Economic Forum', *The Kremlin*, 17 June 2016, accessed 4 November 2018, en.kremlin.ru/events/president/ news/52178.
72 Ziguo Li, 'Da Ou Ya Huo Ban Guan Xi Yu "Yi Dai Yi Lu" Chang Yi?' [The Greater Eurasian Partnership: Remodeling Eurasian Order?], *Overseas Investment & Export Credits* 5 (2017): 37–41.
73 Li, 'Da Ou Ya Huo'.
74 Ka-Ho Wong, 'A Comparative Study of the Greater Eurasian Partnership: The Chinese and Russian Perspectives', *Russia International Affairs Council* (blog), 31 May 2018, accessed 4 November 2018, russiancouncil.ru/en/blogs/frankywongk/a-comparative-study-of-the-greater-eurasian-partnership-the-chinese-an/; Yuqi Zhang, 'Zhongxin He Bianyuan: Lijie "Da Ou Ya"' [The Centre and the Periphery: Understanding Greater Eurasia], *Eluosi Xue Kan [The Academic Journal of Russian Studies]* 7, no. 2 (2017), accessed 4 November 2018, euroasia. cssn.cn/xsyj/xsyj_elswyj/201706/t20170612_3547447.shtml.

75 James N. Mattis, 'Remarks by Secretary Mattis at the U.S. Naval War College Commencement', U.S. Department of Defense, 15 June 2018, accessed 4 November 2018, dod.defense.gov/News/Transcripts/Transcript-View/Article/1551954/remarks-by-secretary-mattis-at-the-us-naval-war-college-commencement-newport-rh/.
76 Sebastian Rosato and John Schuessler, 'A Realist Foreign Policy for the United States', *Perspectives on Politics* 9, no. 4 (December 2011): 813; Brzezinski and Mearsheimer, 'Clash of the Titans'.
77 Peter Frankopan, *The New Silk Roads: The Present and Future of the World* (London: Bloomsbury, 2018), 143–4.
78 Quansheng Zhao, 'America's Response to the Rise of China and Sino-US Relations', *Asian Journal of Political Science* 13, no. 2 (2005): 21–23.
79 Friedberg, 'China's Understanding of Global Order Shouldn't Be Ours', 89.
80 Philip Stephens, 'Bush's China Policy May Outlast His Presidency', *Financial Times*, 26 June 2008, accessed 4 November 2018, www.ft.com/content/5f6d5306-4399-11dd-842e-0000779fd2ac.
81 Cheng Li, 'Assessing U.S.-China Relations under the Obama Administration', *Brookings* (blog), 30 August 2016, accessed 4 November 2018, www.brookings.edu/opinions/assessing-u-s-china-relations-under-the-obama-administration/.
82 John Pomfret, 'America vs. China: A Competitive Face-off between Two Pacific Powers', Washington Post, 18 November 2016, accessed 4 November 2018, www.washingtonpost.com/graphics/national/obama-legacy/relations-with-china.html.
83 Jeffrey A. Bader, 'Obama's China and Asia Policy: A Solid Double', *Brookings* (blog), 29 August 2016, accessed 4 November 2018, www.brookings.edu/blog/order-from-chaos/2016/08/29/obamas-china-and-asia-policy-a-solid-double/.
84 Obama did this by mentioning how the Senkaku Islands were covered under Article 5 of the Treaty of Mutual Cooperation and Security between the United States and Japan. Obama is the first president of the United States to mention the Senkaku Islands in such a way.
85 Barry Naughton et al., 'What Will the TPP Mean for China?', *Foreign Policy* (blog), 7 October 2015, accessed 4 November 2018, foreignpolicy.com/2015/10/07/china-tpp-trans-pacific-partnership-obama-us-trade-xi/.
86 Jin Kai, 'Will the West's Imperialist Past Be China's Future?', *The Diplomat*, 17 October 2018, accessed 4 November 2018, thediplomat.com/2018/10/will-the-wests-imperialist-past-be-chinas-future/.
87 Katie Hunt, 'Trump, Tillerson and the South China Sea: What's at Stake', CNN, 2 February 2017, accessed 4 November 2018, www.cnn.com/2017/02/02/asia/us-china-south-china-sea/index.html.
88 Kevin Liptak, Cristina Alesci, and Jeremy Diamond, 'A Peek inside Trump's Chaotic Trade War', *CNN* (blog), 1 October 2018, accessed 4 November 2018, www.cnn.com/2018/09/24/politics/donald-trump-trade-policy-china/index.html.
89 Elias Groll and Colum Lynch, 'Trump: China Is Out to Get Me', *Foreign Policy* (blog), 26 September 2018, accessed 4 November 2018, foreignpolicy.com/2018/09/26/trump-china-is-out-to-get-me/.
90 Mark Landler and Michael Forsythe, 'Trump Tells Xi Jinping U.S. Will Honor "One China" Policy', *The New York Times*, 22 December 2017, sec. World, accessed 4 November 2018, www.nytimes.com/2017/02/09/world/asia/donald-trump-china-xi-jinping-letter.html.
91 Emily Rauhala and Anna Fifield, 'Trump TPP Move Seen as Win for China, but Beijing Isn't Celebrating', *Washington Post*, 24 January 2017, accessed 4 November 2018, www.washingtonpost.com/world/trump-tpp-move-seen-as-win-for-china-but-beijing-isnt-celebrating/2017/01/24/f0e5ffcc-e188-11e6-a419-eefe8eff0835_story.html.
92 Andrew C. Kuchins, 'What Is Eurasia to US (the U.S.)?', *Journal of Eurasian Studies* 9, no. 2 (July 2018): 126–7.
93 Kuchins, 'What Is Eurasia to US (the U.S.)?', 128.
94 Joshua Kucera, 'Clinton's Dubious Plan to Save Afghanistan with a "New Silk Road"', *The Atlantic* (blog), 2 November 2011, accessed 4 November 2018, www.theatlantic.com/international/archive/2011/11/clintons-dubious-plan-to-save-afghanistan-with-a-new-silk-road/247760/.
95 Alexander Cooley, 'New Silk Route or Classic Developmental Cul-de-Sac? The Prospects and Challenges of China's OBOR Initiative', PONARS Eurasia Policy Memo (Washington,

DC: George Washington University, July 2015), accessed 4 November 2018, www.ponarseurasia.org/sites/default/files/policy-memos-pdf/Pepm372_Cooley_July2015.pdf.
96 Joshua Walker and Kevin Kearney, 'What Central Asia Means to the United States', *The Diplomat* (blog), 16 September 2016, accessed 4 November 2018, thediplomat.com/2016/09/what-central-asia-means-to-the-united-states/.
97 Catherine Putz, 'Will the US Ever Get a New Central Asia Policy?' *The Diplomat* (blog), 3 May 2017, accessed 4 November 2018, thediplomat.com/2017/05/will-the-us-ever-get-a-new-central-asia-policy/.
98 Kuchins, 'What Is Eurasia to US (the U.S.)?', 129.
99 John Hudson, 'China Has a Plan to Take Over Eurasia – and America Loves It', *Foreign Policy* (blog), 18 December 2015, accessed 4 November 2018, foreignpolicy.com/2015/09/18/china-has-a-plan-to-takeover-central-asia-and-america-loves-it.
100 David Dollar, 'The AIIB and the "One Belt, One Road"', *Brookings* (blog), 21 June 2015, accessed 4 November 2018, www.brookings.edu/opinions/the-aiib-and-the-one-belt-one-road/.
101 Frankopan, *The New Silk Roads: The Present and Future of the World*, 221.
102 Xinhua News Agency, 'Commentary: Silk Road Fund's 1st Investment Makes China's Words into Practice', *Xinhua News Agency*, 21 April 2015, accessed 4 November 2018, www.xinhuanet.com//english/2015-04/21/c_134170737.htm.
103 Joshua Kucera, 'US Signals Return to Great Power Competition in Eurasia', *Eurasianet* (blog), 18 December 2017, accessed 4 November 2018, eurasianet.org/us-signals-return-to-great-power-competition-in-eurasia.
104 Mamuka Tsereteli, 'America Needs Clear Strategy for China's Presence in Central Asia', *The Hill* (blog), 15 December 2017, accessed 4 November 2018, 2018/thehill.com/opinion/international/364979-america-needs-clear-strategy-for-chinas-presence-in-central-asia.

Bibliography

Acharya, Amitav. *The End of American World Order*. Cambridge: Polity, 2014.
Acharya, Amitav. *The End of American World Order*. 2nd ed. Cambridge: Polity, 2018.
Acharya, Amitav, and Alastair I. Johnston, eds. *Crafting Cooperation: Regional International Institutions in Comparative Perspective*. Cambridge: Cambridge University Press, 2007.
Allen, Kenneth W., Phillip C. Saunders, and John Chen. 'Chinese Military Diplomacy, 2003–2016: Master Flat File'. National Defense University Press, 2017. Accessed 4 November 2018, ndupress.ndu.edu/Portals/68/Documents/stratperspective/china/PLA-diplomacy-database.xlsx?ver=2017-07-18-133407-147.
Allison, Graham T. *Destined for War: Can America and China Escape Thucydides's Trap?* Boston: Houghton Mifflin Harcourt, 2017.
Bader, Jeffrey A. 'Obama's China and Asia Policy: A Solid Double'. *Brookings* (blog). 29 August 2016. Accessed 4 November 2018, www.brookings.edu/blog/order-from-chaos/2016/08/29/obamas-china-and-asia-policy-a-solid-double/.
Bo, Zhou. 'China Is Reshaping the International Order'. *The Financial Times*. 16 September 2018.
Brautigam, Deborah. *The Dragon's Gift: The Real Story of China in Africa*. Oxford: Oxford University Press, 2009.
Brzezinski, Zbigniew. *The Grand Chessboard: American Primacy and Its Geostrategic Imperatives*. Updated with a new epilogue. New York: Basic Books, 2016.
Brzezinski, Zbigniew, and John J. Mearsheimer. 'Clash of the Titans'. *Foreign Policy*, 2005.
Cheng, Joseph Y. S., and Zhang Wankun. 'Patterns and Dynamics of China's International Strategic Behaviour'. *Journal of Contemporary China* 11, no. 31 (2002): 235–60.
'China, Kyrgyzstan Agree to Establish Comprehensive Strategic Partnership'. *China Daily*, 6 June 2018.
Cooley, Alexander. 'New Silk Route or Classic Developmental Cul-de-Sac? The Prospects and Challenges of China's OBOR Initiative'. *PONARS Eurasia Policy Memo* 372. 2015. Washington, DC: George Washington University.
Dai, Weilai. 'China's Strategic Partnership Diplomacy'. Translated by Weiwei Du. *Contemporary International Relations [Xiandai Guoji Guanxi]* 26, no. 1 (2016): 101–16.

Dai, Xinyuan, and Duu Renn. 'China and International Order: The Limits of Integration'. *Journal of Chinese Political Science* 21, no. 2 (2016): 177–97.
Dollar, David. 'The AIIB and the "One Belt, One Road"'. *Brookings* (blog). 21 June 2015. Accessed 4 November 2018, www.brookings.edu/opinions/the-aiib-and-the-one-belt-one-road/.
Eder, Thomas Stephan. *China-Russia Relations in Central Asia: Energy Policy, Beijing's New Assertiveness and 21st Century Geopolitics*. Research. Wiesbaden: Springer VS, 2014.
Eurasian Economic Commission. 'Perspektivy "Bol'shoi Evrazii" obsudil na Astaninskom Ekonomicheskom Forume – 2017' [Prospects for 'Greater Eurasia' discussed at the Astana Economic Forum – 2017]. *Eurasian Economic Commission*. 16 June 2017. Accessed 4 November 2018, www.eurasiancommission.org/ru/nae/news/Pages/16-06-2017-1.aspx.
Feng, Zhongping, and Jing Huang. 'China's Strategic Partnership Diplomacy'. *SSRN Electronic Journal*, 2014.
Fettweis, Christopher J. 'Trump, China and International Order'. *Survival* 60, no. 5 (2018): 233–42.
Foot, Rosemary. 'Chinese Strategies in a US-Hegemonic Global Order: Accommodating and Hedging'. *International Affairs* 82, no. 1 (2006): 77–94.
Frankopan, Peter. *The New Silk Roads: The Present and Future of the World*. London: Bloomsbury, 2018.
Friedberg, Aaron. 'China's Understanding of Global Order Shouldn't Be Ours'. *Foreign Policy* (blog). 24 January 2018. Accessed 4 November 2018, foreignpolicy.com/2018/01/24/niall-ferguson-isnt-a-contrarian-hes-a-china-apologist/.
Friedberg, Aaron L. *A Contest for Supremacy: China, America, and the Struggle for Mastery in Asia*. New York: W. W. Norton, 2011.
Gabuev, Alexander. 'Friends with Benefits? Russian-Chinese Relations After the Ukraine Crisis'. CP 278. Moscow, Russia: Carnegie Moscow Center, 2016. Accessed 4 November 2018, carnegieendowment.org/files/CEIP_CP278_Gabuev_revised_FINAL.pdf.
Gabuev, Alexander. *A 'Soft Alliance'? Russia-China Relations after the Ukraine Crisis*. ECFR/126. London: European Council on Foreign Relations, 2015. Accessed 4 November 2018, www.ecfr.eu/page/-/ECFR126_-_A_Soft_Alliance_Russia-China_Relations_After_the_Ukraine_Crisis.pdf.
Glaser, Charles. 'Will China's Rise Lead to War? Why Realism Does Not Mean Pessimism'. *Foreign Affairs* 90, no. 2 (2011): 80–91.
Goncharuk, Andriy, Eugenia Hobova, Viktor Kiktenko, Oleksiy Koval, and Serhiy Koshovy. 'Foreign Policy Audit: Ukraine-China'. Discussion Paper. Kyiv, Ukraine: Institute of World Policy, 2016.
Groll, Elias, and Colum Lynch. 'Trump: China Is Out to Get Me'. *Foreign Policy* (blog). 26 September 2018. Accessed 4 November 2018, foreignpolicy.com/2018/09/26/trump-china-is-out-to-get-me/.
Hudson, John. 2015. 'China Has a Plan to Take Over Eurasia – and America Loves It'. *Foreign Policy* (blog). 18 December 2015. Accessed 4 November 2018, foreignpolicy.com/2015/09/18/china-has-a-plan-to-takeover-central-asia-and-america-loves-it/.
Hunt, Katie. 'Trump, Tillerson and the South China Sea: What's at Stake'. CNN. 2 February 2017. Accessed 4 November 2018, www.cnn.com/2017/02/02/asia/us-china-south-china-sea/index.html.
Ikenberry, G. John. 'The End of Liberal International Order?', *International Affairs* 94, no. 1 (2018): 7–23.
Ikenberry, Gilford J. *Liberal Leviathan: The Origins, Crisis, and Transformation of the American World Order*. Princeton Studies in International History and Politics. Princeton, NJ: Princeton University Press, 2011.
Jacques, Martin. *When China Rules the World: The Rise of the Middle Kingdom and the End of the Western World*. London: Allen Lane, 2009.
Kaczmarski, Marcin. 'Two Ways of Influence-Building: The Eurasian Economic Union and the One Belt, One Road Initiative'. *Europe-Asia Studies* 69, no. 7 (2017): 1027–46.
Kai, Jin. 'Will the West's Imperialist Past Be China's Future?'. *The Diplomat*. 17 October 2018. Accessed 4 November 2018, thediplomat.com/2018/10/will-the-wests-imperialist-past-be-chinas-future/.
Karaganov, Sergei. 'From East to West, or Greater Eurasia'. *Russian In Global Affairs* (blog). 25 October 2016. Accessed 4 November 2018, eng.globalaffairs.ru/pubcol/From-East-to-West-or-Greater-Eurasia-18440.

Karrar, Hasan H. *The New Silk Road Diplomacy: China's Central Asian Foreign Policy since the Cold War*. Contemporary Chinese Studies. Vancouver: UBC Press, 2009.

Keohane, Robert O. *After Hegemony: Cooperation and Discord in the World Political Economy*. Princeton, NJ: Princeton University Press, 1984.

Keohane, Robert O., and Joseph S. Nye. *Power and Interdependence*. 4th ed. Boston: Longman, 2012.

Kucera, Joshua. 'Clinton's Dubious Plan to Save Afghanistan with a "New Silk Road"'. *The Atlantic* (blog). 2 November 2011. Accessed 4 November 2018, www.theatlantic.com/international/archive/2011/11/clintons-dubious-plan-to-save-afghanistan-with-a-new-silk-road/247760/.

Kucera, Joshua. 'US Signals Return to Great Power Competition in Eurasia'. *Eurasianet* (blog). 18 December 2017. Accessed 4 November 2018, eurasianet.org/us-signals-return-to-great-power-competition-in-eurasia.

Kuchins, Andrew C. 'What Is Eurasia to US (the U.S.)?'. *Journal of Eurasian Studies* 9, no. 2 (2018): 125–33.

Kupchan, Charles A. 'The Normative Foundations of Hegemony and The Coming Challenge to Pax Americana'. *Security Studies* 23, no. 2 (2014): 219–57.

Lamb, Peter, and Fiona Robertson-Snape. *Historical Dictionary of International Relations*. Historical Dictionaries of International Organizations. Lanham, MD: Rowman & Littlefield, 2017.

Landler, Mark, and Michael Forsythe. 'Trump Tells Xi Jinping U.S. Will Honor "One China" Policy'. *The New York Times*, 22 December 2017, sec. World. Accessed 4 November 2018, www.nytimes.com/2017/02/09/world/asia/donald-trump-china-xi-jinping-letter.html.

Li, Cheng. 'Assessing U.S.-China Relations under the Obama Administration'. *Brookings* (blog). 30 August 2016. Accessed 4 November 2018, www.brookings.edu/opinions/assessing-u-s-china-relations-under-the-obama-administration/.

Li, Ziguo. 'Da Ou Ya Huo Ban Guan Xi Yu "Yi Dai Yi Lu" Chang Yi?' [The Greater Eurasian Partnership: Remodeling Eurasian Order?]. *Overseas Investment & Export Credits* 5 (2017): 37–41.

Liptak, Kevin, Cristina Alesci, and Jeremy Diamond. 'A Peek inside Trump's Chaotic Trade War'. *CNN* (blog). 1 October 2018. Accessed 4 November 2018, www.cnn.com/2018/09/24/politics/donald-trump-trade-policy-china/index.html.

Liu, Zuokui. 'The Analysis of the Relationship between China and Ukraine'. 16 + 1 China CEEC Think Tank Network. 11 January 2016. Accessed 4 November 2018, 16plus1-thinktank.com/1/20160111/1095.html.

Lo, Bobo. *Russia and the New World Disorder*. London: Chatham House; Washington, DC: Brookings Institution Press, 2015.

Lo, Bobo. *A Wary Embrace: A Lowy Institute Paper: Penguin Special: What the Russia-China Relationship Means for the World*. Docklands, Vic: Penguin Random House Australia, 2017.

Lukin, Alexander. 'Russia, China, and the Emerging Greater Eurasia'. In *International Relations and Asia's Northern Tier*, edited by Gilbert Rozman and Sergey Radchenko, 75–91. Singapore: Springer Singapore, 2018.

Lukyanov, Fyodor. 'Otvet v Evraziyskom Stale' [An Answer in the Eurasian Style]. *Russian In Global Affairs* (blog). 14 August 2018. Accessed 4 November 2018, www.globalaffairs.ru/redcol/Otvet-v-evraziiskom-stile-19705.

Mattis, James N. 'Remarks by Secretary Mattis at the U.S. Naval War College Commencement'. U.S. Department of Defense. 15 June 2018. Accessed 4 November 2018, dod.defense.gov/News/Transcripts/Transcript-View/Article/1551954/remarks-by-secretary-mattis-at-the-us-naval-war-college-commencement-newport-rh/.

Mazarr, Michael J. 'The Real History of the Liberal Order'. *Foreign Affairs*, 7 August 2018. Accessed 4 November 2018, www.foreignaffairs.com/articles/2018-08-07/real-history-liberal-order.

Mearsheimer, John J. 'China's Unpeaceful Rise'. *Current History*, 2006.

Mearsheimer, John J. 'The Rise of China Will Not Be Peaceful at All'. *The Australian*, 18 November 2005.

Mearsheimer, John J. *The Tragedy of Great Power Politics*. Updated edition. The Norton Series in World Politics. New York: W. W. Norton, 2014.

Men, Honghua. 'Zhongguo Jueqi Yu Guoji Zhixu Biange' [The Rise of China and Change in International Order]. *Guoji Zhengzhi Kexue [Quarterly Journal of International Politics]* 1, no. 1 (2016): 60–89.

Menges, Constantine Christopher. *China: The Gathering Threat*. Nashville, TN: Nelson Current, 2005.
MFA of the PRC. 'Guojia He Zuzhi' [Countries and Regions]. Ministry of Foreign Affairs of the People's Republic of China. 2018. Accessed 4 November 2018, www.fmprc.gov.cn/web/gjhdq_676201/.
NATO. 1949. *The North Atlantic Treaty*.
Naughton, Barry, Arthur R. Kroeber, Guy De Jonquières, and Graham Webster. 'What Will the TPP Mean for China?'. *Foreign Policy* (blog). 7 October 2015. Accessed 4 November 2018, foreignpolicy.com/2015/10/07/china-tpp-trans-pacific-partnership-obama-us-trade-xi/.
Niblett, Robin. 2017. 'Liberalism in Retreat'. *Foreign Affairs*, 2017.
Pannier, Bruce. 'Analysis: Kazakhstan Confronts China Over Disappearances'. *RadioFreeEurope/RadioLiberty*. 1 June 2018. Accessed 4 November 2018, www.rferl.org/a/qishloq-ovozi-kazakhstan-confronts-china-over-disappearances/29266456.html.
Pomfret, John. 'America vs. China: A Competitive Face-off between Two Pacific Powers'. *Washington Post*. 18 November 2016. Accessed 4 November 2018, www.washingtonpost.com/graphics/national/obama-legacy/relations-with-china.html.
Putin, Vladimir V. 'Novyi integratsionnyi proekt dlia Evrazii – budushchee, kotoroe rozhdaetsia segodnia' [A New Integration Project for Eurasia – A Future that is Being Born Today]. *Izvestia*. 3 October 2011. Accessed 4 November 2018, iz.ru/news/502761.
Putin, Vladimir V. 'Plenary Session of St Petersburg International Economic Forum'. *The Kremlin*. 17 June 2016. Accessed 4 November 2018, en.kremlin.ru/events/president/news/52178.
Putin, Vladimir V. 'Rossiya Na Rubezhe Tysyacheletii' [Russia at the Turn of the Millennium]. *Nezavisimaya Gazeta*, 30 December 1999. Accessed 4 November 2018, www.ng.ru/politics/1999-12-30/4_millenium.html.
Putz, Catherine. 'Kyrgyzstan Navigates Domestic Political Firestorm, Hopes to Avoid Burning China'. *The Diplomat* (blog). 7 June 2018. Accessed 4 November 2018, thediplomat.com/2018/06/kyrgyzstan-navigates-domestic-political-firestorm-hopes-to-avoid-burning-china/.
Putz, Catherine. 'Will the US Ever Get a New Central Asia Policy?'. *The Diplomat* (blog). 3 May 2017. Accessed 4 November 2018, thediplomat.com/2017/05/will-the-us-ever-get-a-new-central-asia-policy/.
Rauhala, Emily, and Anna Fifield. 'Trump TPP Move Seen as Win for China, but Beijing Isn't Celebrating'. *Washington Post*. 24 January 2017. Accessed 4 November 2018, www.washingtonpost.com/world/trump-tpp-move-seen-as-win-for-china-but-beijing-isnt-celebrating/2017/01/24/f0e5ffcc-e188-11e6-a419-eefe8eff0835_story.html.
Rosato, Sebastian, and John Schuessler. 'A Realist Foreign Policy for the United States'. *Perspectives on Politics* 9, no. 4 (2011): 803–19.
Rozman, Gilbert. *The Sino-Russian Challenge to the World Order: National Identities, Bilateral Relations, and East versus West in the 2010s*. Washington, DC: Woodrow Wilson Center Press, 2014.
Sangar, Kaneshko. 'Russia and China as the Yin-and-Yang of 21st Century Eurasia?'. In *Changing Regional Alliances for China and the West*, edited by David Lane and Guichang Zhu, 199–223. London, UK: Lexington Books, 2018.
Schoen, Douglas E., and Melik Kaylan. *Return to Winter: Russia, China, and the New Cold War against America*. New York: Encounter Books, 2015.
Shanghai Cooperation Organization. 'Charter of the Shanghai Cooperation Organization', 2002. Accessed 4 November 2018, en.sco-russia.ru/load/1013181846.
Shanghai Cooperation Organization. 'Declaration on the Establishment of the Shanghai Cooperation Organization'. 2001. Accessed 4 November 2018, eng.sectsco.org/load/193054/.
Shtraks, Gregory. 'Next Steps in the Merger of the Eurasian Economic Union and the Belt and Road Initiative'. *China Brief* 18, no. 11 (2018): 14–17.
Sidaway, James D., and Chih Yuan Woon. 'Chinese Narratives on "One Belt, One Road" (一带一路) in Geopolitical and Imperial Contexts'. *The Professional Geographer* 69, no. 4 (2017): 591–603.
Slobodchikoff, Michael O. 'Strong as Silk: China in the Liberal Order'. In *Changing Regional Alliances for China and the West*, edited by David Lane and Guichang Zhu, 227–248. Russian, Eurasian, and Eastern European Politics. Lanham, MD: Lexington Books, 2018.

Sorokin, Vladimir. *Day of the Oprichnik*. Translated by Jamey Gambrell. New York: Farrar, Straus and Giroux, 2011.
Stephens, Philip. 'Bush's China Policy May Outlast His Presidency'. *Financial Times*, 26 June 2008. Accessed 4 November 2018, www.ft.com/content/5f6d5306-4399-11dd-842e-0000779fd2ac.
Strüver, Georg. 'China's Partnership Diplomacy: International Alignment Based on Interests or Ideology'. *The Chinese Journal of International Politics*, January 2017.
Su, Hao. 'Harmonious World: The Conceived International Order in Framework of China's Foreign Affairs'. Working Paper Joint Research Series 3. Japan: The National Institute for Defense Studies (NIDS), 2009. Accessed 4 November 2018, www.nids.mod.go.jp/english/publication/joint_research/series3/pdf/3-2.pdf.
Tang, Shiping. 2018. 'China and the Future International Order(s)'. *Ethics & International Affairs* 32, no. 1 (2018): 31–43.
Tiezzi, Shannon. 'China Reacts to the Crimea Referendum'. *The Diplomat*. 18 March 2014. Accessed 4 November 2018, thediplomat.com/2014/03/china-reacts-to-the-crimea-referendum/.
Trenin, Dmitri. 'Russia's Evolving Grand Eurasia Strategy: Will It Work?'. *Carnegie Moscow Center* (blog). 20 July 2017. Accessed 4 November 2018, carnegie.ru/2017/07/20/russia-s-evolving-grand-eurasia-strategy-will-it-work-pub-71588.
Tsereteli, Mamuka. 'America Needs Clear Strategy for China's Presence in Central Asia'. *The Hill* (blog). 15 December 2017. Accessed 4 November 2018, thehill.com/opinion/international/364979-america-needs-clear-strategy-for-chinas-presence-in-central-asia.
UN Security Council. 'Peaceful Resolution of Ukraine Crisis Remains Possible, Under-Secretary-General Tells Security Council during Briefing'. SC/11314. New York: United Nations, 2014. Accessed 4 November 2018, www.un.org/press/en/2014/sc11314.doc.htm.
Walker, Joshua, and Kevin Kearney. 'What Central Asia Means to the United States'. *The Diplomat* (blog). 16 September 2016. Accessed 4 November 2018, thediplomat.com/2016/09/what-central-asia-means-to-the-united-states/.
Wilson, Jeanne L. 'The Eurasian Economic Union and China's Silk Road: Implications for the Russian–Chinese Relationship'. *European Politics and Society* 17 (sup. 1) (2016): 113–32.
Wilson, Jeanne Lorraine. *Strategic Partners: Russian-Chinese Relations in the Post-Soviet Era*. Armonk, NY: Sharpe, 2004.
Witte, Michelle. 'Xi Jinping Calls for Regional Cooperation Via New Silk Road'. *The Astana Times*. 11 September 2013. Accessed 4 November 2018, astanatimes.com/2013/09/xi-jinping-calls-for-regional-cooperation-via-new-silk-road/.
Wong, Ka-Ho. 'A Comparative Study of the Greater Eurasian Partnership: The Chinese and Russian Perspectives'. *Russia International Affairs Council* (blog). 31 May 2018. Accessed 4 November 2018, russiancouncil.ru/en/blogs/frankywongk/a-comparative-study-of-the-greater-eurasian-partnership-the-chinese-an/.
World Bank. 'World Bank Country and Lending Groups'. 2017. Accessed 4 November 2018, datahelpdesk.worldbank.org/knowledgebase/articles/906519-world-bank-country-and-lending-groups.
Wu, Xinbo. 'China in Search of a Liberal Partnership International Order'. *International Affairs* 94, no. 5 (2018): 995–1018.
Xi Jinping. 'Full Text of President Xi's Speech at Opening of Belt and Road Forum'. *Xinhua News Agency*, 14 May 2017. Accessed 4 November 2018, www.xinhuanet.com/english/2017-05/14/c_136282982.htm.
Xiao, Xi. 'Guoji Zhixu Bianqe Yu Zhongguo Lujing Yanjiu' [On the Transformation of International Order and China's Path]. *Zhengzhixue Yanjiu [CASS Journal of Political Science]* 4 (2017): 38–48.
Xinhua News Agency. 'Commentary: Silk Road Fund's 1st Investment Makes China's Words into Practice'. *Xinhua News Agency*, 21 April 2015. Accessed 4 November 2018, www.xinhuanet.com//english/2015-04/21/c_134170737.htm.
Yan, Xuetong. 'Wuxu Tixi Zhong de Guoji Zhixu' [International Order in an Anarchical System]. *Guoji Zhengzhi Kexue [Quarterly Journal of International Politics]* 1, no. 1 (2016): 1–32.
Yu Bin. 'In Search for a Normal Relationship: China and Russia into the 21st Century'. *The China and Eurasia Forum Quarterly* 5/4 (2007): 47–81.

Zhang, Yuqi. 'Zhongxin He Bianyuan: Lijie "Da Ou Ya"' [The Centre and the Periphery: Understanding Greater Eurasia]. *Eluosi Xue Kan [The Academic Journal of Russian Studies]* 7, no. 2 (2017).

Zhao, Quansheng. 'America's Response to the Rise of China and Sino-US Relations'. *Asian Journal of Political Science* 13, no. 2 (2005): 1–27.

Zhao, Suisheng, ed. *Chinese Foreign Policy: Pragmatism and Strategic Behavior*. Armonk, NY: M. E. Sharpe, 2004.

Ziegler, Charles E. 'Russia and China in Central Asia'. In *The Future of China-Russia Relations*, 233–65. Lexington: The University Press of Kentucky, 2009.

Part III
Alternatives in the West

8
Neo-liberalism, Keynesianism and the current crisis

Geoffrey Hosking

When the Soviet Union fell, most of us in the West assumed that liberal democracy had proved itself the most successful form of political theory and practice. Yet, a quarter of a century later, we face a crisis which threatens to destroy liberal democracy. The established parties of government and opposition are being overshadowed by populist parties that preach an exclusive nationalism and exalt leaders claiming to represent the mass of ordinary, uncorrupt people against the corrupt elites. What has gone wrong?

In his recent book *Why Liberalism Failed,* Patrick Deneen asserts that liberalism has failed because it succeeded too well. As he variously puts it, 'Liberalism has failed because liberalism has succeeded.' 'As liberalism has become more fully itself, its inner logic has become more evident and its self-contradictions manifest.'[1] The book is in many ways an interesting one, and makes a number of good points. But I do not accept Deneen's basic premise. To my mind what has failed is not liberalism itself, but only one form of liberalism – one might call it a perversion of liberalism – that is, neo-liberalism. For as Deneen admits, the essence of liberalism is contained in certain fundamental and universal human values, to which he does subscribe: freedom, self-realisation, certain basic rights such as free speech, freedom of association and of religious belief, and so forth. Neo-liberalism has failed us by actually limiting these rights in the name of economic growth achieved by a free market economy within balanced state budgets. This is certainly an ideology, as Deneen asserts, but one which *betrays* the inner logic of liberalism, not manifests it. In fact, it begins to remind me of Soviet communism in its rigidity and in the way governments pursued it to its logical end, regardless of its effect on human suffering.

It is ironic, then, that it was the Soviet Union's collapse which convinced so many theorists and policymakers that there really was 'no alternative' (to use Margaret Thatcher's term) to neo-liberalism. It was widely believed in the 1990s that the state-dominated planned economy had utterly failed and had doomed the Soviet Union. Actually, other no less salient factors were involved – notably the fractious relationships between the nationalities and the radical reforms pursued by the Soviet leader, Mikhail Gorbachev.[2]

There was another modern form of liberalism – in Britain that of Lloyd George, Keynes and Beveridge, all of them Liberals both with a capital and a small letter – but represented in most European countries by Social Democrats or Christian Democrats. In Britain, in fact, their ideas were most fully implemented by a Labour government, that of 1945–51 under Attlee. Personal economic freedom was to be reconciled with social justice and strong government through a tacit or explicit socio-economic contract which aimed at 'full employment' (meaning minimum unemployment) and guaranteed all citizens against absolute indigence by means of what I call the 'fiscal covenant' – the tacit agreement that, provided you pay your taxes, the state will look after you, or at least prevent you slipping into utter destitution if you suffer unemployment, a serious accident or illness, or when you reach old age. The fiscal covenant created a way of making social solidarity real: the sharing of national wealth through progressive taxation proved a powerful factor in consolidating the sense of nationhood engendered by war. The national treasury became the clearinghouse through which the whole nation shared the cost of providing mutual security and well-being: defence, communications, education, health services, pensions, welfare benefits and other forms of social good. The fiscal covenant became a major component of national identity.[3] Taken together with the rule of law, it underpinned the basic trust which, in spite of individual crises, the population in general felt towards elites in general and governments in particular.

The fiscal covenant generated three decades of successful economic development, in which most of the British population became markedly wealthier, healthier, better housed and educated. This was effected by deliberate state policy to counteract the processes which during the 1930s had led to economic instability, unemployment and depression. Keynes had pointed out that classical free-market theory ignored crucial features of the economy and became especially misleading in times of depression. The defects he pointed out all turned on questions of trust and confidence. Theory posited that in investing and concluding contracts, all economic actors had good information about the state of the economy as a whole, they could assess the risks with reasonable accuracy, and could therefore take decisions with confidence. But in the real world, information was often imperfect or worse, especially in the fast-changing circumstances of a serious market downturn; hence, most economic actors had little confidence in the future. Risk was replaced by uncertainty, which in Keynes's view was a very different thing.

Classical theory supposed that in a depression prices would fall; money would then flow to where goods were available at favourable prices, or where investment held out good prospects, and in that way market equilibrium would be restored. Keynes countered that in uncertainty or unfavourable conditions, people would lose overall confidence and hoard money as the best hedge against future risk. Thus, by providing individually against possible disaster, they would bring about real disaster in the economy as a whole. The individually rational would precipitate the socially ruinous: a market collapse.

Finally, theory prescribed that states should balance budgets in all circumstances, whereas Keynes recommended that, on the contrary, in an economic depression they should override short-term concerns about the budget and spend more heavily to inject both money and confidence into the economy. It is often forgotten that Keynes also believed that in good times governments should run a budget surplus and save up funds to inject into the economy in a downturn. In short, he favoured balanced budgets as a means of sustaining confidence, but only over long-term cycles. He knew capitalism was liable to cyclical crises, which at their height led to wasteful overproduction and at their depth to mass unemployment and poverty. He therefore recommended that as an economy turned towards recession, the state should break normal budgetary rules by injecting extra spending, even at the cost of budget deficits. It would thus explicitly become the public risk manager, the upholder of generalised economic trust. In particular, it should keep up welfare payments, since they helped to preserve social peace and enabled the poor to make their contribution to the economy, at least as consumers. He did consider it important, though, that the surplus thus financed was spent on projects which would genuinely increase future wealth, since otherwise the result would eventually be uncontrolled inflation.[4]

During the 1970s, a serious economic crisis hit the UK and many countries of the European Economic Community (as it was then). It was caused partly by the end of the Bretton Woods currency system from 1971 and partly by the steep rise in oil prices precipitated by OPEC. But it was also generated partly by inherent tensions in Keynesianism itself. His theory recommended aiming at full employment (in practice, minimum unemployment), and when put into practice, gave workers and their trade unions a permanent institutional position in the state-guided economy, which in circumstances of full or high employment, plus the price rises caused by higher oil prices, empowered them to seek a greater share of the national 'cake'. That in turn provoked employers to seek higher levels of profit. Unless productivity also improved, the combined effect of those pressures was inflation. That is how in the 1970s the British economy moved into 'stagflation': a malign mixture of rising unemployment and rising prices. Keynes had imagined his economic recommendations being implemented by dispassionate and public-spirited bureaucrats, who would steer the economy according to the needs of the nation as a whole. He had not foreseen that they would become the tool of ambitious party politicians always tempted to expand the economy, however recklessly, in the approach to a general election in order to win the votes of a somewhat wealthier electorate. Nor had he anticipated that the decisive role he envisaged for the state would motivate public sector trade unions to make constant demands for their members, which were difficult to resist without plunging the country into chaos. In effect, Keynes had not linked his economics to the state practice which that economics required.[5]

The result of these developments was inflation – and Keynesianism offers little to an economy in an inflationary crisis. That is not to say that it could not be very helpful during a *deflationary* crisis, such as we have been experiencing since 2008: indeed, I shall argue that it could and should be.

In dealing with the 1970s crisis, Western governments, in different ways and at different tempos, have broken away from the ideals and practices of post-1945 liberalism. More and more the mainstream parties have gravitated towards an ideology which gives priority to the globalised and only lightly regulated capitalist market economy. According to this ideology, economic growth is to be stimulated by competition and the privatisation (or de-statisation) of economic resources, transferring them to companies which are structured to direct a large share of their profits to shareholders and directors. The role of the trade unions in the economy should be sharply reduced. To lubricate the finances of growth, clusters of international banks, finance companies and shadow banks have proliferated, poised to extract their own generous revenues from the operations necessitated by these economic processes. The theoretical justification of these policies has been that financial markets were rational and self-correcting and therefore trustworthy, that they brokered actors' self-interest to work for the benefit of all and that state intervention was therefore unnecessary and indeed harmful.[6] Keynes had long ago pointed out the deficiencies of this theory, but from the 1970s he had become so deeply unfashionable, especially after the Soviet collapse, that his objections were well off policymakers' radar.

As a corollary, the ideal of personal freedom has won out over that of social solidarity. A misreading of Adam Smith's 'doctrine' (actually an offhand remark) of the 'invisible hand' has one-sidedly reinterpreted personal freedom to mean above all the freedom to make money, where necessary at others' expense. The watchword is that 'greed is right' and that it will lead to the good of society as a whole.[7]

In the 1980s, many of the long-established industrial areas of Europe, including the UK, started to lose their industries, outbid by competition from abroad, mainly from Asia. State planning having become unfashionable, under Thatcher and subsequent prime ministers, the British government made little or no provision for the establishment of new industries or for the research and development plus the massive retraining programmes which would have been required to make them viable. Instead the 'market' was left to provide, with mixed results: many workers were in effect thrown on the rubbish heap, their skills gradually atrophying and their contribution to family and community devalued. Many of them were driven back on temporary or insecure service jobs in what became known as the 'gig economy', without sickness and holiday pay or pension entitlements. Deindustrialised communities soon had high concentrations of people on social security benefits and suffering mental or physical illness. The consequent degradation of many former workers' lives was sharply further aggravated by the financial crisis of 2007–8, which left the UK, like many European states, with much higher deficits – deficits which they dealt with in a panicked reversion to Keynesianism by bailing out huge banks. To start tackling the resulting deficits, they applied 'austerity' to state budgets, cutting back on welfare benefits and curtailing or closing many public institutions.

At the roots of the crisis was the massively untrustworthy behaviour of banks, financial institutions and building societies. During the 1980s and 1990s, most of the legal restrictions which had previously kept them cautious and undynamic but trustworthy had been weakened or eliminated by governments anxious to promote rapid economic growth. Britain experienced the 'big bang' of 1986, which weakened the regulation of British banks and opened them to full-scale international competition.

In pursuit of the break from Keynesian policy, both governments and local authorities began in the 1980s to privatise public functions or to outsource them to private corporations. In some cases, this process produced more efficient services, at least for a time; but in others it simply replaced a state monopoly with a private monopoly. Hedge funds and private equity funds, largely unregulated, swelled rapidly to acquire such enterprises, usually by amassing huge (lightly taxed) debts to do so. They then devoted a handsome share of the enterprises' profits to paying off those debts and passed most of the rest to their investors and directors. Meanwhile the risks were borne by the taxpayer.

One example of the results must suffice. Carillion, a company to which numerous public functions had been outsourced, including the building of hospitals and schools, the provision of school meals and the maintenance of prisons, went bankrupt in January 2018. The collapse made more than 2,000 employees and subcontractors redundant or bankrupt, left its pension fund £800 million short, and abandoned public projects, including the construction of major hospitals in Birmingham and Liverpool. The parliamentary Committee on Work and Pensions later reported that Carillion's business model was unsustainable, a 'dash for cash . . . with scant regard for the long-term sustainability or the impact on employers, pensioners or suppliers'. Its directors had been content to let the state and the Pension Protection Fund pick up the bill. In its final years, 'The directors rewarded themselves and other shareholders by choosing to pay out more in dividends than the company generated in cash.' The remuneration committee 'paid substantially higher salaries and bonuses to senior staff while financial performance declined'. The committee concluded that Carillion was 'not just the failure of a company, but a failure of a system of corporate accountability which too often leaves those responsible at the top – and the ever-present firms that surround them – as winners while everyone else loses out'. The committee criticised successive governments too, asserting that they 'have nurtured a business environment and pursued a model of service delivery which made such a collapse, if not inevitable, then at least a distinct possibility'.[8]

A major reason for the mounting power and reach of financial services was that the British public was increasingly having recourse to finance to cope with the ordinary risks of life. For the last 50 to 60 years, the middle class has been contributing enthusiastically to the financialisation of society. Whereas previously people usually relied on family, friends, local community, charities, friendly societies or religious institutions to help with facing risks, nowadays most put their trust at least to some extent in savings banks, insurance policies and pension funds. Those who were able to do so also purchased real estate, both as a reliable roof over one's head and as a hedge against inflation. Many of us have, then, made our contribution to the financialisation of the economy, providing ample funds for financial institutions to use or misuse. In 1963, pension and insurance funds owned 19 per cent of UK shares; by 1998 that was 65 per cent.[9] In the USA, total pension fund assets rose astronomically, from $0.2 trillion in 1975, to $3 trillion in 1990, $8 trillion in 1998, and $16 trillion in 2006 – growth by a factor of 80![10] With the deregulation of capital markets, between 1980 and 1995 investments from mutual funds, insurance funds and pension funds grew some tenfold. This growth played a major role in the globalisation of finance, since much of this investment was in foreign markets.[11] This expansion, however, did not fully include those who have never had enough money to invest extensively in insurance, pensions or real estate. Hence its tendency was to polarise society economically.

One of the results of this policy was a soaring increase in real estate prices, especially in the United States, where they grew by 105 per cent between 1997 and 2007; and in the UK, where they grew by 190 per cent in the same period. This abrupt growth was largely fuelled by the reckless provision of mortgage debt. Banks would offer incautious loans – known as 'sub-prime mortgages' – to customers in the knowledge that they could reduce the risk involved by chopping up and reconfiguring the loans into 'securitised' packages which they then sold on to other banks. The idea was that the spreading of risk would dilute its impact. During 2007–8 it suddenly became apparent that the mathematical risk models underpinning these packages were based on insufficient historical data: they did not, for example, take account of the 1930s economic crisis. Once one bank defaulted, then debts, like a cancer, rapidly metastasised, till in September 2008 they climaxed with the collapse of three of the top five US investment banks, including that of Lehman Brothers – the greatest corporate bankruptcy in history – and of the two institutions that provided 80 per cent of US mortgages. In Britain two major banks, Royal Bank of Scotland and Halifax Bank of Scotland, went bankrupt, as did all building societies which had demutualised – that is, had ceased to rely on depositors for their revenue, but allowed themselves to be quoted on the stock exchange.[12]

Stock markets around the world plunged, losing $600 billion in just 36 hours. The immediate cause of the financial crisis was the collapse of the mutual trust without which banks can scarcely limp on from day to day. In some cases, they stopped even making each other overnight loans which normally smooth out the ups and downs of everyday financial business. They also could not realise the assets in their portfolios, since the price of those assets plunged if they tried to sell them. This collapse was totally contrary to the theory of self-regulating markets. Alan Greenspan, former (and once much admired) chairman of the US Federal Reserve, confessed to a congressional committee, 'Those of us who have looked to the self-interest of lending institutions to protect shareholders' equity (myself especially) are in a state of shocked disbelief.'[13]

In the United States, the UK and other western countries, governments rightly overrode decades of free-market dogma, and bailed out the bankrupt institutions, at the cost of enormously increasing the national debt. In the UK, the operation nearly doubled the debt, bringing it up to a level of 76 per cent of annual GDP in 2010–11.[14]

One might have thought that such a sensational collapse would have led to a profound reassessment of the way the market was operating and to radical changes in policy. On the contrary, the British government on the whole returned to slightly corrected versions of its pre-2008 policies. In the following decade, the annual deficit was gradually reduced, but the effect was too slow to affect state debt, which continued to grow inexorably, until at the end of 2017 it reached 87.7 per cent. Meanwhile, to counteract the effects of austerity, household debt also started rising again, until by 2017 it was approaching the dangerous levels of 2008: 133 per cent of household annual income, as against 148 per cent in 2008.[15] Such a level leaves households vulnerable to a deterioration of their own economic position, and also to either an improvement in the national economy (which would bring about higher interest rates) or a downturn in it (which could mean lower income).

The government did not reform economic and financial institutions; but instead, acting in the name of free-market ideology, they made serious cuts in welfare provision, debasing life for the poor, disabled and the disadvantaged generally, including many women in particular. As a result, liberalism has become degraded and detached from social democracy. Today, it no longer aims to secure the maximum personal freedom of all members of the population. Instead it has become an ideology of the establishment, offering support to the well-connected and wealthy, while reducing the resources, legal status and life chances available to the rest of the population. It is scarcely surprising that those whose lives have been blighted by the consequences have lost trust in established political parties and have turned to 'populists' instead.

'Austerity', the policy pursued by the British government in the 2010s, aimed to pay off state debt through balancing the budget year-by-year. Such a policy may have been necessary in the 1970s, but its effects have been slow and inconclusive. There is no reason why we should cling to it in a completely different kind of crisis. If generals fight the last war over again, it seems the same is true of politicians. Most of the politicians in Britain's two major parties are stuck in the 1970s.

The brunt of austerity was borne by the already disadvantaged – that is, by those who rent rather than own their dwellings, and who depend on welfare and social security systems. In the UK, for example, the costs have included funding cuts to hospitals and schools; the closure of numerous public libraries; extreme strain on the facilities of the National Health Service; repeated crises in the prison service caused at least partly by a shortage of prison officers; families forced out of their homes and communities because their housing benefit has been cut, or because the local council or housing association has sold their home to a developer; reductions in invalidity benefits and tax credits, which have left many claimants with anxiety-creating forms to fill in and intimidating tests to undergo; the withdrawal of many youth services and careers advice centres; and reductions in legal aid which exclude many people from access to the law, especially women, recent immigrants and people newly dismissed from employment. One could go on. Cumulatively, these cuts impaired the fiscal covenant and undermined the rule of law. They deprived many people, especially the poor and disadvantaged, of their confidence in the future, of their feeling of being citizens and belonging to a community. That is what has made them willing prey to populist parties which have pledged to restore welfare benefits and recreate the sense of community.

Globalised markets had other effects too: many people from poorer and/or strife-torn countries migrated to European countries, most of which were still relatively prosperous. Many indigenous Europeans were left with the feeling that they had become surrounded by alien inhabitants whom they did not know and could not trust, and that they could no longer have confidence in the safety nets supplied by the state in case of disaster. Islamist terrorism then added extra impetus to their fears. The result was widespread exaggerated distrust of all immigrants and of international institutions generally.

National populations were rejecting the consequences of free-market economic globalisation, which had curtailed the political power of nation-states and their parliaments, and placed it in the hands of EU bureaucrats and unelected international business tycoons who could transfer resources across frontiers at the click of a mouse, regardless of the needs and wishes of local communities.

There is, though, another reason for the government's stubborn adherence to inappropriate remedies: that is because the neo-liberal market doctrines are overwhelmingly in the interest of the already wealthy and powerful. This factor has given those doctrines a powerful grip on our national media and an almost invincible hold on the practices of government officials, corporations and financial institutions all over the country. The result is an ideological syndrome which operates like Soviet Communist ideology, regardless of the implications for the welfare of ordinary human beings.

A lurid symptom of the consequences was the Grenfell Tower fire of the night of 14–15 June 2017, in which 72 people died and a further 70 were injured. Only five years earlier, during a refit, the Royal Borough of Kensington and Chelsea, practising financial rectitude, had deliberately rejected fireproof external cladding in favour of a somewhat cheaper non-fireproof version, something they were enabled to do by recent relaxations in building regulations. The risks of this decision were exacerbated by the fact that the tower's only evacuation route was down a single central staircase. The tenants of the tower, mostly poorer and minority-ethnic people, had reacted by raising concerns about the fire dangers. They had considered taking legal action against the council, but reportedly were prevented from doing so by recent cuts in legal aid. It later transpired that some 600 high-rise blocks in the UK had similar cladding – 57 in Glasgow alone. In some of them *residents*, rather than the government, the local council or the construction firms, were asked to pay the considerable cost of refurbishment.

After the fire, the government promised that funds would be provided for those who had lost their homes in it, and that all would be rehoused as close as possible to Grenfell Tower within three weeks. In actual fact, nearly a year later only 74 out of 210 households had been permanently rehoused. The rest were still living in temporary accommodation or in hotel rooms, mostly whole families to one room. Kensington and Chelsea, the richest borough in the UK, had not even taken the step of compulsorily purchasing premises that were unoccupied in order to rehouse families.[16] The whole episode suggested that the government and the local authority had mentally assigned Grenfell tenants to the category of second-class citizens, with inferior financial and legal status compared to the more affluent property owners living in some cases only a few yards away from them. The effect was especially dramatic in Kensington, where some of London's poorest people lived in high-rise blocks of flats, almost around the corner from fabulously wealthy Russian oligarchs and the sumptuous embassies around Kensington Palace.

Even without such apocalyptic scenarios, the disruption to stable routines and to household budgets, the restriction of access to the law, the impoverishment of collectively provided facilities – all these deprivations loosened the bonds of attachment and routine confidence in the future which most of us take for granted most of the time, and which are the underpinning of democracy and civil society. Not many families follow politics closely, but most have become aware of the gradually increasing disentitlements imposed on them by a national government yielding to the demands of global finance. They also notice that the already wealthy are actually augmenting their wealth at the same time, apparently at everyone else's expense. By 2017, figures showed that FTSE chief executive officers were earning 386 times the national living wage, or more specifically 132 times more than the average police officer, 140 times more than a schoolteacher, 165 times more than a nurse, and 312 times more than a care worker.[17] Moreover, inherited wealth had become a far better determinant of social and economic status than either exceptional talent or hard work.[18] Those with inherited wealth could expect to have it protected and enhanced by dedicated, discreet and extremely confidential wealth managers, handpicked for their trustworthy qualities.[19] Much of it would be placed in minimally regulated private equity funds, hedge funds or in tax havens (many of them in Switzerland or in British dependencies), where it would be concealed from the tax authorities.[20]

The victims of this process feel that the government has violated the tacit social contract that holds democracies together. The result has been summarised by a former staunch supporter of neo-liberal globalisation, the *Financial Times* columnist Martin Wolf. In recent years he has modified his views and now diagnoses a serious mismatch between the current mode of free market capitalism and democracy:

> In democratic societies, a tacit bargain exists between elites and the rest of society. The latter say to the former: we will accept your power, prestige and prosperity, but only if we prosper too. A huge crisis dissolves that bargain. The elites come to be seen as incompetent, rapacious or, in this case, both.

He adds that globalised elites have

> become ever more detached from the countries that produced them. In the process, the glue that binds democracy – the notion of citizenship – has weakened. . . . The loss of confidence in the competence and probity of elites inevitably reduces trust in democratic legitimacy. People feel even more than before that the country is not being governed for them, but for a narrow segment of well-connected insiders who reap most of the gains and, when things go wrong, are not just shielded from loss but impose massive costs on everybody else.[21]

This is a pretty good description of what has been happening to Western societies for several decades, and of what has propelled populist parties into the foreground of politics. Why in an era of increasing economic globalisation and increased mobility around the world should so many people react by demanding the reassertion of national distinctiveness? At the heart of the explanation for this apparent anomaly lies social trust.[22] I shall concentrate here on two forms of social trust in particular: trust in money and economic institutions, and trust derived from the norms of national culture and national institutions. I shall argue that the symbolic attraction of the nation is far stronger than that of the economy – which is why people will often vote in ways detrimental to their economic interests.

The divisions in society resulting from 'austerity' have been summed up by the German political economist, Wolfgang Streeck, who believes globalised free markets are incompatible with liberal democracy. He labels the two categories *Staatsvolk* and *Marktvolk*. The former are the democratic electorate who choose between the main parties' manifestos and leaders and who depend on the safety nets provided by the state; the latter are the financial markets, who guarantee investors' financial security by demanding from governments that they prove their reliability as borrowers. Streeck lays out the main features, demands and expectations of the two categories as follows:

Staatsvolk	*Marktvolk*
national	international
citizens	investors
civil rights	contractual claims
voters	creditors
elections (periodic)	auctions (continual)
loyalty	'confidence'
public opinion	interest rates
public services	debt service[23]

It is evident that the ongoing development and separation of these two categories will tend to generate increasing inequality, since the *Staatsvolk*, more dependent on public services and welfare benefits provided by the state or local government, will tend from the outset to be poorer and more disadvantaged than the *Marktvolk*, and will become progressively more so.

The financial crash of 2007–8 intensified resentments which had been mounting for a decade or two already. The unjustifiable inequalities it exacerbated severely undermined confidence in the political and economic system as a whole and provided a perfect setting for the rise of populist parties. They stood both for the traditionally right-wing ideals of national greatness, restriction of immigration and resistance to international institutions, yet also for the traditionally left-wing cause of generous welfare benefits.

In the UK, the leading populist role was taken by the UK Independence Party. In a futile attempt to prevent them eating into the Conservative vote, Prime Minister Cameron called a referendum for June 2016 on Britain's membership in the European Union. A majority of the electorate voted to leave it. This was the first time that any nation (with the partial exception of Greenland, a Danish federal territory) had opted to quit what had hitherto seemed an inexorably expanding supranational organisation. The margin of the Brexiteers' victory was not huge (51.9 per cent against 48.1 per cent), but it was definite. Examination of the voting patterns revealed that the vote for Remain was highest (57 per cent) in the two top social strata (As and Bs), lower (49 per cent) in the middle (C1s) and at its minimum (36 per cent) in the lowest strata (C2s, Ds and Es). The main fault lines, however, were not social class, but education and age. Sixty-eight per cent of voters with completed higher education voted Remain, while 70 per cent of those who never advanced beyond GCSE (basic secondary school graduation) voted Leave. Of people over 65 years of age, 64 per cent voted Leave, and 36 per cent Remain; while of those aged 18–24, 71 per cent voted Remain and only 29 per cent Leave.[24] The greatest contrasts thus depended on level of education and on stage of life rather than on social class as such, though of course those with better education tend anyway to belong to a higher social class; furthermore, older people will tend to have been less well educated. It is noteworthy too that, while the Remain campaign concentrated on economic arguments, the Leave campaign put questions of identity, national sovereignty and immigration at the forefront, claiming that Britain was losing control of its own frontiers, its nationhood and its political system. 'Give us back our nation!' summed up their campaign in a few words.[25]

Streeck's *Marktvolk/Staatsvolk* dichotomy roughly corresponds to the dichotomy expounded by another thinker concerned with the condition of contemporary British democracy: in a recent book, David Goodhart distinguishes between 'Anywhere' people and 'Somewhere' people.[26]

The people Goodhart classifies as Anywheres are animated by what he calls 'progressive individualism' – that is, they value individual freedom very highly and are prepared to accept its social corollaries. Their worldview 'places a high value on autonomy, mobility and novelty, and a much lower value on group identity, tradition and national social contracts (faith, flag and family)'. They 'are comfortable with immigration, European integration and the spread of human rights legislation, all of which tend to dilute the claims of national citizenship'. By contrast, the Somewheres hold a worldview which Goodhart calls 'decent populism' (though he notes that a small minority of 'hard authoritarians' among them do not qualify as 'decent'). They 'are more socially conservative and communitarian by instinct.... They feel uncomfortable about many aspects of cultural and economic change – such as mass immigration, an achievement society in which they struggle to achieve, the reduced status of non-graduate employment and more fluid gender roles.'[27] They react against both forms of 'double liberalism'.

Drawing on recent opinion polls, Goodhart observes that in recent years more than half of the British people have agreed with the statement 'Britain has changed in recent times beyond recognition. It sometimes feels like a foreign country, and this makes me feel uncomfortable.'[28] One cause of this feeling has been the recent steep growth in immigration: there were approximately 1 million immigrants from EU countries living in Britain in the late 1990s, whereas by 2016 there were 3.3 million.[29] Somewheres are not totally opposed to immigration, but feel there are too many immigrants in the country, that their ubiquity has changed the country beyond recognition, and that their presence has put unacceptable strains on the NHS, the education system, the social welfare budget and the stock of housing, especially in certain localities. Moreover, successive governments have failed to identify the locations under particular strain and help them with extra resources. The perception takes root that immigrants have come to Britain only to claim welfare benefits without having paid their share into the system first. Their dress, their food, their music, their customs and their religion (often Islam) feel alien and even threatening to native Brits, especially in certain towns (usually economically disadvantaged ones) in which immigrants have clustered in large numbers, and in some cases have recreated Pakistani, Bangladeshi or Somali communities as distinct ghetto-like areas. Islamist terrorism has naturally exacerbated this hostile perception.[30]

The term 'nation-state' has two halves. The state underpins the fiscal covenant, while the nation offers a sense of community and the symbolic links which promote generalised social trust. Consider for a moment what the nation symbolises. It is the largest collective – typically many millions of people – with which the individual can feel a sense of community solidarity. A nation is a huge aggregation, each of whose members can know personally only a tiny proportion of its other members. Imagining the unknown members as people to whom one can extend at least a preliminary presumption of trust and with whom one can engage more readily than with those outside the nation's borders requires a symbolic repertoire capable of summing up the nation's identity and projecting it to all its members. A shared language greatly eases mutual understanding and can facilitate the settling of conflicts. A nation can be symbolically evoked through its various emblems: the national flag, the national anthem, a portrait of the head of state. Its ceremonies – connected with anniversaries or occasions of rejoicing or mourning – give people an opportunity to mingle with each other in a heightened emotional setting, in some cases enhanced by the liturgy of a distinctive religion. A shared history or folklore provides points of reference for conversation or public discourse. A common culture in literature, music or the visual arts, communicates feelings connected with the shared experience of homeland.[31]

Symbols are more powerful and more motivating than self-interest. That is one reason why many people in the Brexit referendum voted against their own economic interest (though of course it is also true that calculating one's own long-term economic interest is difficult). Moreover, symbols are especially suited to communication through social media, which as a result have provided further impetus to populist politics. The prevalence of social media in recent years has greatly reduced the incidence of public meetings as well as of membership of collective organisations such as political parties. While it is possible to organise collective activities such as strikes and demonstrations through Twitter and Facebook, the prior communication of the individuals involved is minimal. For these reasons, nowadays class identity has totally lost its connection with political party voting.[32]

Social media also tend to act as an 'echo chamber'. That is, individuals receive the kind of news they want to hear, usually amplified for good measure, and the kind of political commentary whose lines of argument they already find congenial. Extremist content – chauvinist, racist, misogynist – is disseminated with minimal restriction, while moderate, nuanced or complex comments are drowned out. In a parody of Habermas's 'public sphere', public discussion tends to proceed in closed boxes of strongly held and often exaggerated opinions without differentiated mutual debate. This is the milieu in which 'fake news' and 'post-truth' assertions become apparently valid currency. These are all symptoms of fragmented social trust.[33]

What then is to be done? We have seen that the application of Keynesian theory can cause serious problems: it can provide impetus for an inflationary situation that it cannot deal with. However, the remedies launched in the 1970s and stubbornly adhered to up to the present generate even more serious problems – indeed, threaten to destroy liberal democracy itself.

At the heart of any recovery must be massive investment in the existing strengths of our economy, to ensure its future place in the world, and in the facilities that the British people need – above all, housing (applying new environment-friendly technology), infrastructure and green industry. This investment should be handled not directly by the Treasury, but by a National Investment Bank, probably bolstered by Treasury guarantees of some kind. The bank would have no difficulty in attracting investment: there is a lot of money sloshing around in the British economy, some of it going to tax havens, and some into the overblown real estate market. Insurance companies and pension funds are desperate for investment opportunities offering a reliable and reasonably good return. But if yet more investment is needed, there is no reason why governments should not print new money, provided it goes into producing genuine new wealth, not simply increasing the price of existing assets – as was the main result of existing 'quantitative easing' programmes.

Such investment would need to be informed by a well-designed industrial policy, since misplaced investment would lead only to inflation. Since the 1970s, state industrial policy has been more or less taboo, but there is no inherent reason why that should be so. There are many areas in which innovation offers prospects: artificial intelligence, biotechnology, nanotechnology, 3D printing, materials science, and so on. They will all require a serious research and development input which universities and leading companies should be well placed to provide. As far as possible, these new ventures should be sited outside the 'golden triangle' of London and south-east England, in the regions which have suffered worst in what for them has been a very long recession. The rail line HS2 (if it is ultimately built) should be quickly succeeded – or better still replaced – by HS3 from Liverpool via Manchester to Sheffield and Leeds, with eventual extensions to Hull and York. This would link great cities at present plagued by poor communications with everywhere except London.

This kind of revival should be accompanied by a reform of the structure of British corporations. The history of corporations shows that limited liability was necessitated in order to encourage investment in innovative, high-risk enterprises, since investors could not be expected to chance their entire property in such investments. In the nineteenth century, railways would never have been built without limited liability.[34]

But much economic activity does not entail such risks. Health centres, public utilities, public transport, educational institutions and housing do not need daring innovation and seldom incur serious risks, so they do not need to be run as profit-maximising, share-value-driven companies. Rather, they need to be steady, reliable performers offering good service to the public. At the moment even corporations conducting such public functions are structured so as to maximise 'shareholder value' – that is, the products of their successes go to their directors and shareholders, while the costs of their failures are borne mainly by unsecured creditors, employees, customers, those who live in the surrounding areas and, when necessary, by the taxpayer. Corporations have a public purpose: that is why, when they entail risk, they are allowed the privilege of joint-stock ownership and limited liability. They should not abuse that privilege for rewards which go to the very few. They should be reformed to reflect their multifaceted public role. There are many proposals for doing this currently being discussed by communitarian associations, and they should be taken seriously.[35]

The restoration of social security benefits cannot be accomplished overnight but must be a declared aim of parliament from the outset. Investment will create new jobs, with the result that the unemployed and poorly paid will come off benefits and begin to pay taxes. Their product will also have its own value. This is the 'multiplier' of which Keynes spoke, and it tends to promote economic growth. Gradually, moreover, employees will begin to feel that they have a real place in the community and in the productive economy.

In addition, there is no reason other than unimaginative and selfish dogma why taxes should not be raised. The most productive tax would probably be a land value tax. This would be complex to set up, but it would bring enormous benefits. Land cannot be transferred to the Virgin Islands. Moreover, its equitable taxation would encourage better use of land, especially vacant land with planning permission for housing. Britain should cooperate with other countries, including those in the EU, in discovering the true beneficiary ownership of opaquely managed companies registered in tax havens and in requiring them to register their profits on territories where they operate. They could then be taxed in the same way that indigenous companies are (and other countries would enjoy the same benefit). This is something that a single country cannot do on its own: targeted companies would simply smartly transfer their profits to a more compliant jurisdiction.

In short, the situation is extremely serious, but it is not hopeless. Keynesianism has its problems, but those generated by the globalised and financialised free market are much more dangerous to liberal democracy. Intelligent and determined reform of our economic structures would enable the British state and society to deliver the kind of economic and community benefits which are promised by populist parties but cannot possibly be achieved by the methods they propose. One of the principal strengths of democracy, compared to authoritarianism, is its flexibility and its capacity to respond – albeit often belatedly – to unforeseen challenges and dangers.[36] It certainly needs that strength now.

Notes

1 Patrick Deneen, *Why Liberalism Failed* (New Haven, CT: Yale University Press, 2018), 3, 179.
2 For a convincing argument that Gorbachev's reforms were the decisive precipitant, see Archie Brown, *The Gorbachev Factor* (Oxford: Oxford University Press, 1997). Myself, I believe the final precipitant was the clash between the Russian Republic and the Soviet Union. For a full statement of this argument, see Geoffrey Hosking, *Rulers and Victims: The Russians in the Soviet Union* (Cambridge, MA: The Belknap Press of Harvard University Press, 2006).
3 The passing of this system was lamented by Tony Judt in his *Ill Fares the Land: A Treatise on our Present Discontents* (London: Allen Lane, 2010).
4 The best concise summary of Keynesian theory is Robert Skidelsky, *Keynes: The Return of the Master* (London: Allen Lane, 2009).
5 Simon Clarke, *Keynesianism, Monetarism and the Crisis of the State* (Aldershot, UK: Edward Elgar, 1988), chapter 11; David Marquand, *Mammon's Kingdom: An Essay on Britain, Now* (London: Allen Lane, 2014), 33, 43–5.
6 Sue Jaffer, Susanna Knaudt, and Nicholas Morris, 'Failures of Regulation and Governance', in *Capital Failure: Rebuilding Trust in Financial Services*, ed. Nicholas Morris and David Vines (Oxford: Oxford University Press, 2014), 121.
7 Emma Rothschild, *Economic Sentiments: Adam Smith, Condorcet, and the Enlightenment* (Cambridge, MA: Harvard University Press, 2001).
8 Report of the Parliamentary Committee on Work and Pensions, London, 16 May 2018, summary, paragraphs 1, 2, 10, 39, 50.
9 Jonathan Ford, 'A Greedy Giant out of Control', *Prospect,* November 2008, 22–8.
10 Michael J. Clowes, *The Money Flood: How Pension Funds Revolutionized Investing* (New York: John Wiley & Sons, 2000), 277; OECD statistics, accessed 11 May 2017, stats.oecd.org/wbos/Index.aspx?usercontext=sourceoecd.
11 Robert Gilpin, *The Challenge of Global Capitalism: The World Economy in the 21st Century* (Princeton, NJ: Princeton University Press, 2000), 140–1.
12 Graham Turner, *The Credit Crunch: Housing Bubbles, Globalisation and the Worldwide Economic Crisis* (London: Pluto Press, 2008); Gillian Tett, *Fool's Gold: How Unrestrained Greed Corrupted a Dream, Shattered Global Markets and Unleashed a Catastrophe* (London: Abacus, 2010), especially chapter 15.
13 Andrew Clark, 'Greenspan – I Was Wrong About the Economy. Sort of', *The Guardian*, 23 October 2008, accessed 12 May 2018, www.theguardian.com/business/2008/oct/24/economics-creditcrunch-federal-reserve-greenspan.
14 Office for National Statistics, *UK Government Debt and Deficit: September 2018*, Figure 1, accessed 11 June 2017, www.ons.gov.uk/economy/governmentpublicsectorandtaxes/publicspending/bulletins/ukgovernmentdebtanddeficitforeurostatmaast/september2017.
15 Office for National Statistics, *Report on UK Government Debt and Deficits,* December 2017; House of Commons Briefing Paper 7584, 10 May 2018.
16 Chris Johnston, 'Grenfell: Council Seeks New Powers to Acquire Unused Properties', *The Guardian*, 22 May 2018, accessed 11 June 2017, www.theguardian.com/uk-news/2018/oct/06/grenfell-kensington-chelsea-council-unused-properties.

17   Equality Trust report, March 2017, accessed 4 December 2017, www.equalitytrust.org.uk/paytracker.
18   With a few specialised exceptions such as pop singers and international footballers. For a detailed presentation of the thesis that inherited wealth offers better returns than exceptional talent or hard work, see Thomas Piketty, *Capital in the Twenty-First Century,* trans. Arthur Goldhammer (Cambridge, MA: Belknap Press of Harvard University Press, 2014).
19   Brooke Harrington, *Capital without Borders: Wealth Managers and the One Percent* (Cambridge, MA: Harvard University Press, 2016).
20   Philip Coggan, *Paper Promises: Money, Debt and the New World Order* (London: Penguin Books, 2012), 153–4, 189–91; Coggan, *The Money Machine: How the City Works*, rev. ed. (London: Penguin Books, 2009), 82–90; Nicholas Shaxson, *Treasure Islands: Tax Havens and the Men Who Stole the World* (London: Bodley Head, 2011).
21   Martin Wolf, *The Shifts and the Shocks: What We've Learned – and Have Still to Learn – from the Financial Crisis* (London: Allen Lane, 2014), 351–2.
22   On social trust, see my *Trust: A History* (Oxford: Oxford University Press, 2014), especially chapter 2.
23   Wolfgang Streeck, *How Will Capitalism End? Essays on a Failing System* (London: Verso, 2016), 124.
24   'How Britain Voted', accessed 11 August 2017, yougov.co.uk/news/2016/06/27/how-britain-voted/.
25   David Goodhart, *The Road to Somewhere: The Populist Revolt and the Future of Politics* (London: Hurst, 2017), 19–26.
26   Goodhart, *Road*.
27   Goodhart, *Road*, 5–6.
28   Goodhart, *Road,* 2–3.
29   ONS dataset, 'Population of the United Kingdom by country of birth and nationality', August 2016, quoted in Goodhart, *Road*, 122–5.
30   Goodhart, *Road*, 129–31.
31   The power of national symbols is well summed up in Benedict Anderson, *Imagined Communities: Reflections on the Origin and Spread of Nationalism*, rev. ed. (London: Verso, 1991), and Anthony D. Smith, *National Identity* (London: Penguin Books, 1991).
32   Lecture by David Sanders, 'The UK's changing party landscape', British Academy, 4 July 2017.
33   'I can haz all your votes', *Economist*, 4 November 2017, 21–6.
34   James Taylor, *Creating Capitalism: Joint-Stock Enterprise in British Politics and Culture, 1800–1870* (Woodbridge, UK: The Boydell Press, 2006).
35   Colin Mayer, *Firm Commitment: Why the Corporation Is Failing Us and How to Restore Trust in It* (Oxford: Oxford University Press, 2013), especially 32–4, 63–4. Mayer recommends the creation of 'trust firms', of which the cooperative enterprise is an example: see 199–205.
36   David Runciman, *The Confidence Trap: A History of Democracy in Crisis from World War One to the Present* (Princeton, NJ: Princeton University Press, 2013), especially 106.

Bibliography

Anderson, Benedict. *Imagined Communities: Reflections on the Origin and Spread of Nationalism.* Rev. ed. London: Verso, 1991.
Brown, Archie. *The Gorbachev Factor.* Oxford: Oxford University Press, 1997.
Clark, Andrew. 'Greenspan – I Was Wrong About the Economy. Sort of'. *The Guardian*. 23 October 2008. Accessed 12 May 2018, www.theguardian.com/business/2008/oct/24/economics-creditcrunch-federal-reserve-greenspan.
Clarke, Simon. *Keynesianism, Monetarism and the Crisis of the State.* Aldershot, UK: Edward Elgar, 1988.
Clowes, Michael J. *The Money Flood: How Pension Funds Revolutionized Investing.* New York: John Wiley & Sons, 2000.
Coggan, Philip. *The Money Machine: How the City Works.* Rev. ed. London: Penguin Books, 2009.

Coggan, Philip. *Paper Promises: Money, Debt and the New World Order*. London: Penguin Books, 2012.
Deneen, Patrick. *Why Liberalism Failed*. New Haven, CT: Yale University Press, 2018.
Equality Trust Report, March 2017, accessed 7 July 2017, www.equalitytrust.org.uk/paytracer.
Ford, Jonathan. 'A greedy giant out of control'. *Prospect,* November 2008.
Gilpin, Robert. *The Challenge of Global Capitalism: The World Economy in the 21st Century*, Princeton, NJ: Princeton University Press, 2000.
Goodhart, David. *The Road to Somewhere: The Populist Revolt and the Future of Politics.* London: Hurst, 2017.
Harrington, Brooke. *Capital without Borders: Wealth Managers and the One Percent.* Cambridge, MA: Harvard University Press, 2016.
Hosking, Geoffrey. *Rulers and Victims: The Russians in the Soviet Union*. Cambridge, MA: The Belknap Press of Harvard University Press, 2006.
Hosking, Geoffrey. *Trust: A History*. Oxford: Oxford University Press, 2014.
House of Commons Briefing Paper, 7584, 10 May 2018.
'How Britain Voted'. Accessed 11 July 2017, yougov.co.uk/news/2016/06/27/how_britain_voted.
'I can haz all your votes'. *The Economist*, 4 November 2017.
Jaffer, Sue, Susanna Knaudt, and Nicholas Morris. 'Failures of Regulation and Governance'. In *Capital Failure: Rebuilding Trust in Financial Services,* edited by Nicholas Morris and David Vines. Oxford: Oxford University Press, 2014.
Johnston, Chris. 'Grenfell: Council Seeks New Powers to Acquire Unused Properties'. *The Guardian*. 22 May 2018. Accessed 11 June 2017, www.theguardian.com/uk-news/2018/oct/06/grenfell-kensington-chelsea-council-unused-properties.
Judt, Tony. *Ill Fares the Land: A Treatise on our Present Discontents*. London: Allen Lane, 2010.
Marquand, David. *Mammon's Kingdom: An Essay on Britain, Now*. London: Allen Lane, 2014.
Mayer, Colin. *Firm Commitment: Why the Corporation is Failing Us and How to Restore Trust in It*. Oxford: Oxford University Press, 2013.
OECD Statistics. Accessed 10 January 2018, stats.oecd.org/wbos/Index.aspx?usercontext=sourceoecd.
Office for National Statistics. *Report on UK Government Debt and Deficits*. London, December 2017.
Office for National Statistics. *UK Government Debt and Deficit: September 2018*. Figure 1. Accessed 11 June 2017, www.ons.gov.uk/economy/governmentpublicsectorandtaxes/publicspending/bulletins/ukgovernmentdebtanddeficitforeurostatmaast/september2017.
Parliamentary Committee on Work and Pensions: report, 16 May 2018.
Piketty, Thomas. *Capital in the Twenty-First Century*. Translated by Arthur Goldhammer. Cambridge, MA: Belknap Press of Harvard University Press, 2014.
Rothschild, Emma. *Economic Sentiments: Adam Smith, Condorcet and the Enlightenment*. Cambridge, MA: Harvard University Press, 2001.
Runciman, David. *The Confidence Trap: A History of Democracy in Crisis from World War One to the Present*. Princeton, NJ: Princeton University Press, 2013.
Shaxson, Nicholas. *Treasure Islands: Tax Havens and the Men who Stole the World*. London: Bodley Head, 2012.
Skidelsky, Robert. *Keynes: The Return of the Master*. London: Allen Lane, 2009.
Smith, Anthony D. *National Identity*, London: Penguin Books, 1991.
Streeck, Wolfgang. *How Will Capitalism End? Essays on a Failing System*. London: Verso, 2016.
Taylor, James. *Creating Capitalism: Joint-Stock Enterprise in British Politics and Culture, 1800–1870*. Woodbridge, UK: The Boydell Press, 2013.
Tett, Gillian. *Fool's Gold: How Unrestrained Greed Corrupted a Dream, Shattered Global Markets and Unleashed a Catastrophe*. London: Abacus, 2010.
Turner, Graham. *The Credit Crunch: Housing Bubbles, Globalisation and the Worldwide Economic Crisis*. London: Pluto Press, 2008.
Wolf, Martin. *The Shifts and the Shocks: What We've Learned – and Have Still to Learn – from the Financial Crisis*. London: Allen Lane, 2014.

9
Political alternatives on the Western Left
Podemos, Syriza, Sanders and Corbyn

Peter J. S. Duncan

The combined economic, social and ideological crisis which struck the West in 2008 ought to have meant victory for the left. But instead, all over Europe and in the United States, the traditional centre-left in most countries has lost power and appears weak.

This chapter will focus on four of the most effective formations on the left which have emerged in the wake of the crisis, challenging the centre-left: Podemos and Syriza in continental Europe, and the movements behind Bernie Sanders and Jeremy Corbyn in the Democratic Party and the Labour Party.

In most of the main West European countries, the old socialist and social-democratic parties are out of office and losing influence.

In France, the Parti Socialiste, at the end of the presidency of the Socialist François Hollande, failed to make the runoff in the 2017 presidential election, as the Front National (FN) took second place. In Germany, the Social-Democratic Party (SPD) is the junior partner in the coalition led by Angela Merkel's Christian Democratic Union (CDU), and in opinion polls now comes third behind the CDU and the Greens. In Italy, the Partito Democratica (PD), which developed out of the Partito Comunista Italiano (PCI), lost office to a right-populist alliance in March 2018. In Greece, the Pan-Hellenic Socialist Movement, PASOK, has all but disappeared; while in Spain, the Spanish Socialist Workers Party, PSOE, has struggled to hold on as the largest force on the left, but managed to form a minority government. In Sweden, the Social Democrats, who governed for most of the post-war period, won their lowest level of support for a century in the September 2018 elections, although still remained the largest party.

Portugal is an exception, where the Partido Socialista remains the dominant force on the left and since 2015 has led a coalition including the Communists and the Bloco de Esqueirda (Left Bloc) of radical socialists. This coalition has been seeking to mitigate the effects of an EU austerity-oriented bailout programme while under IMF supervision.

In Britain, the Labour Party was voted out of government in 2010 and lost two more elections in 2015 and 2017. The election of Corbyn as leader after the 2015 defeat has pushed the party sharply to the left and seriously frightened the wealthier sections of British society. The acceptability of socialist ideas in the United States has also grown significantly in the wake of Sanders' unsuccessful campaign for the Democratic nomination in 2016.

The most successful groups on the radical left on the European continent have been Syriza and Podemos. Both arose outside the traditional socialist parties, under the impact of the crisis. Syriza has been the senior partner in the Greek government since 2015. Podemos has challenged PSOE for the leadership of the Spanish left, with successes for its associates in Madrid and Barcelona.

This chapter will examine the growth and development of these four movements – Podemos, Syriza, the Sanders campaign and the movement behind Corbyn – since they appear to be the most successful radical groups in Western Europe and North America. Why did some of the movements develop within existing parties, while others emerged as new organisations? How did they grow? How did they approach identity politics? Did the way they organised prefigure the sort of society they wanted to create? How radical were their aims and programmes? Did they succeed in increasing support for a socialist society, as opposed to a capitalist society with egalitarian policies and a welfare state? In other words, have they succeeded in what the English socialist William Morris called 'making socialists', or, in Gramscian terms, in challenging the hegemony of capitalist ideology in their societies?

Valuable research has been done on how the radical left parties in Europe responded to the Western financial crisis. In particular, Luke March has written the monograph *Radical Left Parties in Europe* (2011) and coedited with Daniel Keith *Europe's Radical Left: From Marginality to the Mainstream?* (2016).[1] Both were written too early to analyse the important developments in and after 2015. A penetrating survey of three of the new movements emerging from the crisis – Occupy Wall Street, Movimento Cinque Stella (Five Star Movement) and Podemos – is by Marco Briziarelli and Susana Martinez Guillem. Entitled *Reviving Gramsci: Crisis, Communication, and Change* (2016), it locates these movements within what Antonio Gramsci described as an 'organic crisis' in which the hegemony of the ruling capitalist class is challenged.[2] *The Socialist Challenge Today: Syriza, Sanders, Corbyn,* by Leo Panitch and Sam Gindin (2018), reviews three of the movements discussed in this chapter.[3] Steve Richards' *The Rise of the Outsiders: How Mainstream Politics Lost its Way* (2017) examines the new movements of left and right and the decline of the centre-left and centre-right.[4]

The most substantial study of Podemos in English is Iñigo Errejón and Chantal Mouffe's *Podemos: In the Name of the People* (2016).[5] The movement's founder, Pablo Iglesias, has written *Politics in a Time of Crisis: Podemos and the Future of Democracy in Europe* (2015).[6] The most detailed study in English of Syriza is by Yanis Varoufakis, *Adults in the Room: My Battle with Europe's Deep Establishment* (2017).[7] This is a memoir of his time as finance minister in 2015. An independent analysis of Syriza's first months in power is Kevin Ovenden's *Syriza: Inside the Labyrinth* (2015).[8] Bernie Sanders' own *Our Revolution: A Future to Believe In* (2017) combines autobiography and political manifestos.[9] It is probably the most useful study of his presidential campaign. Heather Gautney's *Crashing the Party: From the Bernie Sanders Campaign to a Progressive Movement* (2018) is somewhat uncritical.[10] There is a substantial literature on Corbyn's rise to the leadership of the Labour Party and his subsequent performance. Particularly noteworthy are two books with a sympathetic but critical approach: Richard Seymour's *Corbyn: The Strange Rebirth of Radical Politics* (2016), and *The Corbyn Effect*, edited by Mark Perryman (2017).[11]

Debates about how to define socialism and new ways of getting there emerged after the 2008 Western financial crisis. The consequences of the crisis presented a new situation and new opportunities. Concerning the historical memory of the new movements, it was important that both Pablo Iglesias, the leader of Podemos (born in 1978), and Alexis Tsipras (born in 1974), who became the leader of Syriza, began their political careers within the Moscow-oriented communist movement, in the youth organisations of the Eurocommunist Spanish Communist Party (PCE) and the more traditional, vanguardist Greek Communist Party (KKE), respectively.[12] This trajectory equipped them with some understanding of historical debates about the relationship between the working class, its party and the state.

The 2008 crisis revived social struggles. They first evolved around single issues or particular economic sectors. Young people were especially involved, not least because many had not found a place in the labour market and were hit disproportionately around the globe. Within the EU, young people in southern member countries – Greece, Spain, Italy and Portugal – suffered most.

The year 2011 may be considered the beginning of the coalescence of these struggles into more general movements. The Arab Spring developed from the beginning of the year as popular movements against repressive regimes in Tunisia, Libya, Egypt, Syria and Bahrain. On 15 May, over 100,000 people demonstrated in 54 Spanish cities against politicians, bankers and what they termed *el Sistema*. This was the movement which became known as the *Indignados* (the outraged or indignant), based particularly on young, educated people.[13] A few days later appeared the *aganaktismenoi* (indignant citizens' movement), also known as the 'Squares' movement', in Greece. From September, the Occupy Wall Street campaign developed in the United States, further strengthened by campus protests against increased tuition fees. This movement, directed against the heart of finance capital, inspired 'Occupy the City' in London, in which scores of people lived for several weeks in tents outside St Paul's Cathedral. In Russia, hundreds of thousands demonstrated in the major cities in protest against fraud perpetrated on behalf of Vladimir Putin's United Russia party in the State Duma elections in December. Common to these protests was the new factor of the use of Internet platforms such as Twitter and Facebook, both to spread information about abuses in government and business and to organise and publicise protest actions.

These movements of political protest across different parts of the globe formed the background to the emergence of the four parties and movements which will be considered here. They appear in the order in which they became important.

Podemos: Left populism and centralisation

This section will show how a movement based on protests in the streets rose to become a major influence in Spanish national politics, able in concert with others to sack governments.

The background to the emergence of the *Indignados* in 2011 was anger at corruption in the Spanish political system, which extended even to the royal family. The two parties that alternated in power after the death of dictator General Francisco Franco in 1975, the conservative Partido Popular (PP) and the socialist PSOE, were losing support. The Eurocommunist PCE had already begun to decline with the transition to democracy and as far back as 1986 had created an alliance with other groups, the United Left (IU). A new centre-right group, *Ciudadanos* (Citizens), was gaining strength.

The rise of Podemos

Seeking to turn the *Indignados* into an electoral force, a number of left-wing groups, including the Trotskyist Anti-Capitalist Left, and intellectuals formed Podemos ('We can') in January 2014. From the start, the leader was the young, pony-tailed, charismatic Pablo Iglesias Turrión, one of a group of political scientists at Complutense University of Madrid who, following Ernesto Laclau,[14] were seeking to build a movement on the basis of populist rather than explicitly socialist or class-based appeals. Some of the group, such as Iñigo Errejón, also at Complutense and arguably the group's principal theoretician, had studied the experience of populism in Bolivia and Hugo Chavez's Venezuela.

In populist fashion, Podemos presented society as divided between 'us', the people, *la gente,* against 'them', the political and economic establishment, referred to as 'La Casta'.[15] Iglesias argued that the Spanish elites were, in Gramscian terms, facing an organic crisis of the loss of hegemony and that this had led to a regime crisis.[16] Podemos also opposed the Lisbon Treaty, increasing the powers of the EU, and Spain's membership of NATO. It argued, unlike the established parties, that political activity could be fun. Helped by Iglesias's status as a popular television presenter, Podemos succeeded in winning 8 per cent of the votes in the May 2014 elections to the European Parliament, doing especially well among the youth voters.

In the course of the first year of its existence, it grew to have the second largest membership of any party in Spain, behind the PP and overtaking PSOE. In November 2014, Podemos organised a 'Citizens' Assembly' to convert itself into a political party. This marked a turning point away from a more open, horizontal approach to organisation to a more centralised, vertical one and was achieved through the adoption of the structures by online voting; the leadership's proposals prevailed over those of a more horizontalist faction. This was followed by the adoption of the party executive by choice between slates rather than voting for individual candidates. The leadership's slate won, and the impression of a return to communist norms seemed reinforced by the election of Iglesias to the new post of general secretary. Alexandros Kioupkiolis, from the Aristotle

University of Thessaloniki, has argued that the stagnation which Podemos suffered after 2015 began with the introduction of the centralist practices within the party, at odds with its proclaimed aims for society.[17]

In its campaigning, however, Podemos retained an open attitude. In the elections in Spain's two largest cities, Madrid and Barcelona, in May and June 2015, it supported anti-austerity coalitions, Barcelona en Comú and Ahora Madrid, rather than standing in its own right. These coalitions had built support in particular by opposing the eviction of tenants who could not afford to pay their rent and mortgage-holders who could not keep up their payments. Neither won outright control of the city councils but formed majorities together with PSOE; and both their candidates for mayor were victorious.

Symbolically, both new mayors were women. Manuela Carmena in Madrid had been active in the communist underground under Franco's dictatorship. Ada Colau, 30 years her junior, was a founder of an anti-eviction group, Mortgage Victims' Platform, in Barcelona; she had once been arrested for occupying a bank in a protest. She spoke of 'feminine values' being applied to 'a deepening of democracy'.[18] Both Carmena and Colau lost office in the May 2019 elections, in Madrid to the resurgent right and in Barcelona to the Catalan Republican Left.

Ahead of the elections to the Cortes (lower house of parliament) of December 2015, Podemos aimed to overtake PSOE. On the way, it suggested joint primaries with the other left parties to agree on candidates; the other parties, including United Left, were unresponsive.[19] Youth unemployment reached 55 per cent in Spain in 2015.[20] Jobless young graduates and others had time to campaign for Podemos. In the elections, Podemos became the third largest party, with 20.65 per cent, behind the PP with 28.71 per cent and PSOE with 22.02 per cent. This effectively ended the two-party system and inaugurated a period of government instability. Another election was called for June 2016. Podemos formed an alliance of left-wing groups, Unidos Podemos ('United we can'), this time including United Left, but their combined vote rose only to 21.2 per cent, still behind PSOE.

Changing the government

Following this election, the PSOE leader, Pedro Sánchez, sought to form a government with the support of Podemos. In October 2016, however, the PSOE right wing overthrew Sánchez. They preferred to support a conservative PP government under Mariano Rojay than allow Podemos into power.

Podemos had to take a position on the issue of Catalonia when the Catalan government held a referendum on 1 October 2017 on the independence of the region from Spain. Barcelona, which with a high proportion of immigrants from other parts of Spain was broadly against independence, was also a centre of support for Podemos. The PP, PSOE and *Ciudadanos* declared the referendum illegal, and the PP government sent police to beat citizens peacefully queuing to take part in the vote. Podemos took a principled position, avoiding the national-populist temptation of supporting the government, while also refusing to support independence. Instead it urged both sides to find a peaceful compromise.

The PP government lasted until June 2018, when a court found the Popular Party guilty of a major act of corruption. Meanwhile, Sánchez had regained the PSOE leadership. He proposed a no-confidence motion on Rajoy in the Cortes. With the support of Podemos it passed. Iglesias then called on Sánchez to include Podemos in a coalition government led by PSOE, but Sánchez refused and formed a minority government, depending on the support of Podemos.

This apparently influential position for Podemos concealed the fact that it was going through a period of splits, stagnation and decline. Iglesias himself had faced and defeated a leadership challenge in February 2017 from the theoretician Iñigo Errejón. In May 2018 Iglesias came under fresh criticism from within the party for supposedly 'joining the bourgeoisie' after buying together with his partner, the parliamentary spokesperson of the party, a €600,000 house with a swimming pool outside Madrid on a 30-year mortgage. They responded by putting their positions to a special confidence vote of the membership, winning easily. By then support for Podemos in the country was down to 18 per cent.[21] The party was further weakened when Errejón left in January 2019. In the parliamentary elections held in the following April, the Unidos Podemos bloc won only 14 per cent of the vote, falling from 71 to 42 seats, while PSOE consolidated its leading position, winning 29 per cent of the vote.

The continuing refusal of Podemos to articulate an avowedly socialist position reinforces the view that it is a populist movement, although clearly oriented towards the left along the lines argued by Chantal Mouffe. It does not promote Spanish nationalism or anti-immigrant feeling, as right-wing populist movements do. It succeeds in attracting not only people on the left, but also those without ideology, even though the leaders are strongly influenced by Marxism. The political scientist David Bailey suggests that the leaders 'have become so focused on winning elections that their adherence to any particular set of political principles appears hard to discern'.[22] A further concern, in the populist tradition of a strong leader, is the high profile of the general secretary, Iglesias, and his apparent invincibility in his position. While all political leaders today can expect to have their personal lives examined under a microscope, mistakes on his part might cause lasting damage to Podemos.

In the meantime, while attracting young, educated people into electoral politics, its failure to analyse the class and systemic roots of the austerity policy it opposes means that it is unable to pose an alternative to capitalist hegemony; or even, in Morris's words, to 'make socialists'.

Syriza: Three victories and a retreat

Like Podemos, Syriza gained support rapidly under the impact of crisis, but unlike Podemos, it succeeded in entering government. Elected in January 2015 on a programme of opposition to the austerity measures to deal with the Greek debt crisis proposed by the 'troika' – the European Central Bank, the European Commission and the International Monetary Fund (IMF) – it secured further support for its resistance in a national referendum in July 2015. Yet within a day of the referendum result, the Syriza government capitulated to the troika and embarked on the harsh austerity programme that they demanded.

Why did Syriza succeed so well in propagating its policies and values, and why did it capitulate? Its resistance to austerity policies was popular. It will be argued that, at the same time, Syriza's commitment to Greece staying in the euro made it a hostage to the rules of the troika; and it failed to prepare the population for the sacrifices that a decisive clash with the Greek ruling class and the troika would entail.

The rise of Syriza

Unlike Podemos, Syriza was openly on the radical left. 'Syriza' is the Greek acronym for the Coalition of the Radical Left, formed in 2004 as an alliance of various ecological, communist, Trotskyist, Maoist and other left groups. Tsipras was elected leader in 2008.

Similarly to the situation in Spain, two parties had alternated in power in Greece since the overthrow of the colonels' dictatorship in 1974: the conservative New Democracy and the socialist PASOK. In May 2010, under the impact of the financial crisis, the PASOK government signed a bailout agreement with the troika. The loan was conditional on the application of an austerity programme of spending cuts and tax rises, known as the 'Memorandum'. In 2011, as austerity continued, and under the impetus of the *Indignados* in Spain, the *aganaktismenoi* appeared and began to occupy public squares. The *aganaktismenoi* were not only opposing austerity but also making political demands for more accountable and direct democracy. Whereas Podemos evolved from the movement on the streets, Syriza already existed when the *aganaktismenoi* emerged, and was able to support and interact with them.

PASOK's implementation of the Memorandum, first on its own and then from November 2011 in coalition with New Democracy, led to the haemorrhaging of its support. The communist party, the KKE, previously the largest party to the left of PASOK, was suspicious of the movement in the squares because it could not control them; it therefore lost influence. Syriza overtook both and became the largest opposition group in the elections of May and June 2012. Syriza's Electoral Declaration proclaimed: 'a socialism with freedom, a fully blossoming democracy where all citizens participate in decision making is the strategic aim'.[23]

Entrenched as the main opposition party, Syriza highlighted the struggles of different sectors of society against austerity, from employees of the broadcasting corporation which the government had closed down to the sacked cleaning ladies of the Ministry of Finance. It gave practical help to the victims of austerity too; it established food banks, known as Solidarity Clubs, all over Greece.

The majority of the Greek people strongly favoured remaining in the euro, despite the austerity policies, because of the association of the euro with political and economic stability and prosperity. Aware of this, Tsipras persuaded Syriza to abandon its opposition to the euro in 2012. Only in 2013 did Syriza transform itself from a coalition into a unitary party, but with an internal opposition, the Left Platform. They favoured leaving the euro and won 30 per cent of the Central Committee seats.

In September 2014 Tsipras unveiled the Thessaloniki Programme. It reflected pressure from the Left Platform. The programme promised the nationalisation of the banks, renegotiation of Greece's debt including a substantial write-off, and the reversal of austerity policies imposed under the Memorandum. All this was, however, to be subject to a balanced budget. The economist Yanis Varoufakis, who had agreed to become finance minister in a Syriza government, denounced the programme for promising more than could be achieved. He called on Syriza to face up to reality and promise, in the immediate term, only 'blood, sweat and tears' in the struggle to get the budget balanced. Tsipras's colleague Nikos Pappas explained to Varoufakis that in fact Varoufakis himself would author the real programme of action; Thessaloniki was only to rally the troops.[24]

It would seem that Tsipras was consciously deceiving the Syriza members and the voters about what a Syriza government would be able to do. In order to ensure their election, they were making promises that could not be fulfilled without a confrontation with the troika.

Varoufakis himself had a broad understanding of the economic crisis facing not only Greece but also European capitalism and the European Union as an institution. His fear was that capitalism might collapse in the crisis before an alternative had been prepared to replace it. Given the weakness of the left in Europe, as a self-styled 'erratic Marxist', he came to the conclusion that the left should seek to stabilise the situation. As he warned in an article written before entering politics:

> Europe's crisis is far less likely to give birth to a better alternative to capitalism than it is to unleash dangerously regressive forces that have the capacity to cause a humanitarian bloodbath, while extinguishing the hope for any progressive moves for generations to come. [. . .] we have a contradictory mission: to arrest the freefall of European capitalism in order to buy the time we need to formulate its alternative.[25]

Resisting the troika

Syriza easily won the election held in January 2015 with 36.3 per cent of the vote and 149 out of 300 seats. The KKE refused to endorse the Syriza project and remained in opposition. Instead of allying with the left-wing parties, Tsipras decided to form a coalition with a small right-wing radical populist group, the Independent Greeks (ANEL). Their 13 seats gave the new coalition a stable majority.

Naturally, Tsipras was criticised for allowing this right-wing group into office. What made the Independent Greeks the right partner for Tsipras was their implacable resistance to austerity; and they promised not to interfere with Syriza's strategy negotiating with the troika.[26] The presence of the Independent Greeks in the coalition also indicated that Syriza was not intending to embark on specifically socialist policies, and could reassure the Greek ruling class of this. This failure to confront entrenched domestic interests weakened Syriza's resistance to the troika.[27]

In the first week after the election, the government moved to stop privatisation, restore pensions, reintroduce the minimum wage, restore free prescriptions and hospital visits, and restore trade union rights. Greece's debt bailout had reached €240 billion, with the final tranche of €7.2 billion due in February to keep the government going. Tsipras appointed Varoufakis as finance minister. He announced that his ministry's cleaning ladies would be among those public employees who would get their jobs back.[28]

The troika continued to insist on the application of the Memorandum. Varoufakis made clear that he wanted to compromise with the troika. Ahead of his first meeting with the EU finance ministers' Eurogroup on 11 February, he said Syriza was willing to implement 70 per cent of the Memorandum. This provoked a sharp protest from the head of the Left Platform, Energy Minister Panagiotis Lafazanis. At the Eurogroup meeting, German Finance Minister Wolfgang Schäuble announced, 'Elections cannot be allowed to change economic policy.'[29]

The Syriza leadership believed that they held a valuable negotiating card: the threat to leave the euro if Brussels was too unreasonable. A key problem with this was that the population was wedded to the euro; and Tsipras was not willing to challenge this publicly. Moreover, as Varoufakis has argued, already in 2012 Schäuble had decided that Greece should be forced out of the euro as an example.[30] Schäuble's refusal to negotiate on the terms of the Memorandum meant deadlock; but this was broken the following day by the intervention of Angela Merkel. She wished Greece to remain in the eurozone, and therefore wanted an agreement and overruled Schäuble.

The reform programme which Varoufakis submitted made a number of concessions to the troika. The raising of the minimum wage was postponed, early retirements would be halted and privatisations would not be reversed. Tsipras sought to maintain domestic support by introducing free electricity and food stamps to the poorest in Greece, further antagonising the creditors.[31] The prime minister's tactics seem to have been to make concessions to the troika formally, but delay their implementation in practice, while presenting himself domestically to have been more successful in the negotiations than he had been. At the same time, he sought to enlarge his negotiating freedom by threatening to default on the IMF debt, when in fact he had no intention of doing so.[32]

Trying to force Syriza to accept its programme, the troika threatened to deny Greece the $7.2 billion of bailout money. Without this, Greece would be unable to meet its due payments and would be declared bankrupt.[33] On 26 June the troika rejected the latest offer from Tsipras of substantial tax increases and presented an ultimatum. Greece had to implement the troika's programme, with harsher tax increases and a rise in the retirement age to 67 by 2022, in exchange for a five-month extension to the bailout. If the prime minister did not agree, the bailout would end in four days.

The referendum and after

Tsipras responded that night by calling a referendum on the bailout terms. The troika was joined by an alliance of German, French and Italian social-democratic leaders, warning that a vote against the terms would mean that Greece would have to leave the euro. Tsipras, Varoufakis and the government nevertheless asked Greeks to vote 'No' to the troika's terms, and Tsipras warned that the government would resign if the vote was 'Yes'.[34]

The referendum campaign split Greece, with right-wing politicians and business leaders accusing Syriza of wanting to bring back the drachma. Trade unions and the left organised demonstrations and strikes for a 'No' vote. Defying Germany and Brussels, Syriza at the referendum on 5 July won a crushing 'No' vote of 61.3 per cent, including 80 per cent of voters under 34. Tsipras now sought the backing of the opposition parties in his efforts to have the debts rescheduled. Varoufakis resigned, blaming pressure from the creditors. Tsipras gave in to the political and economic pressure from Berlin and Brussels and offered a new programme of tough austerity measures to get another bailout and stay in the euro.[35]

Seeking to explain why his colleagues had capitulated to the creditors so soon after winning an impressive victory at the referendum, Varoufakis has argued that Tsipras feared that if they persisted, the Greek right wing would organise a coup through the president and the security services. Instead, Tsipras wanted to continue the policy of pretending to cooperate with the troika while preparing resistance.[36] Whether or not Tsipras really feared a coup, it is undeniable that he would have lost popular support if he had allowed Greece to be pushed out of the euro.

On 13 July, after another ultimatum, this time from Merkel and Hollande, he signed up to the 'Third Memorandum' to gain access to €86 billion in bailout funds. This austerity programme was worse than what he had earlier rejected, and the government conceded control over whole areas of economic and social policy to the troika.[37]

The left wing of Syriza refused to support the deal; in August, with 40 Syriza MPs including Varoufakis rebelling, the programme was passed with support from opposition parties. Varoufakis argued that the deal would make the economy worse and allow Greek oligarchs to maintain their control over it.[38] Lafazanis led the Left Platform out of Syriza and formed Popular Unity. Having lost his majority, Tsipras resigned as prime minister; but the following month he led Syriza to victory in a general election, with 35.5 per cent, only slightly less than in January. Tsipras formed another coalition with the Independent Greeks. He had managed to persuade sufficient numbers of voters that if austerity was the price of staying in the euro, he could be relied on to minimise the impact on ordinary people.[39]

Over the following three years, Syriza presided over more economic decline and cutbacks. Finally, in June 2018 it reached another agreement with the troika, deferring some debt repayments and extending another €15 billion in credits, but marking the official end of the bailout. By then GDP had fallen 26 per cent since 2010, wages nearly 20 per cent and pensions 70 per cent. Unemployment was at 20 per cent and youth unemployment at 43 per cent. Greece promised to maintain a defined budget surplus, excluding debt repayment, until 2060. Syriza was trailing New Democracy in the opinion polls.[40]

The personality of Tsipras was an important factor in building up support for Syriza. Faith in Syriza and in Tsipras himself led to his election victory even after his capitulation to the troika following the referendum. The party's strategy, however, had been flawed from the start. Instead of telling voters in 2012 that there was a choice between austerity imposed from outside and leaving the euro, which at least in the short term would have made things worse, Tsipras made promises he knew he could not keep. He would not allow Greece to be forced out of the euro, although for negotiating purposes he was willing to pretend that he was. Varoufakis, on the other hand, was open about the depth of the crisis and the resulting dilemma, and he was prepared to leave the euro if it was the only way to escape the creditors' dictates. But he was unwilling to seek to bring down the EU structures, which he considered worth defending against chaos and the threat from the right. Neither Tsipras nor Varoufakis were ready to use the Greek crisis to argue for a transition to socialism.

In Spain and Greece, radical leftists believed that the main socialist parties were too enmeshed in the existing system to be agents of social change, and were sufficiently discredited to make the new movements, Podemos and Syriza, serious contenders for power.

In the United States and Britain, on the other hand, the two major parties of right and left were well entrenched. The first-past-the-post electoral systems tended to hinder the development of third parties. On the left, both the Labour Party and the Democratic Party could claim achievements in social reform, and both had strong links with the trade union movement. But the Labour Party's commitment to creating a socialist society was lukewarm, and under its leader Tony Blair removed the traditional aim of an economy based on 'common ownership' from the party constitution in 1995. The Democratic Party never had a socialist orientation and had strong ties to American business. So in both countries, socialists have debated for more than a century about whether it was possible to work inside them, or to create a separate socialist party. In 2015, two white-haired men attempted to move both these parties to the left.[41]

Bernie Sanders and the Democratic Socialists of America: A political revolution?

The American left is still divided between those who fight for their ideas and for elective office through the Democratic Party, in some cases through the Democratic Socialists of America (DSA), and those who maintain their purity in isolated groups or as independent individuals. It is therefore not surprising that Bernie Sanders, the self-described 'democratic socialist' Independent US senator from Vermont, has had an ambiguous relationship with the Democratic Party. As well as seeking to influence Democratic opinion, most obviously in his campaign for the 2016 Democratic presidential nomination, he has sought to appeal to campaigners and members of a variety of disadvantaged groups outside the party. This section will analyse Sanders' campaign and ask whether, despite its ultimate defeat, it had a more lasting impact. First, it will discuss the reasons why the campaign gained momentum but did not succeed. Then it will consider the impact on the DSA.

Bernie Sanders' campaign: Victory in defeat

In 2008, the financial crisis helped bring Barack Obama to office. Although the first Black president was socially progressive, he tended to follow neoliberal economic policies. This was clear in his advocacy of the Trans-Pacific Partnership, which not only aimed to bring down trade barriers but also shifted power from states to corporations. Extra-parliamentary movements gained strength: in response to the crisis, Occupy Wall Street in 2011, campaigns in support of raising the minimum wage, and Black Lives Matter in opposition to police killings of African Americans. Obama was re-elected in 2012, but in the November 2014 midterm elections the Democrats suffered severe losses. Obama's policies were not helping some of his core supporters and inequality was increasing.

The Democratic Party establishment settled on the former senator and Secretary of State, Hillary Clinton, to be the 2016 presidential candidate, and to become the first woman president. While advocating public health insurance, she had generally favoured pro-business, neo-liberal economic policies, deregulation, and open trading. Socially she mixed with the wealthy.

On 26 May 2015, at the age of 73, Senator Sanders announced his candidacy for the Democratic presidential nomination. His speech was entitled 'Today we begin a political revolution'. Using the term 'middle class' in the American sense, to mean the big majority of the population between the wealthy and the very poor, Sanders outlined his programme. He declared it was time for 'millions of working families to come together, to revitalize American democracy, to end the collapse of the American middle class' and bring their descendants 'health, prosperity, security and joy'. His speech promised to fight the domination of the political system by billionaires; income and wealth inequality; unemployment; trade agreements that allowed corporations to move their jobs from America to low-wage countries; and climate change. He advocated raising wages, breaking up the Wall Street finance houses, providing healthcare for all as a right, expanding social security benefits and abolishing tuition fees in public higher education institutions.[42]

Sanders later offered a more detailed exposition of his domestic policy in 'An Agenda for a New America: How We Transform Our Country'. The section 'Ending the Rigged Economy' formed nearly half the document; this was a series of measures aimed at using the power of the federal government to make the economy more efficient and humane, serving workers and consumers rather than the 'oligarchy', and making it easier to form trade unions.[43]

In November 2015, in a speech at Georgetown University in Washington, DC, he explained what he meant by 'democratic socialism'. The text referred back to Franklin D. Roosevelt and Martin Luther King, Jr., not to Marx and Engels. Some of its language nevertheless was posed in terms of class, amended for the American context, and reflecting the slogans of the new social movements.

> If we are serious about transforming our country, if we are serious about rebuilding the middle class, if we are serious about reinvigorating our democracy, we need to develop a political movement which, once again, is prepared to take on and defeat a ruling class whose greed is destroying our nation. The billionaire class cannot have it all. Our government belongs to all of us, not just the one per cent.

As in the speech announcing his candidacy, the programme was similar to what might be found in a manifesto of a mainstream socialist party in Western Europe which was moving away from neo-liberalism. 'Democratic socialism means that we must create an economy that works for all, not just the very wealthy.' But this was not traditional socialism.

> I don't believe the government should own the means of production, but I do believe that the middle class and the working families who produce the wealth of America deserve a fair deal.

> I believe in private companies that thrive and invest and grow in America instead of shipping jobs and profits overseas.[44]

Himself Jewish, Sanders understood the importance of identity issues alongside class. His equality agenda appealed to women and ethnic and sexual minorities. His championing of undocumented immigrants appealed particularly to Latino voters. He was aware, however, of his lack of appeal to Black voters, who were largely loyal to Hillary Clinton.[45] Very early in the campaign it became clear that Sanders was the main opposition to Hillary Clinton for the nomination.

As well as appealing to experienced activists from a variety of progressive causes, Sanders' campaign drew in hundreds of thousands of mainly young people who had not been involved in politics before. These provided the foot soldiers for knocking on doors and speaking directly to registered Democrats. Despite the candidate's age, the campaign made extensive use of the Internet: Facebook and Twitter messages, online advertising, and live streaming of meetings. Lacking wealthy backers, the campaign received most of its income from small online donations. Sanders gained backing from several trade unions. Most importantly, he succeeded in persuading the trade union umbrella body, the American Federation of Labor and Congress of Industrial Organizations (AFL–CIO), who were expected to endorse Clinton as the establishment candidate, to postpone its decision until after the candidate had been chosen.

Some opinion polls showed that Sanders was more likely than Clinton to beat any of the likely Republican candidates. In the primary elections and caucuses, Sanders succeeded in winning 22 states. In view of the historical suspicion of socialism in the United States, reinforced by the Cold War, this was a tremendous achievement for a socialist. He did badly in the southern states, reflecting his lack of support from Black Americans, except for those under 30. At the national convention in Philadelphia in July, Sanders had a substantial minority of the elected pledged delegates, while Clinton had a majority of these plus nearly all the 'superdelegates', establishment figures with *ex officio* voting rights.

Despite losing, Sanders opted to carry on working within the Democratic Party to influence its electoral platform, moving it left in a number of areas, including free tuition in public universities and colleges, expanding community health centres and curbing Wall Street's freedom to play havoc with the economy. He endorsed Hillary Clinton. Donald Trump's victory in the presidential elections, despite Clinton winning the popular vote, reflected a resurgence of White racism in American politics.

The Democratic Socialists of America (DSA)

The youth activism of 2015 and 2016, mobilised in support of Sanders, led to a huge boost in the fortunes of the DSA. Since its formation in 1982, the promotion of socialist ideas and candidates within the Democratic Party has been its main activity.[46] In June 2016 the DSA's strategy document welcomed Sanders' campaign and the rise of Podemos, Syriza and Corbyn with optimism. It put forward a 'vision of democratic socialism' involving 'radical democracy' and, instead of capitalism, 'economic democracy'. The latter would include 'the democratic management of all businesses by the workers who comprise them and by the communities in which they operate. Very large, strategically important sectors of the economy – such as housing, utilities and heavy industry – would be subject to democratic planning outside the market'. This was to the left of Sanders' platform. The document tried to reduce expectations: 'a democratic socialist society cannot produce total social harmony'; it 'will not be the utopia that many socialists of old imagined'.[47]

After Sanders' presidential campaign, many of his supporters' groups converted themselves into DSA chapters. President Trump's Islamophobic, anti-refugee and anti–immigrant attitudes, together with his tax cuts for Wall Street and his anti-environmentalist policies, galvanised the young activists. DSA membership rose from 6,000 before the campaign to 32,000 in late 2017 and 47,000 in July 2018. The median age fell dramatically, from 68 in 2013 to 33 in 2017. The membership is reported as being 75 per cent male and 90 per cent White – repeating Sanders' failure to attract Black Americans.[48]

The focus has been on getting its members elected as Democratic Party candidates to public office, with some success. In 2018, the DSA attracted considerable attention by winning a number of primaries for the midterm elections to federal and state legislatures, defeating established

Democratic incumbents. Among the successful was Alexandria Ocasio-Cortes, a 28-year-old former cocktail waitress of Puerto Rican origin. She won the Democratic nomination and then the election to the House of Representatives from Queens, New York City. She campaigned on social issues and called for the abolition of the border control agency. Following the primary, she declared: 'I think a lot of working-class Americans and voters here have been waiting for an unapologetic champion for economic, social and racial dignity in the United States.'[49] Her victory was part of a wider wave of some success for progressive, mainly young female candidates.

Bernie Sanders did not expect to win the presidency. Jan Rehmann has suggested that Sanders is creating a '"historic bloc" of different subaltern classes and groups, and is particularly aiming at an alliance between working and middle classes'.[50] Sanders does not use Gramsci's terminology, but this description seems fair. The aim of Sanders and of the DSA has been to argue for an alternative way of organising society, 'making socialists'. The DSA has been clearer than Sanders about its desire to abolish the capitalist system. Both have embraced extra-parliamentary social movements and combined this with standing for office as candidates of the established party with its long-standing trade union links.

Jeremy Corbyn and Momentum: Transforming the Labour Party?

The election of Corbyn as leader of the Labour Party in 2015 was even more unexpected than the success of Sanders. He started his campaign with bookmakers' odds of 100-to-1 against him.[51] This section will analyse why he was elected, how he has dealt with challenges from inside the Labour Party and the problems impeding his path to office.

In the general election of May 2015, Labour under its centre-left leader Ed Miliband had reasonable expectations of defeating the Conservative-Liberal Democrat coalition, which had imposed five years of austerity. Instead the Labour vote fell, the Liberal Democrats collapsed and Prime Minister David Cameron was able to form a purely Conservative government. Labour's defeat was due, at least in part, to its inability to tell a convincing story on the economy. It was divided as to whether to address the government deficit with austerity policies, as the majority of MPs seemed to wish; or to make a decisive break and oppose austerity.

Corbyn elected leader, 2015

Ed Miliband resigned after his defeat and a leadership election was called. A handful of Labour MPs agreed that Corbyn, aged 66, would carry the left-wing, anti-austerity standard on this occasion. Within the Parliamentary Labour Party (PLP), he had little support outside the far left. Corbyn's strength was his consistency and the widespread perception that he was honest. He was seen as not like other MPs, but someone who stuck rigidly to his socialist and internationalist principles. He always opposed the 'New Labour' philosophy of Prime Ministers Tony Blair and Gordon Brown, and argued for more democracy and accountability within the party. The other three candidates were united in claiming that Corbyn's left-wing policies made him incapable of leading the party to an election victory.

Corbyn was helped by change in the leadership election rules. This allowed Labour supporters, who were not members, to pay £3 and have a vote of equal value to that of individual party members and affiliated individual trade unionists. Trade unionists, students, environmental activists and young people who had been active in anti-cuts campaigns flocked to register as supporters, and to staff the Corbyn campaign offices.

Much older people, who had supported the left-wing Labour minister Tony Benn in the 1970s but since dropped out of party activity because of outrage at Blair's policies, came back into the party in order to back Corbyn. Trotskyist and Communist organisations which had written off the Labour Party as irretrievably bourgeois also tried to join in. Almost 300,000 people, including nearly 100,000 trade unionists, joined the party, doubling its individual membership. Armed with the support of important trade unions, activists embarked on creating phone banks around the country to contact party members and recruit more supporters.[52]

In September 2015, Corbyn was elected on the first ballot, with 59.5 per cent of first-preference votes. Since then he has faced the suspicion of him held by a majority of Labour MPs, and at least for the first two years, the opposition of the Party apparatus. Corbyn appointed his old far-left comrade John McDonnell to the key post of Shadow Chancellor of the Exchequer but sought to create a shadow cabinet representing the whole parliamentary party.

In October 2015, Corbyn's leadership campaign team began to transform their supporters' groups into a national organisation, Momentum, independent of the parliamentary leadership. The veteran activist Jon Lansman was the founder and leader of Momentum. The aim was to maintain a strong left grouping within the Labour Party, to protect Corbyn from attacks from Labour's right and centre, and build up the Labour Party as a grassroots, campaigning mass organisation.

An early Momentum statement spoke of the need to make the party more democratic, and for 'real progressive change', without explicitly calling for 'socialist' policies. It further declared: 'Momentum is the successor entity to the Jeremy Corbyn for Labour Leader campaign but it is independent of the Labour Party's leadership. It will work with everyone who supports Jeremy's aim of creating a more fair, equal and democratic society'.[53] In the constituency Labour parties (CLPs) and party branches, Momentum sought to enthuse the new and reborn activists, overwhelmingly Corbyn supporters, encouraging them to participate in local campaigns and stand for office and committees within the party. In response, the old guard of the party fought back; several hundred party members were suspended, mainly Corbyn supporters. They were accused of having supported other parties in earlier elections, or retweeting speeches by Green Party members or, most controversially, of anti-Semitism.

Challenge and consolidation: From the Brexit referendum to the 2017 general election

Sharp divisions in the Conservative Party over Britain's membership of the EU should have created opportunities for Labour to make gains in the May 2016 local election. In England and Wales, however, Labour made a small net loss and in Scotland, traditionally a bastion for Labour, fell to third place behind the Scottish National Party and the Conservatives. Tensions between the leader's office and party headquarters impeded the effectiveness of Labour's campaign.

It was the result of the Brexit referendum of 23 June 2016, however, which led to the PLP rebellion against Corbyn. Since 1975, the Labour Party had supported Britain's membership of what became the EU. During the referendum campaign, Corbyn spoke and made videos opposing Brexit. After the referendum vote by a small majority to leave the EU, many Labour MPs accused Corbyn of campaigning ineffectually and even privately supporting Brexit. Corbyn himself gave some currency to this view by calling on the morning after the referendum for Article 50 of the Treaty on European Union, announcing the intention of a member to leave the EU, to be activated at once.

Several resignations from the Labour front bench followed. On 28 June, the PLP passed a motion of no confidence in Corbyn's leadership by an overwhelming majority, 172 to 40. Corbyn had to fight another leadership campaign, this time against a single candidate, Owen Smith. As well as the issues of the elections and the referendum, Corbyn was attacked over his attitude towards women; over 40 female Labour MPs accused him of inattention to the online abuse of women. But the Momentum machine swung into action with its phone calls, emails and social media, and ensured a vote for Corbyn of 61.8 per cent, slightly higher than in the previous year.

Corbyn's victory consolidated his position in the party outside parliament, but the majority of MPs were not reconciled. In January 2017, the new Conservative Prime Minister Theresa May introduced into the House of Commons a measure allowing the government to activate Article 50. Corbyn imposed a three-line whip, forcing Labour MPs to vote in favour of this. Additionally, MPs feared that Momentum was trying to take over CLPs and replace them as Labour candidates with Corbyn supporters. They likened Momentum to Trotskyist groups who had entered the party in the 1970s–80s.

Lansman and his allies on Momentum's Steering Committee responded by abolishing the organisation's National Committee and pushed through a new Momentum constitution. This required all Momentum members to be or become Labour Party members; thus, the leaders hoped, banning Trotskyists. The constitution broadened Momentum's aims to include not only the 'election of a Labour government' but also 'to broaden support for a transformative, socialist programme'.[54]

With Labour divided, and well behind the Tories in opinion polls, Theresa May called a general election for 8 June. Labour was expected to make losses, and the party apparatus based its strategy on protecting existing MPs in marginal constituencies. Corbyn and McDonnell, however, had control of the manifesto, 'For the Many, not the Few'. This was a phrase of Tony Blair's; the content, however, was a decisive rejection of neoliberalism in favour of economic intervention, which recalled the Labour governments between 1945 and 1979. A National Transformation Fund of £250 billion would be established for infrastructure investment. A National Investment Bank would fund economic projects which the finance houses rejected. Water, the railways, energy and the Royal Mail would be renationalised. Workers' rights would be increased substantially, and some benefit cuts would be restored. A National Education Service would be established. Reflecting the experience of Bernie Sanders' campaign, university tuition fees would be abolished, and maintenance grants reintroduced.

Most of these were not, in reality, innovations, but a return to the situation before Margaret Thatcher's government. Indeed, not all the

Conservatives' privatisations were to be reversed, and there was no return to the relatively high rates of income tax accepted by Labour and Conservative governments before 1979. Brexit would go ahead, since 'Labour accepts the referendum result'.[55]

McDonnell produced a companion document costing the policies and outlining the source of funds, and a further paper explaining how Labour would crack down on tax avoidance.[56] At the same time, the Labour leaders tore into the Conservative manifesto, which was poorly costed and included a proposal to make elderly people pay more for their care. Labour dubbed this 'the dementia tax'. The prime minister proved an ineffective campaigner, unable to engage the voters and offering unhelpful, robotic responses.

Corbyn toured the country addressing overflowing meetings and, as the campaign progressed, narrowed the gap with the Tories. Meanwhile, Momentum members were fighting a campaign separately from that of the party apparatus. Advised by some activists from Bernie Sanders' team, they applied what McDonnell called 'the cutting edge use of targeted Facebook advertising'.[57] Momentum branches organised canvassing visits to marginal constituencies. More optimistic than the party apparatus, Momentum targeted marginal seats which might be won for Labour from sitting MPs from other parties.

The Conservatives remained in power as the largest party after the election but lost their majority. Labour increased its share of the vote by the largest amount since the war, from 30.4 per cent in 2015 to 40.0 per cent in 2017, with a net gain of 30 seats.[58] The turn of young people to Labour was most dramatic. Among the 18–24 age group, it reached 62 per cent. Age seemed to replace class as the best predictor of voting.[59] The promise to abolish tuition fees undoubtedly attracted many young people and probably their parents. Corbyn had proved himself as a campaigner among the electorate, not only the party. Momentum's strategy had been validated. Labour MPs, not only the new intake, began to take a more favourable attitude to Corbyn. But with the government's public divisions over Brexit, Labour should have done much better.

Towards a Corbyn government?

On several specific issues, Corbyn's approach was criticised both outside and inside the party. Corbyn was particularly active in solidarity with Palestinian groups and Latin American socialists. He was unfairly accused of sympathy for terrorism or for Venezuela's repressive policies. Corbyn laid himself open to accusations that he was not sufficiently critical of Putin's regime in Russia, or when he was, he tended to balance any criticism by attacking some aspect of Western policy. Parts of the Labour left had traditionally been sympathetic to the Soviet Union, but now communism had fallen and Russia was ruled by an authoritarian kleptocracy which had removed territory from two of its neighbours. It had nothing in common with socialism.

After Russia annexed Crimea, Corbyn wrote in April 2014: 'On Ukraine, I would not condone Russian behaviour or expansion. But it is not unprovoked, and the right of people to seek a federal structure or independence should not be denied. And there are huge questions around the West's intentions in Ukraine.'[60] Such equivocation became harmful in a party leader. In March 2018, when two Russians, Sergei and Yulia Skripal, were poisoned in Salisbury in South West England, not only the British government but also all competent experts were convinced that the action had been ordered by the Russian authorities. In parliament, Corbyn cast doubt on this explanation. Two days later, he repeated his doubts. 'To rush way ahead of the evidence being gathered by the police, in a fevered parliamentary atmosphere, serves neither justice nor our national security.'

At the same time, he distanced the Labour Party from the Putin regime, with 'its conservative authoritarianism, abuse of human rights [and] political and economic corruption'.[61] Corbyn supported proposals from McDonnell to crack down on the use of the City of London by Russian oligarchs for money laundering. But Corbyn's equivocation allowed the Conservatives and his Labour opponents to portray him as soft on Putin. It was only at the Labour Party Conference in September 2018 that Corbyn announced that he now accepted that the Russian state was responsible for the poisonings.[62]

Corbyn and his allies failed to take seriously accusations of anti-Semitism made against them or their supporters. Corbyn was found to have defended a mural depicting ugly capitalists with Jewish features and had to apologise. Against this background, Labour failed to make expected gains in the May 2018 local elections. Some Jewish members of the party demonstrated at Westminster against anti-Semitism inside Labour. By the end of summer 2018, Corbyn acknowledged that the Party had not done enough to fight anti-Semitism in its ranks.

A still larger problem for Corbyn was Brexit. At the 2017 party conference, Momentum helped Corbyn by preventing a debate on the issue. Corbyn was still committed to Brexit, and this had been enshrined in the election manifesto. In 2018, however, as the possible results of Brexit appeared more unfavourable, if not frightening, the new young generation of Labour activists, including many Momentum members, became disenchanted with Corbyn's policy. A YouGov poll in September showed that 90 per cent of party members wanted Britain to remain in the EU.[63] At the party conference at the end of the month, the leadership partially relented. It agreed to allow the possibility of a second referendum; and that the option to remain was not ruled out. This was far, though, from agreeing to campaign against Brexit, as party members seemed to want.

The accusation of populism levelled against Corbyn seems unjustified. He avoids an appeal to 'the people'; he attacks the Tories rather than the establishment or a ruling class; and while he allowed a cult of fandom to develop around him, his personal modesty and political style are the opposite of a strong populist leader.[64] Richard Seymour suggests that, far from the danger of populism, 'Corbynism will struggle to outrun the limits of Labourism'.[65] It is true that much of the 2017 election manifesto would not have seemed out of place as a product of the party mainstream in the 1970s. But Momentum has grown steadily, claiming 40,000 members by April 2018, with increasing influence in the constituencies and seeming willing to hold the leadership to a more radical direction.

Corbyn, McDonnell and Lansman had all battled since the 1970s at 'making socialists' rather than seeking political office. Now they had turned from the fight within the party to the struggle for state power. If they won an election, would they, in the face of adverse circumstances, possibly a post-Brexit crash, and a hostile ruling class, back down, as Syriza did after the referendum, and return to austerity? Unlike Greece, Britain remained a major European power, better able to withstand international pressure. Could a Corbyn government mobilise its supporters outside parliament to carry through its policies?

Conclusion

In order to understand the reasons behind the success of the four movements considered, it should be asked, albeit briefly, why groups in other large West European countries did not achieve the same level of success. Perhaps the most significant other new movement following the crisis was Jean-Luc Mélenchon's La France Insoumise (France Unbowed), which achieved third position and nearly 20 per cent of the vote in the 2017 French presidential election. The French left has long been divided, with three rival trade union federations. Now it is politically split between Mélenchon's supporters; the Parti Socialiste, hammered by Hollande's policy reversals; the communists; and those who moved to back the centrist Emmanuel Macron. In Germany, the left is split between the SPD; the well-established Greens who have become more of a centrist force in recent years; and Die Linke, whose roots lie in the former East German ruling party but which has picked up some radical support in the former West Germany. After it leaves federal office, the SPD is likely to reconnect with its trade union base and move to the left. The most disappointing of the post-crisis radical movements has been Movimento Cinque Stella. This Italian populist movement seemed to express grassroots protest. Unlike Podemos, however, it was led by a charismatic comedian, and then by centrist politicians who were prepared to share power with right-wing populists.

Returning to the questions posed at the start of the chapter, why did the four movements discussed here grow, and why did some develop inside existing parties? Podemos and Syriza, as new parties, were able to grow because of the discrediting of the existing socialist parties and the relative fluidity of southern European party systems. The Democratic Party and the Labour Party, on the other hand, are embedded in the political systems of their states, and protected by the electoral systems. A key factor facilitating the spread of socialist ideas in both parties, despite the conservative political cultures in both states, is the traditional link between the trade union movement and the two parties. This was especially the case with the Labour Party, which was created primarily by the trade unions and remains dependent on them financially.

All four movements discussed here had an open attitude towards cooperating with groups outside their control, including to some extent with other parties. The Democratic Socialists of America allowed its members to oppose Democratic Party candidates, while Momentum decided only in 2017 to require its members to be Labour Party members and work only for Labour candidates.

What of identity politics? All were aware of the importance of identity issues in building support. All sought to promote women. Syriza worked within the strongly pro-European political culture in Greece, while still using anti-German tropes. Sanders and the DSA were both aware of the lack of their support among Black people but did not find much success here. The issue of Britain's European identity was potentially problematic for Corbyn; his adherence to Brexit after the referendum was at odds with the pro-EU feelings of most of his young supporters. Still more problematic was the need to retain Labour's support among Jewish voters.

Did the means pursued by these movements prefigure the sort of society they wanted to create? The record is mixed. Sanders, as candidate, kept control of his own campaign. The DSA remains a decentralised body where the initiative of the local branches is decisive. Iglesias and Tsipras were both accused of limiting democracy within the party in order to ensure their control. Corbyn's three-line whips in favour of Brexit were resented, but he was unable to prevent Labour MPs from voting as they wished. Momentum in early 2017 may have gone beyond its rules in changing the constitution in order to exclude people from Trotskyist organisations. In 2017 it acted to prevent a debate on Brexit at the Labour Party conference. Generally, though, it has acted to build up Labour Party branches and introduce the concept of civilised political debate inside them.

How radical were these movements, and did they succeed in 'making socialists'? They all succeeded in mobilising large numbers of young people, previously uninvolved in politics, and achieving widespread support among the general population. All used the financial crisis to challenge the hegemony of capitalist ideas. While Podemos was not explicitly socialist, the other three all widened support for socialist ideas among the voters. Podemos did not replace PSOE as the main party of the left, but people close to it became mayors of Madrid and Barcelona. Syriza was the only one to form a government, but it was forced to implement austerity policies. Bernie Sanders did not become the presidential candidate, but he spread the concept of socialism among Democratic Party voters and laid the basis for further gains by the DSA. Corbyn became Labour leader but has not yet won an election. Even if he does not, Momentum has potential to keep pushing the Labour Party to the left. All four movements have grown because they have appealed to the real grievances of millions of people and pointed the way to an alternative. Politics in their countries have changed beyond recognition.

What is clear is that the fact that avowedly socialist systems have collapsed in Europe does not mean that the idea of socialism has died. It might even be argued that the collapse of the USSR makes it easier to separate socialism from Russian totalitarianism. It was only the model of one-party rule, combined with central planning, which was discredited. China's hybrid system is as likely to find friends on the right as on the left; few hold it up as an example of socialism to be emulated. The way has become clear for new concepts of socialism to be articulated, drawing not only on class but on issues of race, ethnicity, sex and gender, involving a multiplicity of movements as well as parties, and focussing on the needs of the individual rather than the state.

Notes

1. Luke March, *Radical Left Parties in Europe* (Abingdon, UK: Routledge, 2011); *Europe's Radical Left: From Marginality to the Mainstream?*, ed. Luke March and Daniel Keith (London: Rowman & Littlefield, 2016).
2. Marco Briziarelli and Susana Martinez Guillem, *Reviving Gramsci: Crisis, Communication and Change* (New York: Routledge, 2016).
3. Leo Panitch and Sam Gindin, *The Socialist Challenge Today: Syriza, Sanders, Corbyn* (London: Merlin, 2018).
4. Steve Richards, *The Rise of the Outsiders: How Mainstream Politics Lost its Way* (London: Atlantic, 2017).
5. Iñigo Errejón and Chantal Mouffe, *Podemos: In the Name of the People* (London: Lawrence & Wishart, 2016).
6. Pablo Iglesias, *Politics in a Time of Crisis: Podemos and the Future of Democracy in Europe* (London: Verso, 2015).
7. Yanis Varoufakis, *Adults in the Room: My Battle with Europe's Deep Establishment* (London: Bodley Head, 2017).
8. Kevin Ovenden, *Syriza: Inside the Labyrinth* (London: Verso, 2015).
9. Bernie Sanders, *Our Revolution: A Future to Believe In*, paperback ed. (London: Profile, 2017).
10. Heather Gautney, *Crashing the Party: From the Bernie Sanders Campaign to a Progressive Movement* (London: Verso, 2018).
11. Richard Seymour, *Corbyn: The Strange Rebirth of Radical Politics* (London: Verso, 2016); Mark Perryman, ed., *The Corbyn Effect* (London: Lawrence and Wishart, 2017).
12. 'Introduction to Pablo Iglesias', *New Left Review* 93, May–June (2015): 5; Stathis Kouvelakis, 'Syriza's Rise and Fall', *New Left Review* 97, January–February (2016): 47–8.
13. Briziarelli and Martinez Guillem, *Reviving Gramsci*, 98–102.
14. Ernesto Laclau, *On Populist Reason* (London: Verso, 2005).
15. Alexandros Kioupkiolis, 'Podemos: The Ambiguous Promises of Left-Wing Populism in Contemporary Spain', *Journal of Political Ideologies* 21, no. 2 (2016): 99–110; Briziarelli and Martinez Guillem, *Reviving Gramsci*, 111–3.
16. Pablo Iglesias, 'Understanding Podemos', *New Left Review* 93, May–June (2015): 10.
17. Kioupkiolis, 'Podemos', 111–3.
18. Ashifa Kassam, 'Ex-Communist, Retired Judge, Blogger . . . The Woman Now Poised to Run Spain's Capital', *Observer*, 31 May 2015.
19. Iglesias, 'Understanding Podemos', 21, 15.
20. Martin McQuillan, 'Post-Structuralist Politics', *Times Higher Education*, 26 March 2015.
21. Michael Stothard, 'Spanish Leftwing Leader Wins Confidence Vote after House Furore', *The Financial Times*, 27 May 2018.
22. David J. Bailey, *Protest Movements and Parties of the Left: Affirming Disruption* (London: Rowman & Littlefield, 2017), 209–10.
23. Giorgos Katsembekis, 'Radical Left Populism in Contemporary Greece: Syriza's Trajectory from Minoritarian Opposition to Power', *Constellations* 23, no. 3 (2016): 392–8 (quotation, 398); Michalis Spourdalakis, 'The Miraculous Rise of the "Phenomenon SYRIZA"', *International Critical Thought* 4, no. 3 (2014): 355–7 (voting, 357).
24. Kouvelakis, 'Syriza's Rise and Fall', 52–3; Varoufakis, *Adults in the Room*, 88–90.
25. Republished as Yanis Varoufakis, 'How I Became an Erratic Marxist', *The Guardian*, 18 February 2015.
26. Anthea Carassava, 'Greek Radicals Take Power in Deal with Anti-Migrant Party', *The Times*, 27 January 2015; Paris Aslanidis and Cristóbal Rovira Kaltwasser, 'Dealing with Populists in Government: The SYRIZA-ANEL Coalition in Greece', *Democratization* 23, no. 6 (2016): 1077–81.
27. Ovenden, *Syriza*, 174.
28. Helena Smith, 'Out with Austerity, in with the Cleaners – A New Age Dawns', *The Guardian*, 29 January 2015.
29. Katie Allen and Helena Smith, 'Tsipras in Bold Mood as Crunch Talks Resume in Brussels', *Guardian*, 16 February 2015; Varoufakis, *Adults*, 231–47 (Schäuble quotation, 237).
30. Yanis Varoufakis, 'Germany Won't Spare Greek Pain – It Has an Interest in Breaking Us', *Guardian*, 11 July 2015.

31. Anthea Carassava and Charles Bremner, 'Greece defies EU with handouts for the poor', *The Times*, 19 March 2015.
32. Varoufakis, *Adults*, 351–71.
33. Bruno Waterfield and Helen Womack, 'EU Draws up Secret Plan to Kick Greece out of the Eurozone', *The Times*, 10 April 2015.
34. Larry Elliott, Graeme Weardon, Nicholas Watt, and Helena Smith, 'No Vote Means You Are out of the Euro, Greece Warned', *The Guardian*, 30 June 2015.
35. Phillip Inman, Graeme Weardon, and Helena Smith, 'Greece Seeks Deal with €13bn Package of Reforms and Cuts', *The Guardian*, 10 July 2015.
36. Varoufakis, *Adults*, 467–71.
37. Ian Traynor, Jennifer Rankin, and Helena Smith, 'Europe Takes Revenge on Tsipras', *The Guardian*, 13 July 2015.
38. Phillip Inman, 'Varoufakis Labels Greek Deal a Gift to Tax-Dodging Oligarchs', *The Guardian*, 18 August 2015.
39. Aslanidis and Rovira Kaltwasser, 'Dealing with Populists', 1082–8; Kouvelakis, 'Syriza's Rise and Fall', 63–8; Jon Henley, 'The Voters Saw We Defended the Poor and They Backed Us', *The Guardian*, 21 September 2015.
40. Jon Henley and Daniel Boffey, 'Greece Hails Eurozone Agreement That Will End Eight Years of Austerity', *The Guardian*, 23 June 2018; Helena Smith, 'After the Crash: Has Greece Finally Escaped the Grip of Catastrophe?', *Observer*, 15 July 2018.
41. Canada shows an interesting interaction of both these factors. The New Democratic Party has remained the main arena of left-wing politics, since like the Labour Party it has close links with the trade unions. As a third party in most provinces, however, behind the Liberals and Progressive Conservatives, it loses out under the electoral system.
42. Bernie Sanders, *Our Revolution: A Future to Believe In*, paperback ed. (London: Profile, 2017), 117–28 (quotation, 118).
43. Sanders, *Our Revolution*, 185–444.
44. 'Senator Bernie Sanders on Democratic Socialism in the United States', 19 November 2015, *Bernie*, accessed 15 May 2018, berniesanders.com/democratic-socialism-in-the-united-states/.
45. Sanders, *Our Revolution*, 140, 172.
46. Anna Heyward, 'Since Trump's Victory, Democratic Socialists of America Has Become a Budding Political Force: Why an Army of Young People is Joining DSA', *The Nation*, 15–22 January 2018, accessed 17 November 2018, www.the nation.com/article/in-the-year-since-trumps-victory-democratic-socialists-of-America-has-become-a-budding-political-force/.
47. 'Resistance Rising: Socialist Strategy in the Age of Political Revolution: A Summary of Democratic Socialists of America's Strategy Document, June 2016', accessed 17 November 2018, www.dsausa.org/strategy.
48. Heyward, 'Since Trump's Victory'; Arwa Mahdawi, 'Socialism's No Longer a Dirty Word in the US', *The Guardian*, 30 July 2018.
49. Ben Jacobs and Lauren Gambino, 'The Former Cocktail Waitress Who Has Shaken up America's Ailing Democrats', *The Guardian*, 28 June 2018.
50. Jan Rehmann, 'Bernie Sanders and the Hegemonic Crisis of Neoliberal Capitalism: What Next?' *Socialism and Democracy* 30, no. 3 (2016): 7.
51. Richard Seymour, *Corbyn: The Strange Rebirth of Radical Politics* (London: Verso, 2016), 13.
52. Mark Perryman, 'The Great Moving Left Show', in *The Corbyn Effect*, ed. Mark Perryman (London: Lawrence and Wishart, 2017), 8–9; Hilary Wainwright, 'Mind the Labour Gap', in *The Corbyn Effect*, ed. Mark Perryman, 115–8; Seymour, *Corbyn*, 13–57.
53. Momentum, 'Welcome to Momentum', n.d. [c. November 2015], accessed 29 December 2015, www.peoplesmomentum.com.
54. Momentum, 'Constitution', emailed to members on 10 January 2017.
55. 'For the Many, Not the Few' (London: Labour Party, 2017), quotation, 24.
56. 'Funding Britain's Future', and 'Labour's Tax Transparency and Enforcement Programme' (both London: Labour Party, 2017).
57. John McDonnell, Letter to Party Members, n.d. (March 2018).
58. Peter Dorey, 'Jeremy Corbyn Confounds His Critics: Explaining the Labour Party's Remarkable Resurgence in the 2017 Election', *British Politics* 12 (2017): 320.

59 James Sloam, Rakib Ehsan, and Matt Henn, '"Youthquake": How and Why Young People Reshaped the Political Landscape in 2017', *Political Insight*, April 2018, 4–8.
60 Jeremy Corbyn, 'NATO Belligerence Endangers Us All', *Morning Star*, 16 April 2014, accessed 8 March 2019, https://morningstaronline.co.uk/a-972b-nato-belligerence-endangers-us-all.
61 Jeremy Corbyn, 'Salisbury Was Appalling: But We Must Avoid a Drift to Conflict', *The Guardian*, 16 March 2018.
62 Matthew Taylor, 'Speech's Key Themes: Eyes Fixed on Electorate as Leader Sets Out Stall', *The Guardian*, 27 September 2018.
63 Toby Helm and Andrew Rawnsley, 'We Must Back Members on New Brexit Vote, Watson Tells Corbyn', *Observer*, 23 September 2018.
64 Jonathan Dean and Bice Maiguashca, 'Corbyn's Labour and the Populism Question', *Renewal* 25, no. 3–4 (2017): 56–65.
65 Seymour, *Corbyn*, 219.

Bibliography

Allen, Katie, and Helena Smith. 'Tsipras in Bold Mood as Crunch Talks Resume in Brussels'. *The Guardian*, 16 February 2015.

Aslanidis, Paris, and Cristóbal Rovira Kaltwasser. 'Dealing with Populists in Government: The SYRIZA-ANEL Coalition in Greece'. *Democratization* 23, no. 6 (2016): 1077–91.

Bailey, David J. *Protest Movements and Parties of the Left: Affirming Disruption*. London: Rowman & Littlefield, 2017.

Briziarelli, Marco, and Susana Martinez Guillem. *Reviving Gramsci: Crisis, Communication and Change*. New York: Routledge, 2016.

Carassava, Anthea. 'Greek Radicals Take Power in Deal with Anti-Migrant Party'. *The Times*, 27 January 2015.

Carassava, Anthea, and Charles Bremner. 'Greece Defies EU with Handouts for the Poor'. *The Times*, 19 March 2015.

Corbyn, Jeremy. 'NATO Belligerence Endangers Us All'. *Morning Star*, 16 April 2014. Accessed 8 March 2019, https://morningstaronline.co.uk/a-972b-nato-belligerence-endangers-us-all.

Corbyn, Jeremy. 'Salisbury Was Appalling: But We Must Avoid a Drift to Conflict'. *The Guardian*, 16 March 2018.

Dean, Jonathan, and Bice Maiguashca. 'Corbyn's Labour and the Populism Question'. *Renewal* 25, no. 3–4 (2017): 56–65.

Dorey, Peter. 'Jeremy Corbyn Confounds His Critics: Explaining the Labour Party's Remarkable Resurgence in the 2017 Election'. *British Politics* 12 (2017): 308–34.

Elliott, Larry, Graeme Weardon, Nicholas Watt, and Helena Smith. 'No Vote Means You Are out of the Euro, Greece Warned'. *The Guardian*, 30 June 2015.

Errejón, Iñigo, and Chantal Mouffe. *Podemos: In the Name of the People*. London: Lawrence & Wishart, 2016.

'For the Many, Not the Few'. London: Labour Party, 2017.

'Funding Britain's Future'. London: Labour Party, 2017.

Gautney, Heather. *Crashing the Party: From the Bernie Sanders Campaign to a Progressive Movement*. London: Verso, 2018.

Helm, Toby, and Andrew Rawnsley. 'We Must Back Members on New Brexit Vote, Watson Tells Corbyn'. *Observer*, 23 September 2018.

Henley, Jon. 'The Voters Saw We Defended the Poor and They Backed Us'. *The Guardian*, 21 September 2015.

Henley, Jon, and Daniel Boffey. 'Greece Hails Eurozone Agreement That Will End Eight Years of Austerity'. *The Guardian*, 23 June 2018.

Heyward, Anna. 'Since Trump's Victory, Democratic Socialists of America Has Become a Budding Political Force: Why an Army of Young People is Joining DSA'. *The Nation*, 15–22 January 2018. Accessed 17 November 2018, www.the nation.com/article/in-the-year-since-trumps-victory-democratic-socialists-of-America-has-become-a-budding-political-force/.

Iglesias, Pablo. *Politics in a Time of Crisis: Podemos and the Future of Democracy in Europe*. London: Verso, 2015.
Iglesias, Pablo. 'Understanding Podemos'. *New Left Review* 93, May–June (2015): 7–22.
Inman, Phillip. 'Varoufakis Labels Greek Deal a Gift to Tax-Dodging Oligarchs'. *The Guardian*, 18 August 2015.
Inman, Phillip, Graeme Weardon, and Helena Smith. 'Greece Seeks Deal with €13bn Package of Reforms and Cuts'. *The Guardian*, 10 July 2015.
'Introduction to Pablo Iglesias'. *New Left Review* 93, May–June (2015): 5.
Jacobs, Ben, and Lauren Gambino. 'The Former Cocktail Waitress Who Has Shaken up America's Ailing Democrats'. *The Guardian*, 28 June 2018.
Kassam, Ashifa. 'Ex-Communist, Retired Judge, Blogger . . . The Woman Now Poised to Run Spain's Capital'. *Observer*, 31 May 2015.
Katsembekis, Giorgos. 'Radical Left Populism in Contemporary Greece: Syriza's Trajectory from Minoritarian Opposition to Power'. *Constellations* 23, no. 3 (2016): 391–403.
Kioupkiolis, Alexandros. 'Podemos: The Ambiguous Promises of Left-Wing Populism in Contemporary Spain'. *Journal of Political Ideologies* 21, no. 2 (2016): 99–120.
Kouvelakis, Stathis. 'Syriza's Rise and Fall'. *New Left Review* 97, January–February (2016): 45–70.
'Labour's Tax Transparency and Enforcement Programme'. London: Labour Party, 2017.
Laclau, Ernesto. *On Populist Reason*. London: Verso, 2005.
Mahdawi, Arwa. 'Socialism's No Longer a Dirty Word in the US'. *The Guardian*, 30 July 2018.
March, Luke. *Radical Left Parties in Europe*. Abingdon, UK: Routledge, 2011.
March, Luke, and Daniel Keith, eds. *Europe's Radical Left: From Marginality to the Mainstream?* London: Rowman & Littlefield, 2016.
McDonnell, John. Letter to Party Members. N.d. (March 2018).
McQuillan, Martin. 'Post-Structuralist Politics'. *Times Higher Education*, 26 March 2015.
Momentum. 'Constitution'. Emailed to members on 10 January 2017.
Momentum. 'Welcome to Momentum'. N.d. [c. November 2015]. Accessed 29 December 2015, www.peoplesmomentum.com.
Ovenden, Kevin. *Syriza: Inside the Labyrinth*. London: Verso, 2015.
Panitch, Leo, and Sam Gindin. *The Socialist Challenge Today: Syriza, Sanders, Corbyn*. London: Merlin, 2018.
Perryman, Mark, ed. *The Corbyn Effect*. London: Lawrence and Wishart, 2017.
Rehmann, Jan. 'Bernie Sanders and the Hegemonic Crisis of Neoliberal Capitalism: What Next?' *Socialism and Democracy* 30, no. 3 (2016): 1–11.
'Resistance Rising: Socialist Strategy in the Age of Political Revolution. A Summary of Democratic Socialists of America's Strategy Document, June 2016'. Accessed 17 November 2018, www.dsausa.org/strategy.
Richards, Steve. *The Rise of the Outsiders: How Mainstream Politics Lost Its Way*. London: Atlantic, 2017.
Sanders, Bernie. *Our Revolution: A Future to Believe In*, paperback ed. London: Profile, 2017.
Sanders, Bernie. 'Senator Bernie Sanders on Democratic Socialism in the United States'. 19 November 2015. *Bernie*. Accessed 15 May 2018, berniesanders.com/democratic-socialism-in-the-united-states/.
Seymour, Richard. *Corbyn: The Strange Rebirth of Radical Politics*. London: Verso, 2016.
Sloam, James, Rakib Ehsan, and Matt Henn. '"Youthquake": How and Why Young People Reshaped the Political Landscape in 2017'. *Political Insight*, April 2018, 4–8.
Smith, Helena. 'After the Crash: Has Greece Finally Escaped the Grip of Catastrophe?' *Observer*, 15 July 2018.
Smith, Helena. 'Out with Austerity, in with the Cleaners: A New Age Dawns'. *The Guardian*, 29 January 2015.
Spourdalakis, Michalis. 'The Miraculous Rise of the "Phenomenon SYRIZA"'. *International Critical Thought* 4, no. 3 (2014): 354–66.
Stothard, Michael. 'Spanish Leftwing Leader Wins Confidence Vote after House Furore'. *The Financial Times*, 27 May 2018.
Taylor, Matthew. 'Speech's Key Themes: Eyes Fixed on Electorate as Leader Sets Out Stall'. *The Guardian*, 27 September 2018.
Traynor, Ian, Jennifer Rankin, and Helena Smith. 'Europe Takes Revenge on Tsipras'. *The Guardian*, 13 July 2015.

Varoufakis, Yanis. *Adults in the Room: My Battle with Europe's Deep Establishment*. London: Bodley Head, 2017.

Varoufakis, Yanis. 'Germany Won't Spare Greek Pain – It Has an Interest in Breaking Us'. *The Guardian*, 11 July 2015.

Varoufakis, Yanis. 'How I Became an Erratic Marxist'. *The Guardian*, 18 February 2015.

Wainwright, Hilary. 'Mind the Labour Gap'. In *The Corbyn Effect*, edited by Mark Perryman, 115–8. London: Lawrence and Wishart, 2017.

Waterfield, Bruno, and Helen Womack. 'EU Draws up Secret Plan to Kick Greece out of the Eurozone'. *The Times*, 10 April 2015.

Conclusion

Peter J. S. Duncan and Elisabeth Schimpfössl

Articulating alternatives to capitalism and socialism remains stubbornly difficult. This is a problem because the existing systems of socialism and capitalism are now often seen as hardly appropriate for solving any of the novel, and often unsettling, political developments we are confronted with across the globe. It is clear, however, that both these terms – socialism and capitalism – embrace a wide variety of existing models and potential models. Moreover, looking at a given existing system as in the case of China, it is by no means obvious whether the system is either capitalist or socialist or, as it appears, a hybrid of both. If it is a hybrid, it is not clear which elements, capitalist or socialist, are dominant; and it is not clear in which direction the system is moving. Russia is clearly now a capitalist society, but its capitalism is highly dependent on the state. Although different from China, Russia also has hybrid features.

The book demonstrates clearly that the transition from socialism to capitalism has not delivered what many had promised. In Russia, privatisation has benefitted only a small minority of society. Wealth inequality is one of the world's largest and poverty is again on the rise. The chapters also documented the power and patronage exercised by the wealthy in Russia and China, most of whom are closely tied to the state apparatus. A phenomenon that has accompanied the rise of the rich is ever greater corruption. Attempts by the state to get this under control have been fruitless.

Such practices are replicated on lower levels in society, albeit on a much smaller scale, and yet they are essential for survival. As such, the failure of neo-liberalism to allow ordinary people of the former Soviet states to develop decent living standards has meant that they have maintained their informal practices. An example of this is the *birzha* in Georgia, used by the excluded as a tool to navigate through daily life. Attempts by the authorities to undermine these have had little success.

Yet the issues raised here are only a small selection of the troubles the world is facing today. Revolving around China and the West, the alternatives raised in Parts Two and Three of the book also have relevance for the rest of the world, including the former Soviet bloc and the global South.

Whether China is socialist or capitalist, or a hybrid of the two, undoubtedly it has become a pole of attraction for policymakers in less developed countries around the world. In the tradition of area studies, the book has shown that the Belt and Road Initiative has deep historical and cultural roots. Already before the birth of Christ, products were transported across Eurasia along forerunners of the Silk Road. Today, the image of the Silk Road is powerfully symbolic both in East and West, alarming to some and engaging to others. The appeal of China's role in the world is strengthened by the movement from a unipolar to a bipolar (or multipolar) international system.

More relevant for our topic than the issue of world dominance is the question of what drives China's expansion. While the Belt and Road Initiative may appear perfectly compatible with the current world order and hence with a capitalist mode of production, the mechanism behind it has surprisingly little to do with market-economy stimuli. Instead, the whole project is very much under the control of the Chinese Communist Party, rather than being pushed by private enterprise. Xi Jinping's plans for China's foreign economic policy are closely tied to the enlargement of the party's power inside the country, particularly in relation to developing its western regions.

China's development under the Deng Xiaoping model greatly favoured the coastal east and south of the country and Xi now wishes to reduce the geographical inequalities. This reflects his desire to manage the increasing level of discontent, both among the urban working class and the peasants. While the capitalist policies pursued after Mao's death brought hundreds of millions of Chinese out of poverty, Xi very clearly understands that the system today needs rebalancing, with a greater role for the state to prevent the cycle of capitalist crises from which the West suffers.

With regards to the West, the pathways discussed in this book were either tried and tested previously in contemporary history, such as Keynesianism, or are slowly emerging and trying to find a voice, such as the new left-wing movements. Although sustainable for several decades under favourable conditions, Keynesian policies were abandoned not least because, ultimately, they led to frequent strikes by strong trade unions, high taxation and inflation. Under the pressures of the world market from the late 1970s onwards, capitalism could no longer afford luxuries such as job security and an expensive welfare state.

By now, however, the policies of austerity, promoted by neo-liberalism, have fallen into disfavour with European voters. Despite being the pioneers of European neo-liberalism, the British Conservatives have proclaimed an end to austerity (which does not mean they would not simultaneously proceed with cuts in welfare spending and public services generally). A true return to Keynesian expansionary policies to overcome stagnation should, for a start, require corporations to become what they were meant to be initially: namely accountable to the public rather than just enriching a few shareholders. For society to live and prosper, a clean environment is essential. Hence, any Keynesian policies would have to be linked with investment orientated towards solving global and regional environmental problems, from urban traffic congestion to global climate change.

In the 1970s, Keynesian policies, which were originally intended to preserve the capitalist system, began to threaten it. Decades of full employment had led to stronger and stronger trade unions, which were not afraid to exert their industrial muscle. Strikes disrupted whole industries and many firms became unprofitable. Faced with the cruel competition of the global market, the corporations demanded shackles on trade unions and major cuts in corporate taxation. The labour movements were not willing or able to use their industrial strength to protect their jobs and the welfare state as they had done. Nor were they willing to challenge the existence of the capitalist system. In different parts of the world the Thatcherite slogan 'There is no alternative!' took hold. This implied reversing the gains of the post-war period, a return to large-scale unemployment and the gradual withering away of the welfare state.

Many today, therefore, consider that capitalism can no longer afford to return to measures it previously employed and, as some have argued, can only continue to exist by taking away democratic rights.[1] When social-democratic parties ceased to defend their main achievements, such as the welfare state, and instead adopted austerity measures, they began to lose their support. As a result, especially since the onset of the 2008 crisis, we have seen the mood become more radical, including a return of socialist ideas. The book has shown that the strategy taken by socialists in different countries necessarily reflects differences in their histories and institutions. Where the labour movement has traditionally been associated with one particular party, as in much of the English-speaking world, the socialist movements have focused on gaining influence within these parties. Elsewhere, when existing parties lack such links with the trade unions or have been thoroughly compromised, new movements are likely to develop. As these develop in strength, however, and as the allure of electoral power grows, pressures develop to compromise on policy and principle. Thus, for example, Syriza failed to prepare the Greeks for a clash with international lenders and had to back down. Such dangers will threaten other socialist movements if they are elected to office.

Even among the four movements considered here, there is little unanimity or even clarity as to what sort of socialism they are trying to create. It seems, for example, that Bernie Sanders (at least in the immediate term) is aiming at a mixed economy with a strong social orientation. The Democratic Socialists of America clearly have a more radical direction. There is agreement that there can be no return to the totalitarian, centrally planned societies of the Soviet bloc. For Western socialists the contemporary Chinese model, with its single party rule, suppression of intellectual freedom and massive repression of some ethnic minorities, also has no attraction.

An increasing number of people sense that if capitalism is not guaranteeing economic and social security, then it might well have outlived its usefulness. The most sustainable models to date seem to be those which want to see the power of private corporations severely constrained, through a large-scale extension of democratic control in society, over public services and within the corporations themselves through the involvement of their employees in managerial decisions. On this basis, housing, education and healthcare can be made accessible to all and care for the weakest parts of society can be assured. More radical ideas such as undermining private enterprise itself find little favour today. Instead, there is talk of state ownership existing alongside cooperatives, municipal ownership and private enterprise.[2]

Some advocates of neo-liberalism seem to believe the old adage, 'the worse, the better'. As Naomi Klein has argued, neo-liberals use disasters, whether man-made or natural, to push through changes that they want. They do not even shy away from instrumentalising tragedies such as the war in Iraq and the tsunami in the Pacific to boost private business interests. The disorientation reigning in Eastern European countries after the fall of the Berlin Wall allowed for Western private business and capital to gain a stronghold and influence the privatisation policies to come. They intensively propagated the use of shock therapy, with little concern that this would drive millions of people into poverty.[3]

In Britain, after the Brexit referendum many neo-liberals appeared to believe that the best outcome would be if Britain left the European Union without making a deal with it. In the ensuing chaos, there would be a bonfire of regulations and unbridled capitalism let loose to rage without constraints. This would allow money laundering to reach unseen heights and turn the United Kingdom into a tax paradise similar to those in existing offshore havens. There has been speculation that a pending EU anti-tax avoidance directive, to be implemented from the beginning of 2019, might have been an additional motive to go ahead with Brexit as rapidly as possible.[4]

In the neo-liberals' dream world, which may be in their grasp, there would no longer be any hindrance to breaking up the National Health Service, privatising it further and selling it in bits and pieces to private service providers. Trade unions would lose their remaining protection and Britain would become a low-wage economy. Life expectancy is already now going down in many parts of Britain and infant mortality rose twice in a row from 2016. The last time the latter happened was in 1939–41.[5]

In reaction against the policies of neo-liberalism of the current radicalised shade, the far right has re-emerged across Europe. In classic populist style, while they pretend to represent the interests of the people against the elite and the establishment, in reality they seek to stir up conflict and splits within the population on the basis of identity and ethnicity. Strikingly, Francis Fukuyama's view has evolved from the triumph of liberal democracy to a gloomy awareness of the consequences of identity politics. He sees the rise of the populist right all over the globe as posing fundamental threats to existing liberal-democratic institutions.[6]

Already during the Brexit referendum, violence inspired by the far right increased, with the murder of the Labour MP Jo Cox. After the referendum, there were physical attacks on mosques, Muslims, and ethnic minorities, and a Polish man was murdered for speaking his native language. Trump has justified xenophobic feeling with his rhetoric against Muslim and Latin American immigrants. In Italy, the right-wing-populist coalition has launched criminal charges against the charity *Médecins sans frontiers* for helping refugees. Across Europe, immigrant populations are feeling intimidated, and anti-Semitism is on the rise.

In the former Soviet bloc, there has been a backlash against the consequences of globalisation, privatisation and inequality. This is reflected in the authoritarian and nationalist regimes of Law and Justice in Poland, FIDESZ in Hungary and Vladimir Putin in Russia.

FIDESZ, the ruling party in Hungary, has for some years used anti-Semitic tropes in its attacks on its opponents in the Hungarian intelligentsia. Interfering with academic freedom, the government has forced the Central European University to leave the country, and FIDESZ has openly portrayed the university's founder, George Soros, as an evil Jew. The far right across Europe and in America has repeated these attacks.

In Russia, President Obama was mocked for his race on television. The Kremlin has been financing, indirectly and sometimes covertly, far-right groups in Europe, including France and Britain. Its interference in support of Trump and Brexit in the US elections and British referendum in 2016 shows the danger to democracy posed by right-wing populism backed by Moscow. Indeed, the Russian model of neo-liberal economics combined with authoritarianism may represent the future of Western capitalist societies.

Whether ascribed to the right wing as in most cases, or to the left wing in some exceptional ones such as Hugo Chavez in Venezuela, populism is usually understood as opposing progressive politics. Some conceptualise things differently. Over the last decades, Ernest Laclau together with Chantal Mouffe have attempted to rehabilitate the concept of populism as a democratic movement rather than one with primarily ethnic or cultural undertones. They argue for a new politics, mobilising the people against the establishment.[7]

These socialist and democratic aims are so different from those of the right-wing populists, however, that adoption of the term may lead to great confusion. Unlike some commentators,[8] Jan-Werner Muller is rightly critical of ascribing the populist label to Corbyn's Labour Party, Podemos or Syriza.[9] Crucially for him, neither do these movements claim to represent 'the people' nor do any of them have xenophobic ambitions. Whenever left-wing movements gave in to opportunistic ideas and made xenophobic ideas their own, as did most notoriously the leadership of Die Linke in Germany in the mid-2010s, it backfired in no time.

Left-wing parties all over Europe have a lot to answer for about how history developed throughout the twentieth century. Repeating such mistakes would be a tragedy – and yet it is the kind of tragedy that would save capitalism yet another time. So far, the left has shown little capacity to learn from history. Too often, social-democratic parties have accommodated the demands and needs of those higher up in society instead of those of their own traditional supporters. Along the way, they buried their founding emancipatory ideas and instead surrendered (almost too eagerly) to the fashionable ideas of the ruling class. New Labour was a classic case of this surrender (both ideological and practical), as was in due course almost every social-democratic party in Europe. Almost everywhere, they have failed to challenge the hegemony of dominant ideas, even when those ideas have long been discredited and people have become restless because their representatives are incapable of articulating any alternatives, or unwilling to do so.

As for the more recent alternative social movements, things are very different. Instead of talking their supporters into compromise, they make bold promises of social reform which they cannot possibly keep under the economic circumstances we live in today. Even worse, they tend to fail to prepare their supporters for the resistance their promises will inevitably encounter. The result is predictable: voters will become disillusioned and may turn to unsavoury alternatives.

In order to gain theoretical clarity about aims and methods, we require empirical and conceptual inputs from the most different situations in all their historical, cultural, political and economic aspects.[10] This is what justifies the present volume. The analysis of recent developments offers fresh insight into how capitalism has impacted on society and social structure in countries which, not long ago, moved partly or fully towards market economies. Investigations into models whose systemic nature is not clear-cut provides us with inspirations as to where alternatives might appear. Do we need to ponder over new potential options from scratch, or can we try to combine the best features of both socialism and capitalism in a new way?

Area studies is one of many lenses through which to approach such global questions and these lenses are good at sharpening the eye. This volume is a multidisciplinary contribution to the development of both global theories and area studies. Traditionally, area studies took the Anglo-Saxon world as the norm and regarded the rest as exotic. Not too far off from an approach advocated by Edward Said, we have broken with such outlived ideas and tried to treat any region of the world on its own terms. Today it is the societies of the West which are threatened by the disintegrative forces of protectionism, nationalism and right-wing populism.

Russia and China, in turn, are little-appealing alternatives, given their dismal record in human rights and democracy. And yet, Russia's population has a history of standing up to both the imperialist world and their own elite. China today, gruesome as it is in many aspects, runs social projects on a scale which is beyond our imagination. Revolution started a process where industrialisation followed, and the Soviet Union turned into a superpower. China is following in its footsteps. Both historically (in the case of Russia) and contemporarily (in the case of China), there must be elements which we should not dismiss from the outset. Area studies is meant to identify and critically reflect upon them. If Western Europe and North America are to emerge from the crisis which is threatening them, then they must learn from the experience of the rest of the world. Area studies must come home.

Notes

1. Wolfgang Streeck, *How Will Capitalism End? Essays on a Failing System* (London: Verso, 2016).
2. See, for example, *Alternative Models of Ownership*, which is a report published by the Labour Party as a discussion document in early 2018, accessed 24 November 2018, labour.org.uk/wp-content/uploads/2017/10/Alternative-Models-of-Ownership.pdf.
3. Naomi Klein, *The Shock Doctrine: Rise of Disaster Capitalism* (London: Penguin, 2008).
4. European Union Council, *The Anti Tax Avoidance Directive 2016/1164*, accessed 24 November, ec.europa.eu/taxation_customs/business/company-tax/anti-tax-avoidance-package/anti-tax-avoidance-directive_en. For a discussion see Chevan Ilangaratne and Dami Olatuy, 'Is This the Real Reason Why Farage and Rees-Mogg Want a Speedy Brexit?', *The New European*, 28 August 2018, accessed 24 November 2018, www.theneweuropean.co.uk/top-stories/is-the-anti-tax-avoidance-directive-the-reason-the-rich-want-out-of-eu-1-5669763.
5. Danny Dorling, *Peak Inequality: Britain's Ticking Time Bomb* (Bristol, UK: Policy Press, 2018), 273.
6. Francis Fukuyama, *Identity: Contemporary Identity Politics and the Struggle for Recognition* (London: Profile Books, 2018).
7. Chantal Mouffe, *For A Left Populism* (London: Verso, 2018).
8. Cas Mudde and Cristóbal Rovira Kaltwasser, *Populism: A Very Short Introduction* (New York: Oxford University Press, 2017).
9. Jan-Werner Müller, *What Is Populism?* (London: Penguin, 2017), 1, 12.
10. The need for the new movements to develop firm ideological clarity if they are to succeed is argued in Rafal Soborski, *Ideology and the Future of Progressive Social Movements* (London: Rowman & Littlefield, 2017).

Bibliography

Dorling, Danny. *Peak Inequality: Britain's Ticking Time Bomb*. Bristol, UK: Policy Press, 2018.

European Union Council. *The Anti Tax Avoidance Directive 2016/1164*. Accessed 25 November 2018, ec.europa.eu/taxation_customs/business/company-tax/anti-tax-avoidance-package/anti-tax-avoidance-directive_en.

Fukuyama, Francis. *Identity: Contemporary Identity Politics and the Struggle for Recognition*. London: Profile Books, 2018.

Ilangaratne, Chevan, and Dami Olatuy. 'Is This the Real Reason why Farage and Rees-Mogg Want a Speedy Brexit?' *The New European*, 28 August 2018. Accessed 24 November, www.theneweuropean.co.uk/top-stories/is-the-anti-tax-avoidance-directive-the-reason-the-rich-want-out-of-eu-1-5669763.

Klein, Naomi. *The Shock Doctrine: Rise of Disaster Capitalism*. London: Penguin, 2008.

Mouffe, Chantal. *For A Left Populism*. London: Verso, 2018.

Mudde, Cas, and Cristóbal Rovira Kaltwasser. *Populism: A Very Short Introduction*. New York: Oxford University Press, 2017.

Müller, Jan-Werner. *What Is Populism?* London: Penguin, 2017.

Soborski, Rafal. *Ideology and the Future of Progressive Social Movements*. London: Rowman & Littlefield, 2017.

Streeck, Wolfgang. *How Will Capitalism End? Essays on a Failing System*. London, New York: Verso, 2016.

Index

Note: Page numbers in italics are figures; with 't' are tables.

Abkhazia, 26
accountability, 68, 75, 77, 166, 189, 199, 215
adult care, 202
Adults in the Room: My Battle with Europe's Deep Establishment (Varoufakis), 183
advertising, online, 196, 202
Afghanistan, 4, 143, 144, 145
Agalarov, Aras, 39, 40
Agalarov, Emin, 40
aganaktismenoi (indignant citizens' movement), 184, 189
age, 97, 103t, 104t, 173, 202
'An Agenda for a New America: How we Transform our Country', 195
agriculture, collectivised, 90
Ahora Madrid, 186
aid, international, 58
Akhmedov, Farkhad, 38t
alarmist school, 139
Alekperov, Vagit, 35, 39, 40, 42
Alekperova, Nelli, 40
Alfa Group, 42
Alibaba, 101
All-China Federation of Trade Unions (ACFTU), 121
almsgiving, 60
ambition, as value, 79
America, 4, 10
    See also United States (US)
American elites, 59
American Federation of Labor and Congress of Industrial Organizations (AFL–CIO), 196
American universities, 96
anti-austerity coalitions, 186
Anti-Capitalist Left, 185
anti-corruption campaign, 110, 122, 125

anti-market backlash, 91, 92
anti-Semitism, 6, 200, 203, 217
anti-tax avoidance directive, 217
'Anywhere' people, 173–4
apparat, 73
'appropriating class', 16
Arab Spring, 5, 184
arbitration, 120–1
area studies, 6–10, 219
Article 50 of the Treaty on European Union, 200, 201
arts sector, 59
Asia, 26, 136, 142, 143, 144, 165
    See also Eurasia
Asian financial crisis, 4
Asian Infrastructure and Investment Bank (AIIB), 144
Asian tigers, 91
Association of Muslim Businessmen of the Russian Federation (AMBRF), 39
asymmetrical interdependence, 101, 139
Atlantic integrationists, 25
Attlee, Clement, 162
austerity, 3, 4–5, 49, 165, 172, 188, 215
    in Greece, 189, 190, 192, 193, 206
    in the UK, 168–9, 198
Australia, 28
authoritarianism, 22–3, 178, 218
authoritarian state, 19, 21, 22–3, 29, 217

Bahrain, 184
Bailey, David, 187
bailout, 168, 182, 188, 190, 191, 192, 193
Baisarov, Ruslan, 35, 41
balanced budgets, 163, 168
Bank Avers, 40

221

banking
  China, 115, 118
  Russia, 36
  state, 90, 100
bankruptcy, 167
banks, 5, 164, 165, 167, 176, 189
Barcelona, 186, 187
Barcelona en Comu, 186
Bazhaev, Deni, 39
Bazhaev, Musa, 39, 41
beer, 73
Belt and Road Initiative (BRI), 115, 132, 135–7, 138, 139, 145, 214
  and Russia, 140
  and the US, 133, 141, 144, 146
Berlin Wall, fall of, 3
Beveridge, William Henry, 162
Big Bang, 1986, 57, 165
Bilalov, Akhmed, 36
bilateral relations, 135, 136
billionaires, 93–5, 100, 101
bipolar international system, 133, 145, 214
birzha, 66, 67, 68–80, 213
Black Americans, 196, 197
Black Lives Matter, 194
black-market entrepreneurs, 16
Black people, 205
Blair, Tony, 193–4, 199, 201
Bloco de Esqueirda (Left Bloc), 182
Bolivia, 185
bourgeoisie, 22
Breeze, Beth, 51, 55–6
Bretton Woods currency system, 163
Brexit, 5, 202, 203–4, 205, 206
Brexiteers, 173
Brexit referendum, 173, 175, 176, 200, 216–17, 218
bribery, 22, 75
Britain, 3, 10, 176–7, 178, 182, 193–4, 216–17
  and European identity, 205
  and liberalism, 162–7
  and 'Occupy the City', 184
  and philanthropy, 49, 50, 52, 55–9, 60
  and Russia, 218
  See also United Kingdom (UK)
Briziarelli, Marco, 183
brotherhood, 71
Brown, Gordon, 5, 199
Brzezinski, Zbigniew, 139
Buddhism, 42
budgets, 163
  deficit, 24
  surplus, 193
building regulations, 170
building societies, 165, 167
bureaucracy, 15, 115, 124
bureaucratic authority, 117
bureaucratic economic coordination, 112, 116, 123

bureaucratic networks, 4
bureaucratic planning, 117
bureaucratic power, 117, 118–19
bureaucratic socialism, 109–10
bureaucratisation, 117
Bush, George W., 4
Bush administration, 142, 146
business deals, 72
business elite, 33, 35, 37, 38–9, 39, 40–3

Cadbury, George, 56
cadres, 100, 122, 125
Cameron, David, 5, 173, 198
Capital in the Twenty-First Century (Piketty), 8
capital investment, 91
capitalism, 10, 113, 117, 171, 190, 215, 216, 219
  and cyclical crises, 163
  and inequality, 8
  semi-dependent, 15, 29
  semi-peripheral, 19, 20, 22, 24, 25, 28
  varieties, 7
capitalist elite, 17
Carillion, 166
Carmena, Manuela, 186
Catalonia, 187
Central and Eastern Europe, 3–4
Central Asia, 136, 143–4
Central Bank Law (Russia), 36
Central China, 98
Central European University, 217
centre-left, 181
charities, 50, 56
charity giving, 40–2, 49–54, 55, 56–7, 58, 59–60
Chavez, Hugo, 185, 218
Chechnya, 41
checks and balances, 6
Chen Yun, 94
children, support for, 55, 58
China, 4, 28, 89–104, 206, 213, 214, 219
  and Marxism, 108–26
  rise of, 131–47
Chinese Dream, 101–2
Chinese People's Political Consultative Conference (CPPCC), 95
Christian Democratic Union (CDU), 181
Christian Democrats, 162
churches, 42, 55
cigarettes, 36, 43
citizens
  alienation from political institutions, 76, 78
  protests, 5, 120, 184
City of London, 5
Ciudadanos (Citizens), 185, 187
civil conflict, 68
civil society organisations, 6, 58
cladding, 170
class, 21, 22, 23, 110, 112, 125, 173, 196, 202

classical free-market theory, 162–3
classical socialism, 116, 117, 123, 125
The Class Struggles in France (Marx), 7
climate change, 195, 215
Clinton, Hillary, 25, 143, 144, 194–5, 197
Clinton administration, 142
Colau, Ada, 186
Cold War, 16, 145
collaboration, bilateral, 136
collective enterprises, 124
coloured revolutions, 26, 28
command economy, 90, 100
Commercial Banking Law (Russia), 36
commercial lobbying, 37–9
Committee on Work and Pensions (UK), 166
common ownership, 193–4
communism, 114
   See also China
Communist Manifesto, 2
Communist Party of China (CPC), 94–5, 96, 100, 102t, 108, 110, 125
   and Marxism, 113, 114–15
communist party rule, exclusive, 117
Communists (Portugal), 182
community art, 59
community giving, 53–4
   See also charity giving
community health centres, 197
comparative advantage, 110
competition, 92, 164
compliance, 60, 71
comprehensive strategic partnership, 138
confidence, 163, 173
congagement, 142, 143, 146
conglomerates, 60
conservative governments, 3
Conservative-Liberal Democrat coalition (UK), 5
Conservative Party, 200
Conservatives, 202, 215
conspicuous consumption, 92, 95, 100, 101
constituency Labour parties (CLPs), 200, 201
consumer goods, 36
consumerism, 95
containment, 132, 141–2, 143, 145, 147
control, infrastructure of, 17, 19, 21, 22
cooperation, 135, 136, 137, 142, 143
cooperative banks, 36
cooperative movement, 7
cooperatives, 35–6, 216
cooperative socialism, 7
coordinated market economy, 7
Corbyn, Jeremy, 5, 10, 183, 198, 199–201, 206, 218
   criticism of, 202–3
   and DSA, 197
   and identity politics, 205
   pushed Labour Party to left, 182
The Corbyn Effect (Perryman), 183

Corbyn: The Strange Rebirth of Radical Politics (Seymour), 183
corporate governance, 17, 18
corporate social responsibility, 42
corporate taxation, 215
corporations, 176–7, 215
corruption, 4, 22, 67, 68, 75, 213
   in China, 101, 122
Coutts, 59
Cox, Jo, 217
Crashing the Party: From the Bernie Sanders Campaign to a Progressive Movement (Gautney), 183
crime, 67, 68, 73, 74–5, 78
Crimea, 28, 137, 139, 203
Criminal Code, Georgian, 77
criminal hierarchy, 71–2
criminal structures, 17
criminal world, 75
crises, cyclical, 163
Crocus Group, 40
Cui Zhiyuan, 92
Cultural Revolution, 117
currency bonds, 36–7

Dagestan, 41
Dagestani pilgrims, 41
Day of the Oprichnik (Sorokin), 131
debt, 166, 167, 168, 189
debt bailout, 190, 191, 192, 193
debt crisis (Greece), 188
dedication, 73
defence, 162
deficits, 24, 165
deflationary crisis, 164
deindustrialised communities, 165
'the dementia tax', 202
democracy, 134, 138, 146, 170, 171, 178, 206
Democratic Party, 193, 194, 205, 206
democratic socialism, 195–6
Democratic Socialists of America (DSA), 194, 197–8, 205, 206, 216
Deng Xiaoping, 89, 90, 94, 115, 118, 134, 214
depression, 2, 162, 163
deregulation, 76, 78, 167, 195
development, 110, 111, 112, 117, 136
Die Linke, 205, 218
diplomacy, 135, 136, 138, 146
domestic affairs, non-interference in, 135, 138, 146
domestic consumption, 91
domestic realm/society, 73, 139
donations, 58, 196
   See also charity giving
Donbas uprising, 28
drachma, 192
dual-track approach, 92

INDEX   223

Dynamism, Rivalry, and the Surplus Economy: Two Essays on the Nature of Capitalism (Kornai), 117
dzmak'atsoba, 72
dzveli bich'i, 71–2

Eastern bloc, 145
Eastern Europe, 3–4, 7
Eastern region, China, 98
economic change, 99–100
economic cooperation, 136, 137, 145
economic crisis, 1970s, 163–4
economic democracy, 197
economic development, 110, 111, 112
economic efficiency, 123
economic elites, 101
economic freedom, 116, 162
economic goals, 135
economic growth, 4, 101, 117, 164, 177
    China, 89, 91, 92, 94, 100
economic interest, 175
economic intervention, 201
economic planning, 115
economic policy, 24
economic reforms, 91, 92
economic stimulus programme, 115
education, 96–7, *98*, 101, 103t, 104t, 162, 173, 216
educational causes, 59
educational institutions, 177
efficiency, 123
Egypt, 184
The Eighteenth Brumaire of Louis Bonaparte (Marx), 7
eight-point regulation, 95
electorate, 172
elite, 16, 21, 23, 50, 57, 58, 73
    American, 59
    business, 33, 35, 37, 38–9, 40–3
    capitalist, 17
    globalised, 171
    Jewish business, 39, 41–2
    political, 78, 92, 95, 101
    Russian, 24
    and trust, 162
    Western, 16, 25
    See also wealthy elite
elite philanthropy studies, 50
elite universities, 59
embedded practices, 80
employers, 120, 121, 164, 166
employment, 96, 162, 163–4, 215
engagement, 132, 141
Engels, Friedrich, 2
entrepreneurs, 16, 94, 100
environmental problems, 215
equality, 136, 138
equitable development, 110

equity funds, 166, 171
Errejón, Iñigo, 183, 185, 187
Ertiani Natsionaluri Modzraoba (ENM), 68
Estonia, 19
ethnic conflict, 68
ethnicity, 103t, 104t
EU (European Union), 169, 173, 184, 185, 204, 216
    anti-tax avoidance directive, 217
Eurasia, 132, 135, 136, 138, 139–40, 146, 214
    and US, 133, 142, 143, 144, 145
Eurasian Economic Union (EAEU), 27, 139–40
Eurasian integrationists, 25
euro, 189, 191, 192, 193
Eurogroup, finance ministers, 191
Europe, and Marshall Plan, 135–6
European Central Bank, 188
European Commission, 188
European identity, 205
European universities, 96
Europe's Radical Left: From Marginality to the Mainstream? (Luke and Keith), 182
eurozone, 5
everyday practices, importance and strength of, 79
exploitation, 29, 108, 114
export-led growth, 91
export of private capital, 18
exports, 92
external balancing, 142

Facebook, 184, 196, 202
family, 39–40, 43, 73, 74
fandom, cult of, 204
far right, 5, 217–18
fascist movements, 2
Feldman, Dan, 144
FIDESZ, 217
finance, 36, 167
financial capital, 57
financial crisis, 2007–8, 4–5, 115, 165, 167, 182–3, 194, 206
    and inequality, 8, 172–3
    and social struggles, 184
financial institutions, 5, 16, 164, 165, 169–70
financialisation, 166–7
financial markets, 164, 172
financial services, 166
'financial stabilisation' approach, 17
fiscal covenant, 162–3, 169
five-year plans, 91, 100, 115
food banks, 189
Forbes, 93
    'Golden hundred' of Russians, 22
Forbes Russia, 33, 35, 39, 40, 43, 51, 60
foreign direct investment, 91, 115–16
foreign markets, 167

foreign policy, 24–8, 115, 139, 143, 144, 214
foreign trade, 27, 35–6, 90
foreign trade associations, 36–7
former Soviet republics, 4, 16, 19, 213, 217
foundations, 50, 53–4, 59, 60
fragmentation, 80
France, 5, 7, 181, 204
La France Insoumise (France Unbowed), 204
freedom, 116, 165, 173
free-market capitalism, 171
free-market economic globalisation, 169
free markets, 172, 178
free-market theory, 162
free trade, 100
free tuition, 195, 197, 201, 202
Fridman, Mikhail, 41–2
friendship, 73, 74, 79
Front National (FN), 181
frugality, 101
fuerdai, 95
Fukuyama, Francis, 217
full employment, 162, 163–4, 215
funding cuts, 169

Gan Yang, 92
gas prices, 4
Gautney, Heather, 183
GDP (gross domestic product), 17, 27, 193
 per capita, 19
gender, 102t, 104t
geographical inequality, 214
geographical mobility, 79
Georgia, 26–7, 66–80, 213
Georgian Criminal Code, 77
Germany, 2, 3, 5, 7, 181, 218
gifts, 56
gig economy, 165
Gindin, Sam, 183
Gini coefficient, 93
global collective security, 134
The Global Encyclopaedia of Informality, 8
globalisation, 167, 169, 217
globalised elites, 171
globalised hyper-rich, 60
globalised markets, 169, 172
global wealth, 8, 29
GNI, per capita, 20
Goldman, Marshall, 23
Goodhart, David, 173–4
Gorbachev, Mikhail, 35–6, 116
government policies, 110, 111, 115
Gramsci, Antonio, 19, 183
grants, university, 201
Greater Eurasia Project, 132, 138, 140–1
Great Stagnation, 29
Greece, 5, 10, 182, 188–93, 205, 206, 216
 aganaktismenoi, 184
 PASOK, 181, 188, 189

Greek Communist Party (KKE), 183
green industry, 176
Green Party, 200, 205
Greenspan, Alan, 167–8
Grenfell Tower fire, 170
grey zones, 74, 76, 79
growth, 9, 91, 94, 100, 102, 164, 177
 and inequality, 101
 and wealth, 92
 and working class, 110
guanxi, 101
Guillem, Susana Martinez, 183
Gutseriev, Mikhail, 36, 37–8, 38t, 39, 40, 41, 42, 43
Gutseriev, Sait-Salam, 38t, 39, 40

Habermas, Jürgen, 175
Hajj pilgrimages, 41, 42
Halifax Bank of Scotland, 167
Hall, Peter A., 7
hangouts, 66, 67, 68, 69
hard budget constraint, 123
HDI rank, 20
health care, 162, 195, 216
health centres, 177, 197
heavy industry, 90, 110–11
hedge funds, 166, 171
hegemony, theory of, 19
Hezbollah, 28
higher education, 59
historical memory, 183
Hollande, François, 192, 204–5
honesty, 73
Hong Kong, 91
hospitals, 169, 190
household debt, 168
household income, 96, 97, 102t, 168
housing, 176, 177, 216
housing benefit, 169
HS2, 176
HS3, 176
Hu Jintao, 91
Human Development Index (HDI), 19
human rights, 21, 29, 58, 134, 137, 138, 146
Hungary, 7, 116, 217
Hurun, 93, 95
hyper-rich/wealthy elite, 50, 51, 53–4, 57, 60

identity, 55, 162, 173, 176, 196, 205
identity literature school, 139
identity politics, 205, 217
Iglesias, Pablo, 183, 185, 187, 188, 206
illegal activities, 70
illness, 165
IMF (International Monetary Fund), 3, 144, 188, 191
immigrant populations, 217
immigrants, 169, 196

immigration, 173, 174, 187
income, 18–19, 92, 96, 98, 99, 102t, 136
   and education, 101
   household, 97, 168
income inequality, 93, 96, 102, 195
income tax, 202
Independent Greeks (ANEL), 190, 192
India, 144
Indignados, 184, 185, 189
individualism, progressive, 173
Indo-Pacific region, 144
industrial policy, state, 176
industrial production, 27
Industrial Revolution, 56
industry, 90, 110–11, 165
inequality, 4, 9, 49, 57, 125, 172–3
   in China, 92, 101, 108
   in former Soviet republics, 217
   geographical, 214
   in Georgia, 78, 79
   income, 93, 96, 102, 195
   in Russia, 213
   social, 8, 50, 59
   in the US, 194
infant mortality, 217
inflation, 17, 163, 164, 166
informal control, 17, 18
informality, culture of, 76
informal networks, 74, 101
informal practices, 8, 213
infrastructural investment, 176, 201
infrastructure of control, 17, 19, 21, 22
Ingushetia, 36
inheritance tax, 95
inherited wealth, 51, 171
institutionalist theory, 133–4
institutional ties, 101
insurance companies, 176
insurance funds, 167
insurance policies, 4, 166
intellectual freedom, 116
intellectuals, 185
intelligentsia, 15–16, 54, 55, 217
Interfinance Company, 36
intergenerational mobility, *99*, 100
internal balancing, 142
international aid, 58
international banks, 164
international competition, 92
international cooperation, 135
international institutions, 169, 173
internationalism, liberal, 135, 138
international order, 133, 145, 146
Internet, 196
   platforms, 184
interstices, 71
intimacy networks, 74
invalidity benefits, 169

investment, 135, 176, 177
investment banks, 167
investment hunger, 119
Iran, 28
Iraq, 4
Islam, 41, 42–3
Islamist terrorism, 169, 174
Israel, pilgrimages, 41–2
Italy, 181, 184, 205, 217

Japan, 142
Jewish business elite, 39, 41–2
Jewish voters, 205
Jiang Zemin, 94
Jianlong Steel Holding Company, 121
Jilin State-owned Assets Supervision and
   Administration Commission (SASAC), 121
Jin, Yongai, 96
jobs, 91, 100, 177
job security, 214
joint-stock ownership, 177
joint ventures, 115–16
Judaism, 42

Kabardino-Balkaria, 41, 42
Kanokov, Arsen, 35, 38t, 41, 42
k'anonieri kurdi, 72
Kazakhstan, 137
Keith, Daniel, 182
Kendall, Diana E., 50
Kensington and Chelsea, borough, 170
Kerimov, Said, 40
Kerimov, Suleiman, 33, 38t, 40, 41, 42, 43
Keynes, John Maynard, 9, 162–5, 177
Keynesianism, 9, 10, 162–4, 177, 214, 215
Keynesian theory, 175–6
Khodorkovsky, Mikhail, 52–3
Khodorkovsky Affair, 53
King, Martin Luther, Jr., 195
kinship ties, 74
Kioupkiolis, Alexandros, 185–6
KKE, 189, 190
Klein, Naomi, 216
Komsomol, 74
Konstantinovsky Palace, 41
Kornai, Janos, 7, 108, 109–10, 111, 112–13,
   116–19, 123–4, 125
   on corruption of China's officials, 122
Kremlin group, 24, 25, 28
Kyrgyzstan, 138, 144

labour, 19, 21, 29, 92, 120
Labour government, 5, 162
labour laws, 120
Labour Party, 5, 182, 183, 193–4, 198–204,
   206, 218
Laclau, Ernesto, 185, 218
Lafazanis, Panagiotis, 191, 192

226   INDEX

land sale, 4
land value tax, 177
Lane, David, 15–16
Lansman, Jon, 199, 201, 204
Latin American immigrants, 217
Latin American socialists, 202
Law and Justice party, 217
law enforcement agencies, 17, 25
law of value, 119
Law on Cooperatives (Russia), 35–6
layoffs, 92
Ledeneva, Alena, 43
the left, 10, 181, 190, 192
Left Opposition, 118, 119
Left Platform, 189, 192
left-wing parties, 218
legal aid, 169, 170
Lehman Brothers, 167
Lenin, Vladimir Ilich, 2, 118
Lezgin language, 41
Lezgins, 41
liberal democracy, 172, 178
liberal-democratic institutions, 217
Liberal Democratic Party of Russia (LDPR), 37
Liberal Democrats (UK), 198
liberal hegemonic order, 132, 133, 134, 145, 146, 147
liberal internationalism, 135, 138
liberalism, 161, 162, 164
liberal market economy, 7
liberal partnership order, 134–5, 138, 145, 146
libraries, 169
Libya, 184
life expectancy, 217
liminal spaces, 71, 77
limitationist school, 139
limited liability, 176, 177
Lin, Justin Yifu, 110–11
Die Linke, 205, 218
Lisbon Treaty, 185
Lloyd, Theresa, 51
Lloyd George, David, 162
Lo, Bobo, 140
lobbying, 37–40
local authorities, 165, 170, 184
Lofland, I., 67
London, 5, 184
loyalty, 23, 72, 74, 172
LUKoil, 42
Lukoil charity fund, 40

Ma, Jack, 101
Macron, Emmanuel, 5, 205
Madrid, 186
Magomedov, Magomed, 36, 39
Magomedov, Ziyavudin, 36–7, 39, 41, 42
Maidan uprising, 27
maintenance grants, university, 201

Makhmudov, Iskander, 36, 38, 42
male street socialisation, 66
Manas airbase, 144
'manual management', 24, 28
manufacturing output, 91
Maoist era, 115
Mao Yushi, 92
Mao Zedong, 89, 90, 92, 115, 117
March, Luke, 182
marginalisation, 80
market competition, 109
market-driven decisions, 123
market economics, 135, 136, 138, 145
market economy, 3, 118, 137
marketisation, 91, 92
market reforms, 21, 29, 92, 94
markets
   gradualist evolution of, 110
   open, 135
market socialism, 7
market system, 100
Marktvolk, 172, 173
Marshall Plan, 115, 135–6
Marx, Karl, 2, 7, 113, 114
Marxism, 110, 112, 113, 114
Marxist development theory, 111
Marxist-Leninist ideology, 117
masculinity, 71, 75
Mattis, James, 141, 142
May, Theresa, 201
McDonnell, John, 199, 201, 202, 203, 204
Mearsheimer, John J., 131
Mecca, 41
Médecins sans frontiers, 217
media, 6, 169–70
medical research, 54
Melenchon, Jon-Luc, 204
the Memorandum, 188, 189, 191
memory, historical, 183
mental illness, 165
meritocracy, 79, 101
Merkel, Angela, 5, 191, 192
MFA (Ministry of Foreign Affairs)/China, 135
MFA partnerships, 136
middle class, 195
Middle Kingdom, 90
migration, 95, 169
   See also immigration
Miliband, Ed, 198, 199
minimum wage, 190, 194
mixed economy, 7, 9, 100, 102, 216
mobility, 79, 96, 97, 99, 102, 103t, 104t
modernisation, 77, 78, 136
Modern Silk Road Strategy (MRS), 143, 144
Momentum, 199–200, 201, 202, 203, 204, 205, 206
monetary policy, 17, 23
money, 114

money laundering, 216–17
Morris, William, 182, 188
mortality, conceptions of, 50
mortgage debt, 167
Moscow Cathedral Mosque, 33, 43
mosques, 42
Mouffe, Chantal, 183, 187, 218
Movimento Cinque Stella (Five Star Movement), 183
Muller, Jan-Werner, 5, 218
multilateral governance/multilateralism, 134, 135, 138, 145
multilateral organisations, 137
multipolar international system, 133, 134, 139, 145, 147, 214
'Munich speech', 26
municipal ownership, 216
musharakah, 40, 43
Muslim Business Elite (MBE, Russia), 33, 34t, 36, 37, 38, 39–40, 41, 42–3
Muslims, 33–43, 217
mutual funds, 167
mutual responsibility, 67

national debt, 168
National Education Service, 201
National Health Service (NHS)/UK, 169, 174, 217
national identity, 55, 139, 162
National Investment Bank, 176, 201
nationalisation, 189
nationalism, 187
nationalist regimes, 217
national patriotism, 41
National People's Congress (NPC)/China, 95
national rejuvenation, 101–2
national sovereignty, 173
National Transformation Fund, 201
national wealth, 162
nation-state, 174–5
NATO, 26, 185
neighbourhood, 79
(neo)institutionalist theory, 133
neo-liberal economic policies, 4, 5, 23, 194, 195, 218
neo-liberalism, 9, 10, 67, 79, 110, 161, 162
    and austerity, 215
    and Brexit, 216–17
    and crisis of credibility, 4–5
    and former Soviet states, 213
    in Georgia, 67–8, 76
    rejection of, 201
    and wealthy and powerful, 169–70
neo-liberal reforms, 68, 69
(neo)realist theory, 133
networks, 101
New Democracy, 188, 189, 193
New Economic Policy (NEP), 109, 110, 118, 119, 125

New Labour, 3, 199, 218
New Left, 92
New Silk Road Vision (NSR), 143–4, 145
Nizhnekamenskneftekhim, 37
nomenklatura, 73
non-governmental organisations (NGOs), 53–4, 58
normalcy school, 139
Nuland, Victoria, 27

Obama, Barack, 5, 194, 218
Obama administration, 142–3, 144, 145, 146
obedience, 53
Ocasio-Cortes, Alexandra, 198
Occupy movement, 5
'Occupy the City', 184
Occupy Wall Street, 183, 184, 194
Odendahl, Teresa, 50, 59
officialdom, 73
official institutions, 75
offshore firms, 17, 18
offshore tax havens, 51
oil, 3, 4, 23, 163, 164
oligarchs, 4, 21, 22, 24–5, 52–4, 192, 203
online advertising, 196, 202
online donations, 196
opening up (*gaige kaifang*), 90
openness, 135, 136, 138, 145
open trading, 195
organic crisis, 183
organised crime, 68, 73, 74–5
original socialist accumulation, 109, 110, 119, 125
Ostrower, Francie, 50
Our Revolution: A Future to Believe In (Sanders), 183
outsourcing, 165–6
Ovenden, Kevin, 183
overproduction, 163
Owen, David, 57
ownership, 123, 125, 193–4

Pakistan, 144
Palestinian groups, 202
Pan-Hellenic Socialist Movement (PASOK), 181, 188, 189
Panitch, Leo, 183
Pappas, Nikos, 189
paramilitary squads, 74–5
Parliamentary Labour Party (PLP), 199, 200
Partido Popular (PP), 184–5, 186, 187
Partido Socialista, 182
Parti Socialiste, 181, 204
Partito Demcratica (PD), 181
partnership diplomacy, 135, 136, 138, 146
party affiliation, 96, 101
party cadres, 100, 122, 125
party membership, 96, 97, 98, 99
party-state, 101

228   INDEX

party-state officials, 101
PASOK, 181, 188, 189
Passover, 41–2
paternalism, 53, 60
patriotism, 41
patronage, 43, 213
PCE, 183, 185
Peabody Trust, 56
peasants, 119, 125, 126
Peking University, 114
le Pen, Marine, 5
pension age, 4
pensions, 162, 166–7, 176, 190, 193
per capita GDP, 19
per capita GNI, *20*
Perestroika, 16
peripheral capitalism, 19
Perryman, Mark, 183
personal economic freedom, 162, 165
personal politics, 38
personal ties, 74
petty crime, 77, 78
philanthrocapitalism, 49–50
philanthropy, 40–2, 43, 49–60
Piketty, Thomas, 8, 51, 59
pilgrimages, 41–2
plan-market relations, 116
planned economy, 90, 115, 116, 119
planning, state, 119, 125, 165
Podemos, 5, 10, 182, 183, 185–8, 193, 205, 218
 and DSA, 197
 mayors, 206
Podemos: In the Name of the People (Errejon and Mouffe), 183
Poland, 3, 116, 217
polarity, 133
police patrols, 77–8
political connections, 37
political discourse, openness in, 116
political diversity, 134
political elites, 78, 92, 95, 101
political influence, 43
political institutions, citizens' alienation from, 76
political interaction, 137
political movements, 5
political party voting, 175
political protest, 184
political systems, 137
political ties, 96
Politics in a Time of Crisis: Podemos and the Future of Democracy in Europe (Iglesias), 183
Politkovskaya, Anna, 42
Pompeo, Mike, 144
Popular Unity, 192
populism, 5–6, 174, 185, 204, 217–18
populist parties, 169, 172, 173, 178
Portugal, 182, 184

post-Soviet states, 4, 16, 19–20, 217
Potanin, Vladimir, 53
poverty, 68, 91, 101, 163, 213, 216
power, 21–2, 117, 125, 213
power relations, 17, 50
power transition, 133
Preobrazhensky, Evgeny, 108–9, 110, 111, 112, 113, 118, 119, 125
prescriptions, free, 190
presidential power, 22
prices, 17, 90, 163, 164
prisons, 78, 169
the private
 blurred boundaries with the public, 78, 79
 clear-cut division with the public, 77
private business, 117
private capital, 18, 119
private economic enterprises, 115
private enterprises, 4, 90, 216
private foundations, 53–4
private insurance, 4
private investment, 115–16
private monopoly, 166
private ownership, 21, 36, 113, 116
private property, 16, 21, 75, 113
private relationships, 67
private sector, 16, 91, 94–5, 100, 109, 116, 124, 125
private security firms, 17
private space, 66
private sphere, 74, 75, 79
private wealth, 93
privatisation, 164, 190, 217
 in China, 92, 100, 120, 121
 in Georgia, 76, 78
 in Russia, 16–17, 21, 52, 213
 in the UK, 165–6, 202
privatisation auctions, 37
privileges, 50
productivity, 91, 164
profits, 164, 166, 177
progressive individualism, 173
progressive taxation, 162
property redistribution, 18
property rights, 17, 22, 110, 123
property trading and holdings, 57
protest movements, 5, 184
protests, 120, 184
proto-liberal partnership order, 135, 138
PSOE, 185, 186, 187, 206
public discussion, 175
public health insurance, 195
public institutions, 68, 74–5, 76–7, 79, 165
public libraries, 169
public life, 75
public office, 101
public ownership, 3, 91, 108, 115, 116, 125
 and socialism, 112, 117, 123
public places, 74

INDEX 229

public sector bodies, 115
public sector enterprises., 118
public services, 172
public space, 67, 75, 77
public sphere, 74, 78, 79, 175
public transport, 177
Putin, Vladimir, 4, 5, 19, 22–3, 33, 217
   and Corbyn, 202–3
   discouraged business elite from engaging in politics, 38
   and foreign policy, 25, 28, 139
   and philanthropy, 52, 53
   and religion, 43
   and Syria, 28

racism, 5–6, 197
radical democracy, 197
radical left movements, 10
Radical Left Parties in Europe (March), 182
Rajoy, Mariano, 186, 187
Rappaport, Andrei, 42
Reaganomics, 3
real estate, 57, 166, 167
realist theory, 133, 142
recessions, 9, 163, 176
   See also financial crisis, 2007–8
reciprocity, 60, 67, 79
referendum, 6
   Brexit, 173, 175, 176, 200, 216–17, 218
   Catalan government, 187
   Greek, 188, 192
   second on EU, 204
reform socialism, 113, 116, 117, 123, 125, 126
refugees, 217
regime change, 4, 137–8
regime type, 134
regional patriotism, 41
Rehmann, Jan, 198
Reich, Rob, 50
religions, 41, 42–3
religious causes, 41–2, 43, 55
religious festivals, 41, 42
Remain vote, 173
renationalisation, 201
rent, 18–19, 22, 25, 29
repression, 79, 114, 216
research and development, 165, 176
respect, 69, 79
retirement age, 191
Reviving Gramsci: Crisis, Communication, and Change (Briziarelli and Martinez Guillem), 183
revolutionary transitional era, 112, 113, 116–17
The Revolution Betrayed (Trotsky), 15
the rich, 5, 50, 51, 55, 213
Richards, Steve, 183
richest 200 Russians, 54, 60

rich lists, 33, 43, 51
right-wing populism, 217–18
The Rise of the Outsiders: How Mainstream Politics Lost its Way (Richards), 183
risk, 163, 166, 167, 177
'roofs', 17, 22
Roosevelt, Franklin D., 195
Rose Revolution, 67, 76, 77, 78
Rowntree Foundation, 56
Royal Bank of Scotland, 167
Royal Borough of Kensington and Chelsea, 170
Rubin, Dominic, 35
rule of law, 4, 68, 162, 169
ruling class, 218
ruling elite, 73
Russia, 4, 5, 49, 131, 136, 144, 206, 213, 217, 219
   and China, 138–41, 146–7
   and Corbyn, 202–3
   and Crimea, 137
   and Greater Eurasia Project, 132
   and Obama, 218
   and philanthropy, 50–1, 52–5, 58, 59, 60
   and protests, 184
   and semi-dependent capitalism, 15–29
   and super-rich, 33–43
   and support for Trump and Brexit, 218
   and Washington Consensus, 3
Russian Central Bank, 18, 24
Russian Jewish Congress (RJC), 39, 41–2
Russian Orthodox Church, 42, 43, 55
Russian Revolution, 117
Russian Union of Industrialists and Entrepreneurs (RUIE), 39

Saak'ashvili, Mikheil, 26, 67, 68, 69, 76, 77, 79
SAFMAR, 41, 42
Said, Edward, 219
Sakwa, Richard, 25
Salt, Titus, 56
Sanchez, Pedro, 186, 187
sanctions, 79, 139
Sanders, Bernie, 5, 10, 182, 183, 194, 195–8, 202, 206
   and Black people, 205
   and mixed economy, 216
savings banks, 166
Scandinavia, 7
Schäuble, Wolfgang, 191
Schervish, Paul, 50
Schimpfössl, Elisabeth, 40
schools, 50, 169
science research, 54
Second World War, 2–3
security, 134, 135, 136, 137, 162
security cooperation, 136, 145
security firms, 17
self-interest, 176

self-management, 7, 112, 113, 117, 123–4, 126
semi-dependent capitalism, 15, 29
    See also semi-peripheral capitalism
semi-peripheral capitalism, 19, 20, 22, 24, 25, 28
Senkaku Islands dispute, 142
serfdom, 53
Seymour, Richard, 183, 204
shadow banks, 164
Shaimiev, Airat, 35, 37, 39
Shaimiev, Kamila, 40
Shaimiev, Mintimir, 37
Shaimiev, Radik, 35, 37, 39, 40
Shambaugh, David, 116
Shanghai Cooperation Organization (SCO), 134–5
Shanghai Municipal People's Congress, 124
shareholders, 177, 215
sharing, 72–3
Shigabutdinov, Albert, 37
Shishkhanov, Mikhail, 39
shock therapy, 4, 216
shortage, 109
shortage economy, 119
short-term rent, 18–19, 22
Silk Road, 214
Silk Road Economic Belt (SREB), 136, 144
Singapore, 91
Sino-Russian relationship, 146
Sino-Russian security alliance, 139
Sino-Soviet split, 90
sistema, 43
el Sistema, 184
Skidelsky, Robert, 9
Skripal, Sergei, 203
Skripal, Yulia, 203
Smith, Owen, 201
social class, 22, 110, 173
social contract, 171
social democracy, 10
social-democratic governments, 3
social-democratic parties, 2, 215, 218
Social Democrats, 162, 181–2
social development, 41
social dominance, 50
social-economic rights, 19
social good, 162
social inequality, 8, 50, 59
social initiatives, 40–1
socialism, 7, 108–10, 111–26, 183, 193, 194, 203, 206, 215
    and *birzha*, 74
    with Chinese characteristics, 89–90, 95
    and Sanders, 182, 196, 197–8, 205
The Socialist Challenge Today: Syriza, Sanders, Corbyn (Panitch and Gindin), 183
socialist market economy, 90, 91
The Socialist System (Kornai), 109

Socialist Workers Party (PSOE), 181, 182
social justice, 58, 162
social-market economy, 7
social media, 175
social mobility, 79, 96, 99
social movements, 5
social public space, 75
    See also public space
social realm, 74
social reform, 193, 219
social responsibility, 51, 52
social security, 68, 165, 169, 177, 195
social solidarity, 162
social struggles, 120, 184
social system, 23
social trust, 172, 174, 175, 176
social unrest, 112, 121–2, 124, 125, 126
social welfare, 3, 19
socio-economic contract, 162
soft-budget constraint, 123–4
soft power, 27
solidarity, 79, 162
Solidarity Clubs, 189
'Somewhere' people, 173, 174
Sorokin, Vladimir, 131
Soskice, David, 7
Sotheby's Russian auction, 41
South China Sea, 142, 143
South Korea, 91
South Ossetia, 26
sovereignty, 134, 135, 137, 138, 146, 173
Soviet republics, former, 4, 16, 19–20, 213, 217
Soviet Union, 90, 109, 111–12, 123, 203, 206
    and *birzha*, 68
    and Cold War, 145
    collapse, 3, 52, 143, 161
    intelligentsia, 54
    system, 15–16
Spain, 5, 10, 181, 182, 184–8, 189, 193, 205
SPD (Social-Democratic Party), 3, 181, 205
special economic zones, 90
specialisation, 52, 55–9
spending, 4, 53, 95, 163
spiritual revival, 42
Squares' movement, 184
Staatsvolk, 172, 173
stabilisation, 117
stability, 137, 138
Staff and Workers' Representative Councils (SWRCs), 121, 124
stagflation, 164
stagnation, 215
Stalin, Joseph, 3, 112–13, 119, 125
the state
    intervention, 9, 97, 99, 103t, 164
    and mistrust by citizens, 76–7
    patronage, 43
    role of, 68, 97

INDEX   231

the state *(cont.)*
   support, 104t
   taken over by criminal groups, 74
   theory of, 7
   wealth to private sector, 16
state banking, 90, 100
state capitalism, 118
state corporations, 18, 24, 100
State Duma, 37, 38
state economy, 119
state industrial policy, 176
state institutions, 95
state investment, 115
state law enforcement agencies, 17
state-led development, 91
state-owned enterprises (SOEs), 92, 95, 115, 120, 124, 135
state ownership, 116, 118, 216
state planning, 119, 125, 165
state-private ownership, 116
state sector, 124–5
statist beliefs, 97, 102
Stiglitz, Joseph, 110, 111
stock markets, 167
Strategic Arms Reduction Treaty (START), 25
strategic partnership, 136, 137, 138
Streeck, Wolfgang, 172, 173
street communities, 73, 79
street hangouts, 66, 68, 69
street socialisation, 66
strikes, 214, 215
structural ties, 101
sub-prime mortgages, 167
Suleiman Kerimov Foundation, 41
Sulteev, Diana, 40
Sulteev, Rustem, 36, 37, 40
The Sunday Times, 51, 60
super-wealthy, 52
   See also wealthy elite
Supreme Soviet, 21
surplus economy, 118
Sweden, 181–2
symbols, 175
Syria, 28, 184
Syriza, 10, 182, 183, 188–93, 205, 206, 216, 218
   and DSA, 197
   and protest movements, 5
Syriza: Inside the Labyrinth (Ovenden), 183
systemic collapse, 117

Taiwan, 91
Talbott, Strobe, 21
Tatar American Investments and Finance (TAIF), 37, 40
Tatarstan, 36
Tatneft, 37
tax avoidance, 202

tax credits, 169
taxes, 4, 162, 177, 191, 202, 215
tax havens, 51, 171, 177, 217
taxpayer risk, 166
tax relief, 50
Tbilisi, 71
technical progress, 117
temporary jobs, 165
terrorism, 169, 174, 202
Thatcherism, 3
'There is no alternative!', 215
Thessaloniki Programme, 189
thief-in-law, 72, 77
'Third Memorandum', 192
'Thought on Socialism with Chinese Characteristics for a New Era', 89–90
Three Represents, 94
thrift violations, 95
Thucydides trap, 133
Tiananmen protests, 1989, 94
ties, 69, 72, 74, 79, 96, 101
Tolz, Stefan, 76
Tonghua Iron and Steel Company, 121
totalitarianism, 116, 206
trade, 27, 35–6, 90, 100, 136, 138
trade liberalisation, 92
trade unions, 6, 192, 193, 196, 199, 205, 217
   lose industrial power, 3, 164
   rights, 4, 190
   strikes, 214, 215
trade war, 143
traffic congestion, 215
Trans-Pacific Partnership (TPP), 142–3, 194
transparency, 75–6, 78, 79
transport, 177
treasury bonds, US, 100
the troika, 188, 190, 191, 192, 193
Trotsky, Leon, 15, 108, 109, 111–12
Trump, Donald, 5, 143, 197, 217, 218
Trump administration, 133, 141, 142, 143, 144, 145, 146
trust, 68, 69, 77, 78, 162, 168
   and *birzha*, 67, 72, 73, 79
   social, 172, 174, 175, 176
trusts, 56
Tsipras, Alexis, 183, 188, 189, 190–1, 192–3, 206
tuition fees, 195, 201, 202
Tunisia, 184
Twitter, 184, 196
Two-Century Goals, 113

UGMK, 42
UK Independence Party, 173
Ukraine, 4, 26, 27, 28, 137, 203
uncertainty, 79, 163
unemployment, 162, 163, 164, 186, 193, 195, 215

Unidos Podemos, 186, 187
unipolar system, 145, 214
United Kingdom (UK), 54, 173, 174, 175, 176–7, 184, 216–17
   and 2008 financial crisis, 4–5
   elite, 55–9, 60
   and Labour Party, 198–204, 205
   and liberalism, 162–7, 168
   and populism, 173
   and Russia, 218
   See also Britain
United Left (IU), 185, 186
United National Movement, 68, 79
United Nations, 137
United Russia party, 184
United States (US)
   and bank bailout, 168
   and China, 90, 93, 141–5, 146, 147
   and democratic socialists, 194–8
   and deregulation of capital markets, 167
   electoral system, 193
   and financial crisis, 2007–8, 5
   and liberal hegemonic order, 132–3
   and Marshall Plan, 115, 135–6
   and Occupy Wall Street, 184
   and philanthropy, 50
   and Russia, 25–6, 27, 218
   and Sanders, 10, 193–8
   and socialist ideas, 182, 205
   treasury bonds, 100
   universities, 96
   and wars in Afghanistan and Iraq, 4
universities, 59, 96, 217
   tuition fees, 201
unrest, 125, 126
upward mobility, 97, 99, 102, 103t, 104t
urban-rural income gap, 97
urban spaces, 74
urban working class, 125
Usmanov, Alisher, 35, 36, 39, 41, 42–3
USSR, 206
   See also Soviet Union
utilities, 177

value commitments, 74
varieties of capitalism, 7
varieties of socialism, 7
Varoufakis, Yanis, 183, 189, 190, 191, 192, 193
Vedomosti, 36
Venezuela, 185, 202, 218
violence, 75, 217

wages, 122, 193, 195
Wall Street Crash, 2, 197
Wang Hui, 92
Wang Shaoguang, 92
wars, 2–3, 4, 133
'wary interdependence', 142

Washington Consensus, 3, 16, 91
wealth, 8, 16, 29, 50, 51, 57, 100
   in China, 92, 102, 125
   household, 96
   inequality, 49, 213
   inherited, 171
   national, 162
   private, 93
   transfer across generations, 50
   in the US, 195
wealthy elite, 49, 52–4, 169–70, 171
   in China, 89, 93–4, 95, 100, 101
Wedel, Janine, 16
welfare benefits, 162, 165, 168, 169, 172, 173
welfare rights, 120
welfare state, 3, 19, 99, 214, 215
well-being, 162
Wen Jiabao, 96
Western China, 98
Western Europe, 9, 138, 219
   See also EU (European Union)
Western financial organisations, 16
   See also financial institutions
Western influence, 16
Western political and economic models, importation of, 79
Western ruling elite, 16, 25
Western sanctions, 139
Western universities, 96
   See also universities
White racism, 197
Why Liberalism Failed (Deneen), 161
Whyte, Martin King, 92
Wilson, Rodney, 40
Wolf, Martin, 171
women
   Corbyn's attitude towards, 201
   promoting, 205
Work and Pensions, committee (UK), 166
worker-owned enterprises, 7
workers, 123–4, 125, 164
   congress system, 124
   representative councils, 124
   rights, 4, 114, 201
   unrest, 120–1
working class, 10, 110, 125, 126
World Bank, 91, 110, 144
WTO (World Trade Organization), 2, 92, 142
Wu Xinbo, 132, 134, 135

xenophobia, 217, 218
Xie, Yu, 96
Xi Jinping, 89–90, 96, 108, 110, 126, 131, 134
   and anti-corruption campaign, 122, 125
   and Belt and Road Initiative, 115
   and Chinese Dream, 101
   on communism, 114
   and eight-point regulation, 95

Xi Jinping *(cont.)*
  and foreign economic policy, 214
  on Karl Marx, 113
  and Trump, 143
'Xi Jinping Thought', 89
Xin, Meng, 96
Xinjiang, 137
Xu Chenggang, 117–18, 125

Yakovlev, Andrei, 38
Yeltsin, Boris, 16, 21–2, 52
YouGov poll, 204

young people, 196, 197, 202, 203–4, 205, 206
Young Pioneers, 74
youth activism, 196, 197
youth association, 74
youth unemployment, 186, 193
Yugoslavia, 7, 123, 124
Yu Jianrong, 110, 119–20, 121–2

zero-tolerance approach, 77
Zhang Wangcheng, 121
Zhao Ziyang, 94